CAPTURING THE POLITICAL IMAGINATION

D1611959

E·S·R·C
ECONOMIC
& SOCIAL
RESEARCH
COUNCIL

CAPTURING THE POLITICAL IMAGINATION

Think Tanks and the Policy Process

DIANE STONE

Department of Politics and International Studies
University of Warwick

FRANK CASS
LONDON • PORTLAND, OR.

First published in 1996 in Great Britain by
FRANK CASS & CO. LTD.
2 Park Square, Milton Park, Abingdon,
Oxon, OX14 4RN

and in the United States of America by
FRANK CASS
270 Madison Ave,
New York NY 10016

Transferred to Digital Printing 2005

British Library Cataloguing in Publication Data
Stone, Diane
    Capturing the political imagination : think-tanks and the
    policy process
    1. Research institutes – Great Britain 2. Research institutes
    – United States 3. Research institutes – Great Britain –
    Political aspects 4. Research institutes – United States –
    Political aspects 5. Political planning – Great Britain
    I. Title
    320.6'0941

    ISBN 0-7146-4716-0 (cloth)
    ISBN 0-7146-4263-0 (pbk)

Library of Congress Cataloging-in-Publication Data
Stone, Diane, 1964–
    Capturing the political imagination : think-tanks and the policy
    process / Diane Stone.
        p.   cm.
    Includes bibliographical references and index.
    ISBN 0-7146-4716-0 (hardcover). -- ISBN 0-7146-4263-0 (pbk.)
    1. Policy sciences. 2. Research institutes--United States.
    3. Research institutes--Great Britain.   I. Title.
    H97.S833   1996
    320'.6--dc20   96-12700
                                                      CIP

For Roy and Pauline

Contents

Acknowledgements ix

Abbreviations xi

Time Line of British and American Think-tanks xiii

Introduction: Knowledge, Influence and Agency in Policy 1

1 Identifying Think-tanks 9

2 Explaining and Analysing Think-tanks 26

3 US Exceptionalism and Parliamentary Systems 38

4 Think-tank Organisation and Management 53

5 Innovation, Stagnation and Demise 73

6 Knowledge Communities and Policy Institutes 86

7 Policy Relevance and Effectiveness 105

8 Policy Entrepreneurs, Research Brokerage
and Networking 122

9 Second-Hand Dealers in Ideas 136

10 Public Choice Theory and Think-tanks 152

11 Policy Institutes and Privatisation 167

12 The Foreign Policy Club 184

13 Think-tanks and the Study of
    International Relations   203

Conclusion   215

Appendix : Independent Policy Institutes in Britain and the USA 227

List of Interviews   298

Bibliography   301

Index   325

Acknowledgements

This book has taken far too long – over four years – to write. Accordingly I have many debts to acknowledge. I am very grateful to friends and colleagues at the Australian National University, Murdoch University and the Manchester Metropolitan University who have given me support and encouragement: Tomoko Akami, Jillian Bavin-Mizzi, Frances Daly, Lorraine Elliott, Gillie Kirk, and Halina Zobel-Zubrzycka in Australia, and in the UK, Shafquat Nasir, Gail Hawkes, Kate McGowan and Caroline Ukoumunne. In Australia, my research and writing has benefited from the helpful comments on drafts of my manuscript from John Hart, Martin Painter and Patrick Weller. Beryl Radin at Rockefeller College, University of Albany, in the USA also provided me with useful suggestions and Kent Weaver at the Brookings Institution was helpful early on in providing me with material. I am also grateful to the Australian National University for providing me with the resources to undertake the research on this book. Additionally, since 1994 the Economic and Social Research Council of the UK has generously allowed me the time to finalise my writing on this study of think-tanks through their Research Fellowship scheme. Finally, I am very grateful to Richard Higgott who read everything several times with considerable patience and forbearance.

Abbreviations

AEI	American Enterprise Institute
AIPR	American Institute of Pacific Relations
ASI	Adam Smith Institute
CDI	Center for Defense Information
CED	Committee for Economic Development
CEI	Competitive Enterprise Institute
CEPR	Centre for Economic Policy Research
CFR	Council on Foreign Relations
CGES	Centre for Global Energy Studies
CNP	Center for National Policy
COHA	Council on Hemispheric Affairs
CPRS	Central Policy Review Staff
CPS	Centre for Policy Studies
CRC	Capital Research Center
CSIS	Center for Security and International Studies
CSP	Center for Security Policy
EBRI	Employee Benefit Research Institute
EESI	Environmental and Energy Study Institute
EPF	European Policy Forum
EPI	Economic Policy Institute
EPPC	Ethics and Public Policy Center
ERR	Earth Resources Research
ESI	Economic Strategy Institute
FPRI	Foreign Policy Research Institute
IAV	Institute for American Values
ICS	Institute for Contemporary Studies
IEA	Institute of Economic Affairs
IEDSS	Institute for European Defence and Strategic Studies
IEEP	Institute for European Environmental Policy
IFDP	Institute for Food and Development Policy
IFPA	Institute for Foreign Policy Analysis
IFS	Institute for Fiscal Studies
IGSS	Institute for Global Security Studies
IIED	International Institute for Environment and Development

IIE   Institute for International Economics
IISS   International Institute for Strategic Studies
IPPR   Institute for Public Policy Research
IPR   Institute for Pacific Relations
IPS   Institute for Policy Studies
IR   international relations
IRET   Institute for Research on the Economics of Taxation

NAPA   National Academy of Public Administration
NBER   National Bureau of Economic Research
NCPA   National Center for Policy Analysis
NCPPR   National Center for Public Policy Research
NIESR   National Institute for Social and Economic Research
NPO   non-profit organisation

OCPU   Outer Circle Policy Unit
ODC   Overseas Development Council
ODI   Overseas Development Institute

PERC   Political Economy Research Center
PPI   Progressive Policy Institute
PSI   Policy Studies Institute

RFF   Resources for the Future
RISCT   Research Institute for the Study of Conflict and Terrorism
RIIA   Royal Institute of International Affairs
RSF   Russell Sage Foundation

SAU   Social Affairs Unit
SMF   Social Market Foundation

TPRC   Trade Policy Research Centre

WPI   World Policy Institute
WRI   World Resources Institute

Time Line of British and American Think-tanks

Britain	Year	United States of America
Fabian Society	1884	
	1907	Russell Sage Foundation
Round Table	1909	
	1910	Carnegie Endowment for International Peace
	1911	Cooperative League (renamed Twentieth Century Fund)
	1914	Carnegie Council on Ethics and International Affairs
	1916	Conference Board Institute for Government Research (joined into Brookings)
	1919	Hoover Institution on War, Revolution and Peace Twentieth Century Fund
Royal Institute of International Affairs	1920	National Bureau of Economic Research
	1921	Council on Foreign Relations
	1922	Institute of Economics (joined into Brookings)
	1925	Institute for Pacific Relations (disbanded 1961)
	1927	Brookings Institution
	1929	Population Reference Bureau
Political and Economic Planning	1931	

	1934	National Planning Association
	1937	Tax Foundation
National Institute for Economic and Social Research	1938	
Catholic Institute for International Relations	1940	
	1942	Committee for Economic Development
Economic Research Council	1943	American Enterprise Institute
Federal Trust	1945	
	1948	RAND Corporation World Policy Institute
	1950	Aspen Institute
Bow Group	1951	
	1952	Resources for the Future
Institute of Economic Affairs	1955	Foreign Policy Research Institute
International Institute of Strategic Studies Institute of Race Relations	1958	
	1959	Center for the Study of Democratic Institutions
Overseas Development Institute	1960	
	1961	Atlantic Council of the United States Hudson Institute Potomac Institute (disbanded 1991–92)
	1962	Center for Strategic and International Studies Group Research Inc.

	1963	Institute for Policy Studies
	1967	National Academy of Public Administration
Trade Policy Research Centre	1968	Alan Guttmacher Institute Urban Institute
Institute for Fiscal Studies Institute of Muslim Minority Affairs	1969	Environmental Law Institute Overseas Development Council
	1970	Joint Center for Political and Economic Studies Center for the Analysis of Public Issues
International Institute for Environment and Development	1971	Institute for Educational Leadership Arms Control Association
Center for Studies in Social Policy (merged with PEP to form PSI)	1972	Center for Defense Information Center for Women Policy Studies Lerhman Institute (disbanded)
Earth Resources Research	1973	Heritage Foundation
Center for Policy Studies Low Pay Unit	1974	Center for National Security Studies Institute for Contemporary Studies World Watch
	1975	Center for International Policy Center for Policy Alternatives Council On Hemispheric Affairs Institute for Food and Development Policy International Food Policy Research Institute Keystone Center National Legal Center for the Public Interest Pacific Forum
Institute for European Environmental Policy	1976	Ethics and Public Policy Center Flagstaff Institute Institute for Foreign Policy Analysis Media Institute National Committee for Responsive Philanthropy Rockford Institute
Adam Smith Institute	1977	ACCF Center for Policy Research Cato Institute Free Congress Foundation

                                International Center
                                National Taxpayers Union Foundation
                                Northeast-Midwest Institute
                                The International Center
                                Women's Research and Education Institute

Policy Studies   1978   Employee Benefit Research Institute
  Institute   Lincoln Institute
                                Manhattan Institute
                                Reason Foundation

Arab Research   1979   Center for the Study of Social Policy
  Centre   Claremont Institute
                                Institute for Defense and Disarmament Studies
                                Pacific Research Institute for Public Policy

Social Affairs Unit   1980   Political Economy Research Center
Institute for
  European Defence
  and Strategic Studies
Centre for Policy on
  Ageing

Council for Arms   1981   Atlas Foundation
  Control   Center for National Policy
                                Center on Budget and Policy Priorities
                                Institute for International Economics
                                Institute on Religion and Democracy
                                National Institute for Public Policy

                       1982   Roosevelt Center for American Policy Studies
                                National Center for Public Policy Research
                                Washington Institute for Values in Public Policy
                                  (disbanded)
                                World Resources Institute

Centre for   1983   National Center for Policy Analysis
  Economic   Family Research Council
  Policy Research   Institute of the Americas
Family Policy Studies   Nathan Hale Institute
  Centre

Basic Income   1984   Capital Research Center
  Research Group   Center for Democracy
  now known as   Competitive Enterprise Institute
  Citizens Income   Economic Policy Institute
Public Finance   George C Marshall Institute
  Foundation   Heartland Institute
                                Mid America Institute

David Hume Institute	1985	Environmental and Energy Study Institute Independence Institute Institute for Research on the Economics of Taxation Washington Institute for Near East Policy Washington Institute for Policy Studies

Panos
IPSET
Institute for African
    Alternatives
Institute of Business
    Ethics
New Economics
    Foundation
	1986	Drug Policy Foundation
		East-West Forum
		Foundation for Research on Economics and the
		    Environment
		Hannibal Hamlin Institute
		Institute for Global Security Studies
		South Carolina Policy Council

	1987	Institute for American Values James Madison Institute Mackinac Center Pacific Institute Pioneer Institute for Public Policy Research Wisconsin Public Policy Reseach Institute Yankee Institute for Public Policy Studies

Institute for
    Public Policy
    Research
Institute of
    Employment Rights
	1988	Barry Goldwater Institute
		Center for Security Policy
		Commonwealth Foundation for Public Policy
		    Alternatives

Institute of
    Employment
    Rights
Social Market
    Foundation
Research Institute
    for the Study of
    Conflict and Terrorism
Saferworld
	1989	Henry L. Stimson Center
		Institute for Energy Research
		Indiana Policy Review Foundation
		Monterey Institute
		Progressive Policy Institute
		Texas Public Policy Foundation

Centre for Global Energy Studies	1990	Acton Institute Center for Policy Analysis on Palestine Economic Strategy Institute John Locke Foundation Institute on Religion and Public Life Madison Center for Educational Affairs
	1991	Empire Foundation

European Policy   1992
  Forum
Employment
  Policy Institute

Demos   1993
Foundation for
  Manufacturing and
  Industry

Conservative 2000   1995
  Foundation
Politeia

Introduction:
Knowledge, Influence
and Agency in Policy

Ideas matter. It is also the case that ideas do not matter. If the intellectual weight of ideas alone were sufficient to influence political thinking, then the organisations that are the subject of this book might not exist. Ideas need organisations to propel them within the hearing range of decision-makers. Organisational infrastructure plays a significant role in the influence of ideas alongside the individual agents of ideas – scholars and intellectuals. Accordingly this book argues that independent policy research institutes – better known as think-tanks – have become increasingly visible policy actors. They attempt to participate directly in policy-making through the provision of analysis for policy-makers and more indirectly by fashioning ideas in ways to mould public understanding of issues and problems. Outlining what policy research institutes are, what they do, why they have proliferated and how they make ideas matter in policy circles are aspects of this argument.

Think-Tanks and Policy Inquiry

Although one step removed from formal political arenas, policy research institutes are involved in political activity and public policy in a variety of ways. They move ideas into politics. By attracting leading scholars, think-tanks provide a base from which to market, package and popularise ideas and policy proposals. They provide a platform for the views of those not directly involved in decision making such as senior corporate executives and academics. They are also involved in various forms of public education by holding conferences, providing press releases and organising briefings. Yet, think-tanks fall outside of traditional definitions of politics. Most public policy texts fail to discuss think-tanks as either a source of policy innovation or as a group of organisations that seek to inform policy. Yet, it would seem pertinent for think-tanks to be assessed in terms of agenda setting (Kingdon, 1984) or where they fit in the literature on policy communities (Richardson and Jordon, 1979). Studies of advice systems have rarely discussed these institutes (for example, Plowden, 1987). Until recently the knowledge utilisation literature has not considered the role of policy institutes (Weiss, 1992c). Analyses of intellectual movements usually consider a group of think-tanks as an institutional expression of a broad movement such as the so-called New Right (for example, Gamble, 1989b: ch. 2). In most ruling-class studies, there is only passing reference to think-tanks and their impact on policy (Hoover and Plant, 1987). There is a tendency to treat these organisations as epiphenomena. Consequently a chasm exists between the self-aggrandising literature that think-tanks often produce in their annual reports and a lack of serious analysis from other observers.

q ※   Think-tanks are an organisational expression of the blending of ideas, politics and policy *outside* formal political arenas. The confluence of these elements in institutions other than the executive and legislature warrants further investigation. The separation of the public and the private in many standard political analyses undermines the requirement to address the role played by these non-governmental organisations which occupy an ambiguous position between the market and the state. This book looks at what happens at the 'margins' of government in the two liberal democratic political systems of the USA and Great Britain. It investigates the benefits and disadvantages of this sphere as a base from which to inform policy. In this context the literature on non-profit organisations is useful. One objective is to draw a different set of linkages within the policy process by taking a position one step removed from government. New relationships appear and a different set of actors and institutions can be seen to play a vital role (Wyszomirski, 1989). Fundamental questions arise from a vantage point on the margins.

> Because they are largely self governing, bodies on the margins threaten some of political theory with obsolescence. Concerns about elections, legislatures, chief executives and government departments have limited appeal if governments isolate much of what they do from these devices of control (Sharkansky, 1989: 82–3).

Policy institutes are on the margins of government but not *in* government. There is enormous scope for the investigation of the mechanisms that connect organisations on the margins of government with the conventional structures of government. While the approval of public policy remains with elected representatives and appointed officials, governments draw upon outside sources of advice and information. Even so, the impact of think-tanks on policy is incomplete. Influence is limited to constructing a political agenda, developing policy alternatives and diffusing ideas to shape public understanding of issues. Elected decision-makers remain responsible for the selection and persistence of new ideas in policy. Furthermore, as subsequent chapters discuss, the influence of think-tanks is diffuse, variable, fluid, intangible and usually ephemeral. It is not a quantifiable power that policy institutes wield. Nor is it the case that all institutes at some point in their existence exert political influence.

The concept of epistemic communities, employed in part of this book, provides a fresh perspective on the role of think-tanks among groups of policy experts. An epistemic community is made up of a network of specialists from a variety of positions who share a common world view and seek to translate their beliefs into public policies and programmes. Think-tanks represent one type of organisation in which members of a community may be located. As an analytical tool it is in the early stages of conceptualisation and was only recently introduced to the public policy literature (see Rose, 1991; Bennett, 1992). The concept allows for the analysis of fluctuations and variations of think-tank influence by assessing the effectiveness of think-tanks as organisations in tandem with the motivations of the experts who work through them. Accordingly, think-tanks are most likely to affect political thinking and the climate of opinion on an issue when roused by an epistemic community. Policy institutes can help epistemic communities attract the patronage of decision-makers. Think-tanks highlight new problems in need of policy attention and then seek to gain legitimacy for such issues on public and governmental agendas. However, the ability of an epistemic community to shape policy agendas is never complete. Nor do think-tanks need to be dominated by epistemic communities to function. Aside from their best efforts to influence policy, think-tanks perform other educational and technical roles. Consequently, the objective of the book is not to provide case-studies of epistemic communities, but to use this and other policy network concepts of policy communities and discourse coalitions as devices to explain the policy relevance of think-tanks.

Structure and Approach

The book discusses British and American think-tanks. This approach allows some comparative insight and is a step towards establishing why think-tanks have proliferated primarily in the US. It is remarkable, given the amount of research that has been devoted to American think-tanks, that there is a disinterest in comparative analysis. There has never been a case-study on the influence of the Royal Institute of International Affairs (RIIA) in foreign policy to compare with the studies that have addressed the Council on Foreign Relations (CFR) (*inter alia*, Schulzinger, 1984; Smoot, 1963; Shoup and Minter, 1977). To date, the opportunity to conduct a comparative study of the role and influence of the CFR and the RIIA, both of which have common origins in the Versailles Peace Conference, has been missed. This kind of examination can reveal the political environment in which these organisations have been most powerful or relatively weak. Cultural and institutional factors such as the permeability of the American political system to outsiders and the impermanence of bureaucrats, the division of powers and the weakness of political parties along with a history of generous foundation and philanthropic support are important for explaining the proliferation of think-tanks in the USA, but do not explain the growing numbers of think-tanks in other countries. Comparative analysis reveals that think-tanks are not, as suggested by a few writers (*inter alia*, Alpert and Markusen, 1979; Weaver, 1989), unique to the American political system.

This book primarily addresses the ways in which policy institutes seek to contribute to the policy process while recognising that there are methodological difficulties in assessing the degree to which they actually affect policy. It is impossible to establish a causal link between the activities of think-tanks and policy outcomes. A particular policy and its implementation can rarely be attributed to the influence of one organisation. There are a variety of intermediary forces such as political parties, bureaucracies, interest groups and the media. Furthermore, think-tanks are not successful in all their activities or at all stages of the policy process. They have selective impact according to issue and circumstance, and are involved more in the innovation and diffusion of policy ideas than their adoption or implementation by governments. The complexities of the policy-making process create a gap between the inputs of policy institutes and the outputs of policy-making. It could also mean that think-tanks have zero impact. This hiatus prevents measurement of their impact.

One way to mitigate the problem of quantifying influence is by looking not at the *degree* of influence but at the role think-tanks see themselves playing, the contributions they make to the policy process and how, or if, these contributions are used. These are specific questions of an empirical nature but the analysis originates on the margins of politics, not at the centre as would befit a study of non-profit institutes. Accordingly, the book relies heavily on primary material generated by think-tanks – their published products such as books, monographs, newsletters and annual reports as well as unpublished material such as internal memoranda. In addition, the book draws on over ninety interviews that were conducted in think-tanks in the USA and Britain.

The first half of the book deals with the growth and organisation of think-tanks. The second half addresses the question of influence – whether they have the power to influence policy and in what form it is exerted. There is an unavoidable limitation on the number of organisations that can be assessed in detail. In the USA, there are hundreds of think-tanks. Consequently, some of the leading organisations are given more attention than others. There is, for example, more written about the Brookings Institution, the Council on Foreign Relations (CFR) and the RAND Corporation than most remaining US organisations combined. British institutes are far less numerous and are more easily included in the analysis. However, for reference purposes, the Appendix provides data on a representative number of policy institutes.

Chapter one reviews the literature on think-tanks and the dilemmas of definition. Previous definitions are discarded in favour of the identification of a set of common features or characteristics that can be employed to identify think-tanks and distinguish them from other research and policy related organisations. The term is so well established in the popular mind that it cannot be discarded but it is employed in a specific sense as an alternative term for what I define as an 'independent policy research institute'. These institutes are categorised as either 'old guard' or 'new partisan' in character. Chapter two surveys the existing literature on independent policy research institutes. Pluralists, élite theorists and Marxists, among others, present different pictures of think-tanks. Each perspective has its merits but also its disadvantages.

Although a think-tank boom has occurred internationally, the political, legal and cultural conditions in the USA present a more fertile environment for think-tank growth. Accordingly, chapter three outlines some reasons for the differences in scale of the think-tank industry between the Britain and the USA. Chapters four and five turn inwards on think-tanks. Different from both private and public sector organisations, they face a set of problems peculiar to the non-profit organisation. In order to survive and prosper in a changing world, think-tanks must constantly learn and adapt. The organisational health of a think-tank is a significant factor in its potential for policy relevance and influence.

Chapter six locates the think-tank phenomenon – the scholars and others that inhabit them and the ideas, tactics and proposals that are generated – in an epistemic community framework. Research institutes are 'key locations' for these intellectual activists (Haas, 1992a: 31). They are a medium through which to set agendas, confine debate to safe issues, and induce policy learning. Epistemic communities need not necessarily operate through these organisations but policy institutes potentially work best when dominated by or linked with an epistemic community. Chapter seven turns to the main theme of the remainder of the book – the influence and policy impact of think-tanks. Chapter eight critically analyses the research brokerage and networking activities of policy institutes in their efforts to inform policy. As policy entrepreneurs in the guise of charitable educational institutions but engaged in advocacy and research brokerage, their influence lies in their ability to raise issues to the public agenda and to build a receptive audience to new ideas. Chapter nine further investigates the style of think-tank advocacy by discussing the 'war of ideas', that is, the discursive tactics employed by think-tanks to make certain ideas or policy proposals politically attractive. The argument is extended in Chapter ten by looking at the way some market liberal think-tanks have been responsible for establishing public choice theory as a key framework for reinterpreting policy concerns. Chapter eleven focuses on privatis- ation to exemplify how think-tanks can promote policy learning. Free market think-tanks were extolling the virtues of privatisation long before its popularity with governments in the 1980s. Their research brokerage activities have promoted the international spread of privatisation.

The final two substantive chapters change tack and address aspects of influence among foreign policy institutes. The presence of think-tanks in this field since the turn of century presents a unique opportunity to map not only the changing forms of think-tanks over time but also the ways in which they have contributed to the development of an academic discipline, the extent to which they have, or have not, been significant actors in international affairs and the manner in which they have bridged the divide between the worlds of the analyst and the practitioner.

In conclusion, the book reaffirms the role that ideas can play in policy debates. This is not to say, however, that all think-tanks play a part in the policy process. It is easy to exaggerate the importance of these organisations and dangerous to accept uncritically their own statements of influence. Furthermore, it would be unwarranted to assume that information and ideas are essential to decision-making, particularly when interests have a strong role in policy development. Nevertheless, think-tanks are shown to be a contemporary mode of interaction between the world of scholarship and inquiry and the domain of policy-making. In a world where knowledge, information and expertise is burgeoning, think-tanks are an increasingly important mechanism for filtering and refining such resources in a relevant and usable manner.

In both countries, they are strategic institutions that make ideas more competitive in an environment characterised by multiple and conflicting sources of advice and analysis.

1   Identifying Think-tanks

There is a body of literature which discusses a group of organisations variously known as 'imperial brain trusts' (Shoup and Minter, 1977), 'public policy research institutes' (Polsby 1983; McGann, 1992; McDowell, 1992), 'policy discussion groups' and 'research institutes' (Domhoff, 1983), and 'policy planning organizations' (Peschek, 1987) or 'independent public policy institutes' (Stone, 1991). More often than not they are called 'think-tanks'. Yet, the study of think-tanks is not as extensive as the proliferation of labels. In the literature that does exist there are different disciplinary approaches, differences of opinion on their role as well as a lack of definitional clarity and agreement as to *what is* a think-tank. The term is problematic. 'Think-tank' was first employed as a nickname in the 1940s for the brain – 'brain box' – but acquired new meaning in the 1960s when it appeared in magazine and newspaper articles as a description for the RAND Corporation (Dickson, 1971). This organisation is atypical of contemporary policy institutes because of its vast size and budget, its scientific and technical focus as well as close ties to the Pentagon. 'Think-tank' is an umbrella term that means different things to different people. It has been used to describe central government policy units (Blackstone and Plowden, 1988), the Congressional Research Service in the USA (Robinson, 1992), government research bureaux and advisory bodies as well as commercial research organisations. The term is over-inclusive and evokes images of science, detachment and objective expertise. It is a label sometimes rejected by policy institutes. In the USA, for example, the Aspen Institute denies in all its promotional material that it is a think-tank, while Will Marshall of the Democrat affiliated Progressive Policy Institute (PPI) refers to his 'analytic guerrilla group'. The disadvantage of dispensing with the term is that a commonly acceptable replacement has not been forthcoming. In the popular lexicon 'think-tank' is too well entrenched. The different meanings attached to the term are not an insuperable barrier to analysis provided it is used precisely, as it is here, to mean independent policy research institute.

There are two types of literature seeking to define or categorise think-tanks. One set of writing investigates all manner of organisations engaged in policy and scientific research, either independently of, or for government and business. Paul Dickson was the first to write a book on think-tanks but the organisations he studied included scientific laboratories, consultancies and other American research bodies. The following year, Harold Orlans (1972) published a book on non-profit research institutes. Both books were important for addressing systematically a hitherto unassessed phenomenon and for providing a framework to identify different kinds of research institutes. More recently some have applied the term specifically to *policy* research organisations but this includes university, public sector and private sector research bodies alike (see Marsh, 1991; McDowell, 1994). The *independent* policy research institute – described by Dickson as the 'free advice brigade' – is only one category of organisation among the gamut of think-tanks. Accordingly, while this earlier body of literature identifies an important organisational phenomenon, it has not addressed in any detail the diverse forms and activities of the independent policy research institute.

The second set of observers have attempted to define more precisely the independent policy research institute. While these efforts are individually useful, collectively these discussions confuse rather than clarify understanding. The use of different terms and criteria for identification create contradictions and confound efforts to establish a unifying concept of think-tank. Although authors are usually describing the same organisational creatures, and their typologies in many cases overlap, each stress different attributes. Nelson Polsby (1983) distinguishes between 'public policy research institutes' and what he calls 'true think-tanks'. Policy institutes are defined by their politically attuned research agendas and regular impact on policy whereas the pure think-tank allows researchers to pursue their own intellectual agendas with little regard for policy relevance. In a similar vein, Evert Lindquist argues that the term 'think-tank' is too grand and that institutes should be called 'policy clubs' to reflect their limited aspirations, specific audiences and amateur interests (1993: 476). In his paper on British think-tanks, Simon James (1993) argues that think-tanks must be multi-disciplinary, thereby eliminating many institutes from further consideration.

Instead of trying to define and categorise existing think-tanks, Yehezkel Dror (1980) builds a model of an ideal think-tank. First, he argues that think-tanks have a *mission* of undertaking inter-disciplinary, science based contributions to policy-making. Second, they need a *critical mass* of about 15 to 20 professionals from a range of disciplines. Third, these research professionals employ *research methods* that characterise the organisation as a 'thinking outfit'. Fourth, they are characterised by *research freedom* – although this may conflict with the fifth feature which is *clientele dependency* for financing, information and feedback. Lastly, think-tank *outputs and impacts* have bearing on the policy process. Although Dror's model helps us identify policy-oriented organisations, his model is rigid. The ideal is also heavily influenced by American experience. Dror has in mind large operations prevalent in the USA prior to the 1980s, whereas some organisations discussed here are considerably smaller. For instance, his 'critical mass' criterion would exclude from analysis many American as well as non-American think-tanks. Small policy institutes often have part-time and voluntary staff whose activities are cross subsidised by universities, private companies or bureaucracies. Furthermore, advances in communications technology as well as inter-organisational networks reduce the necessity for Dror's critical mass. Dror also stresses that the ideal think-tank makes 'rational' or 'scientific' contributions to policy formulation. He does not consider their ideological and political functions. By contrast, Winand Gellner (1990: 5) defines research institutes by their political rather than intellectual relevance of generating ideas and ideologies, aiding net-working and assisting political parties in the recruitment and training of political élites.

Samantha Durst and James Thurber (1989) identify traits that are attributable to policy research institutes but not to other research organisations, thereby adding more detail to the character of independent policy research institutes. They note, first, that the majority of them are non-profit organisations. Second, these think-tanks have minimal levels of government funding. Indeed, many reject it as a matter of principle. Third, the primary orientation of these organisations is research. Fourth, unhindered research requires independence. As Dickson notes:

> Their finished work is usually never proprietary in the industrial sense and never has the secret stamp of an agency affixed to it. As a class they try to influence decisions, not in the vested role of contractor, but from the outside (1971: 261).

Fifth, they stress a strong scholarly or analytic orientation. Yet, Durst and Thurber's framework would not meet the satisfaction of all. While some institutes are highly academic, not all are 'real researchers' but act as 'policy boutiques' (Coleman, 1991: 439). Many think-tanks regurgitate research conducted elsewhere in a simplified form. Similarly, it is not clear that policy research institutes function more independently with low proportions of government funding. Diverse funding sources may well enhance the legitimacy of research results but it is also commitment to professional standards that ensures the standing of research. Although their study indicates that Washington DC think-tanks do not have significant government funding in practice and generally as policy, it does not mean that this has always been the case or that it is applicable outside the USA.

Other analysts of think-tanks avoid the dilemmas of models or formal typologies by limiting their definition to one or two sentence descriptions. John Gaffney, for example, defines the essence of British think-tanks as 'intellectually informed policy proposal structures with the express intention of gaining direct access to government' (1991: 2). James Smith refers to American think-tanks as 'private, non-profit research groups that operate on the margins of ... formal political processes' (1991a: xiii). Similarly, Hames and Feasey (1994: 216) describe a think-tank as a 'non-profit public policy research institution with substantial organisational autonomy'. In his study of Washington think-tanks, David Ricci merely states that with a wide spectrum of institutes there is a 'need for generalisation' (1993: 20–21). While avoiding the problems of categorisation, such definitions do not help in establishing the boundaries between independent policy research institutes and other organisations.

In sum, there is no accepted definition of the independent policy research institute. Minimalist definitions allow researchers considerable flexibility in application, but can be too broad and encompassing. Attempts to build models of the type produced by Dror are problematic. The organisational features of independent policy research institutes are too diverse and constantly evolving to be so precisely defined. A flexible model that recognises diversity among policy research institutes would seem more appropriate. One way to conceptualise this body of organisations is to determine from the outset what they are not. Once the distinctiveness of think-tanks from other research-related bodies is established, then it is possible to outline a set of features that characterise the organisations under analysis.

Independent policy research institutes are not interdisciplinary units of the type that are found in universities although they have been referred to as 'universities without students' (Gray, 1978; Critchlow, 1985: 4; Weaver, 1989; Ricci, 1993: 20). While think-tanks are engaged in research and other scholarly activities they do not mimic the universities. They are not involved in undergraduate teaching and do not have the same disciplinary range. Research fellows are employees and not free to 'follow their intellectual priorities without constraint' but are required to pursue organisational objectives (Polsby, 1983:16). It does not follow that academic freedom is circumscribed. Policy relevance is emphasised over pure research, but researchers are generally able to come to their own conclusions. Policy research institutes are also distinguishable from philanthropic foundations which tend to fund research rather than do it themselves. 'Operating foundations' such as the Carnegie Endowment for International Peace and Russell Sage Foundation (RSF) are different from foundations that make grants as they use their own funds to conduct policy analysis and research. Although consultancies conduct policy research they operate on a 'for-profit' basis. The product of their research can be, but is not always made public. It is often held to be 'commercial in confidence' for the client who determined the nature of the research enterprise in the first instance. The research agenda of policy institutes is determined by the organisation's research committee, rarely by outside interests. The primary motivation of the policy research institute is research not profit.

They are also very different from advocacy groups, interest groups and lobbies. As Carol Weiss notes, while many of these groups undertake extensive analysis, it 'is intended primarily to advance the cause of the association and to give them ammunition to use in the policy wars' (1992a: xiii). A former Director of the Policy Studies Institute in London, Bill Daniels, makes a clear distinction between his organisation and interest groups, stating that 'We have no set programme or policies to promote. We have no basic political position or philosophy underpinning our work, other than empiricism and pragmatism' (1989: 24). Nevertheless, policy research institutes are similar to some public interest groups that have a research component to their activities and it can be difficult to distinguish between the two types of organisation. However, the public interest group is more interested in grass-roots activity and advocacy whereas the policy research institute is first and foremost a research outfit. While the line between analysis and advocacy does become blurred, policy institutes aspire to be rigorous and balanced. Or in Weiss's words, they 'do not sweep uncongenial information under the rug'. Instead, they treat data systematically and apply research methods in a consistent fashion. '[I]f the answer is always cut-and-dried before inquiry starts', she says, 'it probably should be classed as an advocacy organization' (1992a: xiii–xiv). It is the case that some policy research institutes such as the Heritage Foundation or Adam Smith Institute (ASI) have predictable policy positions. In spite of their conservative or libertarian positions, the source of predictability is not vested interest. It arises from a consistent set of principles or underlying ideology.

Think-tanks are also unlike government advisory organisations such as policy units, task forces and commissions of inquiry. These government bodies often have short life spans and are established at the behest of government for the purposes of solving a specific problem. Government research bureaux, while they may have some independence, remain tied to government objectives and dictates and, hence, can be regarded as part of the bureaucratic machinery. Colin Gray (1978) also makes a distinction between the policy *research* organisation, of which there are few, and the more technical and defence-oriented organisations in the USA. The latter tend to be profit-making bodies and have been pejoratively referred to as 'Beltway Bandits' operating on the outskirts of Washington DC (*inter alia*, Gray, 1978; Sharkansky, 1989; Ricci, 1993). Public policy institutes are not military research institutes engaged in technical or defence related work – which often maintain a close link with the bureaucracy and armed forces – as part of what Dickson (1971) refers to as the 'military intellectual complex'. Nevertheless, many of the independently funded policy research institutes also engage in studies of strategy, logistics and armaments. The difference is the independence of the policy research institute from government dictates whereas 'federal contract research organisations' are usually entirely dependent on Department of Defense funding.

While think-tanks have many features in common with other research organisations, they are different from university centres, government agencies, consultancies and interest groups. Accordingly, a number of criteria are outlined below as defining characteristics of independent policy research institutes. None of the following criteria are sufficient in themselves but they provide a guide to some of their predominant features and distinguish them from other policy-oriented research bodies.[1]

i) Organisational Independence and Permanency. Policy research institutes usually have formal legal status as an entity outside the public sector and independent from corporate and other interests. Independence can be determined from their status as a charity or non-profit organisation. Generally, they are established on a permanent footing. An obvious consequence of their independence is that they have no responsibility for the implementation of government policies. Additionally, think-tanks have some measure of detachment from government and partisan political debate.

ii) Self Determination of Research Agendas. Think-tanks do not have a fixed or dependent policy position – they are intellectually independent. The nature of their work is determined by the institute rather than any specific interest. 'The research activities and quality of work is not controlled by funders or think-tank managers but by internalized professional standards similar to those of the university setting' (Durst and Thurber, 1990: 11–12). Towards this end, think-tank managers often require that funding be untied so that they may be free in determining the questions they address and in arriving at their findings.

iii) Policy Focus. Independent policy institutes are typified by a desire to inform the policy process. Their research is not disinterested. They seek some involvement with government. Their primary ethos is to establish a dynamic between knowledge and policy-making through policy relevant analysis. Their strong policy focus differentiates them from university research which is often more academic, theoretical and less amenable to general consumption. This interplay of knowledge and policy is complemented by strategic practices to develop advisory ties to government, industry or the public.

iv) Public Purpose. Think-tanks are characterised by public spirit or, at least, the rhetoric of contributing to public debate and educating the community. A consistent claim is that they do not represent the interests of any rent-seeking group but that they desire to conduct research for the sake of building a body of knowledge and improving policy. As a consequence, think-tanks often have a longer term focus of inquiry than is available to policy-makers who must deal with immediate events. One feature of their public interest motivation is a heavy emphasis on communication, that is, on public, not private inquiry (Weiss, 1992a: ix; Lindquist, 1993: 555). Publications and research are accessible to the public and a premium is placed on plain and concise English, executive summaries and practical policy recommendations.

v) Expertise and Professionalism. Staff or scholars are usually trained in the policy and social sciences or have considerable firsthand experience from careers in government service. Their academic credentials, technical skills and methodological approaches are not only the intellectual resources of staff but also a source of legitimacy for their research findings and recommendations. Research staff are engaged in the intellectual analysis of policy and are concerned with the ideas, concepts and assumptions that inform policy.

vi) Organisational Yield. The primary products of think-tanks are research, analysis and advice. Policy advice comes in a variety of formats ranging from the multiple messages of books, journals, newsletters, magazine stories and op-ed pieces to tapes, videos, radio and television programming. More informal but equally important think-tank activities such as seminars, workshops and conferences, social meetings and fund raising functions as well as carefully nurtured networks provide the medium for interaction of scholars with decision-makers, opinion leaders and sponsors. Additionally, think-tanks produce human capital in the form of policy analysts who go into journalism, government or business with think-tank experience and, in the case of RAND, even Ph.D. graduands. Just as the product is diverse, so are the forms of conveying the message.

In summary, independent policy research institutes are usually non-profit organisations engaged in the analysis of public policy issues independent from government, political parties and interest groups. Sources of funding may come from government but these institutes maintain their 'academic' or research freedom and are not beholden to any specific interest. They attempt to influence policy through intellectual argument and analysis rather than lobbying. They are public spirited in the sense of seeking to inform and improve policy, and profess to educate the community and act in the public interest. While commonly displaying a high level of social scientific expertise and/or familiarity with governmental structures and processes there is considerable diversity in style and output of think-tanks.

The above set of characteristics do not add up to create an ideal. Institutes do not need to display such characteristics in equal measure. Some are more academic than policy oriented while others are more accessible to the general public compared with relatively exclusive establishments like the Council on Foreign Relations (CFR) and Atlantic Council. Involvement with government will not only vary from think-tank to think-tank but also from one country to another. While this book concentrates on the USA and Great Britain, it is worth remembering that think-tanks are proliferating around the world. Leading Asian institutes, for example, tend to be closely linked with their governments and play a greater role in policy formulation than their North American and European counterparts.

The boundaries surrounding this group of organisations are not always clearly cut. 'Grey areas' and fuzzy borders persist in the framework. For example, since the 1980s in the USA, 'transition tanks' have emerged to provide advice for new incoming presidents (Kornhauser, 1988). These bodies are often established on a temporary basis. A related development is the trend for presidential hopefuls to set up their own think-tank to develop policy agendas but into which they can also channel campaign contributions. The non-profit status of the think-tank allows the candidate to avoid compliance with federal limits on campaign contributions (Fly, 1986). However, candidate institutes are not think-tanks as the prime purpose is to advance the policy positions of particular candidates and ensure their electoral success rather than to engage in rigorous research (Durst and Thurber, 1990: 12). Another organisation on the boundaries is the Center for Policy Research in Education in Washington DC (Furhman, 1992). Although conducting independent research, it is funded by the Department of Education, located in a university and obliged to provide research relevant to state and local governments. At one border, policy institutes fade into interest groups which are increasingly recognising the value of research and analysis in policy debate. At another border, think-tanks merge with university bodies, while at another frontier they seem to become extra-party political campaigning groups.

Think-tank will always be a slippery term. This may well be a positive feature. An acceptance of the absence of firm boundaries between think-tanks and other organisations allows sensitivity to new or evolving kinds of think-tank. Continual tinkering with organis-ational style is to be welcomed for the potential benefits. What matters is that there is a discernible group of institutions at the core which can be subjected to analysis without discounting from consideration evolving forms and innovations at the margin. Accordingly, the remainder of this chapter is devoted to the ways in which these independent policy research institutes have diversified.

From the turn of the century until the late 1920s think-tanks were an innovative organisational form.[2] They were founded in a number of countries. After the Second World War the number of new American research centres and policy institutes increased dramatically and, especially since the 1970s, numbers have boomed. Growth has been at a more consistent rate in Britain and in other parliamentary systems. Today there is a bewildering array of think-tanks. Accordingly, the following discussion distinguishes between what are designated the 'old guard' and 'new partisan' policy institutes.[3] Prior to the 1970s, less than half the number of institutes that are now in existence were established. The 1970s also represent a period of transition in the think-tank industry. 1970 is used as a rough mid point to distinguish between two different extremes of style. The 'old guard' are a more academic and non-political tradition of think-tank, while the 'new partisans' are increasingly entrepreneurial and likely to be more specialised, more directly policy focused and partisan in their research and analysis.

The Old Guard Institutes

Noteworthy features of the older institutes are their broad research focus and strong academic orientations. They are like a 'university without students' (Weaver, 1989: 564). Institutes employed academics as in-house researchers to write book-length studies and journal articles as the primary research product. These institutes tended to have long-term horizons to educate élite opinion but were politically non-aligned. The old guard can be divided into those focused on national public policy issues and those concerned with international issues. Only a few such as the Institute for Policy Studies (IPS) and Brookings span both domains of research. Think-tanks that tackled domestic policy concerns include the Fabian Society, Political and Economic Planning (PEP, now known as the Policy Studies Institute – PSI), the National Institute for Economic and Social Research (NIESR) and the Institute of Economic Affairs (IEA) in Britain. The domestic policy institutes in the USA are numerous. A few of the well known are the Russell Sage Foundation (RSF), Brookings, the National Bureau of Economic Research (NBER), the Committee for Economic Development (CED) and the Urban Institute. The foreign policy institutes include the Royal Institute for International Affairs (RIIA), the Round Table and the International Institute of Strategic Studies (IISS) in Britain. American bodies include the Council on Foreign Relations (CFR), the Foreign Policy Research Institute (FPRI), and the Atlantic Council. Foreign policy think-tanks burgeoned as the USA became a hegemonic power in world affairs and as the Cold War developed. Through the 1950s and 1960s, strategic and defence studies institutes such as RAND, the Center for

Strategic and International Studies (CSIS) and Hudson Institute were created in the USA. The older organisations were often energised by idealistic aims of ending war and promoting international peace, notably the Carnegie Endowment for International Peace and the Carnegie Council on Ethics and International Affairs. In the US and Britain, the people involved in these organisations sought to alert political élites to the dangers of isolationism.

Among the institutes that addressed domestic policy issues there was also a strong pragmatic idealism. The older American institutes such as the Conference Board, Brookings, and the National Bureau of Economic Research came into being as a result of the social science and scientific management reform movements popular towards the end of the nineteenth century (Critchlow, 1985; Smith, 1991a). For example, the Twentieth Century Fund was created as 'a mechanism for a more disciplined attack on social problems' (Berle, 1986: viii). Similarly, PEP's 'practical aim' was 'to study problems of public concern, to find out the facts, to present them impartially, to suggest ways in which the knowledge can be applied' (Lindsay, 1981: 9). The intervention of governments in social and economic affairs after the Second World War generated new funding for research and analysis, particularly in the USA. New institutes such as the Hudson Institute and RAND grew large on a steady diet of defence funding during the Cold War. Institutes such as Brookings, Urban, the Joint Center and Hudson also benefited from President Johnson's 'War on Poverty' and attracted government research contracts. Along with the contract came a new dynamic in think-tank activity. Research agendas were increasingly determined by what government was prepared to sponsor. The style of research product took the form of reports rather than book-length studies. Institutes often became closely aligned with, and financially dependent on a particular department or agency. Thus, for example, RAND has close ties with the US Department of Defense.[4] Contract research is less extensive in the parliamentary context but is not unknown as a practice. PSI and Earth Resources Research (ERR) in London, for instance, receive a considerable amount of contract work. But, in general, bureaucracies, task forces or Royal Commissions undertake this kind of analytic work.

There are relatively few specialised institutes among the old guard. Aside from the Tax Foundation and the environmental institute, Resources For the Future (RFF), most of the specialised institutes were created only from the late 1960s. Institutes established earlier this century tend to have a broad policy focus. Furthermore, while the Urban Institute was created with a specific mandate, it rapidly encompassed wider interests beyond those concerned with urban issues and poverty. Although the Overseas Development Council (ODC) concentrated initially on US foreign aid it has a considerably broader remit today. Similarly, the Institute of Pacific Relations (IPR) was a regionally focused research institute, but its research dealt with all aspects of Asian–Pacific affairs.

While specialisation evolved slowly, ideological differences between institutes were more apparent. In Britain, the IEA is one of the oldest market-liberal think-tanks. Founded in 1955 as an 'anti-Fabian society' (Cockett, 1994: 134), it was a reactionary response to the dominance of Keynesian perspectives in economic and social policy (IEA, 1989: 3). In the US, a like-minded body, the neo-conservative American Enterprise Institute (AEI) has waged the same kind of battle since 1943.[5] The ideas espoused by these two bodies did not come into fashion until the 1970s, prior to when they were regarded as marginal. The IEA was widely perceived as a 'home for intellectual crackpots' (The Economist, 1991: 24). From the 1950s, the Hoover Institution was also known for its anti-communist disposition. Think-tanks with a socialist or social democratic agenda are not so readily apparent. The Fabian Society in Britain is one. In the USA, the Institute for Policy Studies figures highly in conservative demonology as a 'conspiratorial nest of Marxist-Leninists' (Blumenthal, 1986: D1). Similarly, the Center for the Study of Democratic Institutions (which Dror, 1980: 142, describes as anti-establishment) was a progressive liberal organisation.

Before the 1970s, most institutes claimed to be non-partisan. Some, such as the PSI, also rejected any ideological motivations insisting on their pragmatic and practical recommendations. Think-tanks distanced themselves from overt political positions, professing a scientific approach to social and economic problems. Identifiably conservative or left-wing think-tanks such as IEA and IPS were on the fringes and were regarded as intellectually radical. Think-tanks aspired to be disinterested, engaged in the objective pursuit of knowledge or of making 'rational' and 'scientific' contributions to policy and public administration. An impartial and scholarly image was essential for the public standing of a think-tank. Although the aspirations for pragmatic political discussion and rational policy formulation may be disputed or criticised, these think-tanks make an effort to live up to their rhetoric. They often strive for balance in their publications and conferences and give opportunity for alternative views to be voiced. This 'pragmatic' or 'scientific' tradition can be juxtaposed against a more recent and idealistic tradition arguing the primacy of ideas and values (Landers, 1986; Smith, 1989: 178).

New Partisans

The most apparent trend among institutes created since the 1970s is increasing diversity and specialisation. Especially in the crowded American think-tank industry, product differentiation has become essential. Not only are new organisations competing with other new institutes but also with old guard institutes which have consolidated their financial position and have well established reputations and constituencies. Think-tanks have specialised in one, or a combination, of four ways:

i) *ideological tanks.* Institutes such as the Ethics and Public Policy Center and the Free Congress Foundation are easily identified for their conservatism, or, in the case of Cato, its market liberal ethos. Within these organisations scholars adhere to a common philosophy which consistently pervades their products, although they occasionally produce reports or books that are contrary to their perceived image. Institutes often reflect competing ideological positions; for example, the Heritage Foundation combines a conservative posture on moral and defence issues with a *laissez-faire* attitude towards the market-place. The term 'New Right' is used by many writers to describe this particular mixture of thought (see, *inter alia*, Barry, 1987; Green, 1987). Some of the new institutes such as the Economic Policy Institute (EPI, see Kriz, 1988) in the US were founded as a reaction to these groups, while the Institute of Employment Rights in Britain seeks to redress the 'ideological imbalance' in Britain created by the IEA, the Centre for Policy Studies (CPS) and Adam Smith Institute (ASI).

ii) *specialist tanks.* A number of think-tanks have developed a single issue focus but this specialisation is most pronounced in the USA. There are environmental think-tanks (World Resources Institute (WRI), the Environment and Energy Study Institute and the London based Earth Resources Research); institutes addressing minority concerns (the Lincoln Institute, the Joint Center for Political and Economic Studies); regionally focused operations (Washington Institute for Near East Policy); centres for the study of women's policy (Women's Research and Education Institute); economic policy think-tanks (Institute for International Economics (IIE) and the Centre for Economic Policy Research), and institutes addressing tax and budgetary matters (Center on Budget and Policy Priorities and Institute for Fiscal Studies), while the Centre for Global Energy Studies (CGES) focuses on energy and oil resource issues.

The so-called New Right think-tanks in Britain – IEA, CPS, ASI, Social Affairs Unit (SAU), and the David Hume Institute – also exhibit an informal division of labour and friendly but low level competition which has produced diversification of a different kind. The IEA is the oldest and most academic. It produces books and monographs, often of a theoretical nature, seeking to mould the climate of intellectual opinion. The ASI are more like 'engineers who take theory and translate it for practical application', in the opinion of ASI's Director, Eamonn Butler (interview). Compared with the CPS, the ASI has more of an economic orientation. The CPS is more closely linked with the Conservative Party and is the most political of the institutes. In the words of a former CPS Director of Studies, David Willetts (interview), the institutes have 'different jobs' and have evolved to occupy specific niches. Rather than research specialisation, and despite some differences of opinion and philosophy, the conservative and neo-liberal institutes have developed complementary styles of activity.

iii) *state tanks*. A recent development in the USA has been the creation of think-tanks addressing state and regional issues rather than focusing on national ones. These include the Heartland Institutes and the James Madison Institute among others (see Appendix). The Washington policy environment is becoming saturated. Directors of the state public policy centres perceive greater potential for influence with state legislatures rather than competing with numerous other bodies in the Capitol (Moore, 1988). Not surprisingly, in a unitary political system such as Great Britain, the decentralisation of think-tanks has not occurred.

iv) *think and do tanks*. A number of think-tanks have eschewed the academic style of the older institutes. The Washington based Center for Democracy, for example, has organised a 'Gift of Democracy' programme involving donations of personal computers, printers, copiers, fax machines and other communication facilities to the Polish legislature, as well as the Library of Democracy programme involving gifts of collections of 'classic' works on democracy for distribution to civic groups in Eastern Europe. Staff members of the Center for International Policy (CIP) have been involved as observers in the Arias and Contadora Latin American peace plans, interacting informally between UN negotiators and members of US Congress as a conduit of information (Morrell, interview). Institutes like the Free Congress Foundation engage in grass-roots activities, coalition building and training of activists. At some point, such bodies are no longer think-tanks if they abandon research in favour of other activities. It is, however, a fine line. In classic think-tank style, the East–West Forum was established to 'illuminate the debate' regarding the Soviet Union and Eastern Europe through books, seminars and conferences. It gradually became involved in educational activities that were of a 'more engaged' nature. Exchange arrangements for academics, diplomats, public servants and others in the former Soviet and Eastern European countries to study western style business, economics and management now constitute its main activities (Montgomery, interview).

A common theme among the new institutes is an emphasis on marketing and promotion. Their advocacy in policy debates combines a strong ideological, policy or partisan position with aggressive salesmanship. Rather than conducting long-term scholarly research in the style of the older institutes, these think-tanks synthesise and repackage existing research. These institutes place greater premium on links to the media, building networks within policy communities and tailoring their product to the needs of decision-makers and opinion leaders. A number of institutes also try to involve politicians, political appointees and bureaucrats in their research programmes. CPS in Britain frequently uses Conservative Party MPs as authors for its monographs and many more have participated in their study groups. The progenitor of this style in the USA is the Heritage Foundation. Instead of emphasising books and monographs, Heritage produces short issue briefs of two to five pages with a clear policy agenda along with recommendations on the specific issue. Located close to Capitol Hill, Heritage staff build contacts with legislators and cultivate a network of Congressional aides. Heritage reports are often hand-delivered before key legislative decisions are taken.

Most of the new institutes propound an ideologically identifiable set of policy prescriptions. The most rapid growth has been among the free market or conservative think-tanks. There has been some movement on the Left to respond in like fashion to the ideological offensive of the New Right. In Britain, the Institute for Public Policy Research (IPPR) was established by leading figures from academia, business and the union movement who recognised the need for the Labour Party to regain credibility, 'to fight the battle of ideas, to break the intellectual ascendancy of the right' (*The Economist*, 30 July 1989: 60; Timmins, 1990b). In some circles it is affectionately known as the 'pink tank'. The Institute is different from traditional 'socialist' organisations. It is not committed to particular forms of public provision but investigates new forms of intervention to build an 'enabling state', and it occasionally favours market mechanisms.

In sum, the new partisan think-tank is more attuned to politics. It is generally ideologically identifiable. With the proliferation of think-tanks since the 1970s, competition for media attention, funding and political impact has increased. New entrants to the market have adapted to these circumstances by pursuing activist agendas and taking think-tank policy research beyond its traditionally defined politically neutral character. The research product appears in a variety of forms ranging from op-eds, radio and television interviews and short reports, with less concern to publish books or monographs. Not all of the older institutes have successfully adapted to the greater competition, more aggressive marketing practices and new policy and political priorities. The competition from the new breed has been tough. The AEI, for example, is no longer the torch bearer for the American Right. It has been usurped by the Heritage Foundation to the extent that it looks relatively moderate. In general, the old guard institutes remain more scholarly and their operational style is distinct from that of the new, smaller and more specialised institutes. This is not to suggest an evolutionary scale. The practices and style of the older institutes co-exist alongside the innovations of the new partisan institutes.

NOTES

1. I have drawn upon Wallace (1994), Weiss, (1992a) and Durst and Thurber (1989) in drawing up these criteria, as well as an earlier article (Stone, 1991).
2. A chronological listing of selected think-tanks can be found in the timeline preceding the Introduction. As this chapter discusses dozens of organisations, Appendix 1 will need to be consulted for detailed information on those that are used as examples.
3. The term 'new partisan' is drawn from Landers (1986).
4. Three of RAND's research divisions receive the majority of their funding from government sources. The Domestic Research Division, however, has diverse funding sources. It received $20.5 million in 1990 of which $9.5 came from foundations and other (non-government) sources.

5   The term 'market liberal' will be used interchangeably with libertarian to describe institutes or individuals informed by classical liberal principles and free market economics. In America, the term 'liberal' has been appropriated by US social democrats also known as 'progressives', while 'social democracy' is sometimes equated with socialism. The label of liberalism emerged in the context of the new policies associated with the Roosevelt Administration and the New Deal. Those opposed to it came to be known as conservatives, while the more recent American critics of the Great Society programmes are generally described as neo-conservative, for example, those at institutes such as Heritage who are informed by libertarian and conservative thought. For a discussion of Anglo-American terminology see Beer (1980).

2   Explaining and Analysing Think-tanks

Up until the 1990s, the available academic literature on think-tanks was limited. Even the media did not devote much attention to them and they were only deemed to be newsworthy on the establishment of a new think-tank, in the event of financial or leadership problems or the release of a major report. Dror (1980) suggests that the scarcity of literature is attributable to think-tanks being a relatively new innovation. This is a misconception. Think-tanks have been around for most of this century. They have evolved, proliferated, taken on new shape and identity and, hence, they have become more prominent. What the recent spate of books indicates is that think-tanks have been rediscovered and deemed important. The myth that think-tanks are objective and non-partisan research institutes once lulled many scholars into overlooking their participation in the political sphere. The directors and scholars of policy research institutes are themselves little more forthcoming about the role of their organisations in policy making. Furthermore, their promotional material, while giving some insight into the organisational viewpoint, is neither critical nor substantial. Annual reports tend to be descriptive of activities and are, invariably, self-congratulatory.

As in other areas of political science most of the think-tank literature is American. This is symptomatic of their proliferation in the USA. Predominant among the American literature are pluralist perspectives that portray think-tanks operating in a marketplace of ideas. These accounts are complemented by the interpretations of élite theorists. By contrast, the non-American literature is sparse. In Britain, there are few specific accounts of think-tanks aside from case-studies (for example, Robinson, 1990; Cornford, 1990). Greater attention has been paid to the Central Policy Review Staff (CPRS), a government-sponsored research unit established within 10 Downing Street to provide advice to then Conservative Prime Minister, Edward Heath, than to the independent bodies (see Beloff, 1977; Willetts, 1987; Blackstone and Plowden, 1988). Discussions of British think-tanks are mostly limited to brief accounts within studies on broader subjects. Analyses of the Thatcher government, for example, occasionally mention policy institutes such as the Centre for Policy Studies (CPS) or the Institute of Economic Affairs (IEA) (Young, 1989; Gamble, 1989b; Jordan and Ashford, 1993). Instead, the academic discussion of policy institutes in parliamentary systems in general has often been subsumed in broader studies of intellectual movements such as the New Right (see Levitas, 1986; Jordan and Ashford, 1993), or in analyses of the contribution of social science to policy and political advice (Bulmer, 1987a and b; Brooks and Gagnon, 1990).

There are few comprehensive reviews of the literature on think-tanks. This absence can be attributed to two factors. First, in the absence of a clear definition or a standard term to describe these organisations, policy research institutes have often been categorised with other kinds of organisations such as interest groups, consultancies, foundations, or university-based research and development centres. It is, therefore, difficult to isolate the literature. Second, centres of independent policy research have proliferated since the 1970s. Scholars have only recently undertaken the task of review.

Pluralist Analyses

The various pluralist approaches to political science focus on observable conflict and overt use of power. Accordingly, policy research institutes are an object of analysis when they compete among themselves and with other groups to influence the policy process. The number and diversity of American think-tanks reflects strong competition in ideas as well as competition to win funding. In one account of the American think-tank industry, a CSIS scholar described the system as 'essentially pluralistic. Anybody can play. ... There is free entry. No one institution has a monopoly' (Robert E. Hunter quoted in Stanfield, 1990: 552). As James Smith describes it, '... the American political system seems to have all sorts of gaps and interstices in which research ... organizations can survive' (1989: 80). This includes the division of powers between President and Congress and between state and federal government, the numerous centres of power among congressional committees, agencies and departments, and the relative weakness of the political parties as a cohesive force (Weaver, 1989: 570; Polsby, 1983: 58). It creates what Easterbrook (1986) calls the 'intellectual market', that is, an open system conducive to the growth of private sources of policy research such as think-tanks.

In Britain, as in most other countries, policy institutes are smaller in number, stature and size. Pluralist analyses also tend to be less persuasive where competition of policy ideas is less evident within political parties and with the presence of a strong permanent civil service. Nevertheless, executive directors often speak in pluralist terms. A former director of two think-tanks, James Cornford (1990), for example, writes that the IPPR explores 'alternative views' in competition with the free market think-tanks (see also Portes, 1988; Daniel, 1989; Kay, 1989; Wallace, 1990).

In most pluralist accounts, the growth and diversity of think-tanks is a positive feature of democracy. Their proliferation allows governments and other decision-makers to become better informed of diverse views (McGann, 1992: 738). Not only is the corpus of knowledge increased, competition is constructive and raises the standard of analysis. There are, however, widely varying perspectives among pluralists.[1] Pluralists value the competition among think-tanks to influence policy but some disregard the common values among many institutes which allows particular perspectives to dominate in the policy environment. Differences in staffing, budget and capital base and the consequent effect on the ability to compete is not addressed. The positive aspects of competition and diversity are emphasised. Nevertheless, pluralist approaches are useful in explaining why individual think-tanks are unable to monopolise the attention of government and dominate policy agendas.

Neo-pluralists have accommodated some of the criticisms of élite theorists and Marxists that are discussed below. They recognise that the structural power of business or capital skews the political system and that competition might be limited (Lindblom, 1990: 237). For example, while there is constructive rivalry between the British think-tanks on the right of the political spectrum, it is muted by their shared 'overall political viewpoint' (Gaffney, 1991: 10). Additionally, a group of writers who favour the presence of many and diverse institutes deplore as dysfunctional, the trend towards politicisation (see Easterbrook, 1986; Landers, 1986; Smith, 1991a). These writers argue that non-partisan value-free, problem-solving approaches of the older institutes tempered public debate and built consensus, whereas the overtly ideological and partisan strategies of contemporary institutes is conflict-ridden and fragments political debate in a war of ideas. Smith (1991a) develops further the notion of dysfunction by portraying the growing number and competition among think-tanks as an anti-democratic trend because think-tanks are so highly organised as a community of knowledge that the expert is privileged over the citizen (see also Gaffney, 1991; Fischer, 1993). Yet, they also have the potential, especially in parliamentary systems, to serve as an alternative to the bureaucracy, acting as 'ginger groups' and promoting new policy debates.

Ruling Élites

Élite theorists outline the ways in which think-tanks serve the long-term interest of élites through their influence on policy formulation and the opinion forming processes. Policy-planning institutes are examined in terms of their relationship to the major sources of economic and social power – a relationship that is 'demonstrated' by the interlocking directorates of the corporate, military and administrative hierarchies. These theorists argue that think-tanks are neither apolitical organisations devoted to the advancement of knowledge nor competitively enhancing the democratic formulation of policy.

Those who employ Mills' (1959) 'power élite' perspective argue that think-tanks represent the interests of capital and form part of the policy network of 'corporate liberalism' (Eakins, 1972). Writers who distance themselves from the vaguely socialist notion of corporate liberalism, nonetheless write critically of the role of Brookings and the Council on Foreign Relations as part of the 'Establishment' (Silk and Silk, 1980) or depict policy institutes as a central component of a 'shadow government' (Guttman and Willner, 1976). One study portrays the founders of the Brookings Institution as holding a deep distrust of democracy and seeking to undermine electoral influences on public policy and the existing control of government by representative political parties. Political parties were regarded as spokesmen for special interests that corrupted and distorted the general interests of society. By contrast, the social scientists and businessmen who established Brookings considered that 'learned men' with economic expertise could 'stand above specific economic, political or class interests' and therefore were best able to discern the general welfare (Critchlow, 1985: 4). Of contemporary circumstances, Steinfels (1979) talks about neo-conservative think-tank links with big business. He argues that business, unhappy about the relative lack of intellectual support in the academy, welcomed neo-conservatives into their ranks and invested millions in the 'knowledge industry' to counter the criticisms of the progressive liberal intelligentsia – the so-called 'New Class' (1979: 11). Another writer argues that business associations and think-tanks 'constitute the formal interface between the highest levels of government and large corporations', allowing the inner circle, that is, politicised elements of the upper echelons of business, 'decisive impact on public policies' (Useem, 1984: 72).

Élite theorists portray policy as the values and preferences of the governing élite which decision-makers implement either knowingly or unknowingly. One of the best known proponents is Thomas Dye (1978, 1987a and b). For Dye, all societies are governed by élites and democracy is a 'romantic fiction'. He outlines a 'policy planning oligarchy' in which think-tanks perform the central coordination of the policy-making process. Decision-makers are only involved in the procedure of policy and the details of implementation rather than establishing agendas and priorities. The agenda has long since been set before they are involved. Dye argues that resources for research, planning and policy originate from corporate and personal wealth. This wealth is channelled into foundations and think-tanks in the form of endowments, grants and contracts. Senior corporate figures sit on the governing boards to oversee spending. 'In short, corporate and personal wealth provides both the financial resources and the overall direction of policy research and planning' (Dye, 1978: 311). The directors also play a major role in the recruitment of personnel who might subsequently move on to high posts in the executive branch of government. Élite consensus and decisions are thus communicated to government officials.

In sum, élite theorists focus on the narrow social backgrounds, shared élite values and social insulation of personnel running the state apparatus to infer a causal relationship between social and economic status and political power. The flaw with élite studies is that they focus on surrogates for power rather than on the exercise of power. Élite theorists analyse the social backgrounds and interconnections of different élite groups, interlocking directorates, who is recruited and how, and whom they meet 'as surrogate indicators for how they act, and interact, what their values are, and how cohesive they are as a group' (Dunleavy and O'Leary, 1987: 150). This methodology poses problems in terms of identifying leaders. Either the study focuses upon the formally defined power holders or it seeks to get behind these facades to identify the real power holders. The latter approach presupposes prior knowledge of the real élite in advance of the empirical research. Furthermore, while certain organisations or individuals may have reputations as power holders this does not constitute evidence of power being exerted (Ham and Hill, 1993: 32). The assumption that élite consensus and cohesiveness is translated into strategies of control through think-tanks is also problematic. Not only are policy research institutes very diverse in their political and philosophical dispositions but even those that sympathise with a particular administration or social group do not always confirm élite policy preferences. The relationship of think-tanks to the corporate liberal state or Establishment is multi-dimensional and contradictory. Think-tanks have an autonomy or independence of their own. They occasionally propose unpopular policies and represent an unreliable instrument of élite rule.

Anti-Establishment Views

The portrayal of monolithic élite control is more apparent in a body of populist American literature. This right-wing conspiracy theory is predominantly found in the pages of *American Opinion*, the journal of the American Legion. This literature has concentrated on the CFR and Trilateral Commission, the members of which are supposedly working to bring about a new world order in which 'national sovereignty would be superseded by one supranational authority of global compass' (Evans, 1975: 39; see also Allen, 1972). The élite constitutes an 'invisible government' (Smoot, 1962), while the CFR's journal *Foreign Affairs* is the unofficial voice of US foreign policy in which 'millionaire Socialist conspirators who are trying to enslave us, lay down their line'. Establishment figures and CFR members such as Arthur Schlesinger Jnr. and David Rockefeller are 'high class Marxists' while 'Henry Kissinger is a Soviet agent' (Stang, 1975: 25–26). These analyses lack scholarly credibility. Even prominent conservative William F. Buckley denounced these writers as 'kooks' who 'specialize in ignorance' (*Washington Star*, 10 March 1979). CFR member, Zygmunt Nagorski (1977) has written a more measured rebuttal of both right and left-wing criticisms. He denies conspiracy and outlined the traditional pluralist image of the CFR as a 'marketplace of ideas' and a 'community of intellectual freedom'.

New Left and Neo-Marxist Perspectives

Ironically, the right-wing 'patriots' draw upon New Left writers such as Domhoff (1978; 1980) and Shoup and Minter (1977) who engage in 'power structure research'. They articulate the more orthodox instrumentalist view of the state in neo-marxist thought. The 'power élite' is 'the leadership group for the upper class as a whole, transcending to some degree the business oriented perspective of those who are involved only in corporate activities' (Domhoff, 1983: 83). Although the power élite presides over positions of power, they still need non-profit policy organisations. Think-tanks bring long-term issues affecting power élite security to their attention. They develop the ideology and long range plans that transform problems of political economy into manageable objects of public policy. Furthermore, as the common economic interests and social cohesion among the power élite is insufficient to produce consensus on policies, agreement on such matters requires 'research, consultation and deliberation' to form a coherent sense of long-term class interests (Alpert and Markusen, 1980; Domhoff, 1983: 82). For example, Peschek's (1989) study of Brookings, AEI, Heritage, the Trilateral Commission and the Institute for Contemporary Studies (ICS) sought to demonstrate that these institutes mobilise élites to redefine the terms of debate and in order to translate class interests into state action. Studies of US foreign policy (Shoup and Minter, 1977; Shoup, 1977) portray the CFR as a central node of the ruling class where corporate capitalists develop 'imperialistic' strategies to sustain US capitalist hegemony. Yet, ordinary people do not automatically concur with élite views on policy. Domhoff argues that they are just as likely to have differing perspectives on policy that are detrimental to the interests of the corporate community. Trade unions, women's organisations, minorities and other interest groups may have their own sources of power within the community and espouse policies not favoured by the power élite. Hence, think-tanks also perform an ideological role as part of an opinion shaping network (Domhoff, 1983: 83).

Not unlike the élite perspective, the problem with the instrumentalist position is that it portrays political institutions as a passive tool of a mobilised capitalist class active in promoting ideological hegemony. Not only think-tanks but also the judiciary, the media and other institutions exercise a considerable degree of autonomy from the ruling class and articulate diverse points of view. Structuralists, by contrast, argue that the interests of the capitalist class are best served when the ruling class is not the politically governing class. The ruling class cannot transcend its own short-run interests and profit-oriented consciousness, therefore, the state requires relative autonomy.

Despite there being a viable framework, analyses of think-tanks from the structuralist school of Marxist thought have not emerged. Structuralists tend to focus upon how policy *output* supports capitalist institutions. Instrumentalists focus on how class and corporate interests influence *inputs* into policy formation. As policy institutes are not involved in formal decision-making or policy implementation, that is, output, their role appears marginal. Nevertheless, such an approach might depict think-tanks as organisations that have autonomy from corporate interests and are able to pursue social and economic research independently. Their independence allows them to investigate policies and programmes supportive of the long-term stability of the capitalist system. During social and economic crisis, they are in a position to provide 'reforms to state managers anxiously concerned with preventing a complete rupture in the body politic' (Critchlow, 1985: 7). That is, the relative autonomy of think-tanks from class interests coincides with the relative autonomy of the state.

The study of think-tanks is also amenable to Gramscian analysis of hegemonic control. Within this perspective, the ideological apparatus constrains the parameters of ideas, debate and discourse in civil society and the state (Carnoy, 1984: 69). The marketplace of ideas that pluralists idolise is severely truncated as views and beliefs that are critical or revolutionary are circumscribed or repressed. Institutions such as the mass media and universities set the limits in which public debate of controversial issues takes place. According to Andrew Gamble, 'hegemony exists when the political leadership of a group or a nation is exercised with minimal dispute and resistance' (1989b: 1). Think-tanks can be conceived as apparatuses for propagating the ideological hegemony of capitalism. They are a means for forging a common political identity among powerful individuals representing diverse interests through their research activities and symposiums (Desai, 1994; Gill, 1990). The concept of hegemony is often employed in critical discussions of the New Right (Levitas, 1986). New Right think-tanks 'shift the centre of political debate' and 'dislodge the ideological hegemony of the Keynesian regulators or the "new class"' (Sawer, 1990: 1). Their importance lies in their agenda-setting capabilities and capacity to attract media attention as opinion leaders. Gamble (1989b: 147), for instance, places the British free market think-tanks within a network of organisations and individuals who supported Margaret Thatcher's rise to power in their political project to free the economy and roll back the state. Institutes such as the Centre for Policy Studies and the Institute of Economic Affairs represented a small part of the hegemonic project of Thatcherism. Their role was to replace the discredited social democratic consensus with a new policy paradigm as well as to provide the feasible plans and blueprints that would help build Conservative political dominance and restore conditions for profitable capital accumulation (Desai, 1994).

Confounding notions of hegemonic control is the degree of ideological conflict and competition among policy institutes. The policy organisations addressed in this study do not represent a common ideological standpoint. An ideological consensus is conspicuously absent which is hardly surprising given the great diversity among policy institutes. Even the mainstream bodies do not produce consensus. Additionally, many political and corporate leaders drift between ideological poles and between organisations. There are often disagreements arising between different sectors of capital on, for example, tariff or tax policies. This is reflected in how various sectors of the American business community draw upon the expertise of different institutes such as the Conference Board, Committee for Economic Development (CED) or the specialised Employee Benefit Research Institute (EBRI) (Levitan and Cooper, 1984).

One policy specialist, Hugh Heclo, who has worked in three American think-tanks, argues that Marxists are too structured by their interpretative framework and preconceptions of capitalist hegemony. Their determinism is compounded by being 'on the outside looking in at the names on the boards of trustees, the printed recommendations, the assumption of policy influence'. Marxist analysis neither gets inside think-tanks nor fully understands their good, poor or non-existent relations with politicians, bureaucrats and academics. In contrast to perceptions of the hegemonic control of an interconnected élite sustaining the capitalist order, the picture can be counterbalanced by highlighting the 'PR puffery these enterprises generate about their policy influence, [and] the self important and vacuous big names that sit on their boards with little effect' (Heclo, 1989: 1222–24). Furthermore, many institutes are not politically motivated and resist pressures that might entail ideological mobilisation. It is, therefore, more appropriate to identify 'hegemonic projects'. Aspiring to hegemony is a continual struggle. Drawing on Gamble again, 'no hegemony is ever complete, and many attempts to establish hegemony are never realised. That is why hegemonic projects are encountered more frequently than hegemony itself' (1989b: 1).

The Perspectives Compared

The growing interest in think-tanks since the 1980s has produced little agreement regarding their role in the policy process. The pluralist, élite and Marxist perspectives – the most commonly employed theories – provide contrasting images. At one extreme, there are images of think-tanks as élite-ridden centres of power and governance behind-the-scenes. At the other extreme, think-tanks are portrayed as independent centres of objective policy research guilelessly pursuing public interest goals, their influence counterbalanced by the competitive environment in which they operate. Neither extreme adequately portrays the multi-faceted roles of these non-profit organisations. As following chapters discuss, many are ineffectual in policy and politically irrelevant but find a mission in serving other educational, professional or public purposes.

Nevertheless, from the perspective of a Washington insider, the policy process may well appear highly competitive and pluralistic. No one organisation or individual controls the policy agenda or holds together a consensus. Numerous journalistic analyses reinforce this image of competition. However, for those outside the Washington policy network, the process appears more structured and controlled by élites. These outsiders do not see the daily policy battles, the bickering about think-tank personalities, the fight for funding or the competition for media attention. Instead, they perceive the dominance of certain think-tanks and, despite some differences on means and strategies, broad consensus on goals. It is an important point. The proximity of the observer and access (or lack of) to the policy process and networks of power can compound the conclusions of a particular method-ological and philosophical position (see Dye, 1987b). This does not assert the superiority of the 'insider' view. It may simply mean greater access to information at the cost of detachment.

Ruling class theories do not fully explain the think-tank phenomena. As Jerome Himmelstein (1990: 159) notes, both the instrumentalist and structuralist approaches 'assume capitalist problems yield statist solutions'. Following this logic, it is difficult to account for the growth of business funded think-tanks promoting anti-statist policies. Nor do structuralist theories of a passive capitalist class and relatively autonomous state help explain why corporations fund and support non-profit organisations challenging government positions. Instrumentalist approaches assume, however, that capital will attempt hegemonic projects. In common with élite theorists, they perceive capitalists as more cohesive and active in sustaining privilege. While instrumentalists identify think-tanks as a central component in the political mobilisation of business, the approach has not been used to explain the growing numbers of think-tanks, their increasingly specialised character or their more partisan and ideological stances. Instead, neo-pluralist and structuralist arguments that capital is divided and uncoordinated potentially provide better explanations for the diversity of think-tanks and their fluctuating fortunes.

More recently some policy analysts have drawn on Michel Foucault's ideas on power and knowledge to account for the think-tank phenomenon (Gagnon, 1990; Pal, 1990). They focus on the ways in which knowledge and power is dispersed. Power is not a possession or capacity. Nor is it the property of an individual or class. Power has the character of a network or an open set of relations in society. The discourses of knowledge groups – whether it be think-tanks, professional bodies or scientists – establish them as sources power, domination and force. Many think-tanks would represent a 'site of domination' in the sense that their rationalist policy discourses are used by the state as a source of authority to legitimise laws and policies. However, where there is power there is also resistance. Resistance takes many forms and is not unified. This conception of power is 'reminiscent' of pluralist conceptions of power if the idea of domination and asymmetries of power that are also evident in Foucault's work are disregarded (Conway, 1990: 172). It brings into sight the many small and unknown policy institutes that are discounted or not even discussed in Marxist and élite accounts. Analysis that incorporates these marginalised think-tanks and looks at localised struggles in which knowledge is deployed is necessary to account for the extensiveness of think-tank development rather than focusing on only those that have observable links to the state or élites.

As discussed in later chapters, public policy concepts of networks, discourses and epistemic communities are more useful than system-wide frameworks of 'policy planning network' or 'power élite'. The 'power élite' concept operates at a macro-political level encompassing business, military and government and how these three 'pillars' govern society through their interaction. Similarly, the neo-Marxist literature focuses on system wide forms of class control. Epistemic communities and the policy network literature are a more specific or lower level of analysis focusing on networks and individual actors in policy-making. Such communities do not seek to control society and economy. Instead, they are groups of politically motivated intellectuals seeking to inform limited areas of policy on the basis of their expertise. Where élite theorists stress social and economic control through the high level interaction of élites, the epistemic community concept emphasises the shared norms and causal beliefs of experts and their specific political projects. Within the policy planning networks identified in 'power structure research', expertise is used to bolster corporate power for the upper class. There is little scope for agency or independence from structural forces in this framework. The epistemic community concept represents a partial counter by allowing knowledge and learning to play an independent role in the policy process. Although the role of knowledge and expertise in the service of, for example, the corporate sector is recognised, it is not always the case that these communities serve the interests of capital. Epistemic communities have some autonomy. They can be independent of the 'inner circle'. Indeed, they can be in opposition to it. Unlike those who argue that policy is forged by hidden élites, this approach argues that ideas and expertise are an important force affecting the substance of public policy independently of interest groups, bureaucrats and political parties, although these groups remain significant mediating forces in the acceptance of new ideas. Epistemic communities are knowledge based networks who articulate the cause-and-effect relationships of complex problems whether it be the causes of pollution or the impact of deregulatory policies or the logic of nuclear strategy. These communities help decision-makers without expert knowledge to clarify state interests regarding complex technical problems. The analyses of these communities demonstrate that control over knowledge and information is an important dimension of power and that the diffusion of new ideas and data can lead to new patterns of behaviour and policy innovation. Think-tanks are a strategic location for epistemic communities. In particular, they play a role in the development of an epistemic community's consensual knowledge and the diffusion of this knowledge to influence government agendas.

NOTES

1. This is not the place to outline the different views on the role of the state in the pluralist tradition, but see Dunleavy and O'Leary (1987).

3 US Exceptionalism and Parliamentary Systems

The American political system has provided a fertile environment for the establishment of think-tanks whereas in parliamentary systems there are fewer opportunities for growth. American writers often assert that independent policy research institutes are unique to their political system. While the size and scale of think-tank development is certainly unique to the USA, the organisational form is not. There is a strong tradition of independent policy research outside the USA. However, the prospects for survival and expansion of think-tanks in parliamentary systems, and their avenues of influence, are affected by different tax régimes and philanthropic conditions, the role of the political parties, and the policy-making environment in which they are found. Whilst noting the differences in the degree of development between the USA and elsewhere, this chapter qualifies a prevalent view in the American literature that think-tanks are unique to the USA.

Difference and Diversity

There are considerable differences but also some continuities between think-tanks across the British and American political systems. One of the more noticeable differences between US and British institutes that emerges from glancing through the Appendix is the varying sizes of full-time, in-house staff. A word of caution is necessary here. Annual reports are often 'padded' and staff size inflated by the inclusion of short-term visiting scholars, part-time scholars and office-holders who are employed elsewhere. American institutes, particularly the older ones, have very large staffs. Unfortunately, it is more difficult to establish the staff size of new partisan think-tanks as most are reliant on adjunct scholars or affiliated fellows who are employed in universities, the public service, media and the corporate sector. Demos in London, for example, has chosen not to appoint permanent research staff but to draw upon people outside the organisation.

In the British and US systems, policy institutes are concentrated in the national capitals, and to a lesser extent in the USA, in New York and California. There are, on one estimate, 69 think-tanks, and on another up to 100, based in Washington (Weaver, 1989: 564; Smith, 1989a: 179, respectively). Over 70 are listed in Appendix One. There has also been a trend over the last two decades for larger think-tanks such as the Institute for Foreign Policy Analysis (IFPA), RAND, Hudson and the CFR to establish a second office in the US capital. Of note, a number of London based institutes are international. The membership, board and research staff of the International Institute for Strategic Studies are drawn from around the world and the Institute is strongly international in ethos. The International Institute for Environment and Development (IIED), the Institute for European Environmental Policy (IEEP) and Panos all maintain offices in other countries, while the Centre for Economic Policy Research (CEPR) operates a network of scholars scattered throughout Europe. This is probably symptomatic of both the pace of European integration as well as recognition of the global and interdependent nature of many policy problems.

The US system is characterised by a greater number and diversity and, indeed, hierarchy of think-tanks. The largest American think-tanks, with budgets ranging from nine million to 95 million dollars, tend to be drawn from the old guard. Brookings, AEI, Hoover, CFR and CED tend to be the most well known and highly reputed. A significant source of security for a very small number of institutes, such as the Carnegie Endowment and Brookings, is an endowment. They are not typical of the majority of American institutes which are very much smaller in budget and staff size. The new American institutes operate with smaller budgets – usually below five million dollars with the exception of Heritage and WRI. While the budgets of the older British institutes are considerably less than those of the leading American counterparts, they are, none the less, sizeable. In the British system there is more homogeneity. Differences in the expenditures between the old and new institutes are not extreme. In Britain – and parliamentary systems in general (see Stone, 1991) – there is greater similarity in size and policy scope, perhaps because they are not subject to the intense competition of dozens of think-tanks. Furthermore, it is not apparent that to have hundreds of policy centres is advantageous. The proliferation of think-tanks in the USA does not necessarily equate with a more efficient, rational policy process or even better policy analysis. Indeed, the presence of relatively few policy institutes in parliamentary systems may even be a positive feature. There is less clamour for attention outside the formal policy process and fewer resources are exhausted on promotion.

The American Policy-Making Terrain

Carol Weiss (1992b: 6–8) has developed the most comprehensive set of explanations for the proliferation of policy analysis organisations in the USA. It is on these points that some American discussants of think-tanks base their claim that they are unique or peculiar to America. Although Weiss does not make such an assumption, her framework provides the starting-point for the following discussion of the exceptionalism of the American system. There are important differences in political culture and institutions between the two countries which mean that think-tanks, as well as interest groups and lobbies, potentially play a more visible role in the USA political because of more points of access, whereas in Great Britain such groups are more focused on the executive (Weaver and Rockman, 1993: 28).

The first, and probably most important reason that Weiss offers is the fragmentation of the US governmental system. The separation of powers allows both Congress and the President to initiate legislation. A divided government – with neither the Republicans nor Democrats controlling both the White House and Congress for much of the past 25 years – has fuelled demand for intellectual ammunition on both sides. Executive branch departments are also fragmented. They are 'made up of strong component agencies, each with its own interests, clients and policy preferences' (Weiss, 1992b: 6). These circumstances mean that secretaries have difficulty controlling their 'Balkanised' departments. Additionally, Congress is fragmented. Both the Senate and House of Representatives operate independently when fashioning legislation. Power is dispersed over a large number of committees and sub-committees. As party discipline is weak, members of Congress formulate many of their own policy priorities and pursue their agendas with considerable independence. The final point of fragmentation in the USA system is the division of powers between the state and federal governments. The consequence of fragmentation for policy institutes is twofold. Numerous policy fora are created and demand from several audiences for policy analysis and research has grown in what McGann (1992: 738) calls the 'hyper pluralistic nature of American society'.

Second, Weiss argues that few bodies aggregate interests in the

American political system. Political parties have not played as pre-eminent a role in policy development as in other countries. There are few sanctions with which American parties can control their members and force adherence to party platforms. Nor are there strong corporatist structures and peak associations representing sectors of society such as labour, business and other interests that are evident in some European countries. As a consequence, there are no formal mechanisms to bring these sectors into negotiation with government over policy.

Weiss's third point, also identified by Dror (1984), Marsh (1991) and Ricci (1993), is the increasing complexity of government. Policy problems cannot be treated in a vacuum as they are interconnected with other issues. Furthermore, 'finding an appropriate expert or consultant has become difficult because problems do not present themselves in configurations that match the specialisations of the academic disciplines' (Weiss, 1992b: 7). Policy-makers are frequently encountering situations in which uncertain conditions prevail. Big government, globalisation and the flood of information from interest groups, industry and new government programmes mean that think-tanks become one source of expertise able to explain the nature, causes and remedies of problems. They can be functional for governments and bureaucracies in conditions of cabinet and ministerial overload. They augment in-house research capacities, circumvent time and institutional constraints and alert élites to changing global circumstances.

Fourth, the executive branch of government draws on unelected officials to staff many policy-making positions which weakens the 'prerogatives, privileges and power of the bureaucracy' (Weiss, 1992b: 8). Appointed administrators have turned away from the bureaucracy for alternative sources of advice (see also Smith, 1989a: 180–81). In a similar vein, Nelson Polsby (1983: 16) argues that the growth of policy research institutes has been the result of 'certain characteristics of American Government, most notably its permeability'. Polsby was referring to a continuous reciprocal flow of senior staff in and out of government service. The policy institute 'acts as a revolving door for individuals to come and go from administrative agency to think-tank to agency, to media, back for a sabbatical at [the think-tank] and finally into a high level policy making position in a sympathetic administration' (Feulner, 1985: 24). Alongside the propensity of US government to contract out research, permeability also encourages a dependency on outside organisations for intelligence, advice and analysis.

A fifth point is that the openness of the American system to external sources of advice has evolved over the last half century. The presidency became increasingly institutionalised under Truman and Eisenhower when many positions of a policy advisory nature were created in bodies such as the CIA, the National Security Council, the Council of Economic Advisers and in the State Department. After the Second World War, Congress expanded existing bodies such as the Congressional Research Service or created new bodies like the Congressional Budget Office. Far from displacing advisers outside government in universities and think-tanks, the institutionalisation of advice presented new opportunities. The new advisers, often with academic backgrounds, and put in command of large financial resources, expanded links to think-tanks and universities (Smith, 1991a: 113–16). The Johnson Administration's Great Society programmes, for example, generated contract research work for the urban and social policy think-tanks on poverty and racial issues.[1] The Urban Institute, in particular, was set up by seven individuals hand-picked by President Johnson, to study the needs of US cities (Rich, 1988). The new think-tanks mirrored the rise of a new managerial, expert or technocratic class in areas such as health, finance, the environment, defence, intellectual property, trade, communications and transport. Keynesian-inspired public spending and technocratic prescriptions spurred government involvement in and responsibility for these increasingly technical fields of public policy (Beer, 1980: 18–22). With increasing industrialisation, economic interdependence and government intervention, there was, and remains, a greater role for the creation and dissemination of knowledge.

The British Parliamentary System

British (as well as Canadian and Australian) scholars also identify politico-institutional features of parliamentary systems as the main reason for less extensive think-tank development. Parliamentary systems are portrayed as closed. Claims about the decline of Parliament and concentration of power within Prime Minister, Cabinet and bureaucracy are said to insulate policy-making from outside influences. Think-tanks 'languish for want of access to the policy making processes' (Marsh, 1980: x). The convention of collective ministerial responsibility and an ethos of officialdom compounds the insularity of policy making, creating a 'predisposition for secrecy' (Holmes, 1986: 20). For example, Colin Gray, former Chairman of the National Institute for Public Policy in Virginia, argues that:

American style think-tanks could not function in Canada or Great Britain ... because of the differences in political culture and governmental structure. In Canada and Great Britain the ethos of officialdom is predominantly to the effect that (1) the public does *not* have a right to know, and (2) officials know best (Gray, 1978: 189).

John Kay, once Director of the Institute for Fiscal Studies (IFS) in London, considers that 'The primary motive for government secrecy is a perception by both politicians and officials, that information is power, and that control of information is central to the maintenance of power.' Secrecy allows greater control of the policy agenda. If outsiders are unaware of the principal concerns of decision-makers and the timing of issues, they are less able to influence decisions. 'Control of the policy agenda is thus the key element of civil service control, and secrecy about it is essential – and effective – in limiting the role which others can play in the policy process' (Kay, 1989: 21–22).

Closure compounds the distrust that many politicians have in intellectuals (Galston, 1990: 431). Margaret Thatcher, for example, referred to academics and intellectuals as the 'chattering classes'. Furthermore, politicians often do not have the time or inclination to think beyond the next election. They are driven by immediate political concerns in 'a "pressure cooker" environment' (Seymour-Ure, 1987: 177). Incorporating long-term policy analysis in the political process that think-tanks usually offer is problematic. Nevertheless, the salience of long-term planning has been recognised by a variety of governments with the establishment of bodies such as the CPRS in Britain. However, these bodies have rarely been successful (Weller, 1987: 155). One reason why the CPRS, housed at 10 Downing Street, was abolished was because its long-term policy research interests and motivations clashed with the needs of ministers and Cabinet to respond to short-term political realities (Blackstone and Plowden, 1990: 201). The failure of government think-tanks to survive or maintain their original objectives in the face of political pressure may be one reason for the growth of policy institutes in parliamentary systems. Independent advisory bodies potentially have greater longevity. They are less likely to be affected by bureaucratic and political constraints imposed on internal government think-tanks.

Even though the policy formation process is less public than in the USA, parliamentary systems are not impervious to think-tanks. Parliamentarians, party officials and bureaucrats participate in think-tank functions. Some are think-tank members and others independently seek advice and information. Additionally, there are formal routes for policy research institutes to make submissions to Parliament and contribute to public debate. For example, over the period 1990–92, Earth Resources Research in London 'presented evidence to the European Parliament, a number of Select Committees of both Houses of Parliament, Working Group 1 of the Intergovernmental Panel on Climate Change, the Royal Commission on Environmental Pollution, and various public inquiries' (ERR, 1992: 10). Likewise, the National Institute for Social and Economic Research (NIESR) regularly presents evidence before Committees of the House of Commons.

Not everyone considers that the structure of parliamentary systems so intransigently determines the opportunities for the establishment, survival and influence of think-tanks. Jeremy Richardson (1994: 3–4) disputes the notion that the British policy-making system is closed. He describes the so-called secrecy and closure of British politics as a myth. In practice, he argues, there has been a strong tendency to include groups in decision making through informal policy communities. According to Eamonn Butler at ASI (interview), the policy process has changed in Britain and become 'less of an establishment activity'. Dr Butler felt that more people are educated and interested in politics, think they have a right to participate and are articulate enough to do so. The media is also increasingly 'hungry for ideas' and anxious to get people to comment on policy issues. While not providing the administrative permeability of the US system, the Special Adviser System nevertheless allows some individuals to be seconded into the civil service by a Minister. David Willetts (interview), when based at the CPS, also considered that there was greater use of special political advisers by ministers and that a more pluralistic environment of research and analysis was emerging. Think-tanks are part of this mixed economy of policy advice.

While parliamentary systems are more exclusive, the negative aspects for think-tanks can be emphasised unduly. The centralised character of political affairs and the closed features of British government allow think-tank executives and scholars to more easily target decision-makers. British politics is characterised by a relatively small and easily identifiable set of policy actors. By contrast, the US system is more fluid – and fragmented, with a larger number of participants in policy circles. It is more difficult to discern the loci of power. The larger number of think-tanks targeting both the executive and legislature with their conflicting policy demands adds to the congestion and gridlock of the US system.

The lack of permeability in the British civil service was possibly one factor in Mrs Thatcher's turn towards independent policy bureaux. Willetts (interview) stressed that Margaret Thatcher did not want to be dependent on the bureaucracy for advice, was also 'suspicious' of the Conservative Central Office and used the CPS as an alternative source of advice (see also *The Economist*, 1989: 63). 'One of the frequent fears of the political consumers of policy advice is that of becoming the prisoners of their suppliers', as can occur when there are permanently closed policy advice circuits or when advisors share the same values, perceptions and methodological approaches (Machin, 1987: 166). Mrs Thatcher also drew upon the advice of those who shared her radical vision (Young, 1989: vii). Her style of leadership aided organisations like the CPS, IEA and ASI.

The structure of British government does not present an impenetrable exterior to outside sources of advice. New tools and institutions for policy analysis may evolve to draw in alternative perspectives. Royal Commissions and discussion papers increased opportunities and demand for policy analysis in the past. The revivification of the committee system in the British Parliament potentially represents a source of demand for think-tank research and analysis (Marsh, 1980 and 1991). Of considerable importance are the reforms to the civil service that will possibly open up the policy-making process. Furthermore, as the number of research institutes grows, decision-makers in bureaucracies and political parties as well as leaders in interest groups, may become more conscious of, and more open towards them. Changing mechanisms of policy formation over time may present new opportunities for think-tanks. In the interim, however, institutional and cultural factors remain important.

Tax Structures and Philanthropic Cultures

Although the architecture of the American political system is an important factor promoting think-tank development, it is equally appropriate to consider the tax regime. The American tax structure encourages the formation of foundations and individual giving, creating a massive source of funding for think-tanks and other non-profit organisations (O'Connell, 1983; Bremner, 1988). There are in excess of 6,500 foundations in the USA (Hodgkinson and Weitzman, 1989: 124). In 1991, the net value of foundation assets was more than $163 billion (NCRP, 1994). In Britain, the taxation system has forestalled the development of foundations as well as independent policy research organisations. Nevertheless, the income of policy institutes is derived largely from accepting gifts and grants which are not taxed, which are tax deductible for the donors and which, in the US, are often from tax-exempt foundations. In many cases, organisations would not have been established or survived were it not for tax concessions.

Non-profit organisations are often regarded as being engaged in 'charitable' activities. In Britain, think-tanks that are registered charities are exempt from tax on rents, land and property; interest and dividends; covenanted donations and other gifts. They must not be involved in propaganda and research must be 'objective' or related to the organisation's aims (see the notes preceding the Appendix). Caveats at the front of think-tank publications generally disown a corporate view. Most American think-tanks are classified under section 501(c)(3) of the Internal Revenue Code, and are subject to similar restrictions on their political activity as in Britain. Yet, despite having what is essentially the same legal status, American think-tanks function within a very different tax environment and philanthropic culture. The presence of many foundations combined with a strong tradition of corporate and individual philanthropy represent a major source of financial sustenance.

In America, the largesse of foundations during the 1980s may partially account for the rapid growth in think-tanks in the US.[2] The funding trends of foundations over the period 1982–87 indicate that grants for social science have risen from 6.2 per cent to 8.9 per cent (Hodgkinson and Weitzman, 1989: 127). In a breakdown of recipient organisations, foundation giving to the category of 'research institute' increased significantly over the period 1982–87, from 5.2 per cent of total giving to 10 per cent (1989: 128). That is, from just over $70 million to over $200 million (Clinton, 1987: 37). In addition, non-commercial research institutes were the only component of the education and research sector to improve relative wages and salaries for employees. The total number of employees increased 25 per cent over the decade to 1987 to almost 125,000 people. In Britain, foundations are not so prevalent. In 1987–88, the two hundred largest trusts made grants totalling £7,027995 to 'education'. It is a category much broader in organisational scope than the 'research institute' category for the USA data. The percentage of company pretax profits as charitable giving by British companies (approximately 0.2 per cent) also compares unfavourably with the USA (Davis Smith, 1989: 6). The philanthropic culture is markedly different from that in America. Nevertheless, a more positive attitude to eleemosynary activities among business and community may be encouraged by changes in tax legislation.

Political Parties

In countries with strong political parties there are supposedly fewer points of access at which policy institutes can participate. On the other hand, parties can magnify the influence of an institute if that party's imagination is captured by the thought and writings of a particular think-tank. For political parties, think-tanks can introduce ideas into debate to see if they are unpopular, unworkable or unsound, thus allowing a government to avoid the embarrassment of abandoning legislation. The CPS in Britain, for example, has been described as a place from which 'ideas can be floated unofficially and without commitment by ministers and others to see how public opinion responds to them' (Coleman, 1991: 441). Greater willingness to consort with some of the innovatory policy ideas of the think-tanks reflected in some degree a departure from the traditional style of Conservative policy-making. Long regarded as having a hostile attitude towards intellectuals in favour of pragmatism and a party conference that traditionally ratified rather than created policy agendas, the Conservative Party has been relatively closed to extra-parliamentary policy actors. Under Margaret Thatcher the internal party secrecy over policy was loosened but not removed. Thatcher remained reliant on career civil servants for policy advice and some close to her were sceptical of ideas coming from the CPS (Hames and Feasey, 1993).

Nevertheless, think-tanks can be instrumental in ideological mobilisation that helps to sustain a political party in office, for example, the Conservative Party under Margaret Thatcher and John Major. With such a long tenure in office, the think-tanks were a source of radical energy and renewal at times when the government appeared to falter or drift. Conservative and libertarian policy institutes such as IEA, CPS and ASI, with the ascension of a radical reformist party in 1979, found themselves in an environment where their policy elaboration was welcome and encouraged by the Prime Minister and other sympathetic ministers. These think-tanks were a source of innovation to 'militate against the consensus and compromise oriented procedures of parliament and the inertia of bureaucracies' (Gaffney, 1991: 15). This kind of ideological stimulation and rejuvenation could not come from the civil service.

An important factor was the determination of think-tanks to build contacts within the Conservative Party. For example, the Chairman of the Bow Group invited John Major to specify areas where policy might be extended and in which the Group might create policy units to deliver some policy ideas. After a positive response from Downing Street, the Group initiated studies on housing policy. The IEA helped establish the 'No Turning Back' group of backbenchers which subsequently developed links with the ASI. Other contacts result from the previous work experience that think-tank executives and scholars had in government. David Willetts, for example, left the Policy Unit at Number 10 to become Director of the CPS (James, 1993: 501–02).

The British parties have well developed avenues for policy development through annual conferences, in-house policy units and input from affiliated groups such as trade unions. The Fabian Society has a long established relationship with the Labour Party in Britain. The Institute for Public Policy Research had its genesis among Labour Party supporters, informally linked with Neil Kinnock's office when he was leader of the Labour Party. According to the past Director of IPPR, James Cornford (interview), the Institute has good access to the Labour Party but there is more distance between them compared to the CPS and the Conservative Party. Cornford valued detachment and believed it gave the IPPR more credibility. In his view, the IPPR could expect to be heard by a Labour government but it would not have a 'hand in hand relationship'. Nevertheless, over 1992–94 the IPPR housed and administered the Commission for Social Justice set up by the Labour Party as a contemporary version of the Beveridge inquiry.

Despite the occasional influence of think-tank scholars, it is difficult for a think-tank to engage party leaders and almost impossible to attract political parties as whole. Think-tanks rarely mirror the economic beliefs and political values of the party's power brokers. Prime Ministers are more likely to consult their own advisers, and those within the party, rather than outside it. Additionally, the factional system of many political parties can fragment a party into contending sets of views regarding policy. A think-tank can be marginalised if it becomes too closely identified with a particular faction.

A number of think-tanks in the US are directly identified with political parties such as the former relationship between the Cato Institute and the Libertarian Party, and Heritage, Hoover, and ICS, to name but a few, with the Republicans and the Reagan administration in the 1980s in particular. The Progressive Policy Institute (PPI), the Economic Policy Institute (EPI) and the Center for National Policy (CNP) are associated with the Democrats. The PPI, EPI and CNP do not share common policy positions. Instead, they reflect different strands of thinking evident in the Democratic Party. According to PPI's director Will Marshall (interview), the EPI reflects the 'old lack lustre liberalism'. Steinbruner (interview) said the CNP 'steered clear of factionalism' in the party and advocated a positive role of the political process and government intervention. Marshall mentioned a congruence of PPI ideas with some Republicans and conservatives. Accordingly, Jeff Faux at EPI, which is more labour-oriented, disparages the use of the word 'progressive' in PPI's name (*New York Times*, 28 June 1989). The PPI is associated with a particular faction – the southern market-liberals who established the Democratic Leadership Council with the avowed aim of steering the Democratic Party away from the New Deal liberalism and more in favour of market mechanisms. Before Bill Clinton became a presidential candidate he led the Democratic Leadership Council which now runs the PPI (*The Sunday Times*, 8 November 1992: 2). In Marshall's (interview) opinion, one of the reasons PPI came into existence were the requirements of the Democratic Party, which had 'only recently got into the think-tank game', of developing an intellectual counter-attack. The PPI assists the party by 'sanctioning' certain ideas as 'safe' for Democrats to speak about that were previously 'taboo'.

In many Western liberal democracies, political parties and bureaucracies are the prime means of élite recruitment. They groom individuals for office and parties are often a mechanism for distributing 'plum jobs' to politicians and administrators as they leave political life. One theory that has emerged about American think-tanks is that the political parties are too weak to perform these functions since they are little more than loose electoral coalitions. Furthermore, American parties supposedly 'lack the capacity to provide the right ideas at the right time' (Gellner, 1990: 14). Think-tanks fill the breach as new party-like institutions and a 'clearing station' for political appointments. Winand Gellner argues the adoption of think-tanks by political parties occurred when think-tanks became partisan.

> In reaction to the increased demand for indisputable answers to global questions, which almost indispensably require ideological answers, they gave up on neutrality, became more ideological and thus have replaced the political parties ... (1990: 19).

The traditional view of them as relatively passive providers of research and analysis is dispensed. They are given the status of an 'innovative and elaborated political institution' (Gellner, 1990: 6).

It is an over-statement to argue that think-tanks have replaced political parties. Gellner makes the mistake of treating think-tanks as an undifferentiated category in which the trend towards partisanship has been consistent. Some American institutes, such as the Environmental and Energy Study Institute (EESI) and the Northeast-Midwest Institute are rigorously bipartisan. Indeed, many other organisations such as universities, interest groups, the media, and legal firms also perform some of the functions identified. It can equally be argued that many think-tanks gave up on neutrality because of the increasingly competitive environment in which they operate. Politicisation is a means to differentiate a new think-tank from the traditional institute and to attract support from a targeted constituency.

American Exceptionalism?

Think-tanks are often portrayed as a 'quintessentially American institution' (Toner, 1985). Many go so far as to say they are 'unique' to America (Alpert and Markusen, 1980: 95; McGann, 1992: 733; Critchlow, 1985: 9). Dror (1980), for example, describes think-tanks as an 'invention' emerging from the peculiarities of the American political system. Such views are not untypical notions of the exceptionalism of the US political system (see also Easterbrook, 1986; Weaver, 1989: 577; Gellner, 1990: 5). Furthermore, a few non-American scholars suggest that American-style think-tanks have been cloned in other countries (Holmes, 1986: 16). Marsh (1991: 33) considers that some Australian think-tanks have imitated overseas organisations. Lindquist believes that the Institute for Research on Public Policy in Canada was created because 'The felt need for an independent institute had more to do with the self-image of a nation, or the image held by its policy élite' (1989: 298) in relation to the USA and its numerous think-tanks.

These diffusion arguments neglect the presence of think-tanks in Canada, Australia and the UK well before numbers boomed in the USA. While it is the case that many people are impressed by American think-tanks and in some cases imitate their approaches, it does not mean that they have simply copied American institutes. Indeed, there is some evidence to suggest that learning has been a two-way process. Both the CFR and the RIIA emerged from the interaction of delegates at Versailles. Institutes of international affairs in Australia, New Zealand, Canada and other Commonwealth countries are sister organisations of, and sometimes modelled after, Chatham House in London. Antony Fisher who established the IEA in London, helped create the Fraser Institute in Canada as well as the Manhattan Institute and the Pacific Research Institute in the USA and is described by the Atlas Foundation (1988: 1) as a 'founder of free-market policy research institutes world-wide'. CSIS in Washington DC is partly modelled on the IISS in London.

This is not to suggest that there has not been imitation. Copying does occur (see Tomkin, 1990, for a discussion). For example, Richard Portes, Director of the CEPR in London, modelled his Centre on the National Bureau of Economic Research (NBER). And in Canada, the Brookings Institution was the inspiration for the Institute for Research on Public Policy. Between 1976 and 1977, a proposal to create a British-style Brookings was floated by the then Chair of the Social Science Research Council, Derek Robinson and Ralf Dahrendorf, Director at the London School of Economics (Pinder, 1981). Some argued that such an organisation could not work outside the American political system or in the closed British system (Kay, 1989). But there is a more simple reason. A Brookings-style institution was impractical (Isserlis, 1981: 163). Indeed, it was doubtful that sufficient financial, entrepreneurial and academic resources could have been found to generate an organisation as large as Brookings. To create another Brookings-like organisation, even within the USA, would have been contrary to the trends of concentration and specialisation identified in earlier chapters.

The American think-tank industry is not unique. Admittedly, the scale of think-tank development is extensive and there is greater diversification. This may be as much the consequence of extensive grant giving by American foundations as the more permeable character of, and points of access into, the US governmental system. However, just as the American system of think-tanks has grown and evolved so this is occurring in Britain, albeit slower and on a smaller scale. Assertions of American exceptionalism do not explain the presence of many well established policy institutes outside the USA, nor account for the significant growth in the number of policy research institutes in other countries. Such arguments detract attention from the requirement for comparative study and neglect the emerging international networks among think-tanks.

NOTES

1. Urban was funded almost entirely by federal grants and contracts, especially the Department of Housing and Urban Development (HUD), until it suffered a severe funding drop under the Reagan administration.
2. In 1987, there was a total of 6,615 foundations in the USA (Hodgkinson and Weitzman, 1989: 124). Independent grant making foundations are in the majority (81.7 per cent of foundations), whereas company sponsored foundations (13.7 per cent), community foundations (2.6 per cent) and operating foundations (2.3 per cent) are much smaller in number. In dollar value terms in 1986, American research institutes received predominantly from independent foundations ($178,502000), rather than from company sponsored foundations ($18,889000) or community foundations ($1,996000) (Clinton, 1987: 44–45). The remaining category of foundation are operating foundations. The Carnegie Endowment and the Russell Sage Foundation have assets of $85 million and $103 million respectively (Hodgkinson and Weitzman, 1989: 126).

4   Think-tank Organisation and Management

The effectiveness of independent policy research institutes is dependent on the way they are managed and adjust to change. The health of a think-tank affects its ability to innovate and respond to changed external conditions. Accordingly, this chapter investigates the internal management of policy institutes. That is, their funding, leadership, staffing, research and publication policies. Some institutes are shown to be better equipped than others by virtue of an activist director, financial security or specialisation to succeed in the marketplace of ideas.

Funding and Financial Autonomy

One of the major constraints facing all non-profit organisations (NPOs) is funding. Policy research institutes cannot rely on membership dues to cover operating costs. Nor can they rely upon the sales of publications and services. Philanthropy, corporate support and government contracts are essential to survival. Attracting money has always been difficult. In the USA, pressures on public expenditure since the 1970s have seen the number and size of government contracts reined in. Even though there are fewer institutes in Britain, there are also fewer sources of funding. Large donations from individuals are rare and think-tank directors generally bemoan the lack of a strong philanthropic tradition.

Table 1 provides the funding profiles of selected think-tanks. While it does not indicate the changing balance of funding support within institutes over time, it usefully indicates the mix of funding sources. As different accounting procedures prevail, exact comparison is not feasible. Nevertheless, it is evident that only in a few cases are institutes reliant on a single source of funding. In the main, policy institutes tap several different sources to promote financial stability. Unsurprisingly, the corporate sector is a significant source of financial assistance. But as a proportion of think-tank income, rarely does it rise beyond one-third. For half of the institutes listed in the first column, corporate support represents between ten and 20 per cent of total funding.

Foundations are a major source of support, especially for the American institutes. In many cases, it is more important than corporate support, representing over 80 per cent in the case of the Institute for American Values (IAV) and the Acton Institute, and 50 per cent or more for over a third of the institutes in the second column. In the case of American institutes, support from any single foundation is highly unlikely to exceed 33 per cent of its income. Since the Tax Reform Act of 1969, a foundation providing more than a third of an organisation's budget is subject to 'expenditure responsibility'. This not only involves increased reporting obligations for both the grant giving and recipient organisations, it may also involve the foundation in legal liability for the actions of the think-tank (Culleton Colwell, 1980: 416).

Foundations have been major forces in the establishment of think-tanks, providing 'bricks and mortar' grants to assist in capital projects and general support. For example, the NBER received most of its initial support from the Carnegie Corporation (Lagemann, 1989). When founded, the ODC received half its operating budget from the Ford and Rockefeller Foundations. The Atlas Foundation is currently the major benefactor of the Institute for Energy Research. The IIE was set up with a grant from the German Marshall Fund. In the case of the old guard institutes foundations were aiding the extension of knowledge, often in areas where universities were not involved. As there is now no shortage of policy research institutes in the USA, American foundations are more inclined to fund specific projects directed towards immediate ends rather than provide capital grants. They also show greater interest in the outcomes of research and its public impact. According to an EESI staffer, Michael Witt (interview) foundation executives want to be convinced that grantees are accountable and are not impressed by 'thinking and no action'. A research institute that has specialised or proposes a focused research project or which champions strong positions has an advantage in attracting foundation support. Such funding practices reinforce the trend towards specialisation and advocacy. The implication of changing funding patterns is that institutes cannot rely on three or four big grants but need diverse funding sources. Think-tanks also need to convince foundation executives of the unique and practical consequences of their activities. This involves hiring fund-raising consultants, spending on dinners and retreats to convince donors of the utility of a particular project, and weighing down grant applications with evidence of media coverage and policy impact. Maldistribution of privilege is likely to occur as some groups are invariably better organised and resourced than others.

Individual gifts, fees and donations also represent a sizeable portion of income. The contributions of individuals are highest in organisations that are membership bodies such as the Fabian Society. Rarely does such support rise beyond a third of income and more often than not it represents less than a fifth of income. Heritage and Free Congress both have direct mail programmes, possibly accounting for their high individual contributions. Heritage also receives large donations from very wealthy individuals.

Direct funding from government or through quasi-autonomous agencies is extremely important to a number of institutes although some market-liberal institutes such as Cato reject it as a matter of principle. Of all the institutes listed in the table, less than a fifth indicate government funding. In the UK, IIED receives a large amount (69 per cent) as does NIESR (40 per cent) and in the US, Hudson (38 per cent) and NBER (49 per cent). In most circumstances, government funding is on a contract basis and not stipendiary. Government funding also fluctuates and can have serious consequences. The experience of the Urban Institute is instructive. In the 1970s government contracts represented up to 85 per cent of income (Hallow, 1985). During the early 1980s, Urban experienced a significant funding drop, the result of Reagan administration policies to 'defund the left' (Rich, 1988: H13). While Urban was not specifically targeted – other institutes were also affected – it suffered the consequences of the administration's view that government should not be involved in areas in which Urban was working. Government-sponsored research 'dried up' forcing a significant reduction in staff size. Urban survived only by attracting large foundation grants (Brown *et al.*, interview).

Endowment funds are a significant factor in the financial security of only a small number of policy institutes. Aside from Heritage, it is the old guard institutes that have endowments. The Carnegie Endowment draws most heavily on its assets, and along with Russell Sage, has a degree of financial independence that is atypical. For more than half of the institutes endowment funds represent less than fifteen per cent of revenue. Endowments often afford greater research flexibility. The President of CSIS, David Abshire (1987: 27), argues that the lack of an endowment for his Center is a restriction on CSIS research agenda which, instead of being driven by internally determined priorities, must defer to the availability of outside funding for a project.

TABLE 1: SOURCES OF POLICY INSTITUTE INCOME

	1. Corporate	2. Foundation	3. Individual	4. Grants, Donations and Gifts	5. Government
Acton 1991	2%	85%	5%	6% programmes	
AEI 1993	39%	38%	8%		
ASI 1991				46% business, foundation & individual subscriptions	
Brookings 1993			3.3% trustees & individual	38%	2%
Carnegie Council 1993				18.75% grants, & corporate	
Carnegie Endow 1993				16.9% restricted grants	
Cato Institute 1991	63.5% contributions			88.3% contributions	not accepted
CED 1993	32%			29.3% grants & pledges	
CEI 1994		52%	11%		
CEPR 1992				90%	
CRC 1991	12.7%	59.6%	21.8%		
CSIS 1993				84% private	5%
CSP 1990	24%	61%	16%		
Claremont 1990	46.7%	39.1%	14.2%		
COHA 1991	25%	50%	25%		
Commonwealth 1991		60%	15%		
EPI 1991		40%			
EPPC 1993	2.2%	89.9%	2%	40.2% donations & contributions	
Fabians 1994			39% members	28.2%	
Federal Trust 1993		67% incl. EU & individual			17%
FPRI 1991	15%	50%	8%		
Free Congress 1993	8%	53%	30%		
Heritage 1991	13%	25%	50%		
Hudson 1990	35% restricted grants & other contracts			23% unrestricted grants/donations	38%
Hoover 1992				29%	5%
IAV 1991	9.6%	83.3%	3.2%		
IEA 1990		70%		68% covenants & donations	not accepted
IEDSS 1992				20% company & individual	

	1. Corporate	2. Foundation	3. Individual	4. Grants, Donations and Gifts	5. Government
IFDP 1993				6.3%	
IFPA 1991		46%	70%		27%
IFS 1993			10.5% membership	81.6% research grants	
IGSS 1991			11.4% membership	86.4% grants	
IIED 1992	6%	11.4%			69%
IISS 1990			14.3%	42%	
IPPR 1992	15%	30%	20%	35% trade unions	
Joint Center 1993	28.8%	53.2%			13%
Low Pay Unit 1992		50%	15%		20% local govt
NBER 1992				35% private	49%
NCPA 1993	35%	47%	18%		
NIESR 1991	8.1%	25% and grantors			39.4% ESRC; 0.9% govt
ODC 1990	5%	12%	2%	27.6% grants & contracts	
ODI 1992	10%	60%	30% includes book sales		55%
Pacific Research 1992	20%	30%	50%		
Pioneer 1989	14%	28%	26%		
Reason 1991	17.8%	6.9%	1.5%		
RFF 1993	32.52%				33.2%
RIIA 1993	15%	31.05%	4.33%		4.49%
Rockford 1993		36%	23%		
Russell Sage 1991					

Note: The majority of institutes in their financial statements do not distinguish between grants that originate from corporate, foundation, individual or government sources. Accordingly, the fourth column is a 'catch all' category.

(TABLE 1 continued on page 58)

TABLE 1 (continued)

	6. Endowment & investment	7. Publications	8. Conferences & functions	9. Other (as designated)
Acton Institute 1991			15% incl. sales etc	
AEI 1993			28%	2% interest
ASI 1991		8%	19%	11% tax recovery; 8% royalties etc
Brookings 1993	25%	10%		6% rental revenue, computer services, etc
Carnegie Council 1993	68.3%			6.8% membership fees; 2.7% misc
Carnegie Endow 1993	72.9% interest & dividends			1.3%
Cato Institute 1991		8.6%	6.1% fees	1.2% other
CED 1993	5.5%	4.4%		
CEI 1994		1.4%		5% miscellaneous
CEPR 1992		5.7%		4.2% interest, royalties and misc
CRC 1991				5.9% sales, subscription and other
CSP 1990				
CSIS 1993		1%	5%	5% interest & dividends; 1% other
Claremont 1990				25% sales
COHA 1991				
Commonwealth 1991				
EPI 1991				40% labour and trade unions
EPPC 1993		3.1%		2.8% interest
Fabians 1994		6.1% bookshop		12.7% rent & royalties; 1.7% other
Federal Trust 1993		3%		1.8% interest and other
FPRI 1991				9% sales; 1% other
Free Congress 1993		5% and other		9%
Heritage 1991	7%	2% & misc		
Hoover 1992	44%		1.8% fees	20% university
IAV 1991				1.6% interest, royalties & misc
IEA 1990		10%		22% interest
IEDSS 1992		10%		

	6. Endowment & investment	7. Publications	8. Conferences & functions	9. Other (as designated)
IFDP 1993		19.4%		4.7% royalties, speaking and other
IFPA 1991		1%		26% contract research
IFS 1991			8% incl. publications	
IGSS 1991				
IIED 1992				2.3% interest, fees, events & misc
IISS 1990	28.3%	14.8%		9.9% international agencies; 3.4% other
IPPR 1992				
Joint Center 1993				5% earned income
Low Pay Unit 1992				15% other
NBER 1992	15%			1% other
NCPA 1993				
NIESR 1991	13.1% investment & interest	13.3%		
ODC 1990	12.5%	1.8%		58% contributions
ODI 1992	2%			19% international agencies; 3% NGOs
Pacific Research 1992				
Pioneer 1989				
RFF 1993	37.9%			2.7% other institutions
Reason 1991		31% incl. magazine	15.06%	1% miscellaneous
RIIA 1993	3.9%	6.82%		1.79% other
Rockford 1993	3% & other	26%		
Russell Sage 1991	93.7%	4.6%		1.6 oil, gas rights & royalties

Sources: Annual Reports, Van Der Woerd (1990)

Although not detailed on the table, ownership of facilities provides long-term security for an institute as well as cultivating an image of stability and security. Again, it tends to be the old guard institutes that possess land and buildings whereas the newer institutes occupy leased offices. Simon Crine (interview) spoke of the Fabian Society's premises as its 'greatest asset'. It receives over ten per cent of its income from rent. Yet, paying a mortgage or financing renovations can curtail other activities and divert attention from policy issues. The RIIA is housed in Chatham House, a building listed by the National Trust which involves considerable sums in upkeep and modernisation.

As the figures for publications, conferences and sales reveal (in columns 7, 8 and 9) think-tanks cannot survive from the sale of their services and product. Policy research is not a profitable endeavour. For none of the organisations tabled does such income rise beyond one third of total income. For most institutes, such income is less than 10 per cent. Brookings represents an exceptional case for much of this income comes from its Center for Public Policy Education which provides professional training. Similarly, a number of institutes provide services on a commercial basis such as forecasting, conference organisation and graduate education, usually conducted through a consulting arm of the institute. Other sources of funding include international agencies and non-governmental organisations – for IIED this represents approximately ten per cent of income. The EPI also receives a high proportion of its income from trade unions. The Hoover Institution acquires over a fifth of its revenue base from Stanford University. Most organisations also acquire small proportions of income from interest and royalties.

Many institutes are reliant on voluntary labour in the absence of adequate funding. In the USA the well-established student intern system provides a stream of volunteer labour. Another avenue of support is cross subsidisation from universities. Some institutes, such as CSIS and the Ethics and Public Policy Center, have been located on or affiliated with a university, sometimes receiving free office space and secretarial support if not academic kudos by association. It is also accepted practice for academics to write for a think-tank while in university employ. Other forms of support come from the business sector which might provide services free of charge or on a cost basis only. For example, the European Policy Forum (EPF) has been provided office and meeting facilities in Brussels by the company, Chequepoint International. Until it grew and consolidated, the Social Affairs Unit was provided office space at the IEA. While difficult to quantify, such forms of support are essential to the survival of many organisations.

To minimise the impact of the loss of foundation, individual or corporate support, it is in the interests of policy centres not only to build numerous supporters but also a mix of different kinds of financial support. Even so, a considerable number barely manage to break even from year to year. Yet other institutes prosper. Sometimes this reflects the timeliness of the issues being addressed. At other times it has more to do with the skills of think-tank managers.

Management and Leadership

Leadership is a vexed issue but of critical importance to policy institutes. A significant number of institutes are dominated by charismatic personalities. Ideally, a director of a policy institute is one with a blend of academic and practical experience, a potent public speaker and fund-raiser, comfortable with the media and able to project a reputable image for the institute. The person needs the necessary managerial acumen to deal with trustees and staff while directing research activity, outreach and committee work. In short, institutes require strong leadership or 'policy entrepreneurs' at the helm (Feulner, 1985). As Eleanor Farrar (interview) said of Eddie Williams at the Joint Center, 'he has leadership style, broad experience in the outside world and is someone who can interact with business, foundation people and officials to reinforce the credibility of the Joint Center'.

It is not often easy for institutes to find directors with all these qualifications. Smaller institutes often cannot pay salaries equivalent to those found in the private sector. Most are unable to provide the security usually found in the public sector or universities. Trustees often have little option but to seek out younger candidates who perceive work experience in a policy institute as a stepping stone for future career possibilities or those who are strongly committed to the goals of the institute. Within these parameters, directors tend to be high powered individuals who indelibly stamp an institute with his or her character. Institutes dominated by one personality run the risk of becoming 'vanity tanks' (Wilentz, 1986: 23).

Vanity tanks are usually smaller bodies of less than ten full-time staff, where the founder is the director and motivating force. In such cases, the policy research institute often acts as a vehicle for the director's career. The organisation provides a launching pad into the arena of public debate and legitimates the director as an opinion leader. When people think of IIE they also think of Fred Bergsten, just as in various policy communities Clyde Prestowitz is coupled with the Economic Strategy Institute (ESI), Lester Brown is linked with World Watch, and Frank Gaffney is associated with the Center for Security Policy – the latter, according to his second-in-command, is not suited to the strictures of a large organisation but is a 'maverick' (Bliss-Walters, interview). In Britain, Richard Portes is the personality behind CEPR and Graham Mather leads the EPF. The directors and presidents of larger and older institutes are equally if not better known but they share the limelight with institute scholars who are also well known. Furthermore, older organisations have been shaped by preceding directors, and have an internal dynamic and set of practices that predate current directors. Nevertheless, the think-tank field 'resembles that of religious advocacy, dominated by "institutionalized personalities" whose reputations outrun their organizations' (Jenkins, 1987: 307).

Whether or not an institute is a vanity tank has implications for its long-term existence. Institutes may expand to the extent that the disproportionate influence of a founder is diluted, as in the case of the IIE. Those that do not usually experience difficulty when the director leaves or dies. For example, Herman Kahn was an inspired leader of the Hudson Institute but a poor manager. Upon his death, the Institute encountered a financial crisis compounded by a rapid succession of presidents. The Hudson Institute also developed a poor reputation among some government clients for its delays in delivering reports. The Institute suffered in the 1970s with the general scaling down of government contracts and with a critical General Accounting Office review of its civil defence work. In the 1980s, the Institute's budget plummeted in the more competitive research funding environment. Its estate in New York was sold and the Institute moved to Indianapolis with resuscitating funds provided by the Lily Endowment (Smith, 1991a: 155–59). Notwithstanding such difficulties, the entrepreneurship of individuals who carve out a niche, crystallise issues and galvanise funding and support are necessary to capture political opportunities to build new institutes. In many cases, the individual policy entrepreneur institutes a dynamic of positive reinforcement for both him or herself and the institute.

Boards of trustees have the power to temper and moderate the control of executive directors. The conventional wisdom on non-profit boards is that they are: i) policy-making and monitoring entities; and ii) build a partnership of mutual trust and communication with management (Middleton, 1987: 152). In theory, trustees are responsible for hiring directors, determining operating policies, budgeting and fiscal control, fund-raising, recruitment, public outreach and resolving internal conflicts. Practice often falls short of the theory. The larger the board the less likely it is to meet. If trustees are geographically dispersed, as is often the case with federally structured or international institutes, it is all the more expensive and difficult to bring the board together. A disincentive also operates against trustees becoming closely involved in the affairs of an institute as they usually serve on a voluntary basis with, at most, an honorarium as recompense (Orlans, 1972: 59).

Diverse opinions were expressed during interviews regarding the role of boards. Norman Ture (interview) felt that board members were not sufficiently involved in fund-raising and did not do enough to raise the profile of the Institute for Research on the Economics of Taxation (IRET). Eleanor Farrar (interview) at the Joint Center talked of the board composed of 'civil rights "types", lawyers and people with money and who can raise money'. The board of the Center for the Study of Social Policy was portrayed as a mechanism for networking and developing contacts with senior current and former government officials (Betsy Cole and Charlie Gershenson, interview). David Boaz (interview) talked of Cato's board as a 'fairly distant structure', whereas Cato's President, Ed Crane, 'makes the decisions'. The IISS Council meets twice yearly to discuss general policy issues, outreach and the direction of research, but spends more time organising the annual conference and fund-raising (John Chipman and Gerry Segal, interview). According to Donna Wise (interview), the World Resources Institute Council – which is international in composition – 'typically confirms the direction of WRI, reviews research and is engaged in limited fund-raising'. It is the President, Gustav Speth who 'sets the vision' for WRI. Robert Fri (interview), President of Resources for the Future, argued that NPOs are not subject to much accountability. 'They are not subject to the test of the market, they are not answerable to Congress, the public is relatively unaware of them'. Hence, in his view, a properly functioning board is very important in establishing credibility for the organisation and as the 'guardian of its philosophy'.

Rather than formulate policy, boards and councils tend to ratify the policy that is presented to them. Executive leaders wield considerable power in relation to trustees. They have greater awareness of issues and access to information, considerable agenda setting powers and responsibility for the implementation of policy. In general, and contrary to the élite theory perspective outlined earlier, trustees do not have great involvement in think-tank affairs, nor do they act strategically to communicate 'élite preferences' to government. The process is rather more *ad hoc*. Instead of intervening in internal affairs, boards play an important role linking the institute with the outside world. Trustees can be good external representatives of think-tanks to the extent that their overlapping membership in other institutes, foundations, corporations, community bodies or government committees as well as their personal friendships and social and business circles place them in situations where they can influence resource allocations for policy research (Culleton Colwell, 1980; Useem, 1984; Middleton, 1987: 143). Furthermore, although they are distant from day to day affairs, trustees remain a constant symbol. The names of board members are often listed on an institute's letterhead stationery or in brochures and annual reports. As they are usually powerful, rich or public figures their association with the think-tank bestows credibility. They enhance the public recognition of a policy research institute.

Ideally the relationship between executive and trustees is harmonious but tension can be the norm. Different conceptions of the 'philosophy' of an organisation creates conflict between the board and the executive. It is during crises that boards intervene. In some cases this is positive. For example, in the late 1970s the Ford Foundation cut funds to RFF throwing its continued existence in doubt. These circumstances imposed a re-examination of RFF's mission in which board members were closely involved. Until the Ford Foundation cut funding, RFF activity was directed towards universities in establishing environmental studies as a new academic field. As a consequence, there was a rapid staff turnover as people took up newly created university positions. With the re-examination of purposes, RFF modified its activities to become more policy related. The board considered a merger with Brookings but feared that environmental concerns would be subsumed. Instead, trustees embarked on a 'very difficult period' of transition to preserve and re-fund RFF (Fri, interview).

Raising basic questions of organisational mandate, character and identity can provoke internal disunity. The Rockford Institute, for example, is conservative in ethos and characterised in the popular literature as a key organisation for the 'paleoconservatives'. Paleoconservatives are supposedly distinguishable from neo-conservatives who are concentrated in New York and Washington, retain some commitment to the mixed economy and are often from a Jewish background. This group includes Midge Decter, Norman

Podhoretz and Richard Neuhaus. By contrast, paleoconservatives, who include Pat Buchanan, are often white Anglo-Saxon Protestants and Catholics. Strong differences concerning foreign policy, bordering on anti-Semitism in the case of some paleoconservatives who accuse neo-conservatives of putting Israel's interests before America's, are one reason why the Rockford Institute in 1989 closed its New York offshoot, the Center for Religion and Democracy run by the Revd Richard Neuhaus. As a consequence of Neuhaus's 'departure', three conservative foundations, Olin, Smith Richardson and Bradley, withdrew funding estimated at $700,000 from the Rockford Institute (see Diamond, 1990: 103; Judis, 1990b). Neuhaus set up a new think-tank – the Institute on Religion and Public Life.

A financial crisis can have the same effect as conflict over organisational mission. This was the case in the dismissal of William Baroody Jnr. from the Presidency of AEI. Between 1985 and 1986 AEI's budget fell from $13.9 million to $10 million. Staff numbers were reduced from 154 to 108. Aside from financial mis-management, Baroody had overambitious plans to build grand new headquarters, without the support of endowment funds, and in circumstances where AEI raised its budget from zero every year (Ford, 1992). Alongside this risky financial venture, the board of trustees identified 'creeping centrism' and a 'flirtation with the mainstream' that saw disenchanted conservative foundations divert funds to Heritage (Blumenthal, 1986: D1, D6). In 1986, the new Chair of the AEI Board, accepted his position on condition that Baroody resign (*Newsweek*, 7 July 1986). Trustee intervention subsequently played a vital role in rebuilding the Institute's reputation.

In London a former Director of the IEA, Graham Mather, was the centre of conflict concerning the Institute's future direction. Lord Harris of High Cross and Arthur Seldon, both with a long-standing IEA association, accused Mather of 'sacrificing academic independence for indecently close relations' with the Conservative Government (Chote, 1991). Mather's pro-European stance exacerbated factional differences within the Institute. Issues of principle were clouded by personal vendettas. The Charity Commissioners became involved when Mather's opponents suggested a review of the IEA's charitable status. Despite trustee support, Mather resigned and with IEA's deputy director, Frank Vibert, established the European Policy Forum (EPF). Division in Conservative ranks regarding European Union affairs extends beyond the IEA. Sir Ronald Halstead, CPS Treasurer for ten years, joined the

EPF in 1993 on the basis of its less hostile line on the European Union (*Sunday Times*, 25 April 1990: 3). A CPS stalwart, Hugh Thomas, similarly departed. However, the divisions were better managed at CPS where the dilemma was resolved by focusing on other policy issues, primarily education (James, 1993: 502).

At some point in their existence, most organisations face crises or divisive internal disputes. The difficulties can often be resolved by splits or mergers, sacking directors and appointing new personnel or by redefining organisational mission to suit contemporary circumstances. Despite the problems that were encountered by the IEA, RFF and AEI, these were overcome. When funding problems and feuding are more intractable, then an institute is likely to close.

Personnel

The staff of an institute are its strength. It is paramount that an institute maintain its financial stability and credibility so that the future career prospects of its staff are not endangered, hence triggering a flight of intellectual resources. In all but the largest and most well-endowed institutes salaries do not exceed those found in the private sector or universities. Furthermore, it is unusual to find tenured research staff. Staff are generally attracted for reasons other than pecuniary reward. As Jeffreys (interview), a lawyer at the Competitive Enterprise Institute (CEI) stated, people do not work for the salaries but because of commitment to the values represented by the organisation. The incentives are intangible – the chance to participate in policy politics, the possibility of media exposure, the opportunity to see ideas translated into policy and working with people who share the same principles.

Perhaps a reflection of its expense, researchers employed in-house are becoming rare. The Carnegie Endowment has approximately 20 in-house researchers, most of whom are on fixed two or three year contracts. It also has a paid six-month internship programme. These activities can be supported by endowment funds. The institutes with an in-house research capability tend to be the old guard organisations – Brookings, CFR, AEI and Hoover in the USA and Chatham House, IISS, NIESR, ODI and PSI in Britain. The Overseas Development Council (ODC) once had a large in-house research capacity, but it proved too costly. The ODC now draws upon scholars commissioned to do research.

Unlike universities the older institutes also display a mix of personnel. In the case of RIIA, fellows come from universities, the business community, the Foreign and Commonwealth Office (FCO) and overseas. The previous work experience of former senior public servants or retired politicians is used to enhance the analytic skills of the institute. The phenomenon of people moving in and out of government into think-tanks 'is the advantage which Brookings has over a place like Yale: that people have got their hands dirty' (Bruce MacLaury quoted in Silk and Silk, 1980: 158). But Brookings is also involved in the academic peer review process, and a university career remains a viable exit option for most scholars.

As they are often stepping stones in peoples careers, think-tanks occasionally experience fluctuations in staffing. In some instances these fluctuations can be a positive force of 'cross-fertilisation of people among like minded organisations' (Jeffreys, interview). However, high turnover of staff brings instability in an organisation. For example, when Reagan was elected President the ICS was 'gutted' as staff left to take up political appointments. A victim of its own success, the Institute drifted until its rejuvenation in the mid-1980s (Harper, interview). A major problem that the smaller policy institutes confront is the lack of a career structure for their research scholars. This problem is more pronounced in Britain where it is more difficult to move in and out of government positions. It is unlikely that these think-tanks can guarantee an employment base allowing for predictable careers. While it is relatively easy to find young people or short-term visiting scholars, James Cornford (interview) at the IPPR argued that to establish credibility senior people are essential.

Institutes reliant on adjunct or associate scholars such as Demos, SAU and ASI in Britain and PPI, EPI and CEI amongst many others in the US are a more contemporary feature of the think-tank. Maureen Steinbrunner (interview) calls her institute – the CNP in Washington DC – a 'think-tank without walls'. In London, the IEA calls itself a 'networking organisation'. It has 'very small staff of its own and commissions particular academics or outside experts to write on topics' (Vibert, 1992). Similarly, CPS prepares some papers and monographs in-house but the majority are commissioned from a penumbra of friendly experts. The advantage is that management can draw upon a wider pool of expertise and economies of scale result. At the same time a wide range of viewpoints can be encompassed in the organisational product. CEPR's Director, Richard Portes (interview) suggested that in-house research, such as at RIIA, cultivates an 'institutional line'. Although the network mode is efficient for small institutes with limited resources, it presents its own problems. There is less control over scholars who rarely enjoy an honorarium, if that. There are few sanctions to ensure that a book or report is delivered on time while incentives (such as EPI trying to provide its writers the opportunity to meet journalists or to speak before a Congressional committee) cannot be guaranteed.

Research and Publication Policies

The research and publications are the most tangible product of think-tanks. Books are emblematic of the old guard institutes and endow both the author and the institute with credibility. While an important symbol, a book requires long-term financial investment which may or may not pay off in the bookshops. Some small institutes do not produce books because it is too expensive. As noted earlier, institutes are pursuing more economical and immediate avenues of diffusion through television interviews, op-ed pieces and newsletters.

Interviews illustrated very different approaches to research and publication. David Boaz said that books were the most important activity of the Cato Institute for 'they have the most life and substance'. On the other hand, Richard Caplan at the World Policy Institute (WPI) said books were 'so quickly obsolete' and that 'there are limits to what people will read'. WPI publishes a journal as an alternative to the slower book process. Similarly, Christine Contee at ODC said that decision- makers are 'not going to read a thick, academic book'. Research needs to be put in a format that people in Congress will read, that is, two to 20 pages. Heritage keeps out of the book market. Jeffrey Gayner argued that 'with the current pace of public policy, books came out too late in terms of influencing the debate'. 'People on the Hill do not have time to read books'. Over the past decade the ICS has switched from publishing multi-authored to single-authored books and from academic to more populist books as the way to influence public opinion. The Chief Executive Officer, Sam Harper, preferred ICS publishing accessible non-academic books, that is, 'big type, short, no footnotes, glossy cover design and imaginative, catchy titles'. In Britain, the Fabian Society produces pamphlets for the membership. It has also started producing specialist discussion papers for a more limited audience. The CPS produces pamphlets, the IPPR publishes monographs and the ASI produces reports. These publications are not aimed at the general public but for a politically educated audience. Eamonn Butler at ASI argued that the media finds shorter studies more newsworthy, whereas 'books often end up with the book review editor' rather than discussed on the front pages. In the relatively uncluttered think-tank environment of the first half of the century, book-length studies could be guaranteed to have greater impact. There were fewer sources of information, communication was a slower process and extended research was more feasible. With technological advances, information travels much faster. Even so, those institutes that eschew books tend to be those that do not have the resources to fund long-term book projects. Institutes that produce books tend also to be driven by academic values with a goal of increasing research knowledge in addition to influencing policy.

All policy institutes claim editorial freedom. It is paramount to maintaining intellectual integrity. Outside reviewers of journals, books and reports are used to validate claims to quality and independence. Such practices are based on the principle of academic peer review. As a form of quality control, the process exposes an institute to alternative viewpoints and mobilises organised scepticism to which it may not be open if it directs its product solely towards a client in government. It is also a device to defuse accusations of politicisation. Politicisation can result from clientele dependency, recruitment of politically motivated staff and subtle forms of self censorship such as not raising unprofitable questions. Evidence of censorship, tends to be anecdotal. A report for the Heritage Foundation produced by George W. S. Kuhn, a former army captain, poses questions about Heritage's independence. Kuhn's report was highly critical of some areas of military spending such as weapons that did not work and military commands that were redundant. Despite the initial enthusiasm and publicity blitz mounted by Heritage, the report was buried after rebuttals from Caspar Weinberger and pressure from then Navy Secretary, Lehman on Edwin Feulner. Lehman had been a room-mate of Edwin Feulner, President of Heritage, at Georgetown University. Lehman also wrote to Joseph Coors, a brewing tycoon, who provided $250,000 for Heritage's start up, and who has remained a major sponsor (Reilly, 1981: 110). There was also pressure to scuttle parts of another report (produced by Kuhn's replacement, Theodore Crackel, a retired Army lieutenant colonel) which advocated reform of the Joint Chiefs of Staff. The report was to be published but Lehman persuaded Feulner to withhold it (Easterbrook, 1986). In 1991, a coalition of industry groups which had sponsored a global warming study by CSIS attempted to suppress it after learning that the findings might undermine some arguments against proposed controls on industrial emissions. CSIS released the study disregarding threats from the industry group to withhold funding (*National Journal*, 22 July 1991: 1553).

There are conflicting pressures between satisfying clients and maintaining independence. At RAND this entails a 'sophisticated relationship' with its clients and recognition that 'tension is inevitable'. Sometimes RAND upsets its clients with its research results when at other times it appears to outside observers that RAND is 'pandering to the airforce'. To some extent RAND is compromised by its funding base. It is managed within the organisation by a willingness to take on problems 'that might not come out right from the client's point of view', by 'buffering' individual researchers from the pressure of clients, and by promoting an ethos that is not risk averse. If the Airforce does not like the outcome of a study, RAND is still in a position to publish, usually after 'a six month cooling off period' (Roll, interview).

One way to make sense of the different types and varying quality of research and analysis provided by policy institutes is to think of it being shaped by demand for something that is 'more, better or different'. Following the theory of excess demand (James, 1987), private provision of quasi-public goods and services such as education or health care emerges where large groups of people are dissatisfied with either the amount or kind of government production. Private provision meets the deficit. It is not evident that new think-tanks are meeting demand for 'more' research and analysis. Nonetheless, it is apparent when looking at the history of some of the older institutes that they were providing information, analysis and research in areas not addressed by government or universities. For example, the RIIA and CFR emerged from the dissatisfaction of élite groups in society regarding the parlous state of information about international affairs and politics. Under the auspices of the IPR, a significant amount of material on the Asian region was produced that did not otherwise exist. Today it is less pertinent to argue that think-tanks are meeting excess demand for research given the size and strength of bureaucracies, semi-autonomous government research bureaux and universities. Instead, demand-side models which portray non-profit production of quasi-public goods as a response to differentiated tastes – demand for a 'different' or 'better' kind of product – are more appropriate (James, 1987: 402). As demand for more information, research and analysis has grown so has demand for different kinds of information and research. Demand explanations help explain the market for independent research as well as the nature of its diversification as think-tanks adapt to meet differentiated tastes.

Think-tanks function differently from other research

organisations. As many institutes do not engage in the academic peer process they are also not bound by its restrictions and can engage in 'hands-on' policy analysis. When governments contract research they are often looking for a different kind of analysis from that which could be produced in-house (Dror, 1980). Commissioned research can be used to reinforce government research findings or it can act as a standard against which in-house research work can be compared. Think-tank managers cultivate impressions of difference by arguing that independent research and analysis is of greater academic integrity than that produced by profit-making consultancies or groups representing vested interests, as well as more critical and challenging of public policy than government analysis.

Demand for ideologically informed research from political parties as well as from interest groups or trade unions is different in kind from demand for scholarly studies. These groups want ideas fashioned into a format to bolster their arguments and interests. For instance, interest group activists do not necessarily want analysis that conforms to academic criteria, but analysis in a simplified palatable form that can be used to inform and mobilise their constituencies. Those in Congress who desire policy proposals that would lessen government intervention in the economy are likely to find policy options and analyses of high but accessible standard produced by organisations such as Heritage, IRET and AEI. Sections of the business community fund organisations such as CED in the USA to ensure that a business perspective is articulated in policy discussion. Demand for research informed by conservative values arises from a dissatisfaction of groups which perceive a 'liberal orthodoxy'. Many policy institutes package their research and analysis in such a way as to meet the specific needs of these sources of demand.

Journalists are a significant source of demand and contact think-tanks for three reasons: information; a source of opinion; and a credible source for *independent* analysis that a lobby or political party does not possess. Think-tanks make the jobs of journalists easier in both countries. Most institutes issue press releases, some arrange press conferences for major reports as well as produce registers of public experts that journalists can contact. Think-tank scholars act as a 'bridge between political journalists and political science' (Waldman, 1986: 35; Whittle, 1985). Old guard institutes remain the most favoured sources of commentary despite the plethora of institutes that exist in Washington DC. During the first six months of 1991, in the *New York Times* and the *Washington Post*, Brookings scholars were quoted 184 times, AEI 58 times, Heritage 43 and CSIS 42 times respectively. Another survey conducted after the Gulf War found that Brookings scholars appeared on TV newscasts more frequently than representatives from other think-tanks (Matlack, 1991: 155).

While links with the media are necessary, some consider that it detracts from the 'real work' of the institute that makes it 'credible' in the first place (Parker, interview). Many institutes like RAND or CFR keep an arms-length distance with journalists and do not care for punditry. Saferworld in Bristol maintains a low profile, claiming that inappropriate or excessive publicity can close important doors. By contrast, the Center for Security Policy's automated fax system churns out 600–900 briefs a night, many of which go to newspapers. Other new partisan institutes, such as Heritage, are 'out there hustling' (Boal, 1985). As a consequence, supply outstrips demand. There is considerable competition in the USA for newspaper column space and editors of op-ed pages receive much more unsolicited comment than can be published.

As research and analysis is quasi-public in character, think-tanks encounter the free-rider problem. Thus, while there is demand for think-tank products, some potential supporters perceive that they will benefit from their activities whether they contribute or not. Think-tank managers are compelled to provide selective benefits through membership arrangements to generate financial support. In return for a fee, members often enjoy privileged access to conferences and meetings, newsletters, executive retreats, journals, data banks and libraries. For example, executives who are members of the Conference Board are sometimes able to reduce their consulting costs simply by consulting with their peers through the Board (Conference Board 1993). Selective benefits involve tangible returns to the user. In cases where membership dues are very high, as with CED, fees are a form of gate-keeping and a practice that promotes homogeneity of members, hence a greater likelihood of similar needs and interests. Other forms of gate-keeping also exist. CFR membership is not open. Candidates must be nominated and elected by the membership board. Those who are elected are 'distinguished people', 'up and coming' or who have the potential to 'do great things' in foreign policy. Such procedures are a form of quality control of limiting participants to those who are 'suitably qualified' (Harsh, interview). It is also a means of managing the public standing of a think-tank and indicating that certain organisations are a cut above others. As entry is exclusive, competitive and élite, an organisation can lay claim to superior standards or of being an exceptional distillation of wisdom and expertise. Exclusivity operates as a selective benefit for members.

5 Innovation, Stagnation and Demise

Throughout their existence institutes experience fluctuations in organisational health and effectiveness. Their condition can range from a state of innovation through rejuvenation, reform, adaptation, stagnation, entropy to disestablishment. This chapter asks why particular institutes grow whereas others disband. To conceptualise the patterns of organisational change among think-tanks the discussion draws upon some of Ernst Haas' ideas of organisational change. Think-tanks are treated as 'problem solvers' which create knowledge 'to specify causal relationships in new ways so that the result affects the content of public policy' (Haas, 1990a: 23). It is through learning and adaptation that policy institutes are able to redefine problems.

Three types of behaviour – i) learning, ii) adaptation, and iii) decline and demise – are outlined. Learning is an innovative process and involves the re-examination of organisational purposes. It entails a recognition that problems will be always taken apart, examined from a variety of perspectives and recombined with new solutions. Learning is less common than adaptive responses but this is not to suggest that adaptation is insignificant. Adaptation or habit-driven behaviour can be sustained successfully by an organisation for several decades. Policy research institutes can become 'stale' in their approach to policy problems if habit becomes entrenched. The habit driven actor is typified by behaviour 'developed over time out of memories, traits, beliefs, expectations, scenarios, and prior experiences that lead them to make the same choices that they made previously in the same context' (Rosenau, 1990: 227). To some extent all organisations are habit-driven. As an organisation ages, decision making becomes more formal as standard operating procedures evolve (Light, 1983: 175; Cyert and March, 1963: 119).

The pressures for an institute to innovate are reduced if an institute has an established reputation for providing certain kinds of analysis. Similarly, if institutes are in an environment characterised by minimal competition with other institutes there is less incentive for innovation and risk-taking. Access to endowment income potentially reinforces this conservative tendency. The danger is that institutes become settled, predictable and unconcerned by unfamiliar external events. By contrast, weaker organisations are 'inclined to search for new ways of coping with their situations' (Rosenau, 1990: 235). Paradoxically, learning or innovation is less likely in those bodies that are most able to break with old habits. Forces in favour of the familiar are often far more powerful than those proposing change with the consequence that organisations avoid uncertainty (Cyert and March, 1963: 118–20). It is necessary, therefore, to look at organisational behaviour to understand why some think-tanks prosper whereas others decay.

Decline and Demise

Decline occurs when there is considerable dissatisfaction about the performance of a policy institute. Within the organisation goals are unclear or forgotten or in dispute. The methods of constructing and imparting knowledge, that is, the generally accepted understandings about cause and effect relationships of a given phenomenon considered important by society, is no longer consensual. The think-tank lacks ideological unity or collegiality. It prevents clear definition of programmes. When leadership is weak or divided 'the established routines prevail, giving rise to bureaucratic inertia that slows the pace of organizational learning' (Rosenau, 1990: 232). The organisation is plagued by disputes over administration. Personnel recruitment may occur on the basis of political favouritism or be suspended altogether. Morale tends to be low and staff leave. Membership is static or diminishing. The executive is reactive to outside pressures and responds defensively to new events or the agendas of others rather than being proactive and driven by a coherent organisational mission. Frequently, the financial circumstances of the institute are dire. Decline entails an inability to act on policy. New projects do not get off the ground, publications are not forthcoming. Efforts to forge links with politicians, bureaucrats, the media or other opinion-makers are not initiated. The think-tank suffers diminished intellectual authority and legitimacy. If it is unable to escape this decline, disestablishment is a possibility.

The Round Table, established in 1909, is a good example of disbandment. Its reason for existence disappeared as domestic and international circumstances changed. The Round Table (a proto-think-tank) was an international organisation promoting imperial federation as a measure to stem the decline of the British empire. It was founded by Sir Alfred Milner and the men who worked with him in South Africa, the so-called 'Kindergarten'. Membership was politically conservative. Recruitment into this select group relied on personal friendship, Colonial Office connections and Oxford University association. All members believed in closer imperial ties but there were some divisions among those who favoured co-operation and those who favoured formal institutions such as an imperial cabinet (Foster, 1986: 11). Membership was restricted to a small number to ensure secrecy. As an élite and secretive organisation that shunned publicity, rumour and conspiracy theories abounded. This was one reason for its subsequent problems. There were other internal contributing factors. Branches were established throughout the empire requiring substantial resources to maintain links. By the late 1920s, the central London group let contact with the dominion Round Tables lapse. More importantly, tensions between the dominion branches resulted from the diversity of views that emerged from current or former colonies as each nation developed separately. The London group was plagued by disagreement about the degree and manner of imperial unification and new members recruited in the 1920s were often sceptical of the ideals of the older members (Kendle, 1975: 274). Some members developed wider interests in international affairs – often through the RIIA – rather than a concern solely imperial matters, and a few key members became important public or political figures, sapping the central London group of its vitality.

As the British empire decayed after the Second World War, especially after Suez, imperial federation was implausible. At most, the Round Table could hope for the preservation of Commonwealth links but they could not be substantially strengthened. The organisation's mission remained unchanged and increasingly remote from the manifestly different world in which it was operating. In the end, the Round Table foundered on a bad idea. As one member noted in 1932:

> We were wrong. ... We overstated the argument for federation of the Empire as an immediate and indispensable necessity. We made too little of the practical difficulty of working a world-wide federal system under such institutions as we at present possess. We were wrong to assume that organic union of the Empire as a whole is necessarily the first essential step towards a better world-order (quoted in Kendle, 1975: 288).

That a free but united Commonwealth was a buttress of peace and a
mechanism to promote democratic institutions proved fallacious
when confronted by the nationalistic movements within the former
colonies, fuelled by those not so enamoured with the notion of the
superiority of British civilisation. Overtaken by events and
compounded by an ageing and dwindling membership, the Round
Table study groups ceased in the dominions in the 1960s and 1970s.

Other organisations have lost their sense of purpose. The
Washington-based Potomac Institute, established in 1961, addressed
racial and economic discrimination in the USA. It remained a small
organisation fluctuating between ten and twenty full-time staff
augmented by consultants and project staff. Potomac did not usually
operate projects on a permanent basis – they would be 'spun off'.
Instead, the Institute would act as the 'spark' for new organisations
such as voter education programmes. This meant 'weak
institutionalisation' for Potomac as projects were not perpetuated
within the institute (Fleming, interview). Today, all programme
operations have ceased and the Institute exists in name only. There
are a variety of reasons for its cessation. The President, Harold
Fleming, was not prepared to continue in his position past retirement
age and a successor had not been groomed. He was of the view that
Potomac had served a worthy purpose but 'needed to be put to bed'.
Although the issues which Potomac addressed still persist, the
external situation has changed. No longer are there 'simple black and
white issues'. Economic factors, gender considerations and other
minority concerns required different approaches or what Fleming
called a 'different ball game'. He did not see the point of 'pouring
new wine into an old organisation which was race specific in focus'.
A new body could more effectively deal with the changed
environment.

The idea of a 'throw-away institution' was favoured by James
Cornford (interview) at IPPR in London. The IPPR does not have
much infrastructure or expensive facilities like a library. It is primarily
composed of its 'social capital', that is, staff and their connections
which, said Cornford, could easily be disassembled into another
entity. Between 1976 and 1980 Cornford was the director of the
Outer Circle Policy Unit (OCPU) which was set up with a five-year
grant from the Rowntree Foundation and other funds. Rather than
perpetuate the unit, the three researchers decided to live off the
grant. In Cornford's view it was a sensible decision as they freed
themselves of the requirement for fund-raising and devoted their
efforts to policy work. When obsolescence becomes apparent as in

the case of Potomac or when the research activity rather than the organisational presentation is given precedence, as in the case of the OCPU, disbandment can be appropriate behaviour.

The short-lived Lehrman Institute was established by Lewis Lehrman, a New York businessman. Described as a 'public policy salon' which operated through dinner discussions, it focused on foreign policy and economic policy questions (Mone, interview). The Institute was also a means to boost Lehrman's political aspirations. There were research fellows but they had a low public profile compared with Lehrman. Lehrman had hoped for a position in the Reagan Administration. When that did not materialise he withdrew from politics. The Institute also faltered. Funding was gradually reduced and new funds were not sought. Whatever the merits of the Lehrman Institute's research and seminar activities, it was too closely aligned with Lehrman. It was a vanity tank. Longevity was compromised by dependence on Lehrman for institutional leadership and funding. The Roosevelt Center also foundered on its funding dependence. A Chicago futures trader and multi-millionaire, Richard C. Dennis helped set up the Center in 1982 and over the course of its seven-year existence contributed approximately $15 million. Although it appears that he made it clear from the outset that he would not fund the Center indefinitely, there was little effort by staff to diversify sources of support until it was too late. There was also some speculation that Dennis stopped funding the Roosevelt Center as it did not reflect his political values. Nor did the Center serve as a means of entrée to Congress and the White House, apparently one reason why he dismissed the Center's first President, Doug Bennett. The board of directors decided to close rather than risk running a deficit for several years (*National Journal*, 10 June 1989). Numerous institutes quietly disappear. That many fold without notice suggests that they were not competitive and were unable to develop a recognisable name and image. Financial difficulties are often the reason for closure but other problems usually beset the organisation beforehand.

The demise of the American Council of the Institute of Pacific Relations (AIPR) was more public. The Institute of Pacific Relations was established in 1925 as an international organisation composed of autonomous nationally based councils. The US Council of the IPR was the strongest and best financed. During the first twenty years of its existence, criticisms of the AIPR activities and studies were relatively minor, such as occasional criticism that the Institute was pro-Japanese or pro-Chinese in sympathies. Disputes were internal and based in differing notions of the nature of the organisation and concern about possible conflict of interest between an official's IPR role and outside activities (Thomas, 1974: 36). By the mid-1940s, however, the IPR was accused of being a communist front organisation by groups outside the Institute. After the collapse of the Nationalist Government in China, the US Congress's interest in the IPR was sparked by Senator McCarthy's charge of communists in the State Department and his accusation that AIPR official and editor of *Pacific Affairs*, Owen Lattimore, was a 'top Russian espionage agent' (Thomas, 1974: 67).

The McCarran Committee investigation of the IPR heard charges that the Institute was 'completely under the control of the Communist Party'. Communist agents were supposedly exerting influence over US Far Eastern policy by using the AIPR as intellectual cover and as 'a little red school house for teaching certain people in Washington how to think' (Thomas, 1974: 85). The Committee lacked impartiality and did not investigate strong evidence of internal dispute about the direction of the IPR and the many non-communists who occupied important positions in the organisation. In the paranoia whipped up by McCarthy, the IPR became both a scapegoat and an instrument in the Committee hearings to create a hard-line anti-communist foreign and domestic policy (Thomas, 1974: 95). The AIPR's credibility as a non-partisan organisation for the free intellectual inquiry of Asian affairs was destroyed. The IPR became entwined with charges of treachery and conspiracy. Its intellectual authority was diminished. Staff and membership morale was undermined by the Congressional hearings and the Institute's executive was forced into a defensive position. Already in financial difficulty by the late 1940s, the McCarran Committee inquiry stymied potential donors during the 1950s. The IPR was also competing with newly formed university centres of Asian studies. Funding constraints constricted the IPR's ability to adapt its mode of operation to new developments in Asian-American relations and the growth of Asian studies. Consensus over the role norms and objectives of the organisation dissipated as rivalries between the New York office and other chapters heightened. In 1955, the Internal Revenue Service revoked the IPR's and AIPR's tax exempt status. Over the five years that the IRS ruling was challenged, membership dropped, chapters in San Francisco and Seattle disbanded and the founding chapter in Hawaii was renamed, effectively divorcing it from the IPR. After 1960, when Columbia University agreed to publish *Pacific Affairs* and offered the AIPR Secretary-General a position in its Asian Studies Department, the IPR disbanded.

Incremental Change and Organisational Flux

Many policy institutes reflect an adaptive style of behaviour. From the vantage point of those who run policy institutes a steady and untraumatic growth in task, programme and budget are highly desirable. Habit-driven behaviour is often favoured over the strains resulting from reform and constant reassessment. Change by adaptation involves adding new activities to old ones without questioning or re-evaluating underlying values and theories that provide justification of the think-tank's mission. The emphasis is on altering actions, not the organisation's purpose. Adaptation can be of two kinds. First, incremental growth involves augmentation of tasks without change in an organisation's decision-making dynamics. An organisation is relatively stable experiencing a growth or consolidation of income, staff, programmes and activity. Adaptation of the second kind is more traumatic. Significant changes in organisational decision-making are occurring but lack coherence. The goals, aims or mission of the institute are confused or unclear. Consensus within the organisation dissipates as the means of enacting these goals is contested (Haas, 1990a: chs. 5 and 6). Incremental growth continues while nothing disturbs the leisurely pace at which new demands are introduced. This behaviour flourishes while few new think-tanks enter the intellectual marketplace and while institute membership, clients and sponsors remain happy. Once a number of complex demands engulf an institute the limits of this style of behaviour have been reached. New institutes can upset the equilibrium of older institutes. Competitive factors can set back an institute which previously operated in near monopolistic circumstances, impelling the board, members and clientele to question the mode of operation of an institute.

The starkest example of this is in Washington DC where the old guard institutes have had to adjust. Adjustment does not mean that broad objectives have changed, merely that they are pursued in a different context, through different means and in a different style. To enhance the receptiveness of reports and books, public affairs offices have been established when once they were not needed. Brookings has adopted some of the tactics of the new partisan institutes. In 1991, Brookings hired a PR firm, Hager Sharp Inc., to assist in the launch of a health care report (*National Journal*, 22 July 1991: 1552; see also Toner, 1985). It has also been noted by many that Brookings took a 'rightward turn' to the middle ground to ensure that its policy advice was heard, if not received by the Reagan and Bush administrations (Bernstein, 1984: 96; McGann, 1992). Adjustment has not meant that old guard institutes have mimicked the approaches of the new partisan institutes. Instead, new activities have been encompassed and incorporated with existing approaches.

Many of the older organisations are in a secure position with solid publishing records, recognised expertise and financial security. The financial autonomy and independence of the Carnegie Endowment or Russell Sage allows them to preserve their scholarly style and to resist the trend towards partisanship and marketing – they are very much universities without students. By contrast, Brookings' endowment is not large enough for it to resist change. Instead, it represents a 'buffer' enhancing Brookings' independence and allowing studies to be pursued when funds could not be garnered elsewhere. Even though Brookings, Chatham House, CED and NIESR operate in a fundamentally different environment from when they were established, their character has not changed greatly. They are not evolving to the new partisan style.

Adaptation of the incremental mode will become unmanageable if directors, trustees and scholars stubbornly defend their established mission and resist new demands on the organisation. Routine, an entrenched organisational culture and assured financial resources can promote misperceptions of security. Attrition can also occur with rapid staff turnover and when numerous complex tasks pressing on the institute pose problems of scale. Although budgets may expand, personnel increase or new contracts and tasks be acquired, an institute can still be characterised by disorder and flux. Otherwise known as 'turbulent non-growth' (Haas, 1990a), executives and fellows pursue many activities simultaneously but show little or no co-operation or agreement on common goals. Dominant factions within the institute lose control, leadership is lacking and 'goal compatibility' among staff is low (Light, 1983: 182). Efforts to incorporate new scholars or board members to bolster the established pattern of behaviour either fail or result in further diffusion of the original consensus. Alternatively, new leaders do not completely displace the old faction and warring continues. Organisational evaluation deteriorates as membership or boards lack an agreed set of criteria with which to assess achievement of aims. Coherence among programmes declines. As a consequence, the questioning of goals and norms accelerates (Haas, 1990a: 109).

This kind of decay need not destroy policy institutes. Transcending it requires a crisis, a shared definition of its causes and strong leadership. For example, financial crisis, brought on by reduced corporate support, a diminishing membership base or failed research programmes may impel a critical re-evaluation of organisational mission. As outlined in the previous chapter, RFF adapted to its financial crisis and the changed external environment – of universities developing greater strength in environmental studies – by becoming more policy focused. Hudson adapted through significant restructuring and relocation. The AEI adapted through management changes and a new financial regime. In a different response, the World Policy Institute (WPI) in New York has given up on the vicissitudes of foundation funding and opted for greater financial stability as part of the New School for Social Research. Another adaptive strategy to escape disestablishment is to merge with another think-tank. The PSI in London was created from the merger of PEP and the Centre for Studies in Social Policy (CSSP). In the decade before 1978, PEP experienced a growth of task, programmes and finances, but in an inflationary climate the PEP could not expand its staff base adequately in order to address the new set of social and economic questions that were facing Britain in the 1970s. Consequently, it joined with the CSSP – an organisation that was also pondering its future and which had complementary research interests – to become a much larger research institute (Pinder, 1981: 157–59).

Some institutes have difficulty adjusting to changed external circumstances. Indeed, a number of security studies organisations will need to reassess their future direction with the end of the Cold War. The Nathan Hale Institute which provided research on and support for the US intelligence services is almost inactive in the words of its President because of the 'end of the Cold War and all that'. Over its thirty-year existence, the stature of the Institute for Policy Studies (IPS) in Washington DC has gradually ebbed. Its lack of impact has much to do with over two decades of Republican administrations and the ideological hegemony of neo-conservatism. It has also suffered from a barrage of criticism that it is a communist front organisation (Powell, 1987; Isaac and Isaac, 1983). However, in the 1960s the IPS was an innovative organisation. Its founders did not emulate the non-partisan and value-free style of Brookings and other institutes. Instead, the IPS was a politically engaged institute and a highly visible centre of intellectual opposition during the Johnson and Nixon administrations. IPS achieved fame, or notoriety, for the production of the *Vietnam Reader*, a text for the teach-in movement, and when one of its co-founders was tried in the Boston Five trial.[1] At the time, it was virtually the only radical liberal institute providing a clearly articulated and activist intellectual challenge to US foreign policy.

By the 1970s, the IPS was confronted by a number of competing claims within the organisation. New Left concerns of feminism, minority and gay rights, and third world revolution as an agent of change propelled the Institute in a directionless course. In the words of one of the co-founders, 'there was a kind of pseudo-democracy, an ethos of participation, that excluded establishing priorities' (Barnet quoted in Blumenthal, 1986). The lack of coherence in Institute scholarship reflected splits on the American left. Where once the IPS had been noted for scholars criticising the national security state and popularising the notion of the permanent war economy, many of the New Left exponents 'distorted' liberalism into support for big government. Thus, while the IPS grew larger and added new programmes, the founders and senior fellows who had built the institute and raised the funding lost organisational control. The schism between them and the younger 'cultural revolution faction' became uncontainable when the IPS experienced funding cutbacks in 1976. Staff morale was also badly damaged by the death of IPS fellow and former foreign minister of Chile, Orlando Letelier, and an IPS staff member. The car in which they were travelling was exploded by a bomb placed by Chilean secret agents. The warring between factions resulted in a split when some fellows opposed general cutbacks by forming a union and demanding salary increases and workplace democracy. In the subsequent settlement, the dissident fellows received a third of IPS resources to establish their own institute which has since folded (Blumenthal, 1986).

These internal conflicts severely damaged the capacity of IPS to be actively involved in policy debates. The IPS has not regained the pre-eminence it once had. Funding is more difficult to acquire. The IPS also sold its buildings as part of the settlement and now operates from leased offices. Its organisational history since the mid-1970s has remained turbulent. Since the two co-founders have relinquished the directorship there has been a number of leadership changes. Additionally, it has not been easy for the organisation to adapt to changes in its external environment. As a scholar in another think-tank noted, with the end of the Cold War as well as changes in Latin America and South Africa, the IPS 'has lost its momentum' (Royal, interview).

Learning

Learning or innovation is a reflective process. Organisational goals and practices are questioned. New purposes eventuate when new goals are established and legitimated by consciously developed theories or value explicit programmes that necessitate changed behaviour. The change that results is the consequence of a purpose redefined. This type of think-tank defines for itself the problems that set its tasks. In an organisation that learns the executive directorate is entrepreneurial. It confronts crises by developing a more dynamic partnership with the board of trustees and building new coalitions of support within the institute through a refashioned consensus. Leaders turn from a passive or reactive to an active stance. They take initiative in persuading other, perhaps antagonistic, members to create an inner circle of reformers whilst recognising the need for ideological tolerance and compromise in order to achieve a high level of goal compatibility. Learning is associated with new arrangements and finding new mission (Haas, 1990a: 4). Through learning, bureaucratic entities cope with the unprecedented. It is a rare feat. The stimuli for learning mainly comes from unexpected events in a think-tank's external environment. This can be developments concerning an institute's field of research such as the collapse of the Soviet Union or systemic disruptions like war, depression and social dislocation. Further stimuli for new behaviour can arise with the election of a new government and new laws or political configurations.

The establishment of a new think-tank is frequently a creative act and can involve learning on the part of the founders. The design of a new organisation displays learning when it occurs as the result of a policy trauma, a catastrophic event or the development of concerns of major loss such as might occur with significant economic restructuring (Haas, 1990a: 165). For example, the founders of the RIIA and CFR were responding to the trauma of the First World War and what they perceived as a lack of understanding about international affairs among decision-makers (Wallace, 1990; Higgott and Stone, 1994). Similarly, the establishment of the IEA and AEI were intellectual challenges to the growing predominance of Keynesian thought in government policies. The founders of the IFS in London wanted to prevent British governments introducing far-reaching tax legislation without the benefit of thorough analysis. In the words of one, 'We, the founders, did not just want to start an Institute; we wanted to change the world or, at least, the world of the British fisc' (quoted in Robinson, 1990: 3). These organisations were characterised by principles that represented a clear break with past practices or with perspectives that were deemed unacceptable.

Learning was involved when RAND was restructured from a unit in the US Air Force to a non-governmental organisation independent from the Department of Defense. A group of far-sighted staff within the Pentagon and RAND recognised that the accelerating pace of technological development in military matters required new ways of thinking and new institutions. Technological advance, the reconstruction of Europe and cold war tensions brought uncertainty and ambiguity. Learning featured when RAND expanded its limited aims centring around technical and defence issues to a concern with broader policy issues of strategy. The innovation allowed experts to reassess US military and economic role in the new world order. Yet RAND was in an adaptive mode with the establishment of New York RAND (its office in New York, now closed) and the development of its Domestic Research Division. In these two cases RAND was responding to changes in the external environment as the federal government increasingly funded urban, poverty and social issues. RAND accordingly expanded by developing new programmes.

The creation of a new institute does not always represent learning. The Potomac Institute, for example, was an adaptive response to a new political situation in which black and minority interests acquired greater public attention and legitimacy. It sought to bring effectiveness to policies already instituted and on which a policy consensus regarding equal rights and desegregation had already been established. Although the IPS and Heritage were innovative organisations at their establishment, developing new styles and techniques of activity, many of their imitators exhibit adaptive behaviour rather than learning. The conservative state based think-tanks in America operate very much like Heritage on a smaller scale. They are a successful adaptation at the state level.

The initial innovation or learning associated with new arrangements is very difficult to sustain. An organisation will enter an adaptive pattern when the original guiding spirit of the institute becomes dogma or ossified. Habit-driven behaviour will set in. Social, political and economic stability, and the absence of crisis and conflict over policies undermines the demand for innovative ways of thinking. The intent to be policy-relevant can be diverted by a growing tendency towards disinterested research, that is, by drifting into the orbit of academic disciplines as has occurred with the Hoover Institution and WPI. Subsiding into an adaptive mode is a frequent occurrence. As Ernst Haas notes:

> Do organizations and their founders display insight, energy, and determination to fashion a brighter future, only to fall victim to divergent interests, flagging enthusiasm, and a tired staff? ... If

entropy lurks in the wings, its role remains ill-understood (1990a: 166).

As institutes grow they become more bureaucratic. Professional staff who have a stake in the continued existence and growth of the institute will have a tendency to steer it along a less adversarial and risky course. There is a temptation to accommodate rather than challenge the views of patrons and sponsors. It seems that the organisational cost of commitment to principles and ideals may be to remain small and sidelined to the periphery of the political arena rather than the mainstream (Jenkins, 1987).

Learning, adaptation, attrition and disbandment is not an evolutionary scale or cycle. Although the majority of institutes are habit-driven for most of their existence whereas only a few are innovators, not all organisations begin life in the incremental mode and degenerate. Nor is it apparent that a policy institute will then disband. Rejuvenation or resurrection can occur. Once it is recognised, habit can be transcended. Establishing whether or not think-tanks are in an innovative or creative stage of learning, or whether they are going through a difficult period of turbulence and confusion is important. It has implications for the effectiveness of an organisation. It is not necessarily the case that an institute in a state of learning is more likely to have impact with government, bureaucracies or other constituencies than an institute in an incremental mode. Yet it will be more efficiently managed and less riven by dispute and factionalism. That is, scholars and executives will be in broad agreement and acting jointly to meet the organisation's objectives. Furthermore, the institute that reflects processes of learning is more likely to provide new ways of understanding and resolving problems that are found intractable with current policies. As the next chapter discusses, the people who provide consensual knowledge are often found in epistemic communities.

NOTES

1. The Boston five trial in the late 1960s attracted nation-wide media attention in the USA. Marcus Raskin co-authored a short manifesto *A Call to Resist* against the draft during the Vietnam War. As a consequence, Raskin was indicted as a 'co-conspirator' for organising draft resistance along with four others – Dr Benjamin Spock, Revd William Sloane Coffin, Michael Ferber and Mitchell Godman. Raskin was acquitted.

6 Knowledge Communities and Policy Institutes

Knowledge is a central aspect of power in the epistemic community perspective. It explains how expert forms of advice penetrate bureaucracies and influence decision-makers. The veracity of knowledge is not at issue. Rather the concern is how it is used in policy. The epistemic community approach focuses on expert actors in policy making who share norms, causal beliefs and political projects and who seek change in specific areas of policy. Without explaining why, the main proponent of the theory, Peter Haas (1992a: 31), describes think-tanks as a 'key location' for epistemic communities. This chapter explores this assertion and applies the epistemic community framework with two aims. First, to examine and contrast with other policy network ideas the utility of the concept as an explanatory device for the occasional influence of think-tanks. Second, to elucidate the organisational importance of think-tanks for epistemic communities. Without political access or patronage these communities sometimes find expression through policy research institutes. Furthermore, think-tanks are likely to operate more effectively when dominated by a community. The consensual knowledge of a community promotes the pursuit of innovative research agendas and enhances the policy relevance of an institute. It does not mean, however, that a think-tank needs to be linked to an epistemic community in order to function.

Epistemic Communities

An epistemic community is made up of experts who seek to translate their beliefs through a common policy project into public policies and programmes. They are '... networks of specialists with a common world view about cause and effect relationships which relate to their domain of expertise, and common political values about the type of policies to which they should be applied' (Peter Haas, 1989: 16). As policy *cognoscenti,* members of the community defend what they consider to be true in public and professional domains. Since they come from diverse intellectual backgrounds and institutions, the ties that bind these individuals are neither bureaucratic or institutional nor based on vested interest. They are linked by common ideas and values. Following Haas (1992a: 3), epistemic communities have four defining features:

> i) they have shared normative and principled beliefs which provide the value based rationales for their action;
> ii) they have shared causal beliefs or professional judgements;
> iii) they have common notions of validity based on inter-subjective, internally defined criteria for validating knowledge;
> iv) they have a common policy enterprise.

It is the combination of these characteristics that distinguish epistemic communities from other groups involved in the policy-making process. Self-evidently, interest groups are politically driven by interest rather than causal beliefs. Academic disciplines are too heterodox to be called epistemic communities. However, sub-fields of a discipline such as politically active Keynesian economists could become an epistemic community in a specific policy field (Ikenberry, 1992). Communities also differ from professions. Professions lack the normative basis of an epistemic community and its policy enterprise. The ethical standards of an epistemic community arise from a principled approach to issues not a professional code of conduct. Epistemic communities also differ from groups of administrators and legislators by their unwillingness to advocate or participate in the implementation of policy that conflicts with their normative objectives (Haas, 1992a: 16–20).

Epistemic communities assert their independence from government or vested interest on the basis of their expert knowledge. The professional and educational pedigree of members of a community are institutional barriers to the entry of others into the group. This facilitates coherence and unity but can also promote an unwillingness to challenge their own orthodoxy (Restivo and Laughlin, 1987: 490). Even so, an epistemic community is not static. It is capable of incorporating additional ideas and participants. Notwithstanding the possible onset of intellectual rigidity, one the most important features of a community is its receptivity to new knowledge and the constant re-examination of prevailing beliefs about cause and effect.

More than anything else, members of an epistemic community need to share common causal methods or professional judgement, common notions of validity and a common vocabulary. This is known as consensual knowledge. This type of knowledge is 'the sum of technical information and the theories surrounding it that command sufficient agreement among interested actors at a given time to serve as a guide to public policy' (Haas, 1990a: 74). For example, a commitment to ecological principles or the tenets of neo-classical economics. The truth or validity claims identify an epistemic community. Members are in rough agreement about the causes of problems and the effects of policy interventions. Accordingly, group solidarity is bound by a common purpose and shared norms to the extent that the community does not need to meet formally. The information flow can be achieved through conferences and journals or even e-mail in what is known as an 'invisible college' (Davis and Salasin, 1978: 121). But institutional ties and informal networks are important promoters of solidarity. They provide some means of comparing information and finding moral support for what are, occasionally, marginal views or unpopular sentiments.

The status and prestige associated with epistemic community expertise and their high professional training and authoritative knowledge regarding a particular problem is politically empowering and provides limited access to the political system. The importance of control over knowledge and information for policy has been exhibited in a number of policy areas. The international trade in services came to the fore in the Uruguay Round of GATT negotiations after an epistemic community demonstrated to governments the benefits of the liberalisation of services through removal of non-tariff barriers (Drake and Nicolaidis, 1992). An epistemic community of cetologists has also exerted sufficient influence over the international management of whaling to temper the policy demands of both whaling industry managers and an issue-oriented lobbying coalition of environmentalists (Peterson, 1992). The depletion of stratospheric ozone has seen the emergence of a community of atmospheric scientists and policy-makers pushing for chlorofluorocarbon (CFC) emission regulation (Haas, 1992b). Another community of marine and ecological scientists activated the UN Mediterranean Action Plan that generated interstate co-operation to supervise pollution control (Haas, 1989). Yet another epistemic-like community of free market economists and policy specialists is said to be promoting economic co-operation in the Asia-Pacific region through advocacy of market-led integration, the minimisation of trade distorting measures and promotion of the Asia-Pacific Economic Co-operation movement (Higgott, 1993).

The receptivity of decision-makers to new ideas or scientific insights is not automatic. Policy agendas are more likely to change with disruption and uncertainty. Uncertainty is evident in the degree of misunderstanding or poor comprehension of the long-term effects of pollution on health, agriculture and the atmosphere or the uncertainty surrounding war, future energy sources and AIDS. Leaders turn to experts for advice to help manage these highly complex policy matters. Uncertainty is a situation where decision-makers must make policy choices in the absence of adequate information to assess the potential outcomes of their subsequent course of action. As a result of poor comprehension there is an inability to apply familiar decision models to estimate the costs and benefits of policy options. It implies more than a lack of information. In uncertainty decision-makers are prone to seek out new advisers to explain the causes and consequences of problems such as AIDS or ozone depletion. Specialists are better trained to deal with uncertainty and more knowledgeable about possible solutions. Epistemic communities are potentially at their strongest in conditions of uncertainty as expertise is at a premium. In circumstances of less uncertainty, where interests are clearer or established policy heuristics appear to be working, the policy impact of epistemic communities is of less magnitude. But by introducing new patterns of reasoning and gradually changing the way state actors perceive their situation, state behaviour may be changed incrementally (Haas, 1992a).

To gain political influence an epistemic community requires appointment to party, political or bureaucratic position and regular channels of communication with leaders via commissions of inquiry or scientific councils. Once consulted, policy debates are likely to be 'informed and bounded by the advice leaders receive' (Haas, 1990b: 350). A community can then carve out a niche within the policy-making process (in regulatory agencies, in Parliament, as advisers of senior ministers, as representatives on government delegations) and are ideally located to provide advice consistent with their causal beliefs in their domain of expertise. Embedded in bureaucracies, they limit the realm of policy debate through their agenda setting power of problem definition which allows members to present issues for action and propose solutions. Continued consolidation of bureaucratic power is dependent on a community's abatement of uncertainty, the absence of new epistemic challengers and the sustained intellectual coherence of the dominant community's frame of reference or causal model. Accordingly, the power of the dominant epistemic community can be undercut by a new crisis impelling decision-makers to consult a new group; internal dissension, bureaucratic infighting and loss of consensus within the group; or lack of access to high-level decision making as may occur with the election of a new government. In these circumstances the compliance of the state or leaders with the perceptions and recommendations of the community breaks down.

Competing Policy Network Perspectives

The epistemic community concept bears similarity with other literature on issue networks, advocacy coalitions and policy communities. These can be generically referred to as different kinds of 'policy networks' (Jordan and Schubert, 1992: 7; Smith, 1993b). The main difference is that the policy network literature portrays policy formation and implementation more as the outcome of power struggles over resources among groups, whereas the epistemic community approach stresses knowledge and uncertainty. The 'discourse coalition' concept also shares common ground with epistemic communities in that it is 'a group of actors who share a social construct' (Hajer, 1993: 45). This process of a group constructing or framing political problems is discussed later in regard to agenda setting. It differs from the epistemic community approach in emphasising the role of discourse in shaping our understanding of reality.

An issue network is the most nebulous, atomistic and fluid version of a policy network and mostly associated with the American policy-making milieu (Heclo, 1980). It is characterised by participants with conflicting interests, a lack of common values and little consensus regarding problem definition or the outcomes of policy interventions. Issue networks feature widening group participation rather than gate keeping. The concept would have little in common with epistemic communities were it not that an issue network is a 'shared knowledge group' in which experts are able to reduce the contradictions created by extensive organisational participation (Heclo, 1980: 103). Issue networks create a complex policy-making milieu where it is difficult to identify the locus of decision making among a 'collective but rather unorganized technocracy' (Van Waarden, 1992: 46). By contrast, policy communities are more stable networks with restrictions on participants and insulation from other networks. A policy community is a set of actors bound together by a common interest in a particular policy field such as health, education or telecommunications. The group can be composed of interest group activists and government officials, as well as ministers, parliamentarians, consultants and journalists. A community has a shared commitment to certain policies, programmes and ways of doing things (Sabatier, 1991: 148). Individuals are usually from similar educational and professional backgrounds and their beliefs are reinforced by the conferences and regular meetings promoted by professional association.

While there may be some overlap not all participants of a policy community would be members of an epistemic community but an epistemic community could be a sub-group within a policy community. An epistemic community which favours a course of action not recognised by a policy community may also operate outside the policy community and try to force issues onto the agenda. A policy community is associated with policy continuity and can be a major constraint on change (Rhodes and Marsh, 1992: 197). By contrast, epistemic communities are normally agents of innovation. They are disruptive of old certainties and seek policy change. In general, a policy community is a more diverse congregation of interests. The distinctiveness of the two concepts lies between the coalition of favoured interest groups, bureaucrats and others controlling a policy sector and enjoying mutual benefits, whereas the epistemic community coalesces around 'objectivity', 'expertise' and 'scientific authority'. Policy communities are not characterised by shared principled beliefs or validity tests.

The advocacy coalition concept treats policy change as the consequence of 'fluctuations in the dominant belief systems within a policy area' (Sabatier, 1987: 605). Unlike policy communities and issue networks which portray agendas changing with the play of interests, advocacy coalitions also recognise a process of policy learning. Advocacy coalitions operate in policy sub-systems (not unlike policy communities) with other key actors – policy brokers and decision-makers. An advocacy coalition can include journalists, researchers and policy analysts as well as elected officials and bureaucratic leaders, that is, people 'who share...a set of basic values, causal assumptions, and problem perceptions – and who show a nontrivial degree of co-ordinated activity over time' (Sabatier, 1987: 660).[1] In most policy sub-systems the number of politically significant coalitions is quite small. Policy learning may occur within an advocacy coalition as new arguments and strategies are developed. Yet, a dominant advocacy coalition is unlikely to be unseated merely by analytic debates. It is external events that significantly change the terms of debate or create uncertainty. External stimuli include changes in socio-economic conditions and technology, electoral changes with new governments adopting different agendas, priorities and leaders as well as policy changes in other systems affecting another policy sub-system. In periods of relative stability, routine and incremental decision patterns, advocacy coalitions are unlikely to have significant impact. Policy-makers prefer information that does not question the underlying consensus of a policy programme. If consensus is decaying, the opportunity for influence is increased. With the stress on core beliefs and learning within coalitions, the approach (in common with epistemic communities) 'neglects' actor interests (Sabatier, 1991: 153). Despite the similarities, epistemic communities are closed groupings whereas advocacy coalitions as well as issue networks and policy communities, to varying degrees, are more open. Neither issue networks nor policy communities have clear boundaries. Furthermore, once an epistemic community achieves its policy project it disappears, whereas the other networks are a more persistent feature of policy-making. The role of vested interest is also a more important variable in issue networks and policy communities than for epistemic communities in which ideas, expertise and knowledge are paramount.

These policy network ideas are of additional relevance in understanding think-tank activities. If it is the case that epistemic communities have limited life spans and dissipate once their policy project is in place, they are presumably replaced by other kinds of networks seeking to influence policy as the new knowledge becomes established. New or refashioned networks of public and private actors may be generated by the ideas, institutions and practices promoted by a successful epistemic community. As co-operation becomes institutionalised and new rules are laid down, technical issues of implementation become more important and 'A community based on expertise [gives] way to several communities based on interest' (Bennett, 1992: 16). Accordingly, policy networks are useful in expanding the epistemic community approach. It is possible to account for the changed policy-making milieu that emerges when an epistemic community disintegrates.

Agenda Setting

There are two types of agenda (Cobb, et al., 1976). The public agenda is composed of issues which have achieved a high level of public interest and visibility. The formal agenda is the list of items which decision-makers have accepted for serious consideration.

Given that think-tanks are relatively small, non-profit organisations outside of government and without large constituencies, the public agenda would appear to be their primary domain of activity. They are in the relatively disadvantageous position of raising matters of public interest in competition with other groups similarly seeking to advance issues. Operating within a policy network, however, they are brought closer to decision-making arenas. In general, policy network models cast agenda setting as a relatively closed rather than open process (Smith, 1989b: 151; Rhodes and Marsh, 1992: 200). Agendas are shaped on the basis of shared knowledge *and* the power and bargaining dynamics of vested interests. Epistemic communities claim authority to influence agendas on the basis of their scientific expertise. Agenda-setting is not well theorised in the epistemic community literature. Issues are carried by epistemic communities onto public and formal agendas in conditions of uncertainty. Action is taken once a community gains bureaucratic entrée, and as the issue is resolved and erodes so does the community. The model of policy evolution is static in the sense that it develops in stages. By contrast, John Kingdon's (1984) model of agenda-setting is more dynamic.[2]

Agenda setting can be conceptualised as three largely unrelated streams: i) a policy stream which refers to policy communities of advocates, researchers and other specialists that analyse problems and propose solutions; ii) a problem stream which consists of information about 'real world' problems and feed back from past government policies; and iii) a political stream that includes turnover of key administrators and legislators, and ideological contests among political parties. The government agenda is set in the politics and problems streams. Issues rise and fall on the agenda when policy windows open, that is, when changes in the political or problem streams present an opportunity to 'couple' or join the three streams. Specialists in policy communities first develop solutions for political consideration after a prolonged 'softening' process in the policy stream. Policy entrepreneurs then advocate them and try to take advantage of political receptivity to package the solution with the problem. In other words, policies are attached to problems. Policy entrepreneurs attempt to educate both 'policy communities, which tend to be inertia-bound and resistant to major changes, and larger publics getting them used to new ideas and building acceptance for their proposals' (Kingdon, 1984: 134). This concern with policy entrepreneurship to convey ideas to policy-makers acknowledges that ideas are not inherently persuasive. Knowledge and research does not automatically 'enlighten' policy-makers. The social and political

context in which knowledge is created, synthesised and used will also
have bearing on which form of knowledge and expertise dominates.

Understanding agenda-setting can also be enhanced by drawing on
the nascent discourse coalition literature. Discourse – or the
argumentative turn in policy analysis – is an essential part of the
process known as the 'mobilisation of bias'. In this view, discourse is
a set of 'ideas, concepts and categories through which meaning is
given to phenomena' (Hajer, 1993: 45). Discourses are important as
they shape understanding and can predetermine the definition of a
problem. Accordingly, discourse coalitions are groups that are
engaged in the mobilisation of bias (or 'softening') and which seek to
impose their 'discourse' in policy domains. If their discourse shapes
the way in which society conceptualises the world or a particular
problem, then the coalition has achieved 'discourse structuration'
and agendas are likely to be restricted to a limited spectrum of
possibilities. If a discourse becomes entrenched in the minds of many
as the dominant mode of perception, it can become distilled in
institutions and organisational practices as the conventional mode of
reasoning. This latter process is 'discourse institutionalisation'.
Chapters Nine and Ten pursue this line of analysis by combining an
assessment of the discursive production of reality with an
investigation of the social practices of think-tanks to entrench their
version of reality in policy debates and decisions. Consensual
knowledge is conveyed to decision-makers through both discursive
and social practices. Accordingly, epistemic communities can also be
conceived as a technocratic kind of discourse coalition which
articulates its common values and ideas through discourse.

The Interaction of Policy Institutes with Epistemic Communities

Think-tanks have much in common with epistemic communities.
Both are primarily concerned with knowledge. Both desire to
influence or inform public policy and penetrate government with
their ideas and/or personnel. Both set themselves apart from interest
groups and professional associations. There is a *potential* point of
intersection. Think-tanks clearly form a part of the organisational
dimension of knowledge networks and may represent a means to
trace the emergence and activities of epistemic communities. For
example, it is necessary for an epistemic community to have relative
autonomy in order to resist political pressures, to retain scientific
integrity and legitimacy and to continue to innovate (Adler, 1992:
112). Epistemic communities require a presence in reputable

organisations outside government such as universities, policy institutes, scientific laboratories and international organisations to cultivate and sustain their scientific expertise and authority. Prior to incorporation into government, epistemic communities consolidate intellectually and politically through independent or quasi-autonomous organisations.

The epistemic community approach neither comprehensively explains the think-tank phenomenon nor is it assumed that think-tanks are the organisational centre of epistemic communities. Instead, it is more accurate to portray think-tanks as 'switchboards' through which connections are made, 'rather than being a depository of activity and authority' (Ruggie quoted in Adler, 1992: 105–6). Furthermore, it does not follow that all think-tanks promote the goals of epistemic communities. These organisations do not need to be dominated by a community in order to function. The CFR, RIIA and FPRI, for example, have a common interest in international affairs. Only tenuously can it be argued that the scholars of these institutes share the same causal models or are committed to a joint political project. Notwithstanding these qualifications, the approach helps explain the sense of mission and commitment to policy reform that infuses many individuals who move in and out of think-tanks. The consensual knowledge of a community promotes learning or innovative behaviour in policy institutes of the kind discussed in the previous chapter. That is, epistemic communities can find expression through think-tanks and potentially act as a trigger for learning. In return, think-tank scholars aid the definition of an issue and help build internal agreement within a community on what constitutes relevant knowledge. RAND was an important organisation in the development of an arms control community of strategists in the USA (Adler, 1992). For a select group of economists, the CFR was 'an extraordinary vehicle for the concentration of expertise and planning' on matters of post-World War Two trade and monetary agreements (Ikenberry, 1992). More recently, organisations such as the Trade Policy Research Centre (TPRC), IIE and AEI, among others, have played a central role in a 'trade in services' epistemic community that targeted the GATT Uruguay Round (Drake and Nicolaidis, 1992).

A four-part model of the role of epistemic communities in policy evolution has been developed (Adler and Haas, 1992: 373). That is, i) intellectual innovation, ii) diffusion, iii) policy selection, and iv) policy persistence. It is the first two steps where think-tanks are likely to have greatest input, whereas in the selection and persistence of an epistemic community's ideas, policy-makers play a more important role. The role of policy institutes or their scholars in innovation is apparent. As organisations devoted to policy research it is of little surprise that a number of think-tanks have been or are at the cutting edge of their field of inquiry. Examples of innovative research work in think-tanks include the studies of graduated deterrence at Chatham House and IISS in the 1950s or the pioneering work of the NBER on US national income (Fabricant, n.d.: 11). Scholars connected to the IIE helped mould the intellectual parameters of international political economy in the USA. Environmental resource accounting, an index to ascribe economic value to the environment, is being extended and applied in a number of environmental institutes such as WRI.

Think-tank scholars are also well suited to the tasks of interpretation and outlining the range of defensible policy options for non-specialist audiences, that is, advocacy and agenda-setting. They communicate ideas through joint research projects, conferences and seminars, and the informal networks of individual scholars. Think-tanks provide an institutional mechanism for maintaining links among an epistemic community. A number of institutes have affiliation arrangements whereby they collaborate or exchange publications and hold joint conferences. Such arrangements are often symptomatic of shared ideology and policy preferences. The interaction between various institutes at both a domestic and international level helps create a transnational alliance where information is transmitted and shared, a conduit for funding is established and skills and expertise are diffused. Diffusion is not limited to government circles but also occurs within the media, the business world and among opinion leaders.

Although an epistemic community may exist as an invisible college there are meeting grounds at which some members congregate. The commitment of members to shared principles is not automatic. The common purpose of the group needs to be constantly re-established in the minds of members. Think-tanks provide one mechanism outside formal decision-making arenas to regenerate solidarity. Very occasionally, a new policy institute may be established by an epistemic community to diffuse its knowledge. That is, a think-tank may be the product of the consensual knowledge and learning of a community (Haas, 1990a: 86). The think-tank acts as a glue, bolstering the epistemic community or a particular form of knowledge. Privately, the norms of the group can be reassessed and modified in light of new events or circumstances. Intellectual convergence can be promoted through involvement and interaction among think-tank sponsored research and conferences.

Drake and Nicolaidis' description of a dynamic between a two-tier trade in services epistemic community is illustrative. The first tier included people from governments, international agencies and corporations. The second tier amassed academics, lawyers, industry specialists and journalists whose concerns were 'more purely intellectual or a matter of professional entrepreneurship' (1992: 57). Despite the differing composition of the tiers the individuals of each shared a common conceptual framework. Where the first tier had greater access to senior decision-makers and was engaged in research brokerage, the second tier possessed organisational independence providing legitimacy for the first tier's perspective.

> The first-tier members of the growing epistemic community, who pushed for services negotiations, cultivated a two-way flow of ideas with the second-tier analysts to pursue symbiotically linked objectives. In the outward flow, they promoted their views in the published literature and on the conference circuit, so that the independent second tier would pick up, elaborate on, and legitimate these views as 'scientifically objective' and correct. In the inward flow, they brought the second tier's assessments directly to the meeting room as evidence of the growing consensus among experts who did not stand to gain materially from liberalization (1992: 55).

Most think-tank scholars could easily be placed in the second tier of experts. For example, the Trade Policy Research Centre was involved in 'consciousness raising' and issue identification regarding the trade in services. As a 'liberalization partisan' the Centre produced publications that linked services to trade issues and principles, thereby becoming a 'major intellectual force' in the debate, especially through its journal *The World Economy* (Drake and Nicolaidis, 1992: 41, 50). Analysis in favour of trade liberalisation was complemented and supported by other institutes, including the AEI, NBER, the Conference Board, RIIA and IIE as well as organisations such as Prométhée and CEDES (Centre des Études de l'Economie des Services), both in France, the Institute for Research on Public Policy and the Atwater Institute in Canada, the International Service Institute in Tempe, and the World Services Forum in addition to universities, bureaucracies and international agencies.

The liberalisation arguments and ideas produced by the TPRC and others in the 1970s and 1980s were used by the first-tier actors to convince governments that international service transactions had common trade properties. Indeed, the TPRC's promotional literature describes itself 'playing a pioneering role in getting the problems of trade in services on to the agenda of inter-governmental discussions, first in the OECD, then in the GATT forum – hitherto exclusively concerned with trade in goods' (1988: 16–17).[3] Before institutionalisation in policy occurred there was a mobilisation of independent organisations which set up new research programmes and conference series to broadcast the epistemic community's consensual knowledge.

Once an epistemic community has been adopted by government or its policy advice 'selected', the think-tank may no longer be required as a policy springboard, particularly if scholars acquire more influential positions in political parties, regulatory agencies, the courts or government. Correspondingly, if uncertainty is reduced by the information and analysis produced by the community, then power and bargaining dynamics among re-established interests are likely increasingly to dominate the policy domain and reduce the opportunity for intellectual innovation. As the issue erodes from formal and public agendas, the epistemic coherence of an institute may dissipate. Eventually it will lose its uniqueness and capacity to innovate. Drifting into a disciplinary orbit and focusing on an academic audience may result. Members of an epistemic community are not permanently lodged in policy institutes. People move on to new places and into different positions just as they may develop new interests. Although the community no longer coheres, the individuals, the journals and newsletters, the contacts and the organisations will often remain. A policy institute can still function and prosper on the basis of its reputation and role in a policy community or issue network.

The epistemic community concept may also account for the influence that some policy institutes occasionally enjoy. A community's views, models and principles can give an institute – or a particular research programme – coherence and dynamism. In other words, an epistemic community can put a think-tank at the cutting edge of policy research. As agents of policy innovation, members of epistemic communities would seek to establish a consensus among staff and direct the activities and research of a think-tank towards clear and specific policy goals. If they are successful an institute is likely to be less riven by factionalism or subject to an adaptive organisational style. In accordance with the community's causal vision, think-tank executives and scholars are in broad agreement on policy issues and act jointly to meet the organisation's objective to generate solutions to solve complex problems confronted by governments. This is more feasible in smaller, specialised institutes. The dominance of an epistemic community is less likely in the older organisations that are more academic in style and characterised by competing paradigms and policy frameworks vying for precedence, and where there is likely to be greater emphasis on non-partisanship in the interests of co-operation and organisational stability.

Epistemic Communities and Broader Policy Debates

A problem with epistemic community approaches is that the emergence and policy successes of these communities have not been related to broader policy crises (McDowell, 1994). The trade in services community, for example, needs to be placed in a context of poorly understood global restructuring, the declining credibility of Keynesian demand management and reforms to international trade policies, and electoral changes at the beginning of the 1980s in the US and UK that brought to power governments increasingly receptive to liberalising policies. The new trade in services régime was not an isolated policy development but related to the general trend of free market economists increasingly occupying positions of state authority. To focus on specialised communities in case-studies 'misses and ignores the large overall trends and processes; that different communities do share some elements in common; and that the prevalence of one knowledge community must be linked to these broader social forces' (McDowell, 1994: 32).

While epistemic communities are likely to be more coherent and cohesive on a specific issue, loosely aggregated communities can operate at a broader level, such as, for example, in the paradigm of neo-classical economic thinking (Biersteker, 1992). In such a way, epistemic communities appear less fragmentary or isolated from broader political and economic affairs. Libertarians, for example, have a shared policy preference for 'rolling back the state'. Their shared set of principles are derived from norms stressing the priority of freedom, choice and individual responsibility. Their causal beliefs are informed by classical liberal thought and free market precepts derived from the monetarist, supply side, public choice and Austrian schools of neo-classical economics. Their shared tenets of validity arise from the rational actor model and treating the individual as the primary unit of analysis. Their consensual knowledge (or problem definition) is that while state intervention may be motivated for the public good, it leads to perverse outcomes. The community is made up of economists, historians, political scientists, sociologists and philosophers who may be academics, consultants, bureaucrats, politicians, lawyers, interest group activists as well as think-tank scholars. Their technical expertise lies in their academic and professional qualifications, theoretical models, data bases and politico-bureaucratic knowledge. In think-tanks they have an identity in the Cato Institute in Washington DC and the IEA in London amongst others. Conditions of uncertainty emerged in the 1970s with economic insecurity and growing dissatisfaction with prevailing policy practices. It provided opportunities for intellectual entrepreneurs to promote the new liberal political economy and challenge Keynesian perspectives.

Reducing the role of the state in society and the economy is a project around which many think-tanks are organised, but is a broad and ill-defined project around which an epistemic community might coalesce. Yet epistemic communities crystallise around specific policy issues. For example, in the education field a community may form that advocates privatisation, educational choice and vouchers. At root are shared convictions informed by classical liberal economic thought. These principles establish complementarity with other specialist communities. Different communities share a causal vision but differ in their focus on different policy issues. In other words, they are bound together by a 'discursive affinity' or the same story-line; 'arguments may vary in origin but still have a similar way of conceptualizing the world' (Hajer, 1993: 47). Cato and the IEA are exemplary of a shared faith in free market economics. A number of environmental institutes exhibit a common holistic ecological framework. While differences of opinion persist among such institutes, the interlocking boards, exchange of staff, common conferences and joint publications are used to air differences and identify plausible solutions. Similarly, think-tanks provide an environment for an epistemic community in one policy arena to learn about the successes and tactics of other communities, with the same causal knowledge, that focus on different areas of public policy or that operate in other countries. By setting a precedent or establishing a principle, a new policy approach may 'spillover' from one policy arena to another (Kingdon, 1984: 201). Think-tanks are strategic organisations for combining these discourses into clusters.

To remedy the partial picture that epistemic (and policy) communities present, it is worthwhile to situate them in what Peter Hall calls a 'policy paradigm'. It is 'an overarching framework of ideas that structures policy making in a particular field' (1990: 59). A policy paradigm specifies the set of problems that are addressed and the kind of instruments or heuristics to be deployed in that policy sphere. Conceptually, a paradigm is similar to Jenkin and Eckert's notion of 'policy frameworks', which is 'a general perspective on the nature of some underlying social problem and its solution'. Changes in policy frameworks are rare and once instituted, 'tend to become self-perpetuating until a crisis occurs that spurs attempts to develop new solutions' (1989: 122). An old policy framework in the USA was identified with a network of policy institutes led by the CED, the National Planning Association, the Conference Board and Brookings. These organisations synthesised Keynesian thought to produce a 'commercial Keynesian' framework that guided macro-economic policy. The new conservative framework that emerged in the 1970s and 1980s clustered around a different set of institutes (AEI, Heritage, Hoover, IRET), business associations and intellectuals who developed austerity programs (Jenkins and Eckert, 1989: 125). What is of prime interest is how these paradigms or frameworks change or are overthrown.

It is necessary to recognise conditions of normal policy making and those of paradigm shift. 'Normal policy making' is characterised by 'incrementalism' and 'bounded rationality' whereas a paradigm shift is disruptive of old certainties. Paradigm shifts occur when anomalies or intractable problems threaten the authority and coherence of the existing paradigm, that is, 'uncertainty'. Conceptual challenges emerge in the form of redefined problems and new interpretative frameworks. The conflict results in a political process where 'the competition between paradigms is likely to be resolved only through a process that involves exogenous shifts in the power of key actors and a broader struggle among competing interests in the community' (Hall, 1990: 61). Keynesian economics in the post-Second World War era was the 'prism' through which political actors saw the economy as well as their own role in the economic sphere (Singer, 1990: 437–8). However, unanticipated developments such as stagflation could not be fully explained within the prevailing paradigm or curtailed with the usual policy devices. By the mid-1970s, the theoretical framework and its chief exponents were increasingly discredited by the seemingly intractable nature of problems. A new range of actors entered the policy fray as conflict over the appropriate course of action widened. In the absence of consensus and in a highly competitive context, expertise acquired a politicised character (Hall, 1990: 68).

The decay of the Keynesian framework lead to a multiplication of economic commentary, or what Hall refers to as an expansion in the 'marketplace in economic ideas' with contributions from the media, polling companies, popular publishers as well as more specialised groups such as consultancies and research institutes. In Gramscian terms, a 'war of position' was waged in order to determine what would be the dominant set of ideas about society and economy (Smith, 1993b: 92). In the confrontation between Keynesian and monetarist ideas in Britain, social scientists were divided regarding the validity or superiority of either of the paradigms. Consequently, the paradigms were judged in political rather than purely scientific terms. But it was the conversion of key figures within the Conservative Party to monetarism that propelled the shift to another paradigm and which was 'assisted by the efforts taken by the Center (sic) for Policy Studies, the Institute of Economic Affairs, and a number of individual monetarist economists' (Hall, 1990: 71; see also Smith 1987a: 70; Seldon, 1989; Gaffney, 1991; Wickham-Jones, 1992; Cockett, 1994). With increasing policy failures, greater interest is shown in alternative ideas and 'politicians will have particularly strong incentives to seek out and embrace ideas that challenge the policies of their opponents' (Hall, 1990: 73).

A final ambiguity in the epistemic community approach is that the main connection to power is access to state decision-makers. The state apparatus dominates. In common with policy community and issue network concepts, the relationship of experts with the state is one of direct contact through a 'narrow set of channels characterized by personal communication' (Hall, 1990: 56). The approach can be broadened by portraying epistemic communities seeking to penetrate institutions outside the state. How an epistemic community that is not patronised by decision-makers might penetrate aspects of civil society such as the media, the foundation world, labour movements or business is an important question. Epistemic communities need to mobilise various groups outside the state to build public support for the acceptance of their policy recommendations. For example, a nascent – if somewhat politically powerless – community is evolving in the US around the legalisation of marijuana and cocaine as an alternative path to stemming drug abuse and drug-related crime. One organisational centre is the Drug Policy Foundation. The policy recommendations emanating from the Foundation lack political legitimacy. Consequently, the organisation and other bodies and individuals associated with it (such as Cato) are forced to adopt different tactics. It has produced a highly successful television series.

The Foundation produces materials suitable for use in schools, and it is tightly linked with grass-roots organisations in the USA and has cultivated an international network of policy experts in this field. The Foundation follows an indirect avenue of influence, targeting popular thinking in addition to addressing the legislative and bureaucratic domains. If a community's policy perspective is not politically accepted it must diffuse its knowledge beyond the state. An epistemic community can penetrate public thinking by its members consistently writing newspaper articles or being available for television and radio commentary. Most think-tanks are highly efficient in generating publicity and have well-developed contacts with the media. Likewise, a number of institutes have strong ties with trade unions (such as IPPR or the Institute of Employment Rights in Britain), with interest groups and grass-roots movements (such as IPS or the Institute of Race Relations in Britain) and with business groups (for example, CED and the Conference Board). These are constituencies that can be educated and mobilised by new thinking with think-tanks providing a strategic organisational platform.

The degree to which an epistemic community's principles and causal beliefs are reflected in the ethos, publications and statements emerging from a think-tank will vary according to the concentration of members and their control over it. If a think-tank is characterised by a coherent paradigm of thought to the exclusion of other systems of thought, it is of greater use in the pursuit of specific policy aims by a community. In those think-tanks that are characterised by a diversity of thought, usually the old guard institutes like Brookings, NBER, PSI and NIESR, an epistemic community is unlikely to control the general direction of the institute. Members of communities may, nevertheless, be located in one of these institutes, or indeed be spread through a number of institutes.

NOTES

1. For an application of advocacy coalition ideas to think-tanks see Lindquist (1990).
2. Kingdon adds a third type of agenda, the decision agenda, which involves proposals considered for legislative enactment or subjects under review for imminent decision by Cabinet, Prime Ministers, Presidents or departmental secretaries.
3. The TPRC initiated studies on trade and services in the early 1970s perceiving that service industries would internationalise and become more important in developing countries' economies and thus increasingly marked by pressure for liberalisation in trade and investment. In this context, trade distorting effects of non-tariff barriers would attract intergovernmental attention. In 1971, the OECD

created a high level group – the Rey Group – to consider further liberalisation of world trade. The British member of the group, Sir Richard Powell, consulted the Centre which formed an advisory group to help him. Sir Richard carried many of the Centre's ideas into the Rey Group which were subsequently incorporated in its 1972 OECD report, *Policy Perspectives for International Trade and Economic Relations*. It was not until the 1980s, however, after considerably more research and debate, that trade in services was included in the Uruguay Round of GATT negotiations (TPRC,1988: 17).

7 Policy Relevance and Effectiveness

Many think-tanks are said to be influential but what is meant by influence is invariably imprecise. Conceptual devices such as policy or epistemic communities explain the routes of influence but cannot quantify the impact of think-tanks. It is the aim of the first section of this chapter to explore some further views of think-tank influence, effectiveness and relevance. Too often, discussions of think-tank influence have concentrated solely on political or policy impact to the neglect of other patterns of influence. The following section outlines the way in which policy research institutes establish an identity as independent and educational organisations committed to promoting the public interest. Establishing this identity is important in order to be effective, that is, to be regarded as a reputable and authoritative source of opinion as well as to retain their concessionary tax status as non-profit organisations.

Do Think-tanks Make a Difference?

There are systemic difficulties faced by think-tanks in their interaction with government that limit their potential for influence. As they operate as 'ginger groups' they can be politically and bureaucratically dysfunctional (Dror, 1980). By elaborating on policy options, increasing the number of alternatives and outlining possible problems, these policy research bodies potentially overload collective decision-making processes, disrupt established programmes, undermine consensus and question the legitimacy of a government's chosen policy. They provide the rhetorical weapons for opposition groups. Identifying flaws in policies or promoting superior policy design does not endear these organisations to politicians or bureaucrats. Two former Directors of the IFS, for example, described the think-tank role in the UK as an 'alternative civil service' that works by 'exposing cant' (John Kay and Dick Taverne, quoted in Thomas, 1984). By discrediting expenditures on programmes, they implicitly criticise the relevant agency. Consequently, 'think-tanks are not easy to integrate into policy making systems' (Dror, 1980: 147). They question the accepted and debunk the habitual in contradiction to the inbuilt conservatism of bureaucracies. Traditional machineries of government are likely to dismiss their contributions to policy. Admitting the salience of independent policy research tacitly recognises the flaws in the expertise and authority of bureaucracies. Finally, the desire to maintain their independence and distance from government may result in a self-imposed restraint on the impact that independent policy units can have on policy.

There are multiple sources of policy advice competing for the attention of Prime Ministers and Presidents. Departmental policy advice, advice from cabinet office, party-political advice, political advice from policy units, the recommendations of congressional or parliamentary committees and outside advice are all sources of potentially conflicting forms of advice. The favoured source of advice is subject to a variety of factors such as a leader's personal preferences to the avenues of access to that leader (Weller, 1987). Governments can also be characterised by 'closed advice circuits' or 'group think' where advisers and decision-makers share values and policy approaches effectively excluding alternatives from consideration (Machin, 1987). Decision-makers do not necessarily have time for think-tank research. As Alice Rivlin notes of Brookings scholars, 'None of us draft legislation, sit in committee markups, or even talk more than sporadically to those who do. Presidents do not call to ask What we should do in the Middle East? or How can we balance the budget? Cabinet officers or subcabinet officers also do not call – at least not very often' (1992: 24). Nor is it the case that decision-makers are even aware of think-tanks, least of all their current research programmes. Furthermore, the vast growth of think-tanks has not been replicated with superhuman abilities in decision-makers to read and process the information churned out by think-tanks and other groups. Even if leaders such as Margaret Thatcher were known to read think-tank pamphlets late at night (Hames and Feasey, 1993: 234), it is a quite different thing to say that think-tank policy recommendations thereby percolated into actual policy.

It cannot be denied that the impact of even the best known think-tanks on policy is modest. Policy making is mainly driven by interests, not by ideas. Yet executives are frequently required to produce evidence that they have direct impact on the policy and legislative processes. There is a lot of anecdotal information. Virtually everyone interviewed was able to provide an example of how their institute was directly involved in the initiation of policy or legislative change. To be more systematic, however, most think-tanks devote considerable resources to compiling indicators of influence. It involves keeping track of media citations and requests for commentary. For example, during 1990 IRET recorded over 100 citations by the print media, over 40 op-ed pieces in publications including *The Wall Street Journal*, *International Business*, and *The Washington Times*, over 20 citations by syndicated columnists as well as a few citations in op-eds written by Congressional leaders, and a minimum of 15,000 column inches (IRET, 1991). Think-tanks keep tabs on written and oral requests for information from politicians or their aides and from business and foundation officials, appearances of staff before Congress or parliamentary committees, appointment of staff to government positions, increased membership, increased and diversified funding, attendance at conferences, attraction of important speakers, and so forth. Directors or annual reports often point to the prestigious positions that staff occupy *once they leave* as evidence of the institute's value.

The IIE in Washington DC provides a good example of the search for indicators of influence. Although the Director, Fred Bergsten, recognises the difficulty in gauging impact – of 'proving' influence – in a memorandum to IIE Board Members, Bergsten lists specific incidents of IIE influence. Copies of newspaper articles and supportive letters from members of the US House of Representatives were attached to the memorandum as evidence of media attention and political interest. Also attached was an independent review of the Institute commissioned by the German Marshall Fund (a major IIE funder), stating that the IIE has been a 'spectacular success' in providing 'constructive debate over international economic policy at a time when this policy is of absolutely crucial importance to our future' (Goodwin, 1990: 8). The reviewer based his conclusions on numerous interviews with senior ranking people in bureaucracy, academe, the media, Congress, and other American research organisations.

Virtually half of the 52 page statement of the National Center for Policy Analysis (1990) in Texas outlines the influence of the Center. It claims a 'record breaking' ability to gain media attention. In 1989, NCPA received 60,000 column inches of print media coverage – an average of 18 articles per day in the USA. Not only does the NCPA seek to quantify its impact, it also attempts to measure its *level* of impact by the extent of media coverage in major markets, editorial endorsement by major newspapers and syndicated columnists, endorsements by leading political figures and key interest groups, and legislative change. With the success of its presidential transition document, *Mandate for Leadership*, Heritage President Edwin Feulner claims that 61 per cent of the recommendations in *Mandate* were adopted by the Reagan administration (Bonafede, 1982: 502; Victor, 1988). Similarly, the ASI in London has made the extravagant claim that more than one hundred of its ideas have made their way into public policy (ASI, 1990: 1). Unfortunately, such 'evidence' of direct influence gives an incomplete picture of think-tank achievements which unduly emphasises their successes.

Establishing the progenitors of policy ideas is not easy to discern. The forces that converge to influence policy making often shroud any causal nexus that may exist between think-tanks and policy. Nelson Polsby notes that policy entrepreneurs require allies to move their policy solutions from 'incubation to enactment'. Policy entrepreneurs in think-tanks 'yield up public credit' for their ideas to politicians who need the credit or authorship for policy innovation 'to survive in an election-dependent world' (1984: 171–72). As John Gaffney notes, 'Neither think-tanks nor government would enhance their image if the former claimed that they were the architects of a democratic government's policy or if the latter admitted accepting ready-to-use, off-the-peg policies' (1991: 11). To maintain legitimacy, political parties and leaders must claim authorship or responsibility for devising policy. Thus, the role of institutes is 'an understated one' (Gaffney, 1991: 14). Annual reports state that an institute has 'informed' rather than 'created' or 'initiated' policy. That is, they allow the transfer of credit to politicians.

Occasionally a think-tank report or study group will influence the actions of politicians and bureaucrats. But the more frequent state of affairs, when independent policy analysis is simply ignored, is not so readily recounted. Frequently, think-tanks do not live up to their promise to inform and influence public policy but simply 'revamp the work of academics into more accessible format' (Lindquist, 1989: 289). Despite some individual success stories there is little evidence of consistent and sustained contribution of think-tanks to governance (Langford and Brownsey, 1991: 10). Instead, there are many sceptics who dispute their influence. Some go so far as to suggest that 'not a single good idea has ever emerged from their ruminations' and they only bring 'grief and disaster to any politician foolish enough to listen to their wild warblings' (Wheen, 1994). There is also a considerable amount of back-biting and gossiping within the think-tank industry. In the course of interviews, think-tankers frequently disparaged the work of other institutes or their scholars. Allen Weinstein who heads the Center for Democracy in Washington has been described by others in the think-tank world as a shameless self-promoter and arrogant publicity seeker who rarely accomplishes anything (*Los Angeles Times*, 7 April 1992: E1–2). Those in the more academic institutes criticise think-tanks that are activist for being too political or for work not of a sufficiently high standard. In London, for example, a number of people considered ASI claims of over 100 of its recommendations being adopted to be 'ludicrous' or 'outrageous' and 'presumptuous'. By contrast, people in new partisan institutes often criticise places such as Brookings as being of limited policy relevance and too academic.

A reason for the different perceptions of think-tank effectiveness lies in varying conceptions of influence. A narrow interpretation posits that only direct impact – affecting the course of legislation or persuading decision-makers of a particular course of action – warrants the description of influence. Accordingly, the notion that think-tanks wield political influence is easily criticised. Most politicians and bureaucrats do not have the time or inclination to read book-length studies or even executive summaries (Seymour-Ure, 1987: 177; Chabal, 1992). Furthermore, bureaucrats act as gatekeepers sifting the information that lands on a minister's desk. They may also present it as their own material. On the other hand, they criticise institutes for their lack of appreciation of the complexities of policy initiation and drafting legislation. As think-tanks are usually small organisations without large constituencies, they can be disregarded in policy development. It means that institute analyses and policy recommendations can be completely irrelevant to policy elaboration.

While there are occurrences of think-tanks being consulted by governments, this is *ad hoc*. Furthermore, political influence may be the result of luck or a host of other factors at work. The window of opportunity for think-tanks may be greatest just before an election and early in the term of a new government when political executives are still establishing their priorities and think-tanks are busy producing transition documents.[1] While staff of policy institutes can be shown to have a strong desire to influence policy, and while some are in positions of authority and have scope for influence, it is not unequivocal evidence that influence is exerted. The counter factual argument can be employed to a limited degree. If think-tanks were of negligible relevance, they would not exist or they would close in greater numbers than they do. Yet policy research institutes are proliferating. The counter factual argument has some merit but does not help explain why and in what circumstances think-tanks are influential nor what constrains their potential for influence. Indeed, this growth might mean that think-tanks become a weaker rather than stronger political force, their potential for impact diluted by their proliferation as well as by the 'fragmentation of interest sectors' (Salisbury, 1990: 209–12).

Claims of direct influence on government thinking remain necessary to promote a policy institute as well as to secure further funding. However, self-inflated publicity and flaunting laudatory letters from presidents, senators or ministers conveys a distorted image of the think-tank. Parading their political connections fosters crude notions about how influence works. Collecting statistics on media coverage and correlating government policy initiatives with previous think-tank recommendations does not explain how think-tanks are effective organisations in policy. An outsider could be forgiven for thinking that publicity seeking, self-promotion and the competition for attention in the marketplace of ideas becomes an end in itself.

A broader interpretation of influence which suggests that think-tanks have the power to change the prevailing consensus or to preserve the existing climate of opinion is also not verifiable. Yet there is little doubt that they help provide the conceptual language, the ruling paradigms, the empirical examples that became the accepted assumptions for those in charge of making policy. The market-liberal institutes are widely believed to have pioneered economic rationalist agendas in the 1970s that have subsequently set the frame of discourse for key public servants and media commentators. How and whether this is achieved is not subject to measurement but must be theorised in terms of how public and policy agendas are set. If a group of policy institutes broadly concur with government agendas and the direction of policy, they individually and collectively reinforce non-decision-making by providing the intellectual ammunition to justify why agendas should be established in a particular fashion and why other matters are non-issues (Bachrach and Baratz, 1962). Yet, other think-tanks have the potential to undermine the non-decision-making impetus. For example, the Drug Policy Foundation questions the value of the US 'war on drugs' (Trebach, interview). The Employment Policy Institute in London works to restore the issue of full employment to the top of the political agenda. Environmental research institutes informed by a philosophy of ecological sustainability similarly question the ethos of unrestrained progress and development. Their independence from government and relative autonomy from other groups gives them the scope to pursue issues that may not be recognised in policy development.

Not all institutes pursue policy influence consistently over time or in all their activities. Business, foundations, governments and individuals may fund think-tanks, not necessarily in the hope that they will influence policy but because they are altruistic and think it is good for a democratic society to have people thinking about public issues and offering alternative perspectives. These factors need to be kept in mind for neither the motives of think-tanks nor those of their sponsors and clients are homogeneous. Accordingly, it is worthwhile to look at the terms in which staff and directors of institutes perceive organisational influence. Individuals within an organisation are often best placed to discern success. As Bill Daniel (interview) at PSI said, we have 'our own folklore'. David Willetts (interview) was 'confident' of the role of the CPS. Given the commitment to confidentiality at CPS, outsiders might be dubious of the Centre's impact but Willetts 'knew' that staff had 'participated in discussions' with the Thatcher government just as Roderick Nye (interview) claims that politicians come to the Social Market Foundation (SMF) for closed discussions. In other words, the problem of verification or providing proof of policy influence does not plague the minds of think-tank executives. Many are smugly satisfied with the degree of contact they have with decision-makers and the kinds of contributions they make to policy debates behind-the-scenes. As Vibert (interview) at IEA said, 'We get discreet feedback'.

Perceptions of effectiveness within an organisation and internally determined criteria of relevance are important. For example, Donna Wise (interview) at WRI, talked of influence and impact in terms of how the Institute operationalised its core principles of sustainable development. WRI provides technical assistance to developing countries and works with non-governmental organisations and aid agencies to translate its ideas into practice. In terms of agenda setting for the 1992 UN Conference on the Environment and Development in Brazil, Wise argued that it was sufficient to look at the deliberations in convening the Conference and the work of its Secretariat, to see that the words and concepts of WRI – which was involved in process from the outset – informed much of the structure of the Conference. The Overseas Development Institute (ODI) in London assesses its effectiveness in its ability to place economists in the public sectors of developing countries. Since 1963, over 350

Fellows have been placed in 23 countries. Many former ODI Fellows 'hold responsible positions in agencies and companies dealing with the Third World' (ODI, 1985: 4). Also in London, the CEPR tries to persuade researchers in the economics discipline to 'do things they wouldn't otherwise do' (Portes, interview). The CEPR tries to influence what academic economists consider important and change the incentive structures of the discipline so that it is more attractive to do policy work. CEPR provides some pay-offs for academics in the form of conference and other funding, or enhanced reputation through invitation to become a fellow of the CEPR (which is by invitation).

Throughout interviews, 'access' – the ability to telephone someone in a position of power – was often equated with influence. According to Michael Witt (interview) at EESI, 'if you can't get a committee person to return your call, then you know where you stand'. Many mentioned that the ability to attract senior actors in policy communities to meetings was a sign of an organisation's 'credibility'. Others spoke of effectiveness more vaguely as the ability to bring alternative perspectives to light, that is, 'broadening', 'shifting' or 'contributing to' the public debate (interviews, Krepon, Portes, Zwart). They stress the capacity of think-tanks to intervene in public debate, to publicise views and sustain critique of policy, in itself as a form of influence whether or not legislation or policy is changed.

Clear and unambiguous criteria of influence are absent. Think-tanks address many different audiences. Power is not evenly spread as think-tanks have different resources and are constrained or enabled by differing political cultures. Furthermore, influence can be wielded in many ways. Clearly, some institutes are better known or perceived to be more influential than others. Although many institutes have negligible input to policy and/or espouse politically unpopular views, their staff can still claim that they make a difference simply by being able to articulate and disseminate those views. Even where a policy paradigm is entrenched, considerable competition to mould agendas and attract political patronage between think-tanks with counter-hegemonic or alternative perspectives can exist.

Rather than looking for impact of a single think-tank, it is fruitful to assess the structural impact of the think-tank industry. That is, the extent to which the proliferation of think-tanks has changed the way policy is debated and decided. If it is accepted that many experts based in think-tanks have been integrated into public sector policy processes and the deliberations of political parties then, to some extent, think-tanks are contributing to both the broad political direction and specific policy arguments of decision-makers. As a consequence of the greater inclusion of policy analysis and advocacy, the dynamics of decision making are changed and the agenda setting process extended to groups outside government. Formal decision-makers – whether it be Parliament or Congress, Whitehall or the White House – are only one, albeit dominant, of the actors involved in agenda setting. In other words, agenda setting may have become more contested as many economic, social and scientific issues confronted by the state are too complex to be dealt with by bureaucratic generalists and require recourse to expertise for problem definition. The formal political scene of party competition and legislative development is only the 'visible tip of the iceberg' of a much longer, insulated and technocratic – some say élitist – process. That is, 'the agenda for policy consideration is increasingly shaped and approved by the deliberations of élites outside the government before political parties and formal policy-makers become actively involved in the process' (Fischer, 1993: 33). Accordingly, our attention is again directed towards the margins of government instead of persisting with conventional explanations of policy development that focus on the centre.

Part of the problem in addressing the impact of think-tanks is the ontological distinction between knowledge and power that reigns in social science. Prevalent in much of the policy network literature is an image of 'two cities' or 'two worlds' (Conway, 1990; Pal, 1990). Think-tank promotional material and writers on think-tanks frequently reveal a common image of distinct and autonomous communities – that is, of researchers, social scientists and experts in the scientific and scholarly realm (or 'ivory tower') providing information, analysis and advice to a separate and politicised domain inhabited by politicians, administrators and civil servants. The two spheres are juxtaposed. Wedged in between are think-tanks which act as a 'bridge', a 'conduit' (Seldon, 1989: 83) or 'transmission belt' (Saloma, 1984: 21).[2] These passive metaphors create an artificial divide, yet activity of communication and interpretation undertaken by think-tanks and others draws attention to the organic relationship between knowledge and governance.

Approaching knowledge and policy as symbiotic and interdependent it is possible to come to a broader conception of the power of think-tanks (Gagnon, 1990). The modern state depends on the creation and widespread acceptance of persuasive accounts of 'human nature' as the basis of legitimate and just laws, and on groups of experts whose views on such issues are considered authoritative.

Think-tank scholars are one such category of experts and, in conjunction with foundations, trade unions and business associations, are engaged in the production of knowledge and connected to hegemonic power centres. At the same time, Foucauldian accounts of power and knowledge reject any concept of conspiracy, centralised direction or global strategy of interventions.

> Those that are supported by business or capital in some broad sense are nevertheless 'relatively autonomous' from their benefactors, and rarely if ever join in some giant conspiracy of knowledge to support a given agenda. There is no 'capitalist line', even though these organizations are supported by capitalists (Pal, 1990: 151).

Power is discontinuous and without telos. It does not emanate from a single sovereign source. If knowledge and power are conceived as continuous there can be no knowledge without power. One implies the other. As a consequence, policy institutes cannot be truly independent. They are part of a grid-like network of power in which our sense of reality is shaped, managed and modulated by knowledge. Furthermore, they have ideological commitments and require funding and organisational support which place limits on what is acceptable or legitimate policy analysis. Their policy research is used by them or others to become partisans of particular policy positions. Far from lacking influence, think-tanks are a manifestation of the knowledge/power dynamic and can be argued to be pervasive in their impact in helping to define our social practices and political struggles.

Where there is power there is also resistance. Resistance is plural in form and in intent – it is not single or unified. Instead, power and knowledge are dispersed and take form in regionalised or localised institutions. In 'sites of domination' social scientists can provide 'unique information resources' and help form 'alternative definitions of reality' (Conway, 1990: 172). Power is exerted in different sites and not only by the state. Think-tanks need not be conceived as acting in the monolithic or hegemonic fashion posed by some Marxist theorists. While institutes such as Heritage and Cato or IEA and CPS were broadly, if not completely, synchronised with the ideological foundations of the Reagan/Bush administrations and Thatcher/Major governments respectively, they were not simply mouthpieces for these regimes. They were frequently critical and stringent sources of opposition. The Cato Institute, for example, was implacably opposed to US involvement in the Gulf War (*Washington Times*, 4 January 1990). Nor does it entail that institutes which espouse unorthodox positions, such as the IPS or the Drug Policy Foundation, are ineffectual or hopelessly marginalised. Instead, these institutes operate 'where dominated people form identities through common language and understanding and mobilize resources in resistance' (Conway, 1990: 172). The concept of discontinuous power allows some degree of power for think-tanks perceived as marginal, insignificant or weak players in other perspectives. Policy institutes can represent a source of resistance for marginalised groups. Thus, for example, institutes such as the Center for Women Policy Studies (CWPS) and The Women's Research and Education Institute (WREI) in the USA provide intellectual support for feminist redefinition's of the role of women in society and the economy while the Institute of Employment Rights in London provides technical and intellectual support within the British labour movement. They provide a counter-discourse. Although the direction of policy research is heavily determined by the state agenda – as can be witnessed with the proliferation of market-liberal and conservative institutes since Reagan and Thatcher – alternative pictures of the world with competing ideological principles and policy positions are being produced, in an effort to empower and legitimise other actors that challenge received wisdom on the role of the state and the allocation of public resources.

Charity and Other Good Works

Despite the interdependence of knowledge and power, institutes stridently claim to be independent educational and research bodies. They create a discursive distance between the knowledge related objectives of institutes and the politicised domain of decision-makers. Established as NPOs or charities they stress their pursuit of the public interest by contributing to informed debate. Many also claim special authority to enlighten policy-makers on the basis of their commitment to dispassionate and scholarly research untainted by connection to vested interest or political power. Policy research and analysis is presented in a passive and apolitical form which only gains force as an instrument in the hands of others. There is tension, however, between the rhetoric of independence, public service and impartial research and the commitment of many institutes to inform policy with a particular set of values and principles.

Within the mission statement of most policy institutes, regardless of whether they are American or British, there is reference to an educational aim of improving public awareness and human understanding. The IEA, for example, was established to 'promote and advance learning by research into economic and political science and by educating the public in these subjects' (IEA, 1989: 1). Membership organisations in particular emphasise contributing to a more informed public. In most institutes research is undertaken in an open and publicly accessible manner. Usually, it is compiled in an understandable format. Individuals or other interested groups are usually welcome to peruse the journals of these organisations and, subject to a fee, attend their seminars and conferences. Frequently, the published product is available in bookshops as well as in university and municipal libraries. In sum, they appear to be porous to the public.

Yet, these institutes are élite focused. There are complex processes of exclusion at work through the academic and technical character of institutes. The majority of think-tanks reject the masses. These organisations cater primarily to the economically and politically literate. Although they claim to promote the understanding of their publics, very few ordinary people are aware of them. Furthermore, the commitment to public education is uneven across this industry. In the USA, the ICS publishes popular books and the CNP makes extensive use of public opinion polling. Some executive directors sustain the public image of their organisations through newspaper columns and regular public lectures. Many institutes such as the Drug Policy Foundation provide school materials. Brookings' Center for Public Education 'helps contribute to an informed citizenry and enlightened decisionmaking' (Brookings Institution, 1991: 16), but also brings in substantial revenue from conferences and seminars. Others are more closed, notably RAND which undertakes classified research and EESI which acts as an information and analysis service primarily for Congress.

Independence and impartiality is vigorously proclaimed. RFF, for example, argues that a 'commitment to objective, scholarly research and a scrupulously maintained distance from ideological bias or political pressure have made RFF a source of accurate and untainted information on topics of keen interest to policy makers and general public' (RFF, 1991: 4). Independence in research is a source of 'credibility'. Organisations heavily reliant on government contracts are often perceived by others in the think-tank industry to be compromised by the source of their funding or their closeness to a particular agency or department, for it does not allow 'the think-tank the latitude either to create its own research agenda or freely explore the items on that agenda' (Langford and Brownsey, 1991: 5). Clearly, organisations such as PPI, CNP and EPI have links with the Democrats just as the IPPR and the Fabians have with the Labour Party in Britain. Nevertheless, these organisations do not mirror party platforms although they share similar philosophical positions. Marshall (interview) stressed that the PPI is 'not an organ of the party' but 'strived to speak with a dispassionate voice'. Even so, the political climate can be very restrictive. During the Thatcher period of government certain areas of policy analysis were 'closed off' at CPS, in the opinion of David Willetts, because of the strong views of Thatcher and senior ministers such as Cecil Parkinson and Nigel Lawson. Or as the Director of IEA, Graham Mather, stated,'... if you have someone [Thatcher] who is around for a long time and has known views on particular issues, there are files which have been looked at and marked "closed"' (quoted in Timmins, 1990a).

Independence provides legitimacy. By maintaining their distance policy institutes supposedly have greater ability to 'think about the unthinkable' as they are not aligned with political parties, the corporate sector and public interest groups. The aura of institutional independence is further secured through the diversification of income (membership fees, government grants, gifts, corporate sponsorship, consultancy, foundations). The effectiveness of epistemic communities also depends on 'their relative autonomy from political power, their ability to keep separate from current critical pressures, to retain their scientific integrity and authority, and to continue to innovate' (Adler, 1992: 112). Think-tanks are sufficiently independent and research oriented to assist in the preservation of this integrity.

A theme interwoven with the attribute of independence are appeals to scientific authority, neutrality and rationality. Institutes extol their scientific methodologies, the educational and professional credentials of staff and their adherence to peer review. The scientific reputations of many think-tanks and commitment to 'open inquiry' are grounds from which they claim they are better equipped than other groups to inform policy. The NBER, for example, seeks to 'develop objective economic information' (NBER, n.d.: 3; see also Fabricant, n.d.). Alice Rivlin describes the Brookings Institution's researchers as 'middle-of-the-road pragmatists, technocrats rather than ideologues, and debunkers of zealots who offer simplistic solutions' (1992: 25). While a belief in the progressive force of knowledge and of social science expertise as objective once prevailed, since the 1960s the scientific status of social science and the value neutrality of research organisations and the techniques they employ has been challenged (Conway, 1990). Regardless of the challenge to their quasi-scientific and technical status, claims of objectivity and neutrality continue to be used by institutes to declare the scientific superiority of their research (Alpert and Markusen, 1980).[3] Think-tank discourse is often one of rationality – or purported rationality.

Even so, a number of policy institutes deal explicitly with values and the ideas that are articulated are to the benefit of certain interests. The Heritage Foundation, for example, styles itself as the voice of 'responsible conservatism'. As stated by a former vice-president of Heritage, 'our role is to provide conservative policy makers with arguments to bolster our side' (quoted in Moore and Carpenter, 1987: 146). Policy analysis is inherently political and value-ridden, and some institutes do not attempt to disguise it. Objectivity, as a standard, is elusive. Although direct intellectual support for political parties or legislation is eschewed by think-tanks, it is frequently obvious that a well-defined political agenda is concealed in the principles and language of economics among most free market research institutes. For many institutes to be educational and apolitical is anathema. Accordingly, many of them tread a fine line between 'charitable' and 'political' activity. The AEI, for example, nearly lost its tax-exempt status when William Baroody Snr, AEI's first president, advised and wrote speeches for Barry Goldwater (Ford, 1992). A House Select Committee investigated whether AEI staff involvement in the Goldwater campaign for the Presidency violated the Institute's tax-exempt status. The review took two years but eventually exonerated the AEI. Henceforth, the AEI was scrupulous in avoiding overt political activity, yet the impact of the controversy saw Baroody push the Institute down a more academic route (Smith, 1991a: 177).

Despite strong scepticism about their value neutrality, many consumers of think-tank work are seeking research work that *appears* 'objective', 'independent' and 'authoritative'. For a government agency, commissioning think-tanks can have symbolic value demonstrating that alternative points of view are being canvassed. As noted in earlier chapters, think-tanks are used by the media as a source of independent opinion and punditry. Institute scholars are often capable of providing an acute observation or a pithy quote (Boal, 1985; Waldman, 1986). Statements from think-tank scholars provide credibility, depth and analysis to reporting and the appearance that journalists have sought independent and unbiased views. Think-tanks are a low cost source of expert information geared towards providing instant analysis on contemporary issues in an accessible, jargon-free style. It would be too expensive and time consuming for journalists to undertake their own analysis and research. The comparative advantage that think-tanks scholars possess is that they draw together bits of knowledge and structure it in an accessible yet meaningful way in the public domain.

In interviews many mentioned that one intangible benefit of think-tanks is the enhancement of democracy. Think-tanks support the foundations of a free society by providing competition in ideas. It is a pluralist argument that diverse, non-governmental voices remind decision-makers of their blind spots, highlight new ideas and present possible policy alternatives. It is also an argument used by many non-profit sector advocates that NPOs provide services needed by the public that are not produced by either the state or the market (Ware, 1989). Policy research institutes provide a distinctive service in raising the standard of debate (Harries; Mone; Moritz, interviews) or broadening the agenda (Andreas and Cavanagh, interview). For example, the Joint Center presents a 'black perspective' to policy-makers who may not have minority 'experience' (Farrar, interview). Think-tanks consequently become the self-appointed protectors of the principles and philosophies underlying democratic societies.[4] They claim to stimulate dialogue, as is required of them by their tax exempt status, but in reality many of them are 'out to impose their own monologue' and do not publish reports that are inconsistent with their philosophy (Linden, 1987: 103). As NPOs they potentially act as a counter to the power of government (Ware, 1989). Thus policy institutes serve the public interest by 'functioning as watchdogs over government' (Gray, 1978: 181). They review government activities, scrutinise policies and practices, thereby working to hold government accountable. This function is made more effective by attracting ex-government administrators who can draw upon their previous experience and knowledge to evaluate government. Think-tanks are supposedly best placed to perform this activity as they are independent of government. The Independence Institute portrays one of its roles as a 'fiscal watchdog' not only on government cost-effectiveness but also on public employee unions (Andrews, 1989: 63). The Centre for Defense Information (CDI) monitors government defence spending and issues reports on 'excessive expenditures' in an effort to re-establish civilian control of the military.

Attributed as public spirited and with a steadfast commitment to independence, objectivity and scholarly enterprise bestows great importance on think-tanks in a dynamic that also boosts the reputations of the individuals associated with it. 'These groups legitimate their members as "serious" and "expert" persons capable of government service and selfless pursuit of the national interest' (Domhoff, 1983: 92). Think-tanks are supposedly above politics and profit but ideas are harnessed to political and economic interests under the cover of charitable status. The production of social respectability is reinforced by the media in its quest for objective facts, scientific opinion and authoritative knowledge. Such authority and legitimacy is a necessary component in effectively diffusing ideas and forcing them onto public agendas. Think-tanks, their funders and the media have successfully cultivated a very positive image for the policy research institute.

Educational and research programmes are a strong component in many institutes. Furthermore, most institutes are legally independent organisations. These attributes reinforce the facade of non-politicised research. Nevertheless, independence and an educational orientation are necessary to attain the benefits of charitable tax status. To be considered legitimate, think-tanks need to be perceived as rigorous and scholarly. Their credibility is grounded in the 'two worlds' metaphor. While many policy institutes are clearly ideological, they maintain the distinction between knowledge and power to the extent that their publications disavow any attempt to influence the course of legislation. They merely provide the intellectual arguments and ideas that are used by others. Regardless of this rhetoric, articulating ideas inevitably favours some interests. There is no clear distinction. Instead, as Murray Edelman suggests, 'Ideological argument through a dramaturgy of objective description may be the most common gambit in political language usage' (1985: 16). Despite the inter-connectedness of power and knowledge, it is in the interests of think-tanks in general to maintain the myth of the distinction between knowledge and scholarship on the one hand, and politics, policy and interests on the other. If policy research institutes are 'above' politics, they are not a threat to democracy. Portrayed passively as a bridge or a transmission belt from the scholarly domain, the metaphor of two worlds gives them a safe distance from politics and protects their credibility and charitable status.

When think-tanks claim political influence they tread a fine line between legitimacy and effectiveness. Policy institutes face a dilemma. There are pressures to overstate their role and well as contradictory tensions to play down their role in policy elaboration. The strategy of the new partisans is to market ideas more strenuously. There is little pretence to ideological neutrality. Yet the certainty of influence is no greater. There is no guarantee that decision-makers will take heed. In seeking a competitive edge through their ideological advocacy and adversarial style, they endanger the scientific status and intellectual authority of institutes as a whole. When there were few policy institutes with reputations for objectivity, their analysis and advice held some sway. Today, with greater competition and varying standards of research, policy-makers appear more aware of politicisation (Weaver, 1989: 577). This does not mean that policy-makers and other decision-making élites turn away from them. Instead, they promote their proliferation as think-tanks provide for them the normative arguments, empirical evidence and techno-rational policy language that has become the currency of policy debates. The knowledge and expertise housed in think-tanks has become essential for political leaders, interest groups and business leaders to advance their cause. In other words, most think-tanks are part of discourse coalitions and policy communities where they act in tandem with interests by providing the political symbols, intellectual justifications and decision-making approaches to legitimate policy stances such as, for example, the conservative agenda of small government and free markets (Fischer, 1993: 34–6). An important component is the policy entrepreneurship of think-tank experts and the effectiveness with which think-tanks 'broker' or communicate policy solutions.

NOTES

1. For the Clinton administration, the PPI's *Mandate for Change* is perceived as a major source of ideas for the new President (*Washington Post*, 7 December 1992: A17). In Britain, the report of the Commission on Social Justice, undertaken by the IPPR for the Labour Party, has performed a similar function.
2. For examples of the use of this metaphor see the CEI, CSIS, Center for Democracy, East-West Forum, IAV, Twentieth Century Fund and ODC in Appendix 1.
3. For example, see the organisational statements of the Arab Research Centre, PSI, RIIA, Brookings, NPA and others in Appendix 1.
4. See, in particular, the statements of the Independence Institute, the James Madison Institute and the Reason Foundation in Appendix 1.

8   Policy Entrepreneurs, Research Brokerage and Networking

Research brokerage and networking are the primary means by which think-tanks make ideas matter. The independent, scholarly status of policy research institutes and their skills in networking, advocacy and brokerage also assist in the policy enterprises of epistemic communities. Think-tanks reinforce and amplify their claims of authority and expertise. The following discussion also illustrates how policy research institutes can be vehicles for the diffusion of a community's consensual knowledge. The scholars and executives of think-tanks act as policy entrepreneurs. Drawing on Kingdon (1984), think-tanks serve three functions: i) they promote ideas by pushing them higher on the public agenda; ii) they 'soften up' the system so that when a policy window opens, an epistemic community's ideas meet a receptive audience; and iii) they make the critical coupling of problem, policy and politics when a window of opportunity opens (Levine, 1985: 257).

Research Brokerage

Research brokerage is a process of conveying social scientific knowledge from universities and research organisations to the world of politics and decision making. In this process think-tanks are often conceived as a bridge between academia and decision-makers. They 'occupy a space in the intellectual life of a society between universities, with their preoccupation on teaching and research, and the Civil Service with its preoccupation with day to day management of public policy' (Vibert, 1992: 2). They are run by 'research brokers' – people of initiative who build institutions where intellectuals can work on policy issues – and who could also be called 'discourse managers' (Gagnon, 1990: 5).

The product of the pure researcher is generally not in a form that can be used by the policy-maker, thus successful brokerage requires the intermediary (Sundquist, 1978: 128–29). Academic intermediaries have a flair for interpreting and communicating the technical or theoretical work of their colleagues. They are engaged in the marketing of their discipline and synthesising and popularising its findings. They get social science research into the public domain by seeking appointment to commissions or delegations, and by testifying before Congressional or Parliamentary committees. They write for newspapers or journals such as the *Economist* or *New Republic* and produce short non-technical books. In charge of research institutes, brokers prepare and present social science for the use of policy-makers. As one think-tank director said, 'we take out the footnotes and make it accessible' (Butler, interview). Often noted thinkers in their own right, such people have critical skills in recognising and recruiting talent. They also tend to be strong personalities, an attribute which can often be put to effective use in fund-raising and public relations. David Abshire at the Centre for Strategic and International Studies (CSIS), and Fred Bergsten of the Institute for International Economics (IIE) in the USA and Richard Portes at the Centre for Economic Policy Research (CEPR) and Madsen Pirie at the ASI in the UK are contemporary examples of the breed.

Information provision is a central brokerage activity of policy institutes. Policy analysis that involves assessing alternative courses of action and making recommendations is usually assumed to be the strength of think-tanks. Yet, a small number of think-tanks are heavily involved in data creation. They create and collect information from polling, surveys and census as well as compiling figures on economic activity or legislative, administrative and business activity. The simulation models of both the Urban Institute and NIESR are highly reputed. Similarly, some institutes are involved in basic research over extended periods of time. The majority of institutes combine research with analysis, collaborating with researchers in universities, laboratories and government agencies. The RFF's 'two dimensional' research programme is illustrative.

> Its basic research develops new knowledge through long-term systematic, and balanced investigation of natural resource areas and of large environmental systems. Then, to help define and enrich the national policy agenda, RFF assembles interdisciplinary teams to build upon, integrate, and frequently extend the knowledge developed through its basic research (RFF, 1991: 4).

Brokerage also involves the dissemination of information. Not all institutes are equally placed to market their ideas, scholars and publications. Very few institutes have their own publishing house. Most rely on their media contacts to disperse ideas. The Center for Security Policy (1990) relies on its automated fax system for the expeditious dissemination of information and analysis. Briefing papers, reports and analyses are often distributed free. Seminars, lectures, lunch meetings and conferences are other means of dispersion. According to one think-tank director (Indyk, interview), 'part of the secret' in attracting a high turn out to functions is to provide incentive, that is, food. Policy-makers do not have much time and if a meeting is scheduled at lunch-time they are presented with fewer time constraints if food is provided. For the AEI, 'food is essential' to the conduct of their activities (Ford, 1992: 35).

With the backing of a research institute the works of individual scholars have received greater publicity and attention than they might have achieved through normal publishing channels or academic networks. The way the Manhattan Institute markets its books, such as Charles Murray's *Losing Ground,* is a good example. Since 1984 over 60,000 copies have sold (Manhattan Institute, 1989: 1). *Losing Ground* was 'skilfully handled' by Manhattan's President William Hammett – a competent policy entrepreneur – who 'knew how to generate talk and controversy to keep it in the public eye for many months longer than a publishing house typically commits itself to a book' (Smith, 1991a: 192). The book sparked a national debate in America on welfare reform comparable with that prompted by Michael Harrington's *Other America*, written under the auspices of the now defunct Center for the Study of Democratic Institutions. Harrington's book has been credited as having convinced Kennedy to begin the 'war on poverty'. Harrington is reported as saying that 'There would have been no book without the intellectual atmosphere and advice of the Center' (quoted in Dickson, 1971: 266). Many of the larger institutes have an office for public affairs composed of staff who know how to publicise a book, the author and the institute. Not only involved in the editorial and publishing process, the think-tank also handles the launch and promotion of both the study and the scholar.

Brokerage also occurs through the training and development of staff. Staff are recruited from universities, political parties, law firms, interest groups and government. Staff experience and professional interaction is an important facet of communication. For example, the common feature of staff at EESI is that they have 'work experience on the Hill' (Witt, interview). They have an awareness of and familiarity with how Congress works and, therefore, how most effectively to conduct EESI business there. To aid this process, offices are often physically close to decision-makers. That is, 'on the Hill' in Washington DC. In London, the RIIA is in walking distance from the Foreign and Commonwealth Office, while institutes such as NIESR, ASI, SMF, EPF, CPS and others are in the 'division bell area' of Westminster. Physical proximity aids the chances of 'rubbing shoulders' with bureaucrats and politicians who attend a seminar.

Although engaged by policy issues, think tankers frequently 'dislike the restrictions of partisan attachments and prefer to remain free-floating intellectuals', but 'what they remain bound to is a particular view of the world, a particular way of analysing its problems, and a preference for a particular kind of solution' (Gamble, 1989a: 6). This common desire to propagate their doctrine as widely as possible is another feature that aids epistemic communities. Robert Royal (interview) described the Ethics and Public Policy Center as a receptive environment for conservatives where they 'need not worry about "political correctness" or feuds with colleagues'. In return, think-tanks represent a means of career advancement and avenues to the media, the foundation world and academia. An organisation such as the AEI 'opens doors' (Parker, interview). Policy institutes are places where networks of politicians, bureaucrats, researchers, business people and others meet to communicate. They provide an environment where younger scholars or activists can be introduced to corporate officials, bureaucrats and politicians and, in general, aid the socialisation of a 'successor generation'. Research brokers muster these sources of social and intellectual capital to create 'egocentric information and helping ties' which assist in reducing the social differences between the educational credentials, occupational status and income achievement of participants (Knoke, 1990: 103). Policy institutes are also a means for 'screening' and determining which scholars or trustees are best suited for leadership and government service either as staff aides or as high-level appointees in their own right (Useem, 1984: 100–1).

In the USA the route between government-bureaucracy-academia with think-tank as a conduit is well worn. For example, journalists have frequently depicted Brookings as a Democratic 'government in exile', while the AEI fills the same function for the Republicans as a 'half way house for much of the Ford Administration, including the former president himself' (Yoffe, 1980: 33). In the past, the 'revolving door' phenomenon was an *ad hoc* process. Since Heritage initiated its Resource Bank, the identification of open government positions and promotion of institute staff has become more systematic. The pattern of interchange is less clear in parliamentary systems. With the more truncated career opportunities offered by comparatively fewer and smaller organisations, individuals are not as likely to spend extended periods of full-time employment in an institute. Movement in and out of government is also curtailed to a significant degree by the relatively closed nature of the permanent civil service. There are some exceptions. David Willetts worked as an official in the Treasury and in Thatcher's Policy Unit before becoming Director of Studies at the CPS. In 1992 he was elected to the House of Commons. Graham Mather, who was Director of IEA before establishing the EPF, became a Conservative member of the European Parliament in 1994. Although only a few can use a think-tank as a springboard into political life, other politicians, bureaucrats, lobbyists and political party officials cluster around institutes in other ways – participating in conferences or becoming board members and sponsors. Secondment to policy institutes and invitations to present seminar papers are well-developed avenues of exchange. Governments and political parties sometimes encourage the brokerage activities of particular policy research organisations. For example, the CPS provides a publishing outlet for Conservative Party politicians. The demarcation of CPS outside the political sphere allows 'kites to be flown' without committing the Conservative government to a policy position (Willetts, interview). If a new policy position eventuates, the CPS has played an important intermediary role in softening and moulding political opinion through its publicity and educational activities.

Another form of brokerage occurs when policy institutes act as a forum for discussion and interaction through conferences, workshops, seminars, breakfast and luncheon meetings, television debates, working groups and annual dinners – functions that may be 'invite only' or 'members only', closed to the media or open to the interested public. Both social functions and the more intensive working environment of seminars and meetings serve an intangible purpose of promoting interaction among people from diverse backgrounds who would not ordinarily meet but who have common interests. Importantly, think-tanks provide neutral territory where people feel more comfortable and have an opportunity to mingle. Academics can meet practitioners, business people can discuss regulatory policy with bureaucrats, and activists can confront politicians.

Meetings also bolster solidarity and help forge a common purpose. The Heritage Foundation, for example, sponsored a series of meetings for young conservatives known as the Third Generation Project. The Project was used to cultivate young leaders among an 'army of conservative activists, political strategists, administrators, and intellectuals' in order for the conservative movement to remain 'vibrant and fresh' (Hart, 1987: 12). The meetings which quickly attracted large audiences provided a forum for discussion among the diverse strands of the conservative movement, that is, among libertarians, classical liberals, religiously motivated conservatives as well as neo-conservatives. The 'mission' of the Third Generation was to build lines of communication within the broad conservative movement in order to develop a set of signals to enable concerted action to attain common objectives. The ASI has embarked on a smaller scale endeavour with its 'Next Generation' receptions which combine 'pink champagne, canapés and talkative future leaders'.

Think-Tank Networks

Most institutes act in coalition with other like-minded organisations. Libertarian and conservative think-tanks have particularly well-developed avenues of co-ordination. They are illustrative of the range of contacts and networks think-tanks develop, but they are also exceptional in the degree of formal or institutionalised networks that they have built. The links, networks and affiliations that think-tanks develop not only among other research organisations but also with the media, bureaucracy and government, foundations and universities, are important and effective means for epistemic and/or policy communities to diffuse their message.

An information sharing alliance of state based conservative and libertarian think-tanks, the Madison Group, was founded by the American Legislative Exchange Council (ALEC), Heritage and the Free Congress Foundation in the late 1980s. There is concern among some groups that it is siphoning off funding from 'the infrastructure for a progressive agenda' (NCRP, 1991a: 5). The impetus for the Group was the belief that 'there can be no victory at the national level without strength at the precinct level' (Andrews, 1989: 65). The intention was to establish an institute in each state. During 1991–92, when the Madison Group numbered approximately thirty institutes, links were formalised with the creation of a new organisation, StateNet. StateNet is an ambitious programme to facilitate joint research projects as well as raise funds, provide technical support and develop computer-facilitated communication (see Appendix). There is considerable co-operation. On a number of issues, analysis conducted in one state can be translated to other states. For example, a study sponsored by the James Madison Institute on a Florida state personal income tax also appeared – with the necessary modifications – as a Yankee Institute publication and as a Texas Public Policy Institute report (Cooper, interview). By establishing a principle or policy approach in one state the StateNet institutes hope to promote 'spillover' to other states.

StateNet focuses on US state politics whereas the Atlas Foundation is a forum for international exchange. It was established in 1981 by the founder of the IEA, Antony Fisher, who assisted the development of other policy institutes such as the Fraser Institute in Canada, the Manhattan Institute and the Pacific Research Institute. He formalised this consultative process through the Atlas Foundation. He believed public policy institutes were the means to 'teach opinion leaders of the world' about classical liberalism.

> Each institute in the Atlas world wide network shares the belief that the world's social, economic and political problems can be ameliorated by relying on some fundamental concepts of the free society: the rule of law, the institution of private property, contracts, the advocacy of the ideal of voluntarism in all human relations, and the support of the unhampered market mechanism in economic affairs (Atlas, 1991).

Atlas does not control institutes in its network but provides assistance to people interested in establishing an institute or those seeking assistance for a specific project. Atlas also conducts yearly international workshops to provide technical information on how to run an institute (Kwong, 1991).

To some degree, both Atlas and StateNet are more sophisticated versions of the Mont Pelerin Society (MPS). A private organisation of individuals founded by F. A. Hayek in 1947, it was not intended to become more than a private debating society to bolster solidarity among the 'embattled advocates of liberalism' (Seldon, 1989: 88). It brought together 'intellectuals and politicians united by a common aversion to the whole state oriented direction of post-war policy' and, as Milton Friedman said, 'it showed us we were not alone' (Gunn, 1989: 21). However, the MPS was too nebulous and exclusive to become a think-tank. It was more scholarly and intellectual than policy focused (see Cockett, 1994, for a full discussion). In the course of interviews, a number of people felt that the Society was 'a generational thing' (Vibert, interview) that provided 'a haven for free marketeers' (Anderson, interview) but which 'had run its course' (Hyde, interview).

A number of think-tanks have their origin in an older think-tank. Such a relationship can strengthen the capabilities of a think-tank as well as enhance the likelihood of its survival. The Arms Control Association, for example, had its genesis in the Carnegie Endowment. IPS staff fostered many institutes including the TransNational Institute in Amsterdam. IPS has always acted in tandem with other organisations. Staff consider they are more effective when operating in conjunction with broader constituencies (Andreas and Cavanagh, interview).

Heritage is also surrounded by a network of organisations. For example, the President of Heritage, Edwin Feulner, first conceived the need for the National Center for Public Policy Research. He drew the necessary people together and was the major impetus in the Center's establishment (Moritz, interview). Burton Yale Pines, Senior Vice-President of Heritage, became Chairman of the Center. Aside from sharing the same philosophy and set of policy enterprises, there is no formal relationship between the two organisations. Similarly, the Free Congress Foundation, although independent of Heritage, shares common conservative concerns. Its founder, Paul Weyrich, was also a founder of Heritage. A number of former Heritage scholars find their way into other organisations such as IRET, CEI, CRC and Cato, as well as numerous bodies operating at the state level. These organisations do not mimic Heritage. They are usually much smaller and more specialised. Cato and Free Congress, for example are not at all alike. The former is libertarian and concentrates on economic affairs whereas the latter is socially conservative. Furthermore, Heritage is focused on the Washington political scene whereas the NCPPR mobilises grass-roots organisations beyond the Capitol. A division of labour has evolved. This is not to suggest that a formal distribution of tasks occurs, merely that Heritage is at the centre of a network around which many different kinds of think-tanks revolve. It is manifest in the regularity with which the same names appear on think-tank rosters as board members, staff, academic advisers or adjunct fellows. This is not limited to conservative organisations. Among some of the American environmental institutes, for example, James Gustav Speth of WRI is on the Board of Trustees of the Keystone Center, the Board of Directors of the Environmental Law Institute and is the Chair of the Board of Directors of EESI. Robert Fri, President of RFF, and Donna Wise of WRI are also on the Board of Directors of EESI. William Futrell, President of ELI, is on the Board of Trustees of the Keystone Center.

Yet another form of networking at a regional level clustered around the Heartland Institutes. The first centre was established in Chicago as an outgrowth of a monthly dinner club of business people. Once consolidated, the founders experimented with a three-step approach to 'franchising' the Heartland Institute to other states. The first step was to add a neighbouring state's newspapers and legislators to the Heartland mailing list. Next, the institute identified a group of academics and financial supporters in the targeted state. Finally, an organisation was staffed and spun off as a separate body. A central office in Chicago provided editorial, printing, mailing, book-keeping, public relations and management services to all six offices for a monthly fee. Additionally, each of the institutes was able draw upon a larger pool of expertise. While the new think-tank shared the same name and research profile, it remained an independent entity and focused on issues relevant to its locality (Wheeler, 1986: 51). The scheme produced economies of scale and lasted for a couple of years but failed with the lack of foundation interest in funding the experiment.

Although the process of new institutes emerging from older organisations is not as common in parliamentary systems, it is not unknown. In Britain, the IEA nurtured both IPSET and the Social Affairs Unit. Both were given office space and access to facilities for a peppercorn rent. The Chatham House model for the study of international affairs has been copied around the world. The International Institute for Environment and Development draws upon the support of its counterpart institutes in the European Union.

Hiving-off promotes specialisation and builds networks. Political themes are reinforced by the multiplication of organisations.[1] At the same time, funding sources may be diversified by staff of the new institutes cultivating new sponsors. Potential conflicts and organisational decay can be defused if factions are encouraged to splinter and re-establish. The influence of one organisation can spread beyond one region or city, its publications distributed by other bodies. The new organisation can, at the same time, rely on the fostering of the older organisation until it becomes fully independent. Alternatively, if a unit established within an older organisation is found not to be viable, it can be closed down or streamlined with minimum dislocation.

In addition to spawning new organisations, many institutes provide technical support for independently generated ventures, including institutes overseas (Palmer, 1991). The Atlas Foundation produces documents with information regarding legal requirements for the establishment of an institute, how to set up a board of directors, how to maintain independence, how to select issues, find authors and commission work, how to undertake in-house editing, and how to raise funds (Fisher, 1983). It provides 'nuts and bolts' advice on such detailed matters as the best way to produce and market pamphlets. 'If possible, get a spine on your books; book shops don't like these (sic) thin pamphlets because browsers can't see what it is. Use thick paper and about 40 pages will have a spine, and you will sell a lot more' (Greg Lindsay quoted in Fisher, 1983: 23). The Roe Foundation's (1990) review of twelve state-based policy institutes also provides comparative information to aid institutes to instil conservative beliefs in society. Advice on successful practices of older organisations and sources of help greatly assisted the growth of conservative institutes in the American states.

Alongside strong network relationships among independent policy research institutes, there are generally strong links with other organisations in broader policy networks. Institutes build an infrastructure to maintain contact and keep interested parties abreast of current activities and research. The ODI, for example, maintains four formal networks through its Agricultural Administration Unit to keep practitioners in developing countries who are normally outside the readership of professional journals abreast of research developments and field experience. The National Center for Policy Alternatives (CPA, 1991), a progressive Washington think-tank, plays a co-ordinating and information provision role for groups addressing state policy issues. It sponsors PALs – the Policy Alternatives Leaders network and directory – which is an effort to unify progressive state leaders in the USA, keep them in contact and spread ideas from state to state.

The directories, guides and newsletters are the most tangible brokerage documents that promote the think-tank. Generally, it is the larger organisations which have the resources to publish and distribute directories. Since 1980, the Heritage Foundation's *Annual Guide to Public Policy Experts* has been the most substantial directory and is now over 420 pages in length. The directory is for the benefit of 'Scholars, government officials, the news media and the public [who] will find it a useful tool for finding experts whose knowledge and experience make them valued participants in the public policy process' (Huberty and Hohbach, 1991: iii). The Guide is compiled from Heritage's Resource Bank which is a database of over 400 research institutions and 2,000 individuals around the world. The Bank is 'an information clearing-house and catalyst for interaction among those who share our goals of individual freedom, limited government, and a strong national defense' (Huberty and Hohbach, 1991: iii). It performs two functions. Firstly, it facilitates expert participation in the policy-making processes such as testifying before Congress. It often pays travelling expenses and arranges other opportunities for experts to present their ideas by organising press interviews and talk show appearances (Pines, 1982: 263). Secondly, for Washington policy-makers and opinion leaders the Bank raises awareness of the 'rich diversity of scholarship available on college campuses and at research institutions around the world' (Huberty and Hohbach, 1991: iii) as well as acting as an 'ideological employment agency' extending the conservative network into government (Williams, 1989: 15).

If the majority of think-tanks do not have the resources to produce a directory of scholars or are too small to warrant one, many maintain a database of scholars. The EESI has compiled the names of over 15,000 individuals in the environmental and energy fields. The National Center for Public Policy Research uses its database to compile a 'List of Conservative Groups' to aid people seeking employment and internships in conservative groups, and for organisations requiring public speakers (Moritz, 1991). Annual reports usually serve the same purpose. In an era of computer technology, information retrieval is simple. Enquiries from the media or others for experts on certain issues can often be handled on the telephone. The Capital Research Center has a 'hotline' (CRC, 1990: 12). Similarly, newsletters, such as Heartland's or the IEA's *Economic Affairs*, often contain updates of new addresses and staff movements of institutes.

Equally important, but less tangible than directories and databases, are the personal networks of staff, executive and board members. Much of the success of a think-tanks is dependent on people interacting with others. For example, Donna Wise (interview) talked of WRI's 'access' and of 'working in the shadows'. The organisation has developed relationships with high-placed people around the world and brings onto its board 'elder statesmen types' who have contacts that can be used for WRI. Personal contacts represent an information resource and tool of influence that people can mobilise not only to advance their own career prospects but also to the benefit of their organisation or to promote the concerns of an epistemic community. These relationships are essential to the effectiveness of policy institutes. Think-tanks cannot survive without the personal links that tie them into other networks spreading throughout academe, foundations, international organisations, political parties, regulatory agencies, the media, interest groups, consultancies and lobbies, the corporate world, executive and legislative bodies. For example, James Cornford (interview) said that the IPPR is assisted through a policy network, much of it based in the personal relationships of staff. Coming from an academic background, Cornford said he drew on civil service and academic circles. Before she left IPPR, Patricia Hewitt who had been Neil Kinnock's Press Secretary and a former Director for the National Council of Civil Liberties was 'well plugged into' media and political circles. She is also on the Executive Committee of the Fabian Society. With Tony Blair's ascension to leadership of the Labour Party, a younger member of staff, David Milliband, has become his 'policy guru' (The Times, 23 July 1994: 7). IPPR trustees also have their own networks. There is reciprocity involved. IPPR staff are often consulted by others and sit on committees of other organisations. The advantages of being an active participant in such networks is that it allows an organisation to obtain and disseminate information within a large number of groups, to pool resources, to identify information gaps and to avoid unnecessary duplication of effort.

The social and professional interactions of staff and trustees and their sequential career moves across institutional settings builds a web of personal interaction networks. These links provide relatively direct and unfettered access among individuals and, to a degree, break down the structural distinctions between government and other organisations. The same names reappear in professional, policy and media settings. In Washington DC it is known as the 'Golden Rolodex' phenomenon, where a recurring set of specialists are filed on the rolodexes of news producers, congressional aides and government officials. These relationships embed think-tanks in a broader social and political context. The cultivation of personal contacts makes nonsense of the belief that think-tanks are independent of the political sphere.

Networking of the type promoted by Heritage requires significant resources and organisation. Heritage acts as a core organisation for conservatives providing intellectual initiative as well as technical assistance to smaller, newer or less prestigious think-tanks. It controls intangible resources such as media contacts, well-developed relationships with conservative and mainstream foundations, high public standing in Republican circles, management skills, intellectual capital, and a production capacity that places it in an asymmetrical relationship with similar bodies. Other organisations such as Atlas and Madison act as trade associations. Their emergence is indicative of the extent of think-tank development, diversification and growing professionalisation. Co-ordinating agencies of this kind are not so evident outside the USA. Think-tanks are in sufficiently small number in Britain for co-ordination to be an informal process. It is easy for directors and fellows to keep in contact with organisations reflecting similar ethos through personal interaction.

Networks have also internationalised over the last two to three decades. Some American institutes are expanding overseas. For example, staff members at IEA and CPS talk to and know of people at Heritage, Cato, CEI and NCPA in the USA, just as they know people based in the Fraser Institute in Canada or the Centre for Independent Studies in Australia. Recently, the Carnegie Endowment and Heritage opened offices in Moscow. The Tokyo Club is organised by the Nomura Research Institute (NRI) in Japan. It is a joint research and seminar programme on global issues drawing together Brookings, Chatham House, Institut für Wirtschaftsforschung in Germany and the Institut Français des Relations Internationales in Paris. Nomura is also building an Asian network of think-tanks known as the Asia Club. Overseas visitors who come for a sabbatical, to participate in a conference or to re-forge links are a common think-tank occurrence. Yet it remains difficult to gauge the degree of internationalisation because much networking is on a personal level. Furthermore, while networking is a necessary activity, it is not given the same degree of importance by all think-tanks. For example, the CPS has 'diplomatic relations' with Atlas but does not get closely involved for CPS focuses on the British political domain (Willetts, interview). Additionally, many institutes do not have the resources to build a network or they consider that funds could be better spent on policy research. Often, institutes can keep abreast of developments in institutes in other states or countries simply by swapping newsletters or through informal contact at conferences.

Strictly speaking, networking does not equate with political influence. Networking aids the effectiveness of think-tanks. However, many of the attributes of networks greatly enhance the opportunity for influence. Networking promotes solidarity, loyalty, trust and reciprocity (Thompson, 1993). Conflict and opportunistic behaviour is diminished in favour of co-operation on a common problem or policy project. More resources and intellectual capital can be mobilised in efforts to shape policy agendas.

NOTES

1. Another phenomenon has been the creation of sister/brother organisations in the US. A number of Madison Group institutes have become activist which often involves spinning off a 501(c)(4) group in a brother/sister relationship with the 501(c)(3) institute. The (c)(4) group can undertake lobbying. For example, Don Eberly is President of the Commonwealth Foundation, a 501(c)(3) institute, and he is also associated with Reach, a 501(c)(4) organisation which is an educational interest group A similar arrangement exists with the ACCF and the ACCF Center for Research. It is an efficient means of reproduction as 'extant organizations, including those formed for completely nonpolitical purposes, can generate political arms at substantially lower costs than are required to form completely new political groups' (Berry and Hula, 1991: 8).

9 Second-Hand Dealers in Ideas

There is a symbolic dimension to agenda setting. Think-tanks promote ideas and simplify policy analysis through the use of metaphor and the creation of symbols. The 'educated public' or the busy decision-maker is not likely to respond to and be persuaded by detailed data or extensive theoretical analyses in heavy tomes, but more by the condensed arguments that think-tanks convey through symbolism and their use of language. Knowledge, information and analysis is mostly ignored until it is made important through political actions and speeches that make issues threatening (Edelman, 1973: 170). This chapter argues that in order to understand the impact of policy research institutes it is necessary to consider how their use of metaphor animates them and moulds the way in which they translate research. Policy research is not always inherently persuasive. Rhetorical or discursive strategies are required to enhance the political potency of ideas and mobilise support. Policy emerges from the 'practical processes of argumentation' (Fischer and Forester, 1993: 2). That is, public policy is made of language and that language does not simply mirror the world, it also constitutes it. Accordingly, the first section of this chapter discusses the tactical deployment of ideas. The second section looks at the use of metaphors by think-tanks to make their policy research more compelling.

The Tactical Deployment of Ideas

Noted for his theoretical work, Friedrich von Hayek also left one other legacy – the advice he gave to other intellectuals and classical liberal sympathisers on how to organise ideas for wider acceptance. During the 1940s, Hayek was greatly concerned that liberal thought was about to expire. With the ascendancy of Keynesianism in policy and practice and the growing potency of socialist thought, classical liberalism was of marginal importance. Advocates of free markets and individual liberty were 'a besieged minority on both sides of the

Atlantic' (Blundell, 1990: 1). Hayek was alarmed by the pervasive influence of socialism as a successful paradigm. In his view, socialists had the courage to be utopian and, consequently, the socialist movement attracted the support of intellectuals who could influence public opinion. Although he believed socialism to be harmful and misguided, Hayek considered the source of its potency to be its offer of an 'explicit program of social development, a picture of the future society ... and a set of general principles to guide decisions on particular issues' (1990: 20). By contrast, liberals had neglected the development of the general philosophy of liberalism to the extent that liberalism failed to be a relevant, living or inspiring set of ideas.

Hayek (1967) stressed the role of the intellectual in shaping the future of society. They act as a filter or medium by which ordinary people learn about ideas and events. The distinguishing features of intellectuals are that they may be 'masters of the technique of conveying ideas but are usually amateurs so far as the substance of what they convey is concerned' (Hayek, 1990: 7). Accordingly, there is a difference between the expert or theoretician compared to the intellectual who propagates and purveys ideas. Hayek prefers the phrase 'second-hand dealers in ideas' to describe them. Their character

> ... is neither that of the original thinker nor that of the scholar or expert in a particular field of thought. ...he need not possess special knowledge of anything in particular, nor need he even be particularly intelligent, to perform his role as intermediary in the spreading of ideas. What qualifies him for his job is the wide range of subjects on which he can readily talk and write, and a position or habits through which he becomes acquainted with new ideas sooner than those to whom he addresses himself (1990: 6–7).

Second-hand dealers in ideas are invariably policy entrepreneurs. They are found in educational bodies, think-tanks, journals and foundations from where they can launch their ideas. Within the libertarian think-tanks the staff are generally in agreement that government intervention is coercive and inefficient. They do not invest their energy in theoretical deliberations or disputes with other perspectives but pursue policy related work. Accordingly, they feature many epistemic qualities.

Hayek advised liberals against going into politics. In his view, politicians become imprisoned into implementing the ideas of earlier decades. Likewise, practical people who concern themselves with daily problems of business or bureaucracy lose sight of the goal of long-term influence. Because of their pragmatism, they lack the idealism of the steadfast ideologue. Over the long run, it is a battle of ideas, and it is the intellectual whether it be a journalist, novelist, film maker or schoolteacher who is critically important. The intellectual 'decides what we hear, when we hear it, and how we hear it'. His desire to make 'the philosophic foundations of a free society once more a living intellectual issue' and regain 'a belief in the power of ideas' lead Hayek to establish the Mont Pelerin Society (quoted in Blundell, 1990: 3–4). The idea was to create 'a group of people who are in agreement on the fundamentals, and among whom certain basic conceptions are not questioned at every step' (quoted in Martino, 1990: 1).

These ideas about enhancing the effectiveness of liberal intellectuals were put into practice by a small number of intellectual entrepreneurs who built other organisations (Pirie, 1988: ch. 1). Blundell, who is currently the Director of the IEA, identifies four men in particular – Harold Luhnow, Leonard Read, F. A. Harper and, in Britain, Antony Fisher. Luhnow became President of the William Volker Fund in 1944 and was thus able to channel funds to the cause of liberalism. Read established the Foundation for Economic Education (FEE) in 1946 to disseminate the classical liberal tradition. A former Cornell University professor, Harper joined the staff of FEE and later the staff of the William Volker Fund. On expiration of the Fund in 1961 he established the Institute for Humane Studies (IHS). In Britain, Antony Fisher took the personal advice of Hayek *not* to enter politics and instead created the Institute of Economic Affairs (IEA).

> [Liberalism] required an organisation prepared to translate scholarship into plain English, to show its relevance for the times, and philosophically combative individuals to harness the historic heritage and embolden the academic liberals as effectively as the Fabian Society had done for socialists a century earlier (Seldon, 1989: 88).

Fisher was also a consultant to nascent institutes and created the Atlas Foundation which is located in the same set of buildings as the IHS at George Mason University. The three US men pursued a number of strategies through the Volker Fund. Classical liberal scholars who could not find university positions were supported and others were provided opportunities to meet, discuss and exchange ideas by the Fund. The Fund also published through the Humane Studies Series books that were spurned by other publishers. Many of these books were distributed to colleges and universities in North America by the

National Book Foundation. Blundell (1990: 4) claims that the origins of both 'Law and Economics' and the public choice school were in the early Volker programmes. The Fund also sought young talented people to nurture – a strategy that has been continued by the IHS.

According to Blundell, the explosion of interest in market liberal ideas must be understood in the light of Hayek's strategic insight and the initiative of institution building intellectuals. Without the commitment of many individuals and their mobilisation through new institutes and foundations he believes that there would not have been a world-wide turn towards markets and freedom. However, this victory is not permanent. The experience of the Fabian Society is salutary.

> Following Labour's huge victory at the polls [in 1945] its membership rushed into government and left a vacuum in the battlefield of ideas. This permitted the IEA to grow in influence unchallenged by a socialist counterpart until the Institute for Public Policy Research was established in 1988 (Blundell, 1990: 7).

Strategies that may have been successful in the 1960s and 1970s may not be applicable for the 1990s. While many believe that liberals are winning the war at the intellectual level and that the climate is more favourable to their cause than it was 25 years ago, the changed rhetoric has not always been translated into policy. Until liberals 'produced a workable, realistic plan or blueprint for dismantling the existing statist structure', the liberal project would represent a rhetorical success but not one of policy practice (Martino, 1990: 10). Consequently, the successes of liberals are vulnerable without precautions against complacency.

One of the ways in which the liberal policy network is secured and organised is through the power of language, that is, through argument, debate and persuasion. Networks can be 'articulated in a rhetorical or discursive fashion' to engineer loyalty (Thompson, 1993: 57). Rhetoric plays a large role in disseminating liberal ideas but also in forming a common identity and shared values within the policy network. Or as another says, 'Our language, our rhetoric, is constitutive: it can help reproduce existing communities or create new ones' (Throgmorton, 1993: 121). Think-tanks are key organisations engaged in these discursive practices.

The Mixed Metaphors of Markets, Religion and War

In the world of libertarian and conservative think-tanks, ideas are used 'tactically' and 'aggressively'. Ideas are weapons for 'those who fought in the trenches of freedom' (Blundell, 1990: 1). Alongside the war metaphor, commentators have also likened key intellectual figures, such as Hayek and Ludwig von Mises, as 'entrepreneurial'. Thus, ideas are marketed by the second-hand dealers. Additionally, advocacy of the new liberalism is sometimes portrayed as a matter of faith. These discourses are important as they are 'practices that systematically inform the objects of which they speak' (Sarup, 1993: 64). The use of metaphor and imagery is one way of understanding the transformation of abstract ideas into policy and political usage. Metaphor is a means to simplify the debate. It provides visual imagery to compensate for the indeterminacy and conflict-ridden nature of concepts. For market liberals it is a means of creating allies and enemies. Metaphors also make the theoretical literature accessible, real and tangible to non-specialist audiences by portraying ideas as something by which one wins or loses. The metaphorical language appeals to our individual interests and prejudices and is one means to win acceptance for a cause by means of either praising it or vilifying alternatives. An implicit part of epistemic community activity is to redefine and make irrelevant the expertise and knowledge of others. Following Edelman, the rhetoric and metaphors evoked by policy researchers are a fundamental influence on political beliefs. Language 'structures perceptions of status, authority, merit, deviance, and the causes of social problems' (1977: 21).

War

The metaphor of war permeates Arthur Seldon's analysis of the influence of the IEA. It gives additional meaning to the phrase 'think-tank'.

The ideas were in place: the long-range intellectual artillery of the IEA had been reinforced by the David Hume Institute and complemented by the short-range infantry of the Centre for Policy Studies (and, to continue the military metaphor, the IEA had beaten part of its artillery into anti-tank guns by lowering their sights and dealing with medium-term problems looming ahead) (1989: 92).

The presidents and directors of policy research institutes are most frequently identified as the 'principal strategists' of the conservative movement (Meyerson, 1991: 6). They are the 'heroes' whose 'courage and persistence are inspiring' (Blundell, 1990: 9). The scholars are 'freedom fighters', that is, thinkers who make 'revolutionary' contributions (Martino, 1990: 7) by providing the 'intellectual firepower' (Feulner, 1991: 14) to undermine the collectivist consensus. They undertake the 'moral offensive' in the conservative 'war in the trenches' (Hart, 1987: 22, 139). The battleground constantly shifts between different policy terrain.

> Individual skirmishes are rarely ferocious, typically waged in the staid pages of a scholarly journal or as polite disagreement at a conference of experts. Seldom is there the fireworks of a debate's direct and heated confrontation or the unrelenting grilling of an especially well-informed legislative committee. Critical battles, in fact, can go almost unnoticed until the fighting stops when, in retrospect, the action's contours stand out in relief (Pines, 1982: 249).

In this war, there is no peace. Battles must be constantly fought and the war is never decisively won. 'There's no such thing as a permanent political victory', declares Heritage's President, Edwin Feulner (1991: 10). Eternal vigilance is thus required. Neither peace nor compromise has a place in the discourse. 'We are not winning' says Martino (1990: 10). Yet, neither are the advocates of statism winning. Although socialism is in its 'death throes', renowned economist, James Buchanan (1990: 1) warns against complacency and 'the continuing necessity to prevent the over-reaching of the state-as-Leviathan, which becomes all the more dangerous because it does not depend on an ideology to give it focus'. These policy entrepreneurs do not believe they have achieved hegemony or fully dislodged other paradigms of thinking.

Faith

Religious metaphors of faith and belief are not uncommon. Edwin Feulner (1991: 16) hopes that people will consider the Heritage Foundation like 'their church or synagogue, that will be around for the long haul – for future generations'. Economists are likened to 'preachers' (Martino, 1990: 7; Kasper, 1987: 342). Keith Joseph, a founder of CPS, has been described as the 'mad monk' (Burgess and Alderman, 1990: 14). In less derogatory fashion, Hayek has been described as a 'spiritual father' (Haakonssen, 1985: vii). Others note the 'proselytising influence' of the IEA (in Seldon, 1989: 98). In particular, the IEA knows 'the truth' and its task is to 'evangelise' (Cockett, 1994: 139). Burton Yale Pines, Vice-President of Heritage describes the seminar series at the AEI on Christian social thought as opportunities to 'win new souls for capitalism' (1982: 259). The new conservatives are the 'true believers' says NCPPR's Director, Amy Moritz (in Hart, 1987: 138). They have faith in the possibility of radical social change.

Those who favour collectivist forms of economic organisation are portrayed as 'desperate, hopeless fanatics' (Martino, 1990: 6). Nevertheless, there are those who saw the light and became 'defectors'. Their defection has earned them the label 'neo-conservative'. In the USA, they include former socialists, radical leftists and liberal democrats such as Daniel Bell, Peter Berger, Midge Decter, Nathan Glazer, Jeanne Kirkpatrick, Irving Kristol, Seymour Martin Lipset, Michael Novak, Norman Podhoretz, and Ben Wattenberg. They represent the 'heavy artillery and bring to the right an enormous tactical advantage – a firing position from within the camp of the East Coast intellectual Establishment' (Pines, 1982: 267). In Britain, CPS's first Director of Studies, Alfred Sherman (known as 'machine gunner Sherman') was formerly a communist.[1]

There are many symbols associated with this war and faith. As Scruton (1983) notes in his *Dictionary of Political Thought*, 'icons are, by extension, ideas'. A fictional creature – Hobbes' Leviathan – is incarnate in contemporary times as a 'monster' (Buchanan, 1991: 9). Big government is portrayed as a grotesque enemy. Socialism and, as discussed below, the New Class are similarly portrayed. The enemy is categorised as evil, covert and engaged in secret subversion. It is through this kind of language that intangible or non-visible enemies are identified.

There has also emerged a mythology of great dead war heroes or prophets. The iconography of Adam Smith is the most advanced – reified in a research institute named after him – the Adam Smith Institute. Not only is a small portrait of Adam Smith found on all ASI publications as its insignia, the Institute also markets Adam Smith pins, ties and coins. The Institute holds an annual Adam Smith dinner and convened in 1990 a conference to commemorate his death. No doubt these products and events are essential to fund-raising and the ASI's public image. Yet, by the same token, the Institute's founders have captured the image of Adam Smith for their own symbolic uses. Adam Smith is 'caught up in late twentieth-century politics' as a 'living prophet' (Nurick, 1990: 46) and a symbol of the virtues of the market. It popularises Adam Smith as the patron saint of *laissez-faire* economics. Other theorists, political writers and public figures have also been used as symbols of libertarian and conservative thought. In Britain, the David Hume Institute is the Scottish counterpart of ASI. American think-tanks such as the John Locke Institute and the Barry Goldwater Institute attempt to encapsulate their philosophy by invoking the legacy of historically prominent philosophers or political figures. Name recognition can be a powerful mobilising force.

The metaphors of war and faith merge. The assertion of independence that think-tanks are 'no-one's hired guns' also indicates they are not mercenaries. Instead, they are committed to a cause, 'the good fight' (Nurick, 1987). Think-tanks 'crusade'. As they are not for hire, they are not really on the market. There is some inconsistency as the market metaphor is an equally strong rhetorical strategy in the think-tank mythology. Graham Mather, whilst still at the IEA, said 'We are in some sense almost a priesthood of believers in the market. We will keep a small corner of the shrine with candles burning...because you have never finished convincing people about the benefits of the market' (Timmins, 1990a). Thus the believers in the market must act not only strategically but also in an entrepreneurial fashion to win new converts.

Markets

The market metaphor emphasises the choice and plurality among different kinds of think-tanks. The metaphor also implies that some think-tank products have greater saliency among decision-makers (buyers) because the innate intellectual persuasiveness of certain sources of policy analysis (a superior product) emerges through competition. The language is particularly noticeable in the populist literature where think-tanks are described as 'idea factories' (Fly, 1986) or 'cerebral supermarkets' (Dickson, 1971). Their scholars are portrayed as 'idea brokers' (Smith, 1991a) engaged in 'arbitrage' (Harper, interview), or 'policy entrepreneurs' (Moore, 1988: 2455) who have a 'product line of ideas' (Rauch, 1988: 2656). In 'Washington's marketplace of ideas' (Thomas, 1988), AEI and Brookings are the Bloomingdales of the think-tank business whereas Heritage is K-mart (Matlack, 1991: 1553). Think-tanks are the refiners, packagers and distributors of ideas.

The market metaphor can be extended significantly to explain why some sorts of ideas are given more importance or are in greater demand (Brooks, 1990). Characterising the relationship between think-tanks and policy in terms of a market implies a reciprocal relationship. Not only do the producers of ideas – policy research institutes – seek to influence policy, social science production of the kind undertaken in think-tanks is also influenced by the nature of the political system, that is, by consumer preferences (Portes, 1988: 161). Demand establishes limits on what is a saleable product. Demand for information is unevenly spread throughout society. Direct consumers, such as the state, the media and interest groups are distinguishable from indirect consumers such as the educated public. Furthermore, consumer preferences are not homogeneous. Demand for the raw product – the academic theories produced in thick tomes – is relatively small. Usually there is one single dominant buyer – the state. This is particularly true for organisations heavily reliant on contracts such as Urban and RAND. Labour organisations, religious groups, environmental bodies and minority groups are also a significant source of demand as they are relatively dependent on independent policy analysis for intellectual legitimation of their policy positions. The media, academics, students and foundation officials are also major consumers. The market for policy relevant ideas and information is fragmented by different consumer needs and demand among each is unequal. Dominant sources of demand, in particular, act as 'legitimacy filters' (Brooks, 1990: 81). That is, a cultural process screens or marginalises views and knowledge that do not conform with prevailing cultural beliefs. For example, some peace researchers argue that foundations support research organisations that do not threaten the status quo rather than activist groups that are more disruptive and challenge the basic structures of power and finance (Wright, *et al.*, 1985: 28). The character of demand frames the issues that are researched.

As a consequence, the so-called competition in ideas is unequal or 'lopsided' (Lindblom, 1990: 106). To mix the metaphors again, the marketplace of ideas is not a level playing field. Those who have the capacity to pay for research and policy analysis have greater scope to affect the research agendas of think-tanks. State, foundation and corporate interests are by far the best endowed buyers and largest source of demand. Think-tanks are aware of this reality. Furthermore, 'Some "producers" have greater credibility in the market than others, as well as having superior resources for carrying out research and disseminating their findings and arguments' (Brooks, 1990: 84). Consequently, the marketplace is dominated by 'establishment expertise'. Certain organisations are presumed to be 'credible' sources of expert advice and have an overwhelming presence in the marketplace, not only in their capacity to generate information, ideas, politically competent speakers and timely analysis but also in their ability to attract funds. Supply and demand becomes a closed circuit.

Rather than superior analysis, the best thinking or the most thorough research having greater selling power, the market metaphor can be used differently to identify the sources of demand as the main factor propelling change in the status of different knowledges. For example, the political potency of market liberal perspectives grew with 'changing demand conditions in the business community and the state' (Brooks, 1990: 89). The qualitatively different global and domestic conditions of the 1980s and 1990s experienced by governments and corporations meant that alternative policy courses were investigated. The balance of political forces tilted in favour of free trade and liberalisation, hence demand for much more of this kind of research and analysis which aided a shift in policy paradigms. Extending the market metaphor assists in 'focusing on the unequal exchange relations that characterize the market for social scientific knowledge' (Brooks, 1990: 93). Market imperfections allow the dominance of particular forms of knowledge. If this is accepted, then the marketplace of ideas as the epitome of democracy and good government is illusory.

Figures of Speech

The imagery of war, faith and the market permeates the terminology of the intellectual entrepreneurs. This language is not mere happenstance but is endemic. Although the imagery is obvious, its significance in policy debates is less transparent. The importance of this discourse in relation to the revival of liberalism and the challenge to Keynesianism is generally overlooked. It is given primacy in this chapter to illustrate a power game, that is, 'a struggle, a war with verbal negotiation, pressure, lobbying and other elements designed to gain support, to "enroll" (sic), to mobilize resources, that in the end assures an intellectual monopoly for the "product"' (Rosenau, 1992: 111). In other words, the language employed by policy entrepreneurs based in think-tanks is part of the 'softening up' process of agenda setting.

Carol Cohn's analysis of the use of metaphor and imagery in her discussion of defence intellectuals and nuclear policy is illuminating. She argues that the techno-strategic language employed by defence intellectuals both reflected and shaped the American nuclear strategic project, playing a central role in the way defence intellectuals acted and thought. Likewise, the language of libertarians and conservatives both shapes and reflects the 'free market, strong state' project (Gamble, 1989b). Their language is self reinforcing. Entrepreneurship and marketing is not only a feature of the programmes and rhetoric of libertarians but is also central to its strategy as a viable social movement.

Cohn is interested in how the imagery functions in a cultural

context. She identified the use of euphemism and abstraction as a
means for defence intellectuals to distance themselves emotionally
from the horror of nuclear destruction. As an example of the
language of the defence intellectuals, she discusses the use of the
word 'pat' – 'pat the missile' – as an attempt by defence intellectuals
to dominate the 'phallic missile'. It is 'an assertion of intimacy, sexual
possession, affectionate domination' interwoven with another
meaning of patting something cute, small and harmless in an attempt
to diminish its lethality (1987: 695). The use of metaphor among
libertarian policy entrepreneurs is the means to make the complexity
of their philosophy concrete and real. Their language is the medium
by which they engage the 'thinking public'. The language of the
defence intellectual, usually involving obscure mathematical game
theoretic formulations, acts as a barrier to broader understanding and
participation. For market liberals and conservatives, their language is
a call to arms. The imagery of war, faith and competition in the
advocacy of market liberalism ascribes urgency and importance to
ideas. Classical liberal principles are made to appear worth fighting
for. The language transforms the abstract concerns of the theorist
into matters of real consequence for all citizens. Where Cohn's
techno-strategic language is distancing, esoteric, élite and jargon-
ridden, the language of the policy entrepreneurs is intended to be
inclusionary, accessible, relevant and of immediate interest.

Language communicates power. In the case of Cohn's defence
intellectuals it bestows 'cognitive mastery', a sense of controlling
nuclear technology among a privileged few. A different process
occurs with the imagery of the policy entrepreneurs who seek to
attract customers or converts. Their metaphors enable cognitive
mastery by many people. Those who are interested in the debates are
given access by the language employed. The imagery has the effect of
simplifying, familiarising and transforming the complexities of
different philosophical and political positions. The language
transforms the debates between liberalism and socialism into a
conflict between 'us' and 'them'. The written works, school materials
and media commentary that emanates from the libertarian think-
tanks do not set up academic or technical barriers, rather they seek
to attract new followers. This discourse helps achieve that which
Hayek hoped – it makes liberalism a 'living' intellectual framework.

Cohn also identifies a religious image in nuclear strategy, that is,
the 'nuclear priesthood'. She notes that in a culture of rationality it is
surprising to find religious language and 'imagery of the forces that
science has been defined in *opposition to*' (1987: 702). The language

reveals an underlying contradiction. The use of religious terms lays claim to supernatural insight and is, in Cohn's view, tacit admission that they are really creators of dogma (see also McCloskey, 1985). But not all think-tanks operate with this open evangelical style. Techno-strategists can be found in places such as RAND and IISS in the field of defence and strategy (see Dalby, 1990). The discourse of rationality and deterrence has dominated discussion of strategic and foreign policy in the USA, and is replete with jargon. Cohn also notices that the techno-strategic language is transformative. The speaker/listener begins to adopt the paradigm and mode of thinking of the strategist. This severely circumvents other ways of conceptualising issues. Refusing to learn the techno-strategic language means that oppositionary voices remain outside the politically relevant spectrum of opinion. By contrast, market liberal and conservative intellectuals see themselves as having surmounted a politically marginalised position by developing a politically attractive and policy relevant language. Think-tank scholars along with other intellectual translators make the language of the experts accessible. They allow ordinary people to become converts and advocates of general principles. The language is transformative in the sense that it is inclusionary and in conveying a framework that is paradigmatic. Decision-makers have adopted the language of choice, efficiency, rationality, competition and individualism advanced by market economists and libertarian thinkers.

Cohn's 'world of strategic analysis' is primarily a world of discourse – of words, legitimate voices and discussion. Only in passing does she mention that the defence intellectuals are 'civilians who move in and out of government, working sometimes as administrative officials or consultants, sometimes at universities and think-tanks' (1987: 687–88). On a number of occasions 'the Center' is mentioned, but its location and physical features are minimised. However, these features are important for 'the Center' (or think-tank) reinforces the discourse. In one passage Cohn notes the attractions of the Center as a 'secret kingdom'.

> Part of the appeal was the thrill of being able to ... rub shoulders with them, perhaps even be one yourself ... The whole set-up ... communicated allures of power ... We were provided luxurious accommodations ... we met in lavishly appointed classrooms and lounges ... and [there were] lunches where we could sit next to a prominent political figure (1987: 704).

Places such as 'the Center' separate and isolate intellectuals with a common interest. The discourse consequently develops in a hot-house atmosphere. Furthermore, the Center is a meeting ground. For intellectuals it provides the opportunity to interact with decision-makers. The offices of most policy institutes are located close to policy communities. At the same time, it is a haven from external influences – a means of filtering discordant voices. Intellectual solidarity, cohesiveness and homogeneity is promoted through such collegial environs. The distillation of talent produces a conducive environment for tackling policy issues. The concentration of like-minded scholars helps entrench perceptions and hardens resolve. Perspectives antithetical to the dominant paradigm can be excluded. The organisational commitment to extend philosophical principles into policy is not waylaid or diluted by constantly confronting conflicting perspectives as is often confronted in university settings. In sum, the discourse is not generated solely by words but by the entire context.

The use of political symbols and metaphorical allusion transforms knowledge and information. It serves to make a policy paradigm more politically appealing and comprehensible. But close examination of the metaphors of war, faith and the market exposes inconsistencies. As discussed, it is possible to dispute the notion that ideas compete equally in the market. Furthermore, religious imagery contradicts the claims to neutrality, objectivity, science and dispassionate analysis outlined in the previous chapter. Lastly, in the 'war', the 'enemy' is not often clear. The 'threat' is multi-faceted. Sometimes the enemy is a caricature – Leviathan. In the past, there was a subversive, communist threat. A contemporary threat is the New Class.

The nature of threat is different in conservative and libertarian perspectives. As a consequence, the alliance between the two intellectual traditions, known as the New Right, is not a stable one but is made to appear secure and harmonious. David Boaz (interview) said that Cato had little in common with conservatives at Heritage, and only found points of agreement with their economists. Similarly Eammon Butler (interview) at ASI stated that they often differed with conservative CPS perspectives on family issues. In general, libertarians are not so enamoured with the conservative preoccupation with morals, the decline of the family, racial and sectarian institutions. Similarly, conservatives do not give full endorsement to capitalism. However, the theory of the New Class establishes areas of common ground among conservatives and classical liberals.

The New Class supposedly emerged with the affluence of the post-war middle classes and was activated by the knowledge industries and the professions (Bruce-Briggs, 1981). The New Class represents an 'adversary culture' that denigrates the capitalist ethic for market liberals and represents moral decline and deterioration of the societal fabric for conservatives. The belief is that the New Class is entrenched in universities, the public sector, the media and public interest groups and which erroneously defines American culture. Progressive liberal social scientists are portrayed as power seeking, socialistic élites out of touch with genuine public concerns (Fischer, 1993: 28). Discussion of the New Class is less pronounced in Britain. However, the debate concerning 'political correctness' in both countries is a contemporary manifestation of the 'cultural war' (Bell, 1992: 10). Conservatives place the blame for the loss of legitimacy of political élites and institutions on the disorder in morals and values. Although market liberals are silent in use of the term New Class, they provide economic arguments that the welfare state serves the needs of state employed professionals and that redistribution has done little to alleviate poverty and deprivation. Instead, individual freedoms have been trampled and an under-class of social security dependants has been created.

Armed with this theory (and threat), Irving Kristol, co-editor of the neo-conservative *Public Interest*, and other scholars associated with AEI sought to persuade American corporations and foundations to change their giving patterns and mount a campaign against the New Class by supporting scholars, teachers and intellectuals whose work contributes to the preservation of a strong private sector and traditional values (*Wall Street Journal*, 21 March 1977). A number of think-tanks amplify Kristol's message through their own publications. An Ethics and Public Policy Center monograph provides guide-lines for corporate officers and executives to steer their giving towards support for the free market ethic, in the interests of their shareholders (Lefever, et al., 1982). Similarly, the Capital Research Center, a highly specialised think-tank that monitors American philanthropy argues that 'a unified, sophisticated and well-funded philanthropic élite' is imposing a 'bankrupt ideology' of progressive liberal values on American people, undermining 'faith in American values of individual responsibility and free choice [and]...diversity in the marketplace of ideas' (CRC, 1990: 3).

The theory resonated among the American business sector which was concerned about its general lack of legitimacy since the late 1960s. Business feared a growing anti-business bias in the media and society in general, and a more favourable attitude to minority, consumer and dissident issues. Not only did the theory legitimate capitalism and corporate behaviour, it aligned business with 'the poor and the working class, as ... antagonists of this liberal "new class"' (Dreier, 1982: 125–26). To counter the threat, some sectors of the business community were galvanised to sponsor think-tanks, journals and university chairs as legitimate academic critics of the New Class. For example, the Media Institute monitors television broadcasters for liberal bias. Institutes such as AEI, the Heritage Foundation, ICS and Cato also conducted studies that 'proved' the harmful effects of government regulation, unionism and taxes on business. The 'war of ideas' began in earnest in the 1980s, bankrolled by a corporate community convinced of the impact of ideas, specifically progressive liberal ideas that inspired the Great Society programmes. They initiated a competition among policy-oriented social scientists to provide intellectual justification and arguments which encouraged the proliferation not only of more think-tanks but of think-tanks that are ideologically combative and adversarial. Through think-tanks, élite experts are drawn into a working relationship with traditional political and economic élites. In the 'battle of ideas' access to expertise – or counter expertise – has become necessary for the effective participation of interest groups in policy. For representatives of corporate interests as well as political élites, think-tanks were a means to both mobilise leading experts and manage their policy discourses so that data, information and analyses served their interests rather than others (Fischer, 1993: 30–36).

The New Class was characterised as radical, morally dangerous and licentious. A good example can be found throughout Steven Powell's discussion of the IPS. He describes the IPS building as 'seedy and peculiar', 'deteriorating', 'sullied', 'dark' and 'dingy'. Those who attend IPS functions are a 'motley crowd' of 'scraggly bearded men and testy-looking women in blue jeans and T-shirts' (1987: 3–4). Throughout the book, the author conjures images to denigrate the organisation, and its scholarship as radical, amateurish, unpatriotic and subversive (see also Isaac and Isaac, 1983). According to IPS scholar, John Cavanagh, the book resulted from the 'infiltration' of the IPS by Powell who posed as a Boston newspaper reporter. Cavanagh believed that Powell was indirectly linked to the Heritage Foundation as a consultant and acting at its behest. Cavanagh claims that Heritage used Powell's book on the Institute as a fund-raising technique. The book portrayed IPS as a threat to the nation, a leftist conspiracy and having subversive influence over the media. Portrayed in this fashion, Heritage could point to the danger and by raising fears it could mobilise financial and other support for the conservative cause (Andreas and Cavanagh, interview). It would be easy to dismiss such books as unscholarly and prejudiced. Yet discursive practices such as these serve a purpose. Prejudices are reinforced. A threat is manufactured. The organisation is discredited. By contrast, neo-conservative think-tanks are made to appear as independent, expert, and mainstream.

The battle of ideas is being waged 'within the bastions of the New Class' (Smith, 1991a: 181). In the main, it is a battle of words. The language and the allusions present a qualitatively different image of what policy institutes do compared to the language of furthering the public interest through charitable educational activities, objective discussion and research brokerage. The next chapter outlines how one theory of politics – public choice – is used by free market think-tanks in this endeavour to identify enemies. The use of this theory is part of the larger narrative endeavour of widening the domain of the market.

NOTES

1. For a discussion of many individuals who adjusted their ideological positions, see Coleman's (1989) analysis of the Congress of Cultural Freedom.

10 Public Choice Theory and Think-tanks

Usually discussions of the influence of market-liberal think-tanks, especially the British bodies, focus on monetarism as a set of ideas successfully politicised and popularised (see *inter alia*, Cockett, 1994; Wickham-Jones, 1992). It is but one example. Public choice economics is another example of a theory advanced by many think-tanks in a metaphorical 'battle of ideas'. The purpose here is neither to develop its theoretical parameters nor to criticise public choice. The intention is to show how some institutes have taken the fundamentals of this approach (or discourse), applied them to policy questions and refined the theory for consumption by people in the bureaucratic, political and interest group world. This use of public choice theory is also illustrative of the manner in which some policy institutes – usually of a libertarian disposition – utilise symbolic devices and rhetoric to attract support and convince decision-makers of the superiority of a particular course of action. These tactics help this theory become influential in moulding the parameters of some policy debates.

The Metaphor of Politics as a Market

The majority of public choice research is highly analytical rather than directly policy related. Some schools of public choice are highly mathematical (see Dunleavy, 1991 and Self, 1993). The focus here is on the popular form which arguably has greater currency with policy élites (Quiggin, 1991a: 52). It is followed by a more lengthy discussion of how public choice economics is modified for policy and political interests. Needless to say, this is not to suggest that public choice is of importance to all think-tanks. Nor is the refinement process the same in all think-tanks.

The 'headquarters' of the public choice school is the Center for the Study of Public Choice at George Mason University in Virginia. Its principal intellectual leaders are Professors Gordon Tullock and

James Buchanan. Public choice theory is founded on methodological individualism. People are regarded as rational utility maximisers, motivated by narrow egoistic concerns. This 'self-interest postulate' argues that people working in government are just as likely to be motivated by the pursuit of personal wealth, power and prestige as their counterparts in the private sector. Consequently, it is a fallacy to view government as a benign despot. Politicians are analysed as utility maximisers who have a 'vote motive'. Parties are 'vote seeking coalitions which respond to interest groups by a process of vote-buying at the common expense' (Green, 1987: 100). Politicians switch allegiances from certain ideas or policies according to the possibility of catching votes and winning power. In two-party systems, the application of the model leads to the proposition that party platforms will tend to converge.

Political markets where hundreds of issues are aggregated in the platforms of one political party are regarded as crude devices for discovering citizen preferences on political and economic management. It would be a time-consuming and costly effort for individuals to inform themselves of the public's interest and those parties and/or candidates which most closely advocate the public good since, in the last instance, the individual's vote is negligible. A rationally maximising citizen will vote according to immediate group interest. This creates a political market for votes. Politicians offer bribes to the electorate entrenching the dominance of interest group politics and the dispensation of political favours. These groups supposedly invest in politics rather than production, leading to economic immobility and an atrophy of productive forces. Special interest legislation, such as tariffs and quotas to protect textile, auto and agricultural industries, are argued not to promote the general welfare, as they are denied cheaper products, but are designed to promote the interests of these industries. These interests are successful in the political marketplace as they have incentive to mobilise. But there is no incentive for such groups to economise. By contrast, voters are uninterested and uninformed and have little incentive to oppose the increased tax burden as each concession represents a negligible tax burden (Olsen, 1982). When the political system can be used for personal or interest group gain, rent-seeking behaviour is the outcome. The numbers of lobbyists, expert witnesses, lawyers and consultants will increase as they will be employed to influence public policy. Accordingly, iron triangles or policy communities of self-interested politicians, bureaucrats, lobbyists and other select outsiders are usually perceived as a conspiracy against the public interest that diverts and wastes public resources.

In the bureaucratic sphere, the work of William Niskanen, who is also Chairman of the Cato Institute, has been notable. If business people maximise their utility by pursuing profit, Niskanen posits that bureaucrats also seek to maximise income, improve working conditions and gain power and prestige in addition to any public motivations they may have. Such aspirations lead to budget maximisation and empire building in bureaucracies. Inefficiency through over-supply and over-manning is the probable outcome. By contrast, the market is said to supply to meet consumer demand but not overspill. Bureaucrats over-supply to such an extent that the welfare gain to society is offset by an enlarged budget. When services are provided by government, individuals are denied choice that would otherwise be exercised through the market. Competitive pressures are removed. Also removed is the possibility that the private sector might supply the good or service at less cost. A service is provided beyond demand for it while bureaux size, salaries and programme development are enhanced. Indeed, as bureaux have a strong incentive to satisfy the vested interests of their political powerful clients, they often act as a lobbying agency. United with interest groups, they represent a force for bureau expansion that parliaments or congress often cannot combat.

Some normative consequences are that institutions need to be designed in such a way that self-serving behaviour is channelled towards the common good. The main conclusion arising from public choice theory is that markets are a more efficient force in aggregating individual preferences than democratic systems where choice is only presented to the citizenry every three to five years. By comparison to markets, state decision making is seen to be coercive, non-interactive, insensitive to price and preference signals, inefficient and not cost conscious. Mistakes or policy failures are inevitable. A government of law − constitutions and bills of rights, especially laws limiting the state tax base − is preferred.

The impact of 'ideas' on policy is minimised in this theory. 'Interests' are the paramount force of change. Dennis Meuller, Sam Peltzman, George Stigler and Robert Tollison, in particular, are public choice theorists who deny a role for ideas. Yet, when assessing the use of the theory in think-tanks, we are presented with a 'curious spectacle of professional dealers in ideas arguing strenuously that ideas and arguments are of no importance' (Quiggin, 1991a: 53; but see Olsen 1989 and Seldon 1989: 78). For example, 'up to the mid 1970s, orthodox public choice theory would have predicted the failure of attempts to shift state owned enterprises into the private sector' because the coalition of interests defending the status quo was so strong (James, 1991). However, as discussed in the next chapter, privatisation has been implemented around the world, testifying to the influence of public choice ideas. Consequently, there is some irony presenting of public choice as a set of ideas that have impact on public policy.

Think Tank Metaphors of Public Choice Theory

Think-tanks have become central in the transmission of public choice ideas. In his book on the politics of public choice, Peter Self (1993: 64–69) argues that organisations such as Heritage, AEI and Manhattan in the USA and IEA and CPS in Britain have been particularly influential in imparting such ideas. Although Self states that think-tanks are an 'important link' in the 'long haul from academic theories to actual public policies', he does not specify what it is that these think-tanks do to make these ideas influential. In addition to their policy relevant applications of public choice theory, the research brokers of think-tanks know that the language in which they couch their policy ideas will enhance their receptivity.

By extending the metaphors of war or faith to public choice theory, it can be portrayed as a weapon or a 'sect of economists' (Solomon, 1987: 2837). It is part of the libertarian and neo-conservative arsenal in the sense of being a store of intellectual ammunition. It is also one source of enlightenment in the 'broad church' of economics. The use of these metaphors transforms public choice theory into more than an objective economic theory of politics. It gives an impression of the way in which it is applied and worked and given wider social and political significance. The market metaphor is less apparent in think-tank descriptions of public choice, perhaps because the market metaphor is endemic within the theory in its explanation of politics (Hoogerwerf, 1992). Nevertheless, it is a 'product' in the sense that the theory is refined, distributed and sold to decision-makers in the 'market place of ideas' as a way of conceptualising policy problems.

The neo-conservative faith of public choice is surrounded by an 'evangelistic fervour that somehow – in the future – public choice is about to transform our understanding' (Dunleavy, 1991: 258). According to the Locke Institute based in Virginia, public choice theory allows for 'a more profound understanding' of issues in political economy. Think-tanks are not unlike missions to win over converts to the public choice gospel of Buchanan and Tullock. The evil this faith battles is the pursuit of private interest at the expense of the public. Salvation is to be found in constitutionalism, the rule of law and balanced budgets. One of the more dire atonements that has been suggested by a fellow at the Political Economy Research Centre (PERC), John Baden, is the creation of a 'predatory bureau'. Its operating income would depend on how much it can reduce the budgets of other bureaux (Shaw, 1987: 25). If people remain committed to their 'false beliefs', then Andrew Melnyk of the IEA advocates 'political propagandising' (1989: 126–27). Convincing others of the need to dismantle a bloated bureaucracy and over-extended state requires polemicists to 'assert' the insights of public choice theory with 'more fire and brimstone' (Kasper, 1987: 341).

In the war of ideas, public choice analysis is a sophisticated weapons system. It is wielded by scholars not to compel but to persuade others of the superior intellectual force of markets and individual choice. The theory represents the 'new advantage' for conservatives, says John Andrews of the Independence Institute. It is to be deployed against the 'coercive powers' of the state. With public choice, think-tanks are 'much better armed, whether to defend against mandated benefits and eco-hysteria, or to press the offensive against socialized approaches' (Andrews, 1989: 65). According to one Heritage scholar, the enemy is government which 'acts as umpire, regulator, jailer, warmaker, and sometimes executioner...forc(ing) people to do things for which they would not otherwise volunteer' (Hart, 1987: 194). Although think-tank analyses may not always state that a public choice perspective is employed, in many cases the theory is implicit in efforts to explain the 'tyranny' perpetrated by democratic government paying off favoured voter blocks.

Public choice theory is operationalised in think-tanks differently from universities where academic peer review prevails. Academic social scientists are primarily interested in the intricacies of the theory's elaboration. The consumers of public choice analyses from think-tanks are more diversified. Rather than theoretical development, consumers in the media, government, the corporate and business sector who are interested in public policy require detailed policies or rationales to support public statements. They are consumers of political language that 'acts very largely to win or maintain public support or acquiescence' (Edelman, 1985: 17). Public choice is transformed from theoretical abstraction into a tool that can be used to strengthen and substantiate arguments against state monopoly, regulation and intervention. The theory is refashioned in this manner by institutes such as Manhattan, CEI, IRET and Heritage in the USA as well as the IEA and ASI in the UK and a network of other institutes throughout the world. It is not unusual that public choice is an important form of analysis in free market think-tanks. Public choice theory is mainstream. Testimony to its credibility and acceptance as a powerful economic theory of politics is the increasing frequency of its chief proponents acquiring Nobel Prizes in Economics. For example, Buchanan in 1986 and Gary Becker in 1992.

Heritage does not undertake elaborations of public choice, instead it makes the 'appropriate applications' (Gayner, interview). Similarly, Norman Ture (interview) was of the view that public choice perspectives flowed through IRET analysis of tax and budgetary policy. The Institute does not undertake public choice research work of a 'seminal type'. 'IRET does not want to re-invent the wheel', he said. The Pacific Research Institute applies 'the fundamental principles of market process, property rights, and public choice theory' (Pacific Research Institute, 1991). One area of application, in particular, is the environment. Along with the Political Economy Research Center, Pacific has been at the forefront in the development of free market environmentalism in the USA which criticises government regulation against pollution, hazardous waste and global warming. Environmentally sensitive resource management is to be achieved by ascribing property rights.

Many think-tank scholars habitually employ public choice theory as an explanatory framework. David Boaz (interview) of the Cato Institute stated that he 'would not go through a day without saying the word' – public choice. He frequently had 'water cooler conversations' with Cato colleagues about how they would go about applying the public choice perspective on specific issues. The framework pervades the thought patterns of many at Cato. The editor of the *Cato Journal* is 'into public choice'. In reference to privatisation, for example, Boaz felt that only by bringing the insights of public choice to bear on arguments could special interests and the government be convinced of the benefits of the privatisation policy. This does not mean Cato analysts explain the precepts of the theory. Public choice simply provides a foundation, along with the insights of Austrian economics and the Chicago School, for Cato analysis. The theory has been 'internalised'. Written work may not identify the theory 'but it is there', says Boaz (see, for example, Crane, 1988). In Britain, the IEA has 'helped publicise the ideas of the American 'public choice' school' (Vibert, 1992: 2; Hoover and Plant, 1987:

60). Madsen Pirie (1988), President of the ASI, wrote a book on the subject, *Micropolitics*. In an easily digestible writing style, Pirie lays out the foundations of the theory, its place in the battle of ideas as a form of critique, and most importantly from his point of view, techniques informed by the theory that can change socio-political dynamics.

Arguments about the New Class can also be tied with public choice arguments. Individuals in industries, ministries and agencies associated with the arts, culture and education and welfare have a material interest in the increase of the public sector and/or public spending. Therefore, the New Class places a burden on ordinary taxpayers. Think-tanks educate the community to become more aware of bureaucratic empire building and inefficiency. Public choice ideas are used to 'demystify anti-market, and particularly rent-seeking, political behaviour' (Melnyk, 1989: 128).

A group of think-tanks have been founded in a conscious effort to undermine the incentives that skew the political system in favour of organised interests. In a prospectus promoting conservative think-tanks throughout the United States, policy institutes were cast as the means to break the control of special interest coalitions on Congress. The authors of the Roe Foundation report argue that reduced budgets will not eventuate while the voting incentives for members of Congress are based in the interests of their constituents. Only by changing the interests of their home districts will their voting patterns in Congress change. State-based policy institutes decentralise the conservative movement and are seen as a means to change attitudes at the local level. The authors argue that there is greater scope to influence policy at the state level, as state legislators do not have the large staffs of their Washington counterparts and are, it is assumed, more open to policy analysis from independent sources. The (rather ambitious) anticipated results of more conservative state institutes are: i) 'legislators become better informed and vote more conservatively'; ii) 'knowledgeable and more conservative legislators become Congressmen and a more conservative Congress results'; and iii) 'without state institutes, liberal legislators will continue to become liberal Congressmen' (Roe Foundation, 1990: 58).

Public choice is operationalised in institutes where there are other conflicting and complementary theories. In institutes such as Heritage or AEI an exponent of the public choice perspective can be found alongside followers of Hayek, von Mises or Friedman. A mix of theories is the norm. For example, IEA applications are 'based on classical liberal political economy, refined ... by developments in

'Austrian–Hayekian' market process, Buchanan–Tullock public choice, and later, Muth–Minford 'rational expectations" (Seldon, 1989: 76). These themes in the IEA's research agenda are combined to induce scepticism about state intervention. That is, public choice is part of a discourse coalition that defines itself in opposition to the Keynesian discourse coalition.

The transformation process is not the same in all think-tanks. Among the free market British institutes, the IEA's work on public choice is more scholarly and much more entrenched as part of its organisational ethos. Arthur Seldon and Ralph Harris, for example, applied public choice theory in the 'choice in welfare' surveys of health and education (Green, 1987: 95–98; Barry, 1987: 126). To reinstate the market, they advocated the introduction of educational vouchers and private health cover. The sweeping theoretical economic or moral arguments were left to others while bodies such as the IEA *applied* such systems of thought. By contrast, the Centre for Policy Studies is less wedded to the approach. It is driven as much by its conservative disposition, its party political connections and greater emphasis on practical policy recommendations than by any one theory. Although public choice is a strong theme at the ASI, this institute takes a more pragmatic approach than the IEA. For example, during the Prime Minister's review into the Health Service during 1987–89, there was strong competition among these think-tanks to influence the review. David Willetts of CPS was particularly close to the review and a prominent defender of its proposals. By contrast, the IEA Health Unit recommendations had little impact and its director, David Green, was an early critic of the subsequent White Paper. The radical financing reform agenda of the IEA was not as appealing as the organisational and managerial changes advocated by the CPS and ASI (Griggs (1991: 427).

In old guard institutes, such as Brookings, the Russell Sage Foundation and NIESR, public choice is diluted among a number of approaches and employed by a small proportion of individual scholars. Nor is it necessarily used as part of a political project to roll back the state. Obviously, some think-tank scholars are critical of the public choice model. For example, one EPI writer, Paul Starr (n.d.) criticises the public choice foundations under-lying many privatisation policies. Maureen Steinbruner (interview) at the Center for National Policy is critical of the assumptions of the approach but nevertheless recognised that the theory had 'percolated' from the social sciences into many of the policy recommendations of think-tanks and into decision making. Although public choice increasingly permeates policy analysis, it is contested (Lowi, 1992). The theory is not monolithic but it has been persuasively applied and popularised by the market liberal institutes.

Self-Interestedness in Think-Tanks

Public choice theory potentially provides analytical insight into the motivations of those who populate the think-tank world. Rather than being charitable, educational or public interested bodies, think-tanks are merely vehicles for private interest. Managers and scholars can be portrayed as rational utility maximisers in the pursuit, if not of wealth (since relatively few think-tanks provide competitive salaries or stable career patterns), then of power and prestige. If they are self-interested, it is ludicrous to mount an argument that scholars are dispassionate analysts or that think-tanks are centres of objective and apolitical policy research. Or, indeed, acting in the public interest. The utility maximising policy analyst would switch adherence from one set of ideas and theories for another if it offered increased possibility of advanced career prospects, public accolade or government appointment. This line of thought provides *one* explanation for the ideological conversion of David Willetts, formerly Director of Studies at the CPS where he espoused CPS's brand of Thatcherite conservatism, who is now closely connected to the Social Market Foundation. Through the SMF, a non-libertarian think-tank which is favourable towards communitarian thought and some forms of state intervention, Willetts has 'converted from a gung-ho privatiser and ripper of the social fabric, to an exponent of "civic conservatism"' (*Guardian*, 21 November 1994). However, such an explanation leaves little room for learning and intellectual reflection by an individual that is unrelated to material interest.

Think-tanks also have a club-like character as consumption of their product is limited (Lindquist, 1989). According to club goods theory, members pay a fee to join on the basis of the benefits they expect to receive. Career advancement through networking is a possible private return perceived by the joiner. Similarly, donors and patrons are driven by self-interest. The costs of corporate philanthropy are likely to be relatively light if it is tax deductible and if it represents negligible cost in relation to company assets and income flow. The overall performance of an institute is not necessarily at issue for individual or corporate funders, only that they get the goods and services they expect at a reasonable price. Following the theory, the institutes that produce the most tangible goods and services will acquire the most revenue. Institutes such as the Conference Board and CED offer an impressive array of services ranging from libraries, meeting rooms, data services, luncheons and seminars or simulation models. Most other institutes offer a more limited range of services. 'Solidary benefits' also result from social interaction among people with the same interests. Additionally, for many individuals there are intangible rewards garnered from contributing to the group because of its stated goals, that is, 'purposive benefits'.

Many financial supporters are also motivated by the public service orientation of think-tanks. Contrary to expectations of the public choice model, individuals and groups may well found think-tanks based on principles or philosophies that such organisations contribute to the functioning of a democratic polity and that their absence would be to the intellectual detriment of society. Despite the utility of the club goods theory, it cannot accommodate the notion of altruism (Dunleavy, 1991: 48). People act in ways that are more complex than rational economic models would have us believe.

Presumably, budget maximisation and empire building is likely to be just as rife in the think-tank world as in bureaucracy. Think-tanks devote considerable resources in the competition for foundation finance. Very few policy research institutes advocate the repeal of their tax exempt status. Clearly, it is not in their interest. In fact, for a number of small think-tanks it would be a suicidal suggestion. It is arguable that taxpayers are subsidising more policy research enterprises than would survive in the market. Think-tanks can also be thought of as rent-seeking entities that have invested in politics. The trend towards partisanship and publicity seeking among think-tanks is symptomatic. Think-tankers seek favour with politicians, bureaucrats and other politically significant actors for both personal aggrandisement and organisational gain. It presents a possible explanation for why Cato moved its headquarters from San Francisco to Washington DC. With the election of Reagan, the capital presented more opportunities for policy influence and organisational expansion. The vastly increased number of think-tanks in Washington DC parallels the greatly increased numbers of business associations and lobbies (Gwartney and Wagner, 1988: 23). Indeed, organisations such as the Washington-based ACCF Center or the CGES in London are closely linked with, and funded by specific industries. They provide intellectual support for vested interests and assist their rent-seeking behaviour.

A number of think-tanks are meant to represent defensive action against the power of these groups. That is, they have relative autonomy from the state and from vested interests, acting in the general interest to provide alternative consumer-oriented or taxpayer perspectives. However, this presumes 'the existence of public spirited policy engineers' which, unfortunately, violates the self-interest postulate of public choice (Dryzek, 1992: 413). Such policy engineers would need to excel in the art of advocacy to change public opinion sufficiently to generate electoral changes in favour of a political party committed to small government and public expenditure reduction. If this did occur it would be testimony to the power of ideas thereby undermining a central postulate of public choice – that policy is the outcome of interest (Borins, 1988: 16).

An Epistemic Community?

Do public choice theorists based in free market think-tanks constitute an epistemic community? Potentially, but not in isolation of like-minded experts with other institutional affiliations. These scholars have shared normative beliefs. That is, they display a concern to create institutional arrangements that limit bureaucratic empire building and ballooning budgets; to establish voting rules that most faithfully translate individual preferences into public decisions; and to organise society for the greatest scope of free exchange (Caporaso and Levine, 1992: 135). They have a shared causal belief that people maximise their utilities. They have common notions of validity. This is encapsulated in a common vocabulary of rationality and methodological individualism. Their beliefs and notions of validity are communicated through a journal, *Public Choice*, edited by James Buchanan, and a professional society – the Public Choice Society – which 'consolidate and give focus to what otherwise might be a fragmentary research program' (Caporaso and Levine, 1992: 134).

These public choice theorists do not share a common policy enterprise beyond a 'shared commitment to the application and production of knowledge' (Haas, 1992a: 3). Yet, their shared discursive practices identify a political concern to institute a particular way of understanding of policy problems among decision-making circles. As noted in Chapter Six, a particular school of economic thinking can produce an epistemic community. Their efforts to establish public choice as a dominant conceptual paradigm is evident in the research brokerage and networking activities of think-tanks, and as people trained in its tenets gradually move into decision-making positions. For example, a network of former students and acolytes of James Buchanan have made their way into positions of power allowing discourse structuration to occur. James

C. Miller, a former director of the Office of Management and Budget was his doctoral student. Other students include John H. Moore who was deputy director of the National Science Foundation; Robert D. Tollison, director of the Economic Bureau of the Federal Trade Commission; and Paul Craig Roberts now at CSIS (Solomon, 1986: 2837). There are also specific policy projects in which public choice theorists may be involved. As noted above, the environment is an area where the free market economists are using public choice to redefine environmental degradation as a consequence of government intervention and advocating property rights as a more effective means of environmental protection. Their political importance is popularising a new way of thinking about policy problems to be exploited as and when policy windows open. By gaining adherents to the public choice perspective, these policy intellectuals limit and shape the policy alternatives considered.

Metaphorical allusions cannot substitute for theoretical argument and analysis. Yet, not only is the discursive strategy a successful marketing technique to popularise a new way of thinking, it also helps identify the advocates as part of an epistemic-like community. As a former deputy director of the IEA remarked, economic problems and policy disputes will persist; 'what matters is the language in which it is discussed' (Wood, 1987).

Some Political Consequences of Economic Theory

Independent policy research institutes help develop the academic discourse of public choice theory but they also refashion it for wider use. Economic theory is refined as a political discourse. In other words, public choice economists have 'invaded the realm of research on government administration – surely the camp of the enemy' (Dionne, 1991: 281). They promote public choice as a way to reinterpret the world more accurately and scientifically than sociologists, historians, political scientists and others. Through this process, the market liberal users of the theory attempt to acquire greater agenda setting powers by asserting greater scientific authority.

Over the course of the century, economics has developed as a separate and distinct discipline. The trend in the development of the economic discipline from its origins in political economy has been an endeavour to escape the subjectivity that is inherent to politics/philosophy, and reach the realm of the apolitical, measurable and empirical. Economics attempted to establish itself as the true science of the social whereas 'the realm of normative prescription is reserved for political economy' (Gamble, 1989a: 3). Part of this process involved extricating the vocabulary of economics from the value laden language of politics. Economics has drawn from politics terms that have been redefined and depoliticised as 'neutral economic terms that speak of the truth rather than of interests' (Pemberton, 1988: 196). Presented as a science, it is better positioned to offer a more valid perspective on economic problems and the public interest than views derived from interests which are partial and promote the aims of minorities. 'Public choice brings ... an intellectual sophistication that reflects its origins in the discipline of economics rather than political science' (James, 1985: 33).

The route to the acceptance of public choice analysis is not educating the populace of its theoretical tenets. Instead, most policy institutes deal with concrete issues of which the public is aware and outline a solution, such as balanced budgets, which is derived from public choice insights. Although it is clearly the case that many scholars based in policy research institutes are well versed in the intricacies of economic and political theories, public debate does not always accommodate full explanation of the premises of an argument. Instead, think-tank work is given a commonsensical appeal in an effort to give public choice, as well as other theories, greater political cogency. The discourse in the libertarian think-tanks such as Cato or PERC is not the same as the academic discourse, for it operates in a broader political spectrum of bureaucrats, journalists, consultants and politicians who require greater policy relevance and simplicity.

At the risk of caricature, one of the maxims derived from public choice is the statement that 'trade unions have too much power'. Implicit is a theoretical standard. The maxim is 'a disguised way of saying that individuals have more power through a collectivity than they *should* have according to the theory of the free market'. Such claims are simple but are vague and ambiguous without their premises. It allows 'different members of the audience to fill in the blanks in different ways, and thus appeal to a whole range of prejudices'. Public choice can be equally employed to state that business lobbies have too much power. In the public arena, however, it is far less frequently heard as such criticisms of business are not usually in demand with the corporate sponsors of policy research institutes. In the absence of strongly stated alternative views, debate becomes severely truncated. Such rhetoric can change the culture of debate as 'the barriers of acceptable subject matter continue to close in on the speaker' (Maddox and Hagan, 1987: 31–32).

These constraints on debate have also been noted by the American political scientist, Theodore Lowi, who argues that public choice is 'hegemonic' in political science for 'reasons of state'. He argues that economics has become the 'language of state'. What political science took as 'science', politicians took as 'weaponry'. In other words, by accepting the theory as psuedo-scientific, the politics discipline failed to subject the theory to political analysis. In a political sense, the dominance of public choice in the USA is 'consonant' with the politics of the Republicans and the rise of *laissez-faire* thought within that party. As the 'language of state', its political utility rests in the way it 'closes off debate' in representative assemblies such as Congress. Policy-making powers are devolved 'less to the agency and more to the decision making formulas residing in the agency' (Lowi, 1992: 5). The language used to describe and analyse institutions has consequences for the way these institutions are perceived, hence managed and reformed. John Dryzek has also suggested that the diffusion of public choice theory beyond the academy possibly 'corrodes trust and civic virtue within government'. The veracity of public choice analysis is less important than the process by which its hypotheses may become more true, 'helped perhaps by individuals trained in public choice attaining high rank in government' which may allow the discourse to become institutionalised (1992: 413). For example, in Britain public choice principles underlined the failed poll tax experiment (Bailey, 1993). A manifestation of, and a link in the symbiosis between social science and the state is the policy research role of the free market think-tanks that help make public choice attractive to policy-makers and bureaucrats. The ASI, in particular, was a strong advocate of the poll tax.

A political analysis of the theory recognises that it is not abstract and detached, or hermetically sealed from its environment. Instead, it is operationalised in a political context where the free market policy institutes are aiming for discourse structuration and its institutionalisation by government. While policy institutes say they are independent and scholarly bodies engaged in dispassionate policy analysis (as discussed in an earlier chapter), they also employ a different language that gives an entirely different impression. The metaphors of war and weapons, markets and competition, or religious faith contradict the apolitical language of enlightenment, science and objectivity. Despite the inconsistencies in the rhetoric, the metaphorical language serves an important research brokerage purpose in making ideas, policy analyses and political and economic theory accessible and relevant. The language of war, markets and faith is necessary to mobilise opinion and set agendas for public debate. At the same time, the language of science is necessary to legitimise the role of the policy research institute, establish their authority and bestow academic credibility on their policy recommendations.

Policy research is not inherently persuasive, hence discursive strategies are required to enhance its political potency. As second-hand dealers in ideas, many policy research institutes are determined to make complex theories and analyses appealing to non-expert audiences. Public choice theory is an example of an abstract economic theory that is transformed by the discursive strategies and applied policy work of free market policy institutes. The theory has been an important pillar in the revival of market liberalism. The next chapter outlines a policy practice – that is, privatisation – through which aspects of the public choice discourse has been institutionalised. Think-tanks have also played a key role in advocating privatisation and promoting its international spread.

11 Policy Institutes and Privatisation

The global spread of privatisation has been given impetus by the intellectual advocacy of privatisation. This promotes learning about and emulation of privatisation policies among different countries. During the 1980s, a group of policy institutes acted as policy innovators, provided intellectual legitimation for privatisation policies and helped diffuse the consensual knowledge of a privatisation epistemic community.[1] Unsurprisingly, most of the work on privatisation among the policy research institutes has come from the conservative or free market think-tanks. On the whole, social democratic or progressive institutes have given less attention to it as a policy tool. Accordingly, institutes such as the Heritage Foundation, CEI and the StateNet institutes in the USA and the IEA, CPS and ASI in Britain – principal players in privatisation debates – are discussed in most detail.

Policy Innovation and Diffusion Among Think-tanks

Although the world-wide trend towards privatisation has occurred in the context of a common international pattern of slower economic growth, the international spread of privatisation is not inevitable. It has been facilitated and shaped by the diffusion of knowledge. This knowledge has allowed decision-makers to 'draw lessons' (Rose, 1991 and 1993) and aided 'cross national policy transfers' (Wolman, 1992). It has resulted in policy convergence across nations.

There are three processes of diffusion of ideas about privatisation (Ikenberry, 1990: 99–106). The first – 'external inducement' – is relevant for less developed countries and the former communist countries of Europe. Foreign aid agencies and international organisations such as the World Bank may make loans and aid contingent on these countries adopting liberalising policies (Biersteker, 1992: 110). The second form of diffusion – 'policy bandwagoning' or emulation – occurs when other governments copy the privatisation policies of another country. This happens when the decision making élite in one country believes that importing innovatory policies successful in another country will also bring them economic benefit or electoral advantage. When old political and economic strategies appear to be failing, decision-makers turn to the successes of other governments as a guide to action. Bandwagoning can be for pragmatic or tactical reasons. Economists and administrators have a pragmatic desire to achieve the efficiency of public or private service delivery. The tactical use of privatisation involves specific political or economic goals such as revenue raising or appeasing the party faithful (Henig, *et al.*, 1988).

The third process – 'social learning' – involves the active diffusion of policy relevant ideas. The concept of consensual knowledge, outlined in chapter six, is relevant here. Consensual knowledge regarding privatisation concerns theories about how it is likely to effect the economy and society. This knowledge is diffused not simply for pragmatic reasons but to effect 'regime change' that will shift the whole system towards a market economy and away from dependency upon the state (Henig, *et al.*, 1988). This knowledge was spread among specialists from different countries and commanded sufficient agreement within domestic and international policy communities during the 1980s to serve as a guide to public policy. In order for policy diffusion to occur, however, consensual knowledge must penetrate policy-making processes and institutions. 'Convergence under this process results from an interaction and consensus amongst an élite that operates, in the first instance, above the fray of domestic politics' (Bennett, 1991: 225).

The international exchange of information can be through formal avenues such as fact-finding missions or more informally through the advice and information of academics, consultants, think-tanks and journalists. Sometimes it prompts reform and change. As Schneider and Ingram note:

> Cross national policy comparisons contribute to innovation. National governments are introverted and career officials identify with particular ministries. Unless the examples of other countries are brought to light through analysis, changes will be incremental (1988: 67).

This international interaction helps create an international policy community of experts on privatisation. Many think-tank scholars researching privatisation were part of an international policy community. They aided the diffusion process by developing and communicating consensual knowledge about privatisation. This knowledge was a necessary but not sufficient component of the diffusion of privatisation. The spread of privatisation ideas also occurred through inducement and emulation.

For many of the market liberal think-tanks, their advocacy of privatisation arises from theorising about the functioning of the state in modern industrial societies and faith in the superiority of private provision. Sometimes this inquiry rests on public choice insights (Goodman, 1985; Kuttner, 1989). Among other scholars it lies with Austrian–Hayekian notions of efficiency. While many bureaucrats and elected officials may regard privatisation primarily as a mechanism to reduce the cost of services, the scholars of the free market institutes are usually distinctive in making more principled claims about the benefits of privatisation. They are less concerned about cost savings and more interested in the proper scope and consequences of government provision and regulation (Butler, 1989: 115). Their concern to reduce state intervention is not simply pragmatic but based on various market liberal economic theories which define them as part of a privatisation epistemic community. The market liberal institutes can be contrasted with other institutes that adopt a more pragmatic and sometimes critical perspective on privatisation. The researchers associated with these institutes are not necessarily interested in 'rolling back the state' but in using privatisation as tool of reform, efficiency and adjustment. They are 'indifferent whether the stimulus to better performance comes in the form of internal competition among government agencies or between government agencies and private firms' (Starr, 1990: 41). Institutes such as Urban or the PSI are not part of the privatisation epistemic community.

Britain

With many years of research on choice, competitiveness and efficiency, the IEA could provide the consensual knowledge of why privatisation was needed. The IEA was sponsoring work that provided '"blueprints" for privatisation long before the policy became a viable political reality' (Veljanovski, 1989: ix). Despite the available consensual knowledge, not until the election of the Conservatives in 1979 did the political opportunity for the implementation of privatisation emerge. Returning to Kingdon's agenda-setting model, the three streams converged. Think-tanks generated policy alternatives in the policy stream but operated independently from the political and problem streams until the 1980s. The political stream changed with Margaret Thatcher's election. In the problem stream, the difficulties of financing and managing nationalised industries and the welfare state were manifest. The 'coupling' of the problem and political streams created a policy window for action which think-tanks exploited through their advocacy of the privatisation 'solution'.

The neo-classical economists working through IEA articulated their dissatisfaction with the performance of the nationalised industries. They brought new modes of economic thought to explain the root causes of inefficiency in public enterprise. These views regarding the 'inherent' inefficiency of nationalised industry were amplified by the publication programmes, seminars, conferences and public speaking engagements organised by think-tanks to 'educate' both policy-makers and the general public. Yet, the approaches of the three main free market think-tanks were different. The IEA looked at broader economic questions and theoretical issues. Instead of a slavish devotion to the Conservative Party's practice of privatisation, IEA scholars regarded privatisation as a subject of continuing examination, criticism and dialogue. Although not denying the political and financial success of the policy, contributors to one IEA book, *Privatisation and Competition,* are critical of the deficiencies in the UK privatisation programme such as 'the continuing inefficiencies which it has fostered' with the sale of monopolies, continued state intervention via regulation and the sacrifice of greater competition (Veljanovski, 1989: x).

The CPS also played an important role in developing privatisation ideas, especially through its Nationalised Industries Study Group. For example Frank Vibert (interview), a former deputy director of the IEA, expressed the view that CPS was a great initiator of privatisation, especially Alfred Sherman. Indeed, Sherman is credited not only with introducing Keith Joseph and Margaret Thatcher to the ideas of Hayek (Todd, 1991), but also as the 'author' of the 'privatisation label' (Burgess and Alderman, 1990: 14). However, the Centre was (and still is) more closely connected with the Conservative Party and able to diffuse its expertise through informal channels of access to sympathetic ministers. In the early days of CPS, the principled case for privatisation, that is the superiority of market forces and private ownership, was extolled as a means for getting the 'privatisation ball rolling' (Willetts, interview). By the mid-1980s, the nature of advice regarding privatisation had changed. It had become an acceptable policy tool. Consequently, CPS publications and research agenda increasingly looked towards new areas 'ripe' for reform. The battle of ideas had been won and the requirement of a privatising government was for more technical information on how to implement privatisation ideas. These new emphases were reflected in the CPS monographs. From the late 1980s, for example, CPS publications addressed the technical questions of how to privatise the electricity supply, the Forestry Commission, postal services and British Coal, as well as measures to institute greater competition, efficiency and choice for consumers in health care. Earlier in the decade publications made a broader intellectual case. It was necessary to clarify the benefits, 'persuade the doubters' and 'allay the fears of employees' of a policy mechanism that was then poorly understood (Moore, 1992: 26–7). By 1992, the cautious analytical approach had given way to more hyperbole. John Moore MP was declaring at the CPS Winter Address that privatisation was a 'proven process' to halt economic decline and that the British experience was being adopted world wide (1992: 5). Nowadays, the CPS is convening conferences entitled, for example, 'Privatisation – Maintaining the Momentum', not only as an opportunity to reflect on past practices and missed opportunities but to ensure further innovations in privatisation.

The Adam Smith Institute claims to have briefed government leaders in over fifty countries regarding the techniques and advantages of privatisation. It has also produced a 200 page *Manual on Privatisation* advising on techniques and sources of privatisation expertise in Britain (Butler and Pirie, 1989; see also ASI, 1985). Since 1987 the ASI has held an annual international conference on privatisation. The Conference attracts hundreds of representatives based in government, international aid agencies, privatised companies, law firms, regulatory organisations and corporations from around the world. It is the Institute's primary means of exporting privatisation ideas to other countries. A specialised event, it allows people involved in privatisation to meet, and through issue specific sessions such as 'developing a stock market', to pursue technical issues in depth. It is an example of other countries seeking to learn from British experience and the transmission of consensual knowledge from an epistemic community operating within broader domestic and international policy communities. At the sixth Conference, Prime Minister John Major stated that 'Britain has led the way on privatization supported by the work of the Adam Smith Institute' (ASI, 'Conference on Privatization' flyer, 1992). While bestowing some credibility on the Institute, such a statement does not mean that the ASI was a principal buttress of the government's privatisation programme. Instead, ASI Director, Eamonn Butler (interview), described the ASI role as distant and *ad hoc*. They try to look at problems from a politician's perspective: how do you privatise? what are the options? what are the problems and logistics? In his view, politicians need people to think about the circumstances, to design a blueprint for privatisation.

The privatisation debate of the 1990s is of a different character to that of the early 1980s. In Butler's view, the case for privatisation had been accepted. Ideological and political opposition is more diffuse. He described the changing status of privatisation as a shift 'from lunacy to respectability'. This shift occurred because organisations such as think-tanks had established legitimacy for it years in advance. An informal division of labour evolved among the free market institutes. Both the CPS and IEA provided the initial intellectual impetus for privatisation. At the IEA, this was done in a more theoretical fashion by advocating the virtues of the market and perils of state intervention. The CPS promoted the idea of privatisation not only in its publications, study groups and public meetings but through established contacts in government. In comparison to the other institutes, the ASI's approach was more practical than academic; it saw its main strength as problem solving, that is, the 'mechanics of public policy, quite prepared to see their hands dirtied with the grease of the real world' (ASI, 1988: 2).

The privatisation programme of the Thatcher government did not conform to the consensual knowledge developed at the IEA. The IEA's journal, *Economic Affairs*, frequently featured articles critical of the Thatcher government's privatisation programme.[2] Efficiency concerns were often sacrificed for revenue generation and other politically expedient objectives such as the desire to undermine unions. The IEA maintained its epistemic integrity. The CPS was also relatively aggressive in its promotion of privatisation and frustration with the pace of reform was often voiced by Alfred Sherman. At the ASI, Madsen Pirie (1988: 175) recognised that while increased competition is the 'ideal solution', it is not always politically possible to break up large bodies like British Telecom. For Pirie, it is enough that the balance of ownership is shifted from the state to the private sector because a private monopoly is more vulnerable to technological innovation and more likely to be eroded over time. By contrast, state sector monopolies are protected from competitive pressures by new legislation (1988: 184–5). Pirie argues that there is a difference between those who stress full free market solutions and those who 'start from the analysis of the public choice school and devise policies to work within the political markets' (1988: 181). The former group criticise government privatisation policies for not instituting markets and competition, and consider the willingness of government to trade benefits with interest groups as a lack of commitment. According to Pirie, such critics do not understand that it is these trade-offs with labour and management that make privatisation politically feasible in the first place. A public choice approach recognises that slimming the state and efficiency reforms inevitably provoke confrontation with established interests (Self, 1993: 59). Those who stress the superiority of the market, forget that state owned firms also operate in a political market and are subjected to similar pressures faced by legislators. A reform-minded government needs to build coalitions in favour of privatisation before policy can be implemented.

Other British institutes, such as IFS, the Fabian Society and PSI, have been less enthusiastic about privatisation. None, however, have mounted a sustained critique of privatisation.[3] As popular attitudes to privatisation have changed and as the Labour Party dropped its blanket opposition to privatisation, a more pragmatic stance has been adopted. Where Fabian Tracts and Research Series papers once strongly advocated the virtues of nationalisation, during the 1980s the Fabians were relatively silent about privatisation. On the whole, Fabian publications attempted a 'restatement of democratic socialism as an effective public policy' (Fabian Society, 1985), whilst criticising the underlying free market philosophy of the Thatcher government's public sector reform (see Kaldor, 1982). The nature of IPPR's work on privatisation is indicative that privatisation has become an acceptable tool of policy. As a general rule, whether IPPR studies favour or oppose privatisation depends upon the features of the industry. That is, privatisation is assessed on a case by case basis (Cornford, interview). Of the privatisation that has occurred in the health and welfare domain, the IPPR Annual Report for 1990–91 states that as it has 'receded from the political agenda, an ideological gulf between the political parties has given way to a common interest in shifting the balance of power from the welfare provider to the welfare user'. The more important issues for the IPPR are policy questions regarding 'empowerment' of consumers and welfare recipients regardless of public or private sector delivery including how to define needs, how to enforce rights and how to improve service quality (IPPR, 1991: 7).

United States of America
Under the Bush and Reagan administrations there has been strong rhetoric about privatisation but little implementation at the federal level. Indeed, there are very few state-owned enterprises owned by

federal government. Instead, contracting-out by state and municipal governments and deregulation are the most common forms of privatisation. Government lack of interest in privatisation was reflected in the degree to which it was being researched and advocated in Washington DC. Although the Competitive Enterprise Institute (CEI) had done some advocacy of privatisation, by the 1990s it was a 'dying issue' (Jeffreys, interview). Nor was privatisation central to Cato's research agenda. Instead, this institute preferred to address the issue of government deregulation. IRET also focused on deregulation as did the Democrat-affiliated CNP, albeit favouring more regulation to overcome imperfect information, social inequities, the existence of externalities such as pollution, and the tendency of some markets to become monopolised (Foreman and Steinbruner, 1991: 14). The AEI also addressed privatisation within its research programme on regulatory policy, but in the words of one AEI scholar, Marvin Kosters, 'Deregulation is dead as a national political issue' (*San Francisco Chronicle*, 2 January 1990).

   While the election of Reagan opened a policy window, that window also closed. Unlike Thatcher's and Major's control of the legislature, the Reagan and Bush administrations were unable to fully control the House of Representatives. Furthermore, the Reagan administration was more of a conservative ideological disposition and lacked the commitment to privatise (Riddell, 1994: 23). According to CEI President, Fred Smith, privatisation was seen as a money-making scheme, approached in budgetary rather than political terms. Politically powerful groups benefiting from public programmes were alienated by the prospect of reduced public funding or job losses and deteriorating working conditions. The inability to generate a wide consensus on a more limited role for government was one factor that stalled the implementation of privatisation at the federal level. The Office of Management and Budget A-76 and A-25 circulars, which legislated for contracting out and user-pays respectively were of mixed success. Although A-76 specifies that if a private sector organisation can provide a service at lower cost than government, it should be given the contract, bureaucrats have become adept at producing favourable cost comparisons. With the A-25 circular, user groups have managed to keep fees and charges low through political action. An IPS scholar, however, argues that too many functions have been contracted out leading to disorganisation in policy delivery (MacLennan, 1988).

   According to Stuart Butler (1989: 115) – director of domestic policy studies at Heritage – the privatisation proponents won the efficiency argument but not the political war. Ideas do not necessarily prevail in the face of political opposition particularly as 'Congress is strongly resistant to program cuts that affect sensitive constituencies' (Moore and Butler, 1988: 1). Nevertheless, Butler considered that privatisation could be successfully pursued provided governments paid attention to the social and political dynamics involved. Similar to Madsen Pirie at the ASI, he argued that private gain could help build coalitions in favour of privatisation. Not only does privatisation shrink the state and claw back the deficit, it also dismantles the constituency for government spending. It is replaced by a 'mirror image coalition' made up of prospective contractors who have the 'incentive to campaign hard for stepped-up privatization' (Butler quoted in Kuttner, 1989: 21). Think-tanks supposedly play a key role in coalition building as organisers and in educating various groups how to redefine their interests.

Despite the continuing agitation of bodies such as Heritage, CEI and Cato, among others, for the federal government to rein in the deficit and privatise, little headway has been made. In response, some American institutes redirected their attention to promoting the spread of privatisation elsewhere. The ICS, for example, through its International Center for Economic Growth, promoted privatisation as an aid to development in developing countries, producing a handbook on techniques of privatisation for this purpose (Hanke, 1987). Heritage *Backgrounders* often addressed the potential for privatisation in the Third World (for example, Roth, 1989; Salinas, 1990). Other institutes applied privatisation principles to new issues. Free market environmentalists advocated the privatisation of public lands – from national parks to the continental sea shelf – as a means of countering environmental degradation. Institutes such as the Political Economy Research Center (PERC) in particular, and the Reason Foundation, the Pacific Research Institute and the Cato Institute provided an outlet for these New Resource Economists.

Unlike think-tankers based in Washington DC, Robert Poole says privatisation is 'blossoming all over the country' (1990: 1). Poole is President of the Reason Foundation which has specialised in privatisation issues since 1976, producing a *Privatization Yearbook* on privatisation trends and a monthly newsletter, *Privatization Watch*. Under fiscal pressure and the threat of tax revolts, privatisation represented an opportunity for state and local officials to 'make better use of tax payer dollars' (1991). The financial dilemmas of state and local governments established a dynamic for policy innovation and heightened receptivity to proposals that would solve funding difficulties. These circumstances provided a policy window for the new locally based conservative think-tanks such as the Commonwealth Foundation, the Mackinac Center, the Washington Institute for Policy Studies, the John Locke Institute and the Heartland Institute to diffuse privatisation ideas. They produced a plethora of studies on the privatisation of prisons; sports facilities and stadia; airports, roads and bridges; and city services such as rubbish collection, water purification and zoos. Privatisation became the hallmark of the state conservative movement.

The old guard institutes such as Brookings, Urban, the Carnegie Council, NBER and others have also conducted studies on privatisation. Unlike the free market institutes, privatisation is not a strong component of their research programmes or reflective of an ideological commitment to small government. Individual studies may well advocate privatisation but studies are more likely to have been instituted in response to the general questioning of the role of government, the growing cogency of the privatisation movement, and its increasing implementation. In general, these institutes provide pragmatic assessments of both the pros and cons of privatisation on a case by case basis (Salamon, 1989). The Joint Center for Political and Economic Studies, for example, has sponsored one substantive study of the effect of privatisation on the social and economic mobility of minorities. While the Center is not, in principle, opposed to privatisation, this particular study argues that as a consequence of contracting-out, the absolute size of the public workforce shrunk, resulting in a loss of earnings, benefits and jobs in the lower ranking service and maintenance positions where minorities are concentrated. While minorities were absorbed into the contracted firms at almost the same rate of their employment with municipalities, they generally earned lower wages (Suggs, 1989: xv–xvi).

More substantial criticism of privatisation has emerged from the Economic Policy Institute (EPI). Max Sawicky (1991) depicts privatisation as a cynical means to reduce the federal deficit and a scheme 'masterminded' by Stuart Butler at Heritage. He attempts to expose and undermine attempts at coalition building in favour of privatisation (see also Sclar, et al., 1989). Paul Starr, another EPI writer, challenges the neo-conservative position that touts privatisation as a 'sovereign cure for virtually all ailments of the body politic' (n.d.: 1). His strongest criticism is reserved for the public choice theorists. He argues, contrary to the public choice perspective, that contracting out does not undermine the incentive of groups pressuring for larger budgets. The producers would be turned into advocates for higher public spending on roads, medicine and education. Starr argues that the most tangible evidence of pressure on the budget is from the 'outsourcing' of defence equipment to private contractors. These private producers make aggressive lobbyists. Privatisation does not necessarily reduce special interest power or reduce the size of the federal budget.

While the consensual knowledge of free market economists was given lip service by the Reagan and Bush administrations, the prevailing configuration of political forces prevented the implementation of an extensive privatisation programme. Although the consensual knowledge on privatisation developed by British and American free market institutes converged – that is, rested on the same theories and principles – the form and extent of privatisation implemented varied considerably between countries. Strong institutional forces endogenous to these political systems shaped the forms of privatisation adopted. Thus, privatisation was adopted for pragmatic reasons by state governments in the USA, not for the principled reasons outlined by free market economists and public choice theorists.

From Lunacy to Respectability: The Spread of Privatisation Ideas

Once a collection of 'scholarly nuts', the advocates of privatisation have 'come of age' (Moe, 1987: 453). Policy research institutes popularised privatisation in public, professional and scholarly domains. Some think-tank analysis, such as that published by the Urban Institute or the IEA, is of academic quality. Much of it elsewhere is derivative. The smaller and poorly resourced institutes often draw heavily upon the work of the larger research oriented institutes or university research to produce short issue-briefs or monographs. CEI, for example, sought to 'implement the ideas produced by academic oriented institutes' (Smith, 1986–87: 29). Their aim was to broaden understanding about privatisation and adapt its practical applications to local or regional conditions.

Accordingly, some think-tanks act as intellectual innovators whereas others are more active as diffusers – through their networks and brokerage activities – of privatisation ideas. Thus, privatisation in Britain 'started out as the idea of a few academic economists and business people which was germinated in the "think-tanks" in the mid 1970s' (Holmes, 1990). The diffusion of the consensual knowledge of the free market policy institutes into government policy was possible once the Conservative Party was elected but these ideas also made their way across the Atlantic to the USA. Jeffrey Gayner (interview) at the Heritage Foundation described privatisation as an idea that has been imported from Britain and adapted to the US context. At Heritage, one route of importation has been through Stuart Butler whose brother, Eamonn Butler, is director of the Adam Smith Institute. Both Eamonn Butler and Madsen Pirie worked at Heritage where they learned about the mechanics of running a public policy institute before founding the ASI. In 1988, the CPS sent a 'small team of British experts to brief President Reagan's Privatisation Commission' (CPS, 1988: 2). As John Goodman of the NCPA notes, 'this movement of people and ideas across the Atlantic can help to propel a movement'. Furthermore, events in one country can be used by institutes and individuals exchanging ideas and techniques to reinforce similar events in another (1985: xi–xii). The NCPA claims that it was the first American institute to 'publish a comprehensive account of the 22 different techniques Margaret Thatcher used', as well as to document the world-wide trend to privatisation, especially in Latin America (1990: 4). Collaborative ventures are another avenue of diffusion. A senior associate of PERC in the US has published with the free market Centre for Independent Studies (CIS) in Australia (Anderson, 1991), John Goodman, Director of NCPA in Dallas, has co-authored another monograph with CIS (Goodman and Nichols, 1990), while the NCPA commissioned Madsen Pirie to write a book on British privatisation techniques. Robert Poole was a contributor to the ASI's *Manual on Privatisation* (Butler and Pirie, 1989). The diffusion of privatisation ideas is also a prime concern of the Reason Foundation. In the words of its Director, Robert Poole, 'The responsibility of the Reason Foundation is to find and publicize examples of privatization for their teaching value' (1985: 59). These policy institutes and individuals were promoting social learning and bandwagoning.

A growing area of interest among many think-tanks is the transition of former communist societies in Europe. Here again, the three streams converged giving think-tanks the opportunity to influence agendas. The 1989 revolutions represented a significant change in the political stream. The difficulties of economic transition from communism combined with the long-standing inefficiency of state industry, thrust privatisation ideas onto government agendas. It presented a window of opportunity for the transfer of policy alternatives generated in other political systems (Wolman, 1992: 42–3). Over the past five years, the Urban Institute has provided technical advice on, and funded a study of the privatisation of housing in Hungary (Urban Institute, 1991: 24). The Reason Foundation has provided advice and assistance to business leaders in the former Yugoslavia. The ASI has studied the potential for privatisation in Eastern Europe (Butler, 1992). Heritage opened a branch office in Moscow to advise Boris Yeltsin on economic reform. A PERC senior associate advised the Bulgarian government on the privatisation of farmland (*PERC Reports*, May, 1991: 2). In September 1990, the Cato Institute organised a conference in Moscow on the Soviet transition process, which also addressed privatisation.

In 1991, the Carnegie Council on Ethics and International Affairs initiated an international privatisation project conducted through luncheon seminars as well as more private off-the-record dinners. In the main, the American discussants outline the potential for privatisation in the USA and the obstacles that persist. Most European speakers have been of the view that the crumbling command economies require privatisation on their path to democracy (Doherty, 1991; Pomeroy, 1991; Reimnitz, 1992). Some warn that privatisation in former communist societies was not comparable to experience in Western industrialised nations. In Britain, privatisation did not result in massive unemployment but this is likely in Eastern Europe. The current world-wide capital shortage also means that these countries are competing for scarce funds. Weak or emergent legal systems combined with underdeveloped accounting practices and management skills compound the difficulties in the transition from communism to capitalism. Consequently, the privatisation process is unlikely to be smooth despite a high degree of political will in these countries (Bell, 1991). The published transcripts of the dinner speeches are not very informative. Instead, the value of the project lies in the way the Carnegie Council acts as a research broker and draws in overseas speakers and matches them with an audience of business leaders, government officials and media figures. The project allows Russian or Eastern European speakers to declare their need for assistance and the opportunities for foreign investment to a select group of high powered New York business people. They, in turn, have the chance to ask specific business questions about the repatriation of profits and rules regarding foreign ownership of land in an informal context. Having established personal contact with Russian government representatives, the German Treuhand representative or Czech politicians, future business negotiations may be facilitated.

Research brokerage and the transmission of knowledge also

occurs among locally based policy communities. The Commonwealth Foundation established the Pennsylvania Privatization Council, the 'state's only clearing-house of expertise on the subject' (Commonwealth Foundation, n.d.: 7). The Council is a group of policy-makers, academics and business people who seek to educate and provide advice for officials and the media on the merits of privatisation (*The Bottom Line*, June 1991: 1). Likewise, the Reason Foundation opened a Privatisation Center as a clearing-house of information with a privatisation database and a 'hotline' open to anyone with questions about privatisation. In its journal, *Intellectual Ammunition*, Heartland published brief notes on privatisation research produced in other institutes and also convened conferences on privatisation for county and municipal government officials.

Think-tanks are by no means the only organisations involved in the export of the idea. Privatisation is also being marketed by banks as well as law and consultancy firms like Price Waterhouse (see Wright, 1994; Towle, 1994). These companies are selling their regulatory and legal expertise for the implementation of privatisation, whereas think-tanks are more often involved in a prior process of discourse structuration and getting such a policy accepted and onto policy agendas. Think-tanks are less likely to be involved in the detailed technical issues of policy design and implementation. Nevertheless, the activities of different groups and actors reinforce the dynamic for privatisation.

Think Tanks and Privatisation

Not all advocates of privatisation share the same commitment to markets and competition as do many scholars in the free market institutes. In these institutes, the public choice perspective is often evident as a set of underlying principles and causal explanation of the growth of government. Similarly, economic theories of regulation provide explanations for the problems of regulated industries (Tullock, *et al.*, 1983). Austrian–Hayekian analyses were a source of inspiration for those promoting the superiority of markets and competition (Shenoy, 1987). Monetarists and supply siders also provided input to the debate. These theoretical themes are often conflated and described as 'free market economic thought', the 'economic rationalist agenda' or as 'New Right thinking'. It is not possible to identify a distinct theory that informs this epistemic-like community. While a policy project is evident – privatisation – it was advocated by various experts and economists for different reasons. These overlapping themes allowed Terry Moe (1987) to talk of a

'Privatization Movement'. Similar to the solidarity of epistemic communities, this movement was unwilling to challenge its own orthodoxy in the pursuit of its cause.

> As long as the premises of privatization do not extend beyond the relatively narrow confines of the public choice and free market paradigm and are not challenged or modified by significant issues of public law, then its advocates admit to few recognizable limits to the efficacy of privatization (Moe, 1987: 458).

There are disagreements within this community. For example, Cento Veljanovski (1987a: 2), a former Research and Editorial Director at IEA, described the ASI's approach to privatisation as 'euphoric' and uncritical. There were also differences over methods of privatisation. The ASI and CPS have proposed two different schemes for the privatisation of British Rail (see Redwood, 1988, and Irvine, 1987 respectively). There is, however, broad agreement between the two on the need for privatisation. Think-tank scholars, academics and other free market intellectuals usually presented a united front against those favouring government ownership and regulation. They diffused policy relevant knowledge that was broadly consensual. These advocates also forged alliances or built coalitions with other groups interested in privatisation but who did not necessarily subscribe to their causal vision. For example, most executives and officials of municipal and state governments in America were not driven by consensual knowledge to seek out privatisation experts for advice. Rather, fiscal pressures generated a pragmatic interest in privatisation. Unable to sustain increasing costs, and uncertain as to how to maintain services, these officials were more open to new ideas. Their adoption of contracting-out indicates bandwagoning not learning.

Think-tanks, along with other organisations and individuals, facilitated the international spread of privatisation ideas. However, the adoption of privatisation policies around the world occurred 'because domestic groups and state officials found their own reasons to pursue them' (Ikenberry, 1990: 107). Inflationary conditions and slower economic growth in industrialised countries caused many political actors to reassess their interests and beliefs. Shifts in public opinion regarding welfare expenditure and tax increases aided the election of conservative parties. Changes of attitude also took place within parties. Once, the state-owned enterprises in Britain were political assets. As productivity suffered, labour disputes intensified and subsidies increased, they became a liability. The 'adoption of new market-minded policies like privatization served party interests in distancing themselves from earlier policies now widely viewed as failures' (Starr, 1990: 37). The waning influence of the Keynesian policy paradigm and economic disorder paved the way for policy experimentation.

Policy change cannot be explained simply by the dominance of free market ideas. Cento Veljanovski argues that the IEA had little input into the Conservative government's privatisation programme and that IEA schemes such as education vouchers and pricing social services failed to move from an intellectual proposition to a policy position. Privatisation in Britain was undertaken *not* because the Conservative Party found it an intellectually coherent idea or because Thatcher was an ideologue, but because privatisation was the best way to achieve the government's objective of reducing state intervention in the economy in response to the pressure of vested interest. Think-tanks did not have great influence over the Conservative Party but simply provided the 'intellectual backdrop' (Veljanovski, 1987a: 25). Similarly, in her study of contracting-out in Britain, Kate Ascher identifies three primary sets of actors – contractors, New Right 'ideologists' and Conservative Party members. The private sector contractors and trade associations played the prime role in lobbying for contracting-out and used the ASI, as one of the most active think-tanks supporting government privatisation policy, to assist in expressing their grievances (1987: 4). The ASI was significant because its 'regular radical publications on the virtues of free enterprise gave the contractor's campaign intellectual credentials' (1987: 50). The ASI not only provided 'moral support' to the contractors, it 'engaged' Conservative Party members as protagonists in the debate.⁴ However, the ASI was not the initiator of the policy of competitive tendering, but became supportive of it in response to the needs of local authorities which put it on the agenda. In other words, the ASI publications were evidence of the direction of government thinking, not a substitute for it. In these two perspectives, think-tanks acted in conjunction with interests. They provided academic legitimacy and gave privatisation further impetus through means peculiar to think-tanks: research, publication and advocacy.

Yet, the role of think-tanks in the privatisation debate was more complicated than simply servicing the information requirements of political parties and vested interests. These organisations built links with the business, media, public interest groups and trade unions to influence broader thinking. Think-tanks also developed policy alternatives, independently of interests, which were advocated years before a short-run opportunity to press their ideas appeared on the agenda. The adoption of privatisation policies was shaped and bolstered by the arguments put forward by intellectuals and scholars in think-tanks, universities, the media and elsewhere, who were able to use their networks and contacts with policy-makers to push new ideas into circulation. They undertook an equally important role in diffusing ideas about privatisation internationally and for reasons unrelated to domestic politics, but rooted in the desire of an epistemic-like community to share expertise and propagate consensual knowledge. In the right circumstances, such as Haas' conditions of uncertainty or when problem and political streams couple in Kingdon's model, epistemic communities can exert considerable agenda-setting powers. Although epistemic communities are a source of new ideas and policy innovation, as Richard Rose notes, 'they lack the political authority to impose binding solutions' (1991: 17). Their influence is, accordingly, limited. Nevertheless, their ideas and policy recommendations affect the substance of public policy through research brokerage at critical moments.

NOTES

1. Privatisation is an umbrella term to describe the transfer of responsibility for certain activities from the state to the private sector. This can be achieved through the privatisation of finance (*user*-charges), the privatisation of production (contracting-out), denationalisation (sale of public sector enterprises) or liberalisation (deregulation) (Heald, 1983).
2. See, for example, the articles by Veljanovski (1987b), Dowd (1987) and Sampson (1987) in the 1987 survey on privatisation as well as the six articles in the June 1993 'Privatisation special' of *Economic Affairs*.
3. This is not to suggest that the privatisation issue has been ignored. Privatisation is addressed in the PSI's journal, *Policy Studies*, and IFS's, *Fiscal Studies*, just as individual PSI and IFS scholars have written about privatisation.
4. The contractors' campaign for the private provision of such services as catering, laundry and security in the NHS and competitive tendering in general was 'considerably strengthened' by two ASI publications by Michael Forsyth (1982 and 1980), *Reservicing Health* and *Reservicing Britain* respectively (Ascher, 1987: 37).

12   The Foreign Policy Club

Foreign policy think-tanks aspire to inform foreign policy making and some have been part of the dynamic of change and internationalisation in the international sphere. In their evolving research agendas, foreign policy research institutes are an important barometer and dynamic of the changing nature of international relations over time. Policy institute research interests have evolved as new issues and problems emerged in the international system. But they not only react to new issues. They also play a strategic role in conceptualising change. Furthermore, a small number of institutes, sometimes in conjunction with an epistemic community, have had substantial impact on foreign policy processes. For the majority of institutes, however, there are limits on influence.[1]

The Evolution of Relevance

Prior to the First World War there were few organisations through which individuals could discuss foreign affairs. The absence of fora for discussion was not unusual since very few people outside those directly concerned with foreign affairs required such specialised information. However, increasing interdependence brought about by trade and technological advances along with the crises of war, regional instability and ethnic or nationalistic tensions, generated a new interest in international affairs. Domestically, wider literacy, trends towards democratisation and pressure for participation from a growing and educated middle class impelled reform-minded efforts to open up the foreign policy-making process – not to the public but to an educated and interested élite – via private policy institutes. Characteristically, these institutes were idealistic and founded by figures imbued by a strong sense of moral duty and mission to preserve peace though educational activities. In the period after the First World War, E. H. Carr noted that 'the passionate desire to prevent war determined the whole initial course and direction' of studies conducted by private citizens in institutes. 'Like other infant sciences', he said, 'the science of international politics has been markedly and frankly utopian' (quoted in Carnegie Council, 1989: 7). Stephen King-Hall, a former officer of Chatham House in the 1920–30s, captured the ethos of these organisations in this era with his comment that 'No progress will or can be made so long as that aspect of human relations known as "foreign affairs" remains largely in an atmosphere of prejudice and sentiment' (1937: 3). Reasoned argument and greater democratic input, it was thought, would raise the standard of public debate and help prevent some of the mistakes of the past.

Both the Carnegie Endowment of International Peace and the Carnegie Council for International Ethics were established with the idealistic task of searching for world peace and were strongly Protestant in character. The Carnegie Council, for example, pioneered concern about minority and human rights in the 1920s, denounced German concentration camps – while the State Department denied allegations of their existence – during the Second World War, and has generally engaged in energetic criticism of US foreign policy throughout its existence. The Twentieth Century Fund sponsored peace studies such as research on economic boycotts in the 1920s (Berle, 1986: 21). A number of institutes were established following the Versailles Peace Conference by discontented participants and observers to the negotiations who feared a reversion to the closed, élite and secretive style of diplomacy and foreign policy making that was evident before 1914. The two most well-known bodies are the Council on Foreign Relations and the Royal Institute for International Affairs (RIIA).[2] Members of the German delegation to Versailles also established a body in Hamburg, the Institut für Auswärtige Politik, which was disbanded in the 1930s. There was some talk of forming an international federation of institutes. However, the difficulties of international communication and travel, compounded by the tensions within Europe created by the treaty settlement defeated this optimistic attempt to promote co-operation via scholarship and discussion in private bodies. Instead of the cumbersome international branch structure associated with the Round Table, national bodies were created. Institutes emerged as state-centric entities. The structure of the international system and nature of decision-making impelled institutes to direct their analysis at a nation-state level.

Not surprisingly, the intention to establish an independent foreign policy institute in London was viewed in some quarters of the British government as an attempt to build a rival civil service. Yet, by the mid-1920s, the RIIA was being criticised as a vehicle for foreign propaganda. However, the more frequent complaint was that its connections with parliamentarians and members of the civil service gave it some kind of semi-official status (Wallace, 1990: 76). The most pronounced period of collaboration with government was the 'wartime mobilisation' of Chatham House. With the aid of a government grant, the RIIA established the Foreign Research and Press Service in Oxford in 1939 under the guidance of Arnold Toynbee, the first Director of Studies at RIIA. In 1943, the Service was transformed into the Foreign Office Research Department (FORD) whilst still under Toynbee's direction. Its contribution to the war effort was 'the provision of raw material in the form of historical background studies and surveys of factors that might come to play a part in the future' (Thorne, 1978: 9). FORD played a research brokerage role that was formalised in the exceptional circumstances surrounding the war. With the establishment of this official link, Toynbee was to have considerable influence later in shaping FCO perceptions of many Middle Eastern issues. The influence of Chatham House scholarship was magnified as it was virtually the only centre in the English speaking world, up until the 1960s, to systematically assess Middle Eastern affairs. It led one critic, Elie Kedourie, to portray the RIIA as an informal branch of the Foreign Office which exhibits 'assumptions, attitudes, and a whole intellectual style which made it possible to speak of the Chatham House version' of Middle Eastern foreign policy (1984: 351).

The dividing line between Chatham House and the official world was also blurred regarding RIIA's relations with the Institute of Pacific Relations. The RIIA acted as the UK office of the IPR. Between 1941 and 1945, the IPR acquired some significance as a forum for debating Allied war aims in Asia. Foreign Office attention was drawn to the strong anti-colonial attitudes expressed in this group. The Conferences were deemed important as they 'were attended by officials from both sides of the Atlantic who, under their conference guise of private citizens, felt able to address one another with a forthrightness not usually indulged in within the confines of formal diplomacy' (Thorne, 1978: 17). Through the RIIA, the Foreign Office sought to counterbalance Chinese and Sino-American voices at two North American IPR conferences in 1942 and 1945. Funding for RIIA delegations to both conferences was made available from government coffers. Along with the finances, however, there were suggestions within Whitehall that the delegates be given guidance. In the final event, it was 'accepted' that it was appropriate only that the Foreign Office give 'informal' advice to one member of the first delegation, Lord Hailey, 'leaving him to keep the delegation more or less within bounds' (Thorne, 1978: 23).

There have been only a few *recorded* instances where the Foreign Office pressured Chatham House affairs and encountered an assertion of independence. In 1938, the Foreign Office tried to persuade Toynbee to delay publishing Elizabeth Wiskeman's book, *Czechs and Germans*, until after the Sudeten crisis had been resolved. Christopher Thorne (1978: 2) notes, however, that although Toynbee did not succumb, he 'corrected' its pro-Czech bias. In 1978, Ministry of Defence officials expressed disapproval of the publication of a paper by Ian Smart called *Beyond Polaris*, as 'sensitive' domestically and internationally (Wallace, 1990: 76). In specific instances, the RIIA has been protective of its independence and its role of providing a podium and outlet for controversial speakers and authors.

Notwithstanding a few difficulties, the RIIA has maintained a strong relationship with the FCO for several decades. FCO personnel regularly attend lunchtime seminars or conferences. The FCO is a corporate member of the RIIA. It contributes approximately £50,000 of the Institute's research project income of approximately £1 million (Dickie, 1992: 299). Yet, the level of government funding has declined significantly since the Thatcher government's regime of financial restraint. Chatham House often responds to requests from Downing Street to organise round table discussions among academic and political figures such as has occurred, in the past, with East Germans, the Soviets and the Yugoslavs (Dickie, 1992: 298–99). More prominently, Chatham House hosted Prime Minister John Major's EC Presidency Conference in August 1992. While it undertook all the organisation, the RIIA had little input into the selection of speakers. A less successful arrangement resulted when the Department of Trade and Industry (DTI) commissioned a RIIA study which enmeshed the Institute in internal bureaucratic battles between protectionists and free traders in the DTI (Hill, 1994: 18). In the eyes of some, including a few RIIA staff, these forms of interaction compromise the academic integrity of the RIIA. Particularly so when the Foreign Office has the opportunity to vet RIIA papers prior to publication. Vetting usually occurs through the study group system whereby 'All manuscripts submitted for publication have to pass the scrutiny of specialists from relevant government departments, the academic world, the business community and the media' (Spence, 1992).

The Second World War also drew the Council on Foreign Relations into policy-making circles (Parmar, 1995). At the outbreak of war in Europe in 1939, the Council approached the Roosevelt administration to conduct, on behalf of the State Department, an investigation into the impact of the war and subsequent peace on US interests (Kraft, 1958: 67–68). The State Department lacked the necessary funds and personnel to conduct such investigations while Congress was cautious of action that hinted at US intervention. With financial assistance from the Rockefeller Foundation, the CFR established four separate planning groups: i) Security and Armaments; ii) Economic and Financial; iii) Political; and iv) Territorial. A fifth group, created in 1941, considered the problems of exiled governments. Upon US entry into the war, the administration created an Advisory Committee on Post-war Foreign Policy to manage the CFR's research agenda for the War and Peace Programme. Each week the study groups would meet in New York for discussion, after which the research secretary of each group would travel to Washington to report to the Advisory Committee and for further advice and instruction (Silk and Silk, 1980: 198).

The CFR study groups rejected the principle of a 'self contained' American economy (Berman, 1983: 44). In particular, the CFR served to heighten awareness within policy-making circles that the USA was increasingly dependent on imported raw resources and could not afford to ignore unfriendly powers closing off access. Many of the ideas that shaped US foreign policy and the post-Second World War international order were discussed in the CFR. For example, Harry Dexter White's formulation of the plan for the International Monetary Fund. A few members of the Economic and Financial study group were either senior US Treasury officials like White or well known to him and Henry Morganthau who was then Secretary of Treasury (Ikenberry, 1992: 301). As a venue for informal discussions with British economists, the CFR group allowed the planners to discover and explore many points of agreement in their thinking. Later, other study groups were also important in establishing a consensus on US geo-political and economic interests in Southeast Asia that subsequently provided a rationale for US involvement in Vietnam (Silk and Silk, 1980: 203; Domhoff, 1983: 87). Twelve of the fourteen members of President Johnson's Senior Advisory Group on Vietnam – the so-called 'wise men' – were CFR members or leaders (Shoup, 1977: 26). However, the policy failures of the Vietnam war destroyed consensus thinking in the Council, a deterioration that was accelerated as its élite character was diluted in the 1970s by efforts to incorporate a wider cross-section of society among its membership. Today, the Council plays a more modest role as an 'agenda defining institution' which attempts 'to make a difference at the margin by asking some key questions' (Peterson in Mandelstam, 1989: 3).

From the 1920s to the early 1940s the CFR and RIIA were formed around an influential internationalist epistemic community. It was a distinctive community given the strong nationalist sentiments and isolationist tendencies prior to the Second World War. Originally, the CFR was unique in America. As a former Secretary of Commerce has stated, 'a handful of people in the Administration, who also happened to be Council members, formed a fraternity of sorts and made decisions' (Peterson quoted in Mandelstam, 1989: 3). The CFR was an innovation, established by a community which wished to see the US adopt an anti-isolationist global role. This common policy project was pursued in more substantive and detailed form through specific study groups which provided the shared causal beliefs and professional policy judgements. It was a community that subsequently found access and entrée into formal decision-making arenas where it was able to inform and influence others. The onset of the Second World War, the crumbling of Britain as a world power and the decay of other colonial empires produced considerable uncertainty about US foreign policy interests. It presented a window of opportunity for those associated with the Council. The expertise within the CFR was drawn upon not solely because of the skill and knowledge of its members and study groups but also because the Council was a well-connected, establishment body. The RIIA under Toynbee's influence, and the general pro-Arab stance prevalent in the Foreign Office at the time, also suggest a strong consensus indicative of a community. Chatham House scholarship was a key component in the constellation of forces residing close to the state and able to inform the causal vision that shaped policy.

The consensus, internationalist and establishment world view of this group has decayed. Views on foreign affairs have become more diverse and complex, suggesting that, although an epistemic community did exist, it was diluted or dissolved by competing paradigms as the number of participants in the study and practice of international relations increased. The CFR and RIIA developed more diverse interests and with an increasingly academic character they became habit-driven actors of the kind outlined in earlier chapters. In the first two decades of their existence, however, these institutes were visionary and innovative. Their establishment was a creative act and

involved learning on the part of founders who were responding to
the trauma of the First World War and what they perceived as a lack
of understanding about international affairs among decision-makers.
Yet, continued innovation is difficult if a think-tank has an established
reputation and route of bureaucratic influence, where there is
minimal competition with other institutes and where financial
security reinforces conservative behaviour. Institutes can become
settled and predictable. The RIIA, for example, has been portrayed as
a 'stuffy' and 'effete talking shop' (*Times Higher Education*, 20
November 1992: 150).

The Cold War Tanks

No longer is US foreign policy the preserve of a few educated and
wealthy men. First, it is not as difficult to attain information
regarding foreign policy. Second, more universities teach and
research foreign policy and competing schools of thought have
emerged regarding the appropriate US international role. With the
increasing internationalisation of the US business sector in outlook,
and many more people travelling in contemporary times, more
sources of information about international affairs abound. Third, as
US commitments overseas expanded, with corresponding
bureaucratic expansion, and the increasing role of Congress in the
wake of Vietnam, more organisations addressed foreign affairs
(Fauriol, 1985: 481). Alongside new institutional developments,
there has been an expansion and professionalisation of the élite that
deals with foreign policy (Polsby, 1993).

The idealism of the élite old guard think-tanks was diluted with
the emergence of the Cold War tanks established after the Second
World War. More technical forms of scholarship, such as that
pioneered by RAND, emerged. Idealism was undermined by an
increasing emphasis on realist approaches to foreign policy
accompanied by rationalist methodologies. For example, the
founders of the International Institute of Strategic Studies (IISS) in
Britain, many of them lay church people, expressed similar idealistic
and ethical concerns that characterised the two Carnegie institutes.
However, the founding director, Alister Buchan was much more
imbued with the culture of rationality perpetrated by RAND and was
able to stamp his character and views on the fledgeling institute
(Groom, 1974: 336; Howard, 1989: 12). The evolution of IISS
paralleled a general shift in defence and security debates from
questions on disarmanent to issues of deterrence and arms control.
IISS's research agenda also reflected a closer integration of

scholarship with American counterparts (Hill, 1989: 267–68). Although the idealist debate characteristic of the 1920s to build institutions of lasting peace resurfaced after the Second World War, it was 'nipped in the bud' by Cold War scholars who feared that 'the study of world affairs might again become mired in naive and dangerous utopianism' (Knutsen, 1992: 218).

Many conservative institutes emerged in America. The Hudson Institute was founded by Max Singer and Herman Kahn, and its analytical style is captured in Kahn's famous phrase, 'thinking about the unthinkable'. The Foreign Policy Research Institute (FPRI), in contrast with RAND's air force connection, has more of an army orientation and greater emphasis on 'hands-on warfare' (Abshire, 1982: 84). The Center for Strategic and International Studies (CSIS) is less technically focused than RAND and usually adopts a traditional realist conception of international relations. The Hoover Institution should also be included as a Cold War tank. Although founded in 1919, it operated in its first three decades primarily as an archive and library. Only in the 1950s did it experience a redefinition of purpose, with an elderly Herbert Hoover declaring that it would 'demonstrate the evils of the doctrines of Karl Marx' (Smith, 1991a: 186). The majority of the new think-tanks did not have the close relationship with government that RAND enjoyed, but they remained essential in helping to entrench a new language that framed and constrained policy debate on defence and security.

It is arguable that an epistemic community of civilian security intellectuals operated through a few strategic studies institutes during the Cold War. Emanuel Adler (1992) and Colin Gray, a former think-tank director, argue that a small group of academic strategists in the 1950s constructed an edifice of strategic theory which had profound implications for US policy. Gray describes them as a 'transnational community of strategic analysts...marked by more points of agreement than division' in the development of strategic thought (1970–71: 773–74). In the 1950s there was a vacuum in US government and the military regarding the qualitatively different strategic environment in the post-Second World War era. Civilian strategists filled the void. The group of academics was small but most had links with the RAND Corporation (Lawrence, 1992: 108). The IISS in London was also a 'stamping ground' (Gray, 1970–71: 774). The civilian strategists criticised the prevailing strategic orthodoxies of massive retaliation and advocated limited war. The community shared the belief that nuclear war could not be won and was best avoided by collaboration among the superpowers, forces and tactics to prevent a first strike, and a high threshold of nuclear weapon use. In their professional judgement, arms control was a 'technical path to improved management of conflict' (Gray, 1971a: 116).

The RAND researchers saw strategy as an economic problem. Their assumption of rationality formed the foundation of their internally defined criteria for validating knowledge, and was complemented by realist assumptions about the nature and resolution of conflicts, and by a fear of communism (Adler, 1992: 114). To be part of the strategic scholars community, the acolyte needed proficiency in game theory and in systems analysis. The group at RAND included Herman Kahn, Albert Wohlstetter, Henry Rowen, Alain Enthoven, Charles Hitch, and William Kaufmann.[3] The community was also complemented by realists such as Henry Kissinger who established his early reputation in diplomatic history at the CFR. Other important community members in arms control were based at MIT and Harvard – the so-called Charles River Gang (Adler, 1992). Albert Wohlstetter was one of the first to combine game theory with systems analysis. He produced with two others a major study that criticised the Air Force's strategy of overseas bomber bases which left them vulnerable to enemy attack. The development of the concept of vulnerability and the determination of RAND and Wohlstetter to communicate the results of the study to political and military leaders – in some 92 briefings – contributed to a long-term change in strategic thinking and policy (Smith, 1991a: 121; see also Williams and Palmatier, 1992: 53).

It was not simply the intellectual force of ideas that captured the political imagination but RAND's research brokerage. Furthermore, both President Kennedy and Secretary for Defense, Robert McNamara encouraged the institutionalisation of this source of expertise.

> In effect RAND personnel 'occupied' the Pentagon as the effective personal instrument of a Secretary engaged in sweeping strategic changes. Leading RAND figures ... were coopted to guide the implementation of a more rational mode of defense management and to engage in a sweeping review of general limited war, and counter-insurgency strategies ... Their intellectual dominance in the early 1960s was nearly absolute. Although the Administration might dilute or reject a proposal, the mode of reasoning, the terms employed were those popularized by Kissinger, Wohlstetter, Kahn, Schelling and others (Gray, 1971a: 119).

This community was able to 'occupy' the Pentagon for three reasons. First, the RAND Corporation acted as an *alma mater* for the academic strategists. Second, from its nascence, RAND was linked to the Air Force. Hence, it was provided a route of bureaucratic influence not open to others. Third, nuclear strategy was an area in need of urgent government attention but which was considered to be out of the realm of expertise of the professional soldier given its highly technical nature and its amenability to quantitative analysis.

RAND's pre-eminence in the study of strategy gradually eroded. The community's power declined with US involvement in the Vietnam War, that is, a regional rather than global entanglement characterised by conventional warfare. Furthermore, the nuclear strategists became insular and their innovativeness dissipated once incorporated into positions of power. They had little time for fundamental reflection, for to be 'wired into a policy process' involved joining a team that demanded 'loyalty, no dysfunctional challenges to the *esprit de corps*, and, above all, agreement of the nature and purpose of the game' (Gray, 1970–71: 783). Preoccupied with implementing their ideas under a congenial defence regime left these theorists vulnerable to challenges from new centres of strategic analysis, such as CSIS, while their dominance of security analysis was undermined by the growth of the academic study of strategy. Re-evaluation of such questions as involvement in Vietnam, technological developments and other policy failures opened spaces for new voices to be heard, to complicate the debate and challenge prevailing orthodoxies. Although RAND no longer operates as one of the key institutions of a strategic analysis epistemic community, it still functions as a prosperous and influential research organisation. But RAND's high profile in the 1950s and 1960s was historically contingent. It nurtured a new school of scholars who were important in developing a 'calculus of war' (Zacher, 1991). The strategists shared: (i) normative beliefs; (ii) causal beliefs and professional judgements; (iii) a common policy enterprise; and (iv) a facility for research brokerage in a time of uncertainty. The role of RAND is a clear example of an institute's ability – given a window of opportunity – to help establish a new agenda in international relations and act as a force of innovation.

The Cold War tanks – RAND, Hudson, CSIS, IISS – have defied obsolescence. They have not lost their rationale for existence with the collapse of communism in the former Soviet Union and eastern European states but have redefined their purpose. First, a number of think-tanks have redirected their efforts to aiding former communist societies in their transition to democracy and the market. During 1990, the Hoover Institution's Foreign Diplomat Training Programme brought young diplomats from former Soviet bloc countries to undertake courses offering Western perspectives on international relations, economics, statecraft and diplomacy. Similarly, some Hoover scholars are conducting research into privatisation and the establishment of legal structures to promote free market entrepreneurialism in Central and Eastern European states. Second, think-tanks have transformed concerns about security, peace and disarmament to other regions of the globe such as the Middle East, or directed research questions towards the foreign and defence policies of the newly formed states. While the economic aspects of security were not overlooked in strategic studies in the past, this dimension has become a stronger component of current research. RAND, for example, initiated in 1988 an International Economic Studies Programme focusing on relationships and interactions between international and domestic policies especially in the areas of international trade, technology, finance and economic development. The dangers of terrorism or smuggling of weapons grade plutonium have also been propelled higher onto research and analysis agendas. Similarly, technological issues such as communications security, cultural factors such as Muslim fundamentalism or ethnic divisions, and resource issues such as energy, have increasingly been incorporated in strategic studies (Abshire, 1982: 95–101). In another response to the end of the Cold War, some institutes have turned inwards and focused on domestic issues. For institutes such as IPS this can be done with relative ease as it always had that domain of interest. With IPS, however, it is equally a reflection of its internal difficulties and loss of direction. At CSIS a broader meaning to the word 'strategy' has been stressed. Traditional political-military concerns are being woven with questions of economic and environmental security as well as American domestic problems.

A Foreign Policy Growth Industry

From the mid-1960s, a number of progressive liberal institutes were established as dissatisfaction with the US global role mounted, with the escalation of hostilities in Vietnam and the increased visibility of third world issues. The Institute for Policy Studies provided an alternative perspective to mainstream thinking on security, foreign policy and development issues and, in addition, developed strengths in the areas of human rights, development and the world economic order (Friedman, 1983). The Center for Defense Information monitored military waste and conducted statistical studies disputing claims of Soviet superiority in the forces of the Warsaw Pact. The Overseas Development Council (ODC) was established to confront the problems of developing countries and US foreign aid responses to these problems (Berman, 1983). It was fashioned after the Overseas Development Institute in London which also addresses development concerns. The founders of these latter two institutes exhibited an idealism of a different kind to that evident before the Second World War. They were concerned to prick Western consciousness of the needs of former colonies, the plight of developing countries and the responsibility to assist of the industrialised world.

Similarly, there is a new generation of strategic studies institutes. The Research Institute for the Study of Conflict and Terrorism (RISCT) and the conservative Institute for European Defence and Strategic Studies (IEDSS) were established in Britain in the 1970s and Saferworld in the 1980s. But growth is especially noticeable in Washington DC. The Henry Stimson Center concentrates on arms control and international security in areas where policy, technology and politics intersect. The conservative Center for Security Policy has a zealous commitment to a strong national security posture. Another security and international affairs think-tank, the National Institute for Public Policy, was established by Colin Gray – a 'nuclear hard-liner' (Easterbrook, 1986). Where the Center for Security Policy adopts a conservative formula to assess international events and foreign policy, both the National Institute and the Stimson Center are more inquiring and analytical. The Institute for Defense and Disarmament Studies (IDDS) also has a commitment to rigorous research but can be characterised as progressive. Although occurring later than the growth experienced in the USA, British entry to the European Community provides yet another forum for think-tank activity and has prompted the establishment of bodies such as IEDSS and European Policy Forum (EPF).

By the 1980s the think-tank form was markedly different from the old guard institutes like the CFR, Brookings or RIIA. The conservative Institute for Foreign Policy Analysis (IFPA) and the similarly conservative but more academic Monterey Institute of International Studies are far less idealistic and much more professional in tone than those established early this century. Equally important, as the foreign policy and defence policy-making fields became more complex, contested and segmented into specialised sub-fields, so too the think-tank industry reflected these developments in both countries. Many new think-tanks are focused on single issue concerns such as the regional studies institutes. Although they spring from different intellectual and philosophical assumptions, the progressive Center for International Policy (CIP), the Council of Hemispheric Affairs (COHA) and the Washington Institute for Near East Policy, in Washington DC, address the nature of US involvement in specific regions of the world. The former two address US involvement in Latin and Central America (and COHA also addresses Canada), while the latter seeks to 'advance a balanced and realistic understanding of US national interests' in the Middle East and is regarded as pro-Israeli.

Environmental pollution and degradation generally know no boundaries and, in accordance, environmental institutes have often developed a global focus of research although they speak primarily to national audiences. Thus, while a body like the World Resources Institute holds most of its briefings, seminars and conferences in the USA, it also provides technical assistance, policy analysis and other services for developing countries and non-governmental organisations (WRI, 1991: 3). WRI also maintains links with International Institute for Environment and Development (IIED) based in London. The World Watch Institute – significant for its annual *State of the World* which catalogues the destruction of the world's resources – is global in its research orientation. By contrast, the Institute for European Environmental Policy (IEEP) is regionally oriented. Trans-border problems of pollution and environmental crisis, such as ozone depletion, and pandemic diseases such as AIDS diminish the utility of traditional concepts of national boundaries and sovereignty. These problems require co-operation, joint action and education. Environmental institutes often regard the world rather than the state as their policy domain and are competent in the analysis of fuzzy border problems. Indeed, they proclaim the inadequacy of treating such problems on a state by state basis although recognising the limits imposed on action by the state system.

Think-tanks have played an important role in promoting understanding of economic globalisation at a number of levels. The search for national economic welfare in an increasingly volatile global economy has given impetus to the development of economic and trade policy institutes in the USA such as the free trade oriented Institute for International Economics, the neo-protectionist Economic Strategy Institute which criticises the post-Second World War foreign policy-making establishment for 'fighting communism over cultivating economic power' (Prestowitz, *et al.*, 1991: xvii), and the

Economic Policy Institute which challenges the free trade orthodoxy.

The economic and the environmental research institutes exhibit some of the qualities of epistemic-like communities. In organisations such as the IIE and the Trade Policy Research Centre it is not difficult to identify: (i) a broadly shared set of normative and principled beliefs in the virtues of free trade and open markets; (ii) an internalised and self-validating set of causal and methodological principles arising from the canons of rational individualism that drive modern liberal economics; (iii) a common policy goal of a more rational and efficient management of the international economic order – especially in the commitment to multilateralism; and (iv) a network of formal, semi formal and informal institutions that, in a period characterised by uncertainty, provide a framework within which to broker a set of policy options drawn from their normative beliefs and amenable to their causal and explanatory principles.

The IIE was established in the US at a fortuitous time. International economic questions were ascending on the foreign policy agenda and while international political economy is still regarded as 'low diplomacy', economic issues are increasingly *linked* with foreign policy. The IIE describes itself as a 'central node in the community of those engaged in the global inquiry into international economic issues' (IIE, 1991). According to Thomas Bayard (interview), they represent a 'fairly tight' community of a relatively small number of people interested in foreign economic policy including US Treasury and Finance people, a small subset of academics who have a policy interest, the specialised press, and a nebulous group of trade representatives, former public servants, diplomats, consultants and analysts of large corporations who have an interest in the field. IIE's nodal function is that of research brokerage. The IIE is particularly effective in this role as the institute has a concentration of international economists not evident in other institutes. A number of like-minded experts work together in the Institute, complementing the tighter or more cohesive communities that may evolve around specific issues such as GATT and the Uruguay Round, US–Japan relations or global energy markets, which extend in networks beyond the institute. While the IIE occupies a niche by focusing on international political economy, it is not issue-specific in the sense that Peter Haas describes an epistemic community. None the less, a particular view of the world – one that favours open world markets – permeates the majority of IIE research and recommendations.

Many environmental and development studies institutes have a common commitment to aid efforts towards sustainable development. Within the broad church of sustainable development, however, reside specialists ranging from deep ecologists through to free market environmentalists – groups with vastly different political philosophies and strategies. While environmental institutes share principled beliefs, that is, the need for environmental protection and conservation, they do not share causal beliefs and, accordingly, have more in common with social movements and interest groups than an epistemic community. Yet, free market environmentalists potentially represent an epistemic community with one organisational manifestation in think-tanks such as Cato, PERC and the Pacific Institute in the USA and the IEA in Britain. Their causal beliefs are informed by classical liberal thought and free market precepts derived from neo-classical economics. Their shared tenets of validity arise from the rational actor model and methodological individualism. Their consensual knowledge is that while environmental regulation may be motivated for the public good, it has worsened or not alleviated environmental problems. Accordingly, the policy projects of free market environmentalists include ascribing property rights to pollution and privatising national parks on the assumption that private ownership will lead to better environmental management and circumvent the phenomenon known as the 'tragedy of the commons'. The AIDS pandemic is also a problem of considerable uncertainty requiring the research and advice of scientists and medical experts. Combating the pandemic has become entwined with development questions in Africa and Asia. The Panos Institute (1991: 15–16) is involved in an emerging transnational community which hopes to reduce the rate of infection and promote learning among governments in developing countries about prevention and the social and economic effects of its spread.

In contemporary circumstances, it is less likely that an epistemic community can be as readily identified with an institute or set of institutes comparable to the CFR and RIIA in their early history. The development and articulation of professional judgements on foreign policy questions and the establishment of common notions of validity are constructed by individuals, found in a number of different kinds of organisations, and correspond to the growth of international organisations. Nevertheless, research institutes remain useful organisations to promote a community's policy enterprise prior to gaining access to the political domain as a base from which to educate, transform and force the pace of change in establishing new agenda issues domestically and in international relations.

From Relevance to Influence

The new institutes have not monopolised the new fields of study. Older institutes readily incorporate new research agendas. The research agenda of the Council on Foreign Relations in the last decade has given special consideration to questions of global economic management. Pacific Forum (which merged with CSIS in 1989) recently created the Ocean Policy Institute to address ocean use and resource management. The role of the think-tank has not been static. The foreign policy institutes not only mirror but are part of the changing international order. The preoccupations of these institutes have widened from the 'high politics' of diplomacy and strategy to the 'low politics' of trade, international economic interdependence and environmental protection. At the same time, the expansion of the international agenda has meant that strategic studies institutes operate in a different network from regional or environmental institutes. The potential for policy influence is accordingly fragmented. Institutes are not likely to have a pervasive influence enjoyed by generalist foreign policy institutes such as the CFR or RIIA during the inter-war years and immediately after when foreign policy élites remained small. Strategic studies institutes interact with ministries of defence, arms suppliers, specialist journals and staff colleges, whereas the environmental institutes interact with a different set of actors such as emerging ministries of environment, international organisations devoted to conservation, scientific agencies, environmental lobbies and the environmental press. Just as foreign policy has become more complex in a post-Cold War era, so too the think-tank industry has diversified, specialised and become transnational in order to remain relevant. But the concern with relevance does not equate with influence.

RAND's early work on game theory and nuclear deterrence did play a significant role in the calculations of officials as they dealt with the evolving arms race. But such long-term impact on the perception of policy problems would appear to be rare. Reasons for the policy decisions of the American foreign policy and national security establishment are more likely to be found in its own responses to evolving circumstances rather than the input of think-tanks. Although foreign policy think-tanks keep abreast of policy developments and have developed new strategies of communication to cope with the immediacy of foreign policy developments, they face a major impediment. This is the necessity for secrecy in foreign policy and strategy. Consultation is limited as it takes months to 'vet' someone before they have access to secret information. In Britain the Official Secrets Act is a barrier to communication, and for civil servants, 'an excuse for non-disclosure' (Webb, 1994b: 89). Nevertheless, the US State Department and the Foreign and Commonwealth Office and DTI consider a number of think-tanks to be influential groups that can be informally used to further official objectives. There is a two-way flow where government departments acquire new ideas and information from think-tanks whilst using them to broadcast official policy thinking to opinion leaders.

Concentrating on the larger, older and best known think-tanks like CFR, IPR, RIIA and Brookings conveys a distorted image of foreign policy think-tanks. The policy successes of a very small number of institutes are given undue weight. It obscures the role and activities of bodies such as FPRI, IFPA and the Atlantic Council in the USA, and IIED, RISCT and EPF in Britain. Undoubtedly some institutes are more esteemed than others. However, the power of bodies such as the CFR or Chatham House is not monolithic. Internally, these are diverse organisations which encompass different and often contradictory viewpoints. Also, their indirect incorporation into policy-making is usually time-bound and issue specific. Furthermore, it is not as feasible in contemporary circumstances for a new institute to have the same kind of impact that was once wielded by the older, wealthier general policy institutes. With specialisation and the competition from increasing numbers of foreign policy think-tanks, in addition to other stronger sources of foreign policy advice, the influence of one organisation is not only likely to be more diffuse but also limited to a narrower policy domain.

This does not mean that smaller or lesser known institutes are of no consequence. They analyse and articulate policy positions, and act as a 'sounding board for new ideas' for policy-makers. Furthermore, they provide services. The Carnegie Council, for example, has participated in the Ethics Training Round Table, an inter-agency initiative of the US federal government designed to offer ethics training to mid-level government employees involved in international affairs. Think-tanks also organise conferences, study groups and establish networks in which officials from a number of governments can participate under the convenient and polite fiction that they are acting in a private capacity. These organisations are amenable to, indeed, eager to offer their services as vehicles for, 'second track' or informal diplomacy. For example, it has been suggested that IIE be used to explore ways of including Eastern European countries in

GATT, whereby it would act as the 'honest broker' inviting all interested parties to sit down behind closed doors to address the problem (Goodwin, 1990: 16). Similarly, the International Peace Academy in New York hopes to provide 'a middle ground' where settlement options in international conflicts can be explored 'in an off-the-record setting'. In other words, many think-tanks are willing to take their 'lead' from government departments or agencies and be guided towards activities that are useful.

Informal diplomacy involves playing a facilitating role. Such an activity is all the more useful if the think-tank is a prominent organisation of which foreigners have heard and, more importantly, if it can draw upon a network of distinguished states-people, business leaders, diplomats, military officers, and scholars. For instance, the International Center in Washington DC arranges visiting delegations both to and from the USA of current and former government officials. During a visit from the Vietnamese deputy Prime Minister Phan Van Khai in 1993, the International Center arranged appointments for his delegation with the Secretary of State, Warren Christopher and United Nations Ambassador, Madeleine Albright, among others. Institutes perform a valued service for the State Department in 'staging forums for visiting diplomats whom the department doesn't quite know what to do with...and sometimes conducting semi-sanctioned negotiations that avoid the tortuosities of official government contact' (Easterbrook, 1986: 8). Informal dialogues are also valuable at times when for whatever reason, official dialogues are stalled or official relations strained. At the time of the Beijing Massacre in 1989, RAND was hosting Chinese government visitors in Santa Monica regarding a UN and World Bank project to introduce market-oriented initiatives on Hainan Island. RAND contemplated postponing the project. However, RAND administrators were persuaded by the National Security Council to proceed as RAND was 'viewed as a liberalising influence on China' (Roll, interview). However, not all institutes are of such use. Some, such as the Center for Security Policy are too small and unknown. Governments and bureaucrats also eschew interaction with institutes perceived to be politically hostile or too radical. Institutes espousing unorthodox positions are not ineffectual or hopelessly marginalised but prefer to remain autonomous of government. They resist co-option and consequently, their deference to power is contradictory and incomplete.

NOTES

1. This chapter is a revised version of a co-authored paper that appeared in the *Review of International Studies* (see Higgott and Stone, 1994).
2. First known as the British Institute for International Relations, it received a Royal Charter in 1926. Initially, the American institute faltered as many of the Versailles contingent dispersed to their universities or other positions on their return to the US. In New York, the intended location of the Institute, there already existed a Foreign Policy Association and a Council of Foreign relations, both established in 1918. The US Institute eventually took flesh in 1921, severing its British connection and merging with the CFR (Silk and Silk, 1980: 186).
3. This school of strategy was not the only one at RAND. Bernard Brodie's approach was historical but he gradually became estranged from mainstream defence intellectuals (Lawrence, 1992: 108).

13   Think-tanks and the Study of International Relations

The desire for policy influence is one major aspect of think-tank activity. But many foreign policy institutes hope to add, if only marginally, to the corpus of international relations (IR) and strategic studies literature. There is, however, a tension between sustaining academic legitimacy and speaking to the discipline, on the one hand, and the brokerage function and engagement with policy making that eschews disinterestedness, on the other. The balancing of these two roles differs substantially from one policy institute to another. The following discussion outlines some points of intersection between scholarship and policy.

Some of the older foreign policy think-tanks stimulated the academic development of IR and comparative politics. Prior to the Second World War, there were few academic centres devoted to the study of international affairs. Private bodies were important generators of information and publishers of scholarly studies. The IPR, for example, was a significant sponsor of research in Asian affairs, then a largely undeveloped field of research, and its two main journals, *Pacific Affairs* and *Far Eastern Survey,* were consulted widely. After the Second World War, when university systems expanded, the foreign policy institutes continued to play an important role in the growth of IR and related fields such as strategic studies. As William Olson and John Groom note in their history of the development of IR, 'the central ideas of massive retaliation and graduated deterrence – later flexible response – were set out, stimulated enormously' by the IISS and RAND (1991: 292). Chatham House was a forerunner – through the scholarship of Susan Strange – of international political economy (IPE), at a time when international economists did not engage in dialogue with international relations specialists or political scientists (see Higgott, 1992; also Hill, 1989: 269).

Unlike universities and colleges, the foreign policy institutes are not usually engaged in teaching. There are a few exceptions. RAND operates a Ph.D. degree programme. RISCT in Britain once organised graduate education and training in its specialised field through its research arm based at the University of St Andrews. Association with a university bestows academic credibility on an institute but is not without its difficulties. CSIS was affiliated with Georgetown University in Washington DC but severed the relationship after differences with the University administration regarding fund-raising and academic standards. According to one version of events, the split was the culmination of tensions running back to the late 1960s, when some faculty members and students criticised the CSIS for its conservative bias and tried to get the University to close the Center, believing it to be supported by CIA covert funds (Muscatine, 1986). In another account, the separation has been portrayed as much more amicable and an assertion of CSIS independence (Smith 1993: 138–40). Similarly, there is a stormy relationship between the Hoover Institution and Stanford University, where some faculty members are critical of not only the Institution's conservatism and political influence but also its very presence on the campus (Bethall, 1984).

The publications of leading research institutes are useful not only for academic research but also for teaching. In some instances, institutes seek to aid directly teaching and research in universities. For example, in 1990 the Carnegie Council began publishing case-studies on ethics and international affairs to provide curriculum materials for college and university professors. The IIE 1994 publications catalogue is replete with recommendations for classroom texts, 'based on our own staff's teaching experience and especially on the invaluable feedback we receive from professors who use our books in their classrooms'. It is an indication of the high regard in which many institutes are held by academics when books published by think-tanks are used as course materials. The annual publication of Worldwatch, *State of the World 1990*, is a good case in point. In the US alone, this book was adopted for use in 1,379 courses through 633 colleges and universities.

Many institutes are not scholarly and do not pretend to contribute to disciplinary development. For example, Earth Resources Research in London generally produces technical policy reports for local government, international agencies or environmental organisations such as Greenpeace. Notwithstanding the technical orientation of the institute, a number of ERR researchers have their own academic networks extending into universities and have contributed to scholarly collections, as well as books produced by RIIA, on an individual basis. The research carried out by RIIA, Brookings, AEI, CFR and RAND is in some ways analogous to that undertaken in universities. However, think-tanks are arguably more eclectic in their approach to the study of international relations. A frequent argument of think-tank executives is that they are not as narrowly academic as the universities or divorced from the needs of policy-makers (Indyk, interview). Some characterised the academic world as theoretical whereas think-tank research is applied (Roll, interview), or suggested that universities are less equipped for integrative or team work that traverses disciplines. The study of IR and strategy in the foreign policy institutes is different from the academic development of international relations. Independent research institutes are not so rigidly bound to the discipline where tenure considerations and peer review produce incentives that steer research towards discipline generated questions rather than policy-driven questions. This difference is reflected in the organisational make-up of foreign policy institutes and the resources at their disposal.

Study Groups

The study group method of research, analysis and discussion was a key feature of the old guard institutes such as CFR, RIIA, IPR and the Carnegie Council. From the outset, the CFR's principal mode of operation was the dinner forum at which members convened to listen to a speaker. There were also smaller discussion groups, complemented by study groups, both of which brought into contact business knowledge, government policy-makers and scholars. Usually, the study group contributed to the production of a book. Probably the best known is Henry Kissinger's *Nuclear Weapons and Foreign Policy,* a seminal critique of massive retaliation. At Chatham House study groups were originally formed on the principle that 'members with an expert interest in any aspect of world affairs could and should form a group to keep their knowledge up to date', although the Council of the RIIA gradually established authority for selecting the subjects for study (Morgan, 1979: 243). One historian of the RIIA, Roger Morgan, argues they 'contributed substantially to the contemporary debate, both in their published form and through the mutual enlightenment of members of the groups' (1979: 246). Another, Stephen King-Hall (1937: 37) describes the study group method more grandly as 'innovative', acting as 'unofficial Royal Commissions'. In the post-Second World War period, however, the study group method of research was seriously questioned within the

Institute. The RIIA Planning Committee argued that there was a 'tendency to compromise' which was 'unsatisfactory as a method of research' (quoted in Morgan, 1979: 247).

The study group method of analysis and discussion may well have been innovative in the 1920s and 1930s when foreign policy was a relatively exclusive activity. Knowledge was limited and experts and foreign policy élites were sufficiently few to sit down together to converse. The approach was a feature of the era. Fewer books were published and audiences were not fragmented as they are today. Although study groups remain an important component of RIIA activities, particularly as they are an effective device for drawing in government officials and corporate and financial leaders, the production of individually authored books and monographs at RIIA, and elsewhere, is more a feature of the post-Second World War era. To an extent, the study group method has been adapted to contemporary circumstances by bodies such as the Atlantic Council and CSIS in the form of closed Congressional Study Groups. This practice was re-instituted at CSIS, partly as a consequence of the 'breakdown of the foreign policy and defense consensus following Vietnam and Watergate, the frequent stalemates between the President and Congress, and the search for new ideas around which to build a new consensus' (Abshire, 1982: 101). At CSIS the groups serve as educational and policy seminars providing members of Congress with a forum for discussion with CSIS experts. Members 'often use their project's findings as a tool to introduce legislation' (CSIS, 1989: 69). Study groups foster a two-way dialogue by bringing politicians, business people and bureaucrats in contact with academics and experts in a private and informal domain. Any reports or publications which emerge usually have the names of Senators or members listed. Their imprimatur not only gives the report political credibility but also eases its circulation within policy-making circles. For the new and smaller institutes without a critical mass of scholars, such as the Henry Stimson Center, study groups conducted on a regular or an *ad hoc* basis are a means not only to extend the public profile of the institute but to draw in external sources of expertise.

Study groups or more informal arrangements to encourage discussion are an important element of the *modus operandi* of think-tanks. They are the means to draw in people of different professions. The academic is not privileged in such a setting. Instead the purpose is to facilitate the exchange of ideas between academics and bureaucrats, military officers and senior journalists, diplomats and campaigners, business leaders and politicians.

Public Scholarship and the Policy Intellectuals

Think-tank scholars are often academics. However, they are distinguishable from the majority of university researchers by their interest in policy. The unfortunate term 'action intellectual' signifies the difference (Van Dyne, 1985; Abshire, 1982). Many academics sneer at these policy intellectuals who have deserted the academy, if only temporarily. Yet, a sojourn in a research institute usually frees academics from teaching to concentrate on research and policy related questions. Except in the most academic institutes, researchers are not disinterested but directly address foreign policy and try to play the entrepreneur. A research institute consciously combining scholarship with practice is the IPS. In the words of one fellow, Arthur Waskow, '... to develop social theory one must be involved in social action and in social experiment' (quoted in Isaac and Isaac, 1983: 112). In this regard, the IPS is distinguishable from older institutes which were less activist, seeking only to inform and educate or, if not, to engage in political activity at a more closed and official level. The IPS seeks a dynamic relationship as both an educational research institute and a political organisation. This was most clear during the Vietnam War when IPS acted as a locus for anti-war scholarship and teach-ins.

In some instances, research institutes are havens for retiring politicians and bureaucrats. Such people are given the time to reflect and write on their government or bureaucratic work and are a significant resource for other scholars associated with the institute. They frequently retain strong links within their past domain of employ and their networks of contacts are useful for acquiring information as well as aiding the circulation of institute research and analysis. The AEI was able to attract former US President Gerald Ford. After his appointment as President Carter's National Security Adviser, Zbigniew Brzezinski accepted a position at CSIS, joining other former political luminaries such as Henry Kissinger and former Secretary of Defense James Schlesinger. Chatham House frequently employs FCO officers on secondment. Such people may not be easily incorporated into universities if they are without academic experience. But the think-tank provides them with some intellectual respectability. In return, these people perform a pivotal role in positioning think-tanks closer to decision-makers. Government occasionally favours giving its senior members the opportunity to write, conduct research and deliver lectures. The State Department's Diplomat in Residence programme is a good example. However, it tends only to send diplomats to well-known bodies such as AEI, Hoover, CSIS, RAND, CFR and the Carnegie Endowment, which serves to further enhance their prestige in the Washington policy environment.

Resources

The resources of institutes have been invaluable aids to scholarship. The Hoover Institution's archives and library (of 53 million items and 1.6 million volumes respectively) constitute one of the world's largest repositories on twentieth century social, economic and political change. Until well after the Second World War, the RIIA was exceptional in the resources that could be placed at the disposal of scholars by its library, the press-cutting service, the Information Departments, as well as its extensive contacts. Today, universities, the bureaucracy and other organisations surpass the resources and capabilities of these institutes, but they remain important as a concentration of expertise and information. The newer institutes cannot boast the facilities or match the reputations of older institutes. But such institutes can represent a readily identifiable source of information and analysis by aggregating a critical mass of expertise or the provision of a specialised service such as databases. For example, the IISS produces the *Military Balance*, a survey of the armed forces throughout the world. With a circulation of approximately 17,000, it is the most influential and authoritative publication of its kind in the world. In another sense, think-tanks are a resource as a facilitator or conduit of academic exchange and knowledge transfer. Academics on sabbatical are frequently to be found based in a policy institute in another state or country. Sabbatical in or secondment to a think-tank provides opportunity to expand contacts and develop networks not just into government but also among previously untapped university circles.

Journals

Journals are central to the identity of a foreign policy institute. The CFR produces *Foreign Affairs* and *Critical Issues*, and Chatham House publishes *International Affairs* and *The World Today*. Since 1970 the Carnegie Endowment has published *Foreign Policy* while the Carnegie Council launched *Ethics and International Affairs* in 1987. IISS is responsible for *Survival* and the CSIS produces the *Washington Quarterly*. Some institutes are either too small or too recently established to have launched a journal. In line with the trend towards specialisation, journals of the new partisan institutes are often specialised, such as, for example, RISCT's quarterly *Terrorism and Political Violence*. These journals are widely recognised as scholarly publications and represent a significant proportion of the general body of foreign policy and international relations journals. On occasion, articles have been seminal and influential, such as the article in *Foreign Affairs* in July 1947 by X (that is, George Kennan), outlining the concept of containment. Some of its most famous contributors include Leon Trotsky, Anthony Eden, Franklin D Roosevelt, W. E. B. DuBois, John Foster Dulles, John F. Kennedy, and Golda Meir, among many others (see Hyland, 1992). *Foreign Affairs* is believed by some to 'reflect official Washington thinking' (Berman, 1983: 47; Kondracke, 1978).

Some of the older institutes hoped to promote the objective and scientific study of international relations through their journals. In doing so, they helped establish the foundations of the international relations discipline. For example, the Carnegie Endowment's *International Conciliation*, now defunct, is described by Olson and Groom as the first professional journal in IR and which applied 'the highest academic standards in its editorial policy' for over half a century. Although the Endowment was created with the political goal of promoting peace, its journal 'created a professional norm...for the discipline that was to emerge after the war' (1991: 48). One of the earliest initiatives of the Carnegie Endowment was to institute, from 1911, the periodic Conferences of Teachers of International Law. The Endowment also distributed books on international relations to numerous US libraries, promoting the development of 'International Relations Clubs' that debated foreign policy questions (Olson and Groom, 1991: 64, 75).

As flagship publications, the standing and quality of journals are scrupulously cultivated through refereeing and editorial care to protect the institute's independent standing. This usually entails participation in the academic peer review process which ties institutes into disciplinary developments. Nevertheless, journals usually reflect the ethos or specialisation of an institute. The focus of *Arms Control Today* of the Arms Control Association (ACA) is self-evident, whereas Heritage's *Policy Review* is conservative in tone. Journals are not equally scholarly. Traditionally, the editors of *Foreign Affairs* have been less focused on disciplinary and theoretical development than educating business, financial and legal élites. By contrast, Chatham House publications were more devoted, initially, to the scientific and objective '*study* of IR along with the study of international affairs *qua* politics' (Olson and Groom, 1991: 107). Even so, the *Atlantic Community Quarterly* of the Atlantic Council or the *Development Policy Review* of the ODI in London are not in the same class as either the CFR or RIIA journals.

Curriculum Support for Schools, Colleges and Universities

A related facet of think-tank scholarly activities is the assistance that many provide to schools and colleges. For example, the FPRI in Philadelphia has been providing classroom material for schoolteachers of history, social studies and foreign languages. Similarly, the Washington based Atlantic Council through its International Education programme seeks to strengthen teaching of post-Second World War international relations in colleges and secondary schools in the USA and Europe. Atlantic Council services include summer institutes for contemporary history teachers and the promotion of curriculum reform as well as the organisation of civic education programmes in conjunction with the Council of Europe for Central and East European educators. This concern to help build the educational credentials of teachers and create new teaching materials indicates that the 'public service' orientation of many think-tanks cannot easily be discounted as mere rhetoric. Substantial resources are devoted by a number of institutes towards this task.

The IR Discipline, Foreign Policy and Policy Institutes

The oldest foreign policy institutes stimulated the study of international relations. The CFR and Chatham House succeeded in 'by-passing the more rigid, conservative university institutions... aiming specifically at analysing the causes of the breakdown of the pre-war order for the explicit purpose of learning from it for the future' (Krippendorff, 1989: 34). The older institutes not only mirrored but helped shaped the initial idealistic character of the discipline. The development of IR was influenced by the determination of founders and members to 'maximize the free flow of information and remove barriers to accurate perception' (Hollis and Smith, 1990: 42). The causes of war were believed to rest in misunderstanding and the lack of democratic accountability of leaders which the private research centres sought to overcome.

The volume of IR research in and its attraction as a subject of study in the universities today masks the early formative role of the private research institutes. Academic surveys of IR do not often discuss the contributions of think-tanks, and when they do, it is rarely in detail (but see the essays in Dyer and Mangasarian, 1989). Today, the resources and personnel of the universities outweigh considerably those of the foreign policy institutes, but they did not earlier in the century. Where the older institutes such as Chatham House and the Carnegie Endowment could make a substantial contribution to the discipline, and still do, this is less feasible for new centres. The discipline expanded and consolidated in the university system. The new institutes are unlikely to break new territory in an academic sense – although there are exceptions such as the IIE, CEPR and some environmental institutes. Many are too small to sustain an in-house research staff and competitive factors drive them in a more political or activist direction. Most of them conduct little original research and simply translate the ideas and research produced in universities for policy consumption. While they may not make original contributions to the IR discipline, they extend new thinking beyond the academic realm. For example, the Institute for Defense and Disarmament Studies (IDDS) in Cambridge, Massachusetts 'serves the public interest sector' and seeks to 'strengthen' the work of other researchers, scholars and activists by 'promoting broadly defined alternative policy proposals' for common security (1990: 10).

Think-tanks perform an additional important function that universities and colleges sometimes find difficult; that is, inter-disciplinary research. The physical, social and intellectual estrangement of disciplines and their compartmentalisation into university departments frequently curtails the potential for inter-disciplinarity. Debates occur within rather than across disciplines. In other words, the disciplines within universities are 'balkanised' (Abshire, 1993: 28). As most think-tanks are not constrained by strong academic cultures that maintain the distance between disciplines, they can be more innovative about the content of research projects. This is particularly the case concerning think-tanks that are issue focused where experts from a variety of disciplines can address a common issue. In the realm of security, for example, the CSIS claims that for 30 years it has been preaching that security is 'not only military but also political, and above all, economic'. Not only was it necessary to preach the interlinkages, the CSIS felt compelled to gather leading strategists and economists to help reach some 'mutuality of views about the security of the nation'. CSIS attempts to be 'synergistic – to break down the compartments and barriers, to look and interrelate all the angles' (Abshire, 1993: 17, 28).

The world of the foreign policy professional based in a think-tank is different from that of an academic based in a university. The two perform quite different roles and, in the main, speak to different audiences. Think-tanks are engaged in more of an applied form of IR, whereas university-based IR focuses on the theoretical and educational. But there are many points of similarity. The exaggerated distance between the two roles will be maintained while think-tanks remain relatively small in number, as in Britain and most other countries, or when they are geographically concentrated in a hot-house political environment such as Washington DC.

Two Worlds

Many academics based in universities are disdainful of policy intellectuals and eschew the world of practice. A frequently heard prejudice is that such intellectuals forgo 'the dispassion which is the hallmark of scholarship', and 'rather than being a free-floating disputatious spirit, the academic will of necessity be forced to adopt a party line' (Webb, 1994a: 22). That is, when an academic becomes a foreign policy professional, that person becomes entrapped by past policy commitments, subordinate to organisational prerogatives and unable to freely set their own agenda of inquiry. Such a view maintains that the imperatives of power and scholarship lead in different directions. Yet, the independence of academics can be too easily overstated and evidence that many university researchers are tied to one perspective and close off debate is too easily ignored (see also Hill, 1994). Furthermore, as William Wallace reminds us, the distinction between 'academic' and 'policy' research 'scarcely existed' in Britain of the 1920s and 1930s where the conventional political wisdom was still shaped in 'the world of London dinner parties and country house weekends'.

> Enlightened men, of learning and leisure, moved in and out of the worlds of academia, government and politics without observing too closely the boundaries between them ... The very small circles of those actively interested in ideas and international issues meant that each man ... played many parts, and institutions and activities overlapped (1994: 140).

However, as government grew in size and scope and as the higher education system changed from an élite-based to a mass-based focus, the divide between the academic and political worlds became more pronounced. The links became more tenuous with the professionalisation and fragmentation of foreign policy élites.

Although the tension between the scholar and the practitioner is unlikely to be resolved, think-tanks can act as centres for communication between practitioners and academics. There is common ground. Both policy-makers and think-tank scholars are likely to have attended university and many of them would have studied the social sciences. Hence, they read the classics along with the textbooks. They may well be familiar with current debates in the discipline through personal contacts or an abiding interest in IR. The ideas and analyses of IR specialists do percolate through but the process is long and attenuated. Think-tanks can be regarded as a means to shorten this in-built delay. At the same time, think-tanks can possibly be conceived as a buffer preventing the concerns of practitioners and policy becoming predominant within the university. In other words, think-tanks are the 'demi-monde' of IR, linking but also keeping apart the two worlds of IR – practitioners and academics (Wallace, 1994: 160).

Nevertheless, think-tanks are not simply a neutral instrument of knowledge transmission or a bridge between the scholarly and political worlds. They build a body of knowledge, from a position of authority and expertise, on which the state or other sources of power can draw for legitimation. The integral character of politics and knowledge is evident from the nascence of IR. Most of the private research institutes were founded with explicit idealist political motives. Reasoned argument, persuasion and debate in the independent and non-partisan think-tank had the clear political objective of promoting peace, consensus and improved intergovernmental relations. The Cold War clarified the political uses of knowledge. Regardless of appeals to science and rationality, as the discussion of nuclear policy in the previous chapter indicated, key strategic studies institutes were not independent centres of inquiry. By recasting nuclear strategy as a technical problem to be addressed by experts, the security intellectuals at RAND, IISS and elsewhere displaced public political discussion and dominated the security agenda. From their position in think-tanks, universities and scientific laboratories, a community of experts were able to 'use their supposedly expert, and often classified, knowledge to specify the "issues" in ways that maintain the foreign policy themes of containment and nuclear deterrence of the "Soviet threat"' (Dalby, 1990: 11).

Policy institutes have not only reflected but have been part of the dynamic of the movement of IR from the 'high politics' of statecraft and diplomacy to the 'low politics' of trade and environmentalism, helping to establish the intellectual frameworks within which contemporary decision-makers operate. The power-knowledge relationship is apparent in the fate of the IPR. As discussed earlier, the IPR was a victim of the cold war and over-inflated perceptions of its influence among the McArthyite anti-communists. For example, Senator Pat McCarran, who chaired the Senate Judiciary Sub Committee on Internal Security, asserted that, 'but for the machinations of a small group that controlled and activated the IPR, China today would be free...' (quoted in Thorne, 1978: 14). The McCarran hearings, which involved the testimony of some conservative scholars, helped generate a rift among Asian specialists. A few scholars feared or experienced loss of employment or public stigma as a consequence of their IPR connections. For different reasons, the CSIS as a target of student demonstrations and the IPS as a centre of opposition to the Vietnam War during the 1960s, reveal the interconnection between the study of IR and foreign policy practice. The interconnections are not consistent over time nor always as obvious as are these examples. Less apparent meshing occurs informally at conferences, in study groups and through networking. The movement back and forth of scholars between academe, government or bureaucracy and the think-tank illustrates the interconnectedness of the private research institute not only with foreign policy but also with the development of the IR discipline.

Conclusion

Think-tanks are an increasingly noticeable mechanism for refining and presenting knowledge and expertise in a relevant and usable manner. Accordingly, one of the main objectives in this book was to provide a picture of the independent policy research industry in Britain and the USA as a whole. That is, to look at the largest and best-known institutes as well as small and unknown bodies and to examine the way in which these organisations have evolved. A further objective was to investigate their policy relevance and the strategies by which think-tanks hope to sensitise decision-makers to change and educate them into specific solutions. Ideas may lack force without the applied work and policy entrepreneurship of policy institutes and the quasi-academic legitimacy that they provide. But not all institutes do this well. Not all policy institutes make their ideas matter.

Policy impact is a difficult task from the margins. Think-tanks are not part of government processes. Yet neither are think-tanks in a non-profit sector vacuum. These organisations overlap with the educational, philanthropic and political worlds. Although the extent of overlap varies among different political cultures and from one institute to another, the boundaries between think-tanks and these other sectors have become blurred. For example, not only are they creeping into the policy process, they are being pulled into it. Many institutes are connected to government through contract research and especially through policy networks. The social and professional interactions of institute staff and trustees, and their career moves across different organisations, create a matrix of personal networks. These personal links break down the structural distinctions between government and other organisations. It is also the case that governments find these organisations useful from time to time. 'In the symbolism of power, the non-governmental policy analysis organization with a particular policy orientation will continue to be used to "signal" shifts in policy' (Smith, 1977: 257). Consequently, the politicisation of think-tanks that has been observed by so many is not a one-way process. Think-tanks have become more political, ideological or partisan in response to the competitive environment of funding, policy advice and media attention. But they have also been politicised by political parties and interest groups which have recognised not only the importance of ideas in policy but the need for intellectual legitimation. As such, the claims to independence and autonomy of most think-tanks are highly questionable.

Think-tanks are not likely to fade from the political or policy scene. They will continue to proliferate although some will be vanity tanks and others will be ill-conceived and closed shop. Accordingly, the think-tank phenomenon will confront social science scholars with questions. This study has focused on the development of the non-profit think-tank industry as a whole and issues of relevance, effectiveness and influence. But other questions are open for further research. What are the relationships between think-tanks and interest groups or, indeed, political parties? What are the implications of the penetration of think-tank analyses into policy for democratic politics? What shape will think-tanks take in other countries?

The Growth of Independent Policy Research

The global spread of independent policy research institutes will impel further study in this area. There are numerous free market institutes in Latin America which are part of the Atlas Foundation network. Think-tanks are burgeoning in Eastern and Central Europe (Palmer, 1991). A returned émigré from Canada, Bohdan Kravchenko, has set up a 'western-style public-policy institute' in the Ukraine (*Economist*, 26 December 1992–8 January 1993: 53). In particular, there has been considerable growth of policy institutes in Asia where think-tanks often play a much more important role in the policy and political domains of their respective countries than do their Western counterparts (Langford and Brownsey, 1991). Although domestic political reasons are the prime determinants for new institutes being established, think-tank growth is also propelled by the process of learning and networking based on both informal personal contacts and new institutional linkages that establish conduits of funding. The transnational networks managed by the Heritage Foundation, Atlas Foundation or the IISS are indicative of the extent of think-tank development, diversification and a growing professionalisation within the industry.

The extent of think-tank development in other countries will be shaped by domestic forces. In the USA it is not only political factors such as the permeability of the American system, the impermanence of bureaucrats, the division of powers and the weakness of political parties, but also a strong philanthropic culture and generous tax regime that encourages the proliferation of think-tanks. A significant constraint on the more extensive development of think-tanks in Commonwealth countries such as Australia and Canada, for example, is the absence of a philanthropic tradition and unfavourable tax regimes. Comparative analysis reveals that they are not, as suggested by a few writers (*inter alia*, Alpert and Markusen, 1980; Weaver, 1989), exceptional to the American political system. From the establishment of the Fabian Society, a number of independent institutes have had long and illustrious histories in Britain. Yet, British think-tanks tend to be smaller in both budgetary and staff size, and fewer in number, than their American counterparts. The scale of think-tank growth in the USA, along with differences in political culture and institutions, mean that American think-tanks appear to function in a more pluralistic environment. By contrast, the British parliamentary system is both more closed and centralised and, accordingly, think-tanks are less visible and appear to be excluded. Such differences do not necessarily mean that American think-tanks are better placed or have more opportunities to inform policy. There are avenues by which British think-tanks can be informally incorporated into decision-making – most often through policy communities or more rarely through the patronage of political leaders.

Dwelling on the differences detracts attention from the similarities. Both countries have experienced a boom in the number of think-tanks, albeit of a different scale. Furthermore, there are similar patterns of development away from the scholarly style of the 'old guard' institutes towards the more specialised 'new partisan' approach among American and British think-tanks. These institutes also face common problems in fund-raising or personnel management, and sometimes internal dissension and conflict over organisational goals. Additionally, think-tanks in both countries have adopted a similar language and set of tactics as 'second-hand dealers in ideas' when marketing their research and policy analysis.

The Rhetoric of Scientific Integrity

Think-tanks appeal to scientific authority, neutrality and rationality based on their scientific methodologies, the educational and professional credentials of staff, peer review and a competence based on impartiality and technical expertise. They stress how they aid the democratic functioning of society by contributing to informed debate. Such claims are important in establishing think-tank legitimacy but also make a false distinction between knowledge and power. In most think-tanks there is a tension between their rhetoric of independence and their commitment to inform policy with a particular set of values and principles. Under competitive pressures to market their policy analysis in a more entrepreneurial and politicised form, many policy institutes endanger their 'scientific' status and intellectual authority by their ideological stance. In order to sustain their public image of authority and impartial research, policy institutes have a stake in maintaining a distinction between knowledge production and power as distinct spheres of activity. Despite their efforts, policy institutes are part of the dynamic that establishes the intellectual frameworks within which decision-makers operate. This is revealed in the language employed by institutes.

The rhetorical or discursive strategies of think-tanks enhance the political potency of ideas and mobilise support. To understand the impact of policy research institutes it is necessary to consider how their use of metaphor animates them and transforms policy research into a 'battle of ideas'. The use of metaphor and imagery is a way of understanding the transformation of abstract ideas into policy and political usage. It is a means to simplify the debate. The language that the 'second-hand dealers in ideas' use to advocate their policy analyses and recommendations both reflects and shapes the perceptions of others. Metaphors also make the theoretical literature accessible, real and tangible to non-academic or non-specialist audiences. Public choice theory can be transformed by scholars in policy institutes from theoretical abstraction into a tool that can be used to strengthen and substantiate arguments against state monopoly, regulation and intervention. The tropological language is an attempt to acquire greater agenda setting powers. As Arthur Seldon of the IEA states, 'ideas require advertising' (1989: 94).

The Elusiveness of Influence

Although the Japanese government deemed Washington think-tanks to be so influential that it appointed a diplomatic official to monitor their activities (Judis, 1990a), most observers are more dubious of the policy impact of think-tanks. The prevalence of such scepticism is because think-tanks are 'hidden participants' in policy (Kingdon,

1984: 209), whereas decision making in the formal political arenas by political parties, legislatures and executives is a more transparent process. While think-tanks do not have a clear, consistent or legally designated route to policy influence, their policy entrepreneurship in policy and epistemic communities provides informal but haphazard access and opportunities for agenda-setting. They invest in a gradual, incremental creep of new ideas into prevailing thinking. This process is captured in the oft quoted statement by Keynes (see *inter alia*, Pirie, 1988: 18; Solomon 1986: 2837; Fisher, 1983: 5).

> Practical men, who believe themselves to be quite exempt from any intellectual influences, are usually the slaves of some defunct economist. Madmen in authority who hear voices in the air are distilling their frenzy from some academic scribbler of a few years back.

Rarely is there a one-to-one correspondence between a book or a study and a particular policy change. There are numerous intervening forces that mediate and alter the impact of research that shroud any cause and effect relationship that may exist between policy institutes and government decision-making. Hence, influence cannot be measured. Proof of it is elusive and, at best, anecdotal. Think-tank indicators such as media citations or appearances of staff before Congress and parliamentary committees merely signify that think-tanks have attracted the attention of the media and politicians. It does not demonstrate that the thinking or perceptions of the public or politicians has been influenced or that some policy initiative or reform has resulted. Asking the question, 'How do you measure the influence of independent policy research institutes?' misses the point. It is more important to ask first, 'What do they do that is policy relevant, and how?'

Despite the absence of proof, the impact of many institutes in helping to forge a consensus on foreign policy, raising consciousness about environmental, social and other problems, or reasserting liberal ideas of free markets, has been and remains pervasive. Knowledge and ideas are a source of power. The modern state depends on experts whose views on issues can provide the theories and rationales for policy and legislation. State structures are the dominant but not the only source of policy innovation as there is a need to consult other interests for information. Think-tanks seek to provide this kind of information and occasionally play a dynamic role in identifying problems. Policy research institutes are most likely to inform policy when they are part of an epistemic community, a wider policy community or discourse coalition. These analytical frameworks are concerned with agenda-setting, networking, research brokerage and the ways in which policy actors operate to establish a discourse that frames understanding of problems and policy. In particular, institutes help forge common identities and shared values among experts and opinion leaders through their conferences, workshops and study groups, and thereby help determine the ubiquitous climate of opinion. Ideas about networks allow an assessment of think-tank influence or effectiveness that gets beyond proving or measuring the input of some of these organisations into a given policy or legislative act. In other words, power is not narrowly conceived as behavioural and observable, but that power is structural and operates through exclusion and non-decision-making (Smith, 1993b: 74). Through both informal and formal avenues, think-tanks become linked to centres of power such as the state or the corporate sector. Yet, this potential for influence is not realised by all institutes or sustained consistently over time and policy area. Furthermore, this potential is limited to policy innovation and the dissemination of ideas. There are a number of reasons why the policy impact of institutes is limited.

First, outside the formal arenas of politics and without large constituencies, think-tanks have little political power other than the intrinsic persuasiveness of their policy analysis. Most institutes face a continual battle for survival. The constant quest for funding, and for new members and supporters, significantly restricts what may be achieved. Politicians and bureaucrats are often unaware of policy institutes or have neither the time nor the inclination to read their product. Independent research and analysis competes with many other sources of advice which often have more direct routes of access to decision-makers. Indeed, it may be that the end result of the interaction among academics, politicians, bureaucrats and other practitioners and experts that think-tanks so enthusiastically pursue represents no more than the opportunity to interact.

Second, the commitment of most institutes to be educational, analytical organisations that adhere to standards of dispassionate and rigorous research limits their political activity and erects professional or scholarly standards that restricts complete identification with the state, political parties or other sectional interests. Tax laws that curtail lobbying by these organisations further institutionalise their distinctive identity. Accordingly, the influence of policy research institutes cannot be of a direct kind. Should institutes become too policy-oriented and their staff co-opted into policy-making, they may lose what makes them interesting and distinctive – their capacity for innovation and sensitivity to new and emerging problems. Under pressure to conform to bureaucratic agendas and procedures, they may become myopic and less able to learn and generate consensual knowledge. There is a paradox here. Even though their knowledge and expertise might be required by individuals and agencies within the state for policy-making, policy institutes need to resist complete politicisation and maintain their academic integrity to pursue their research agendas freely if the capacity for innovation is to be sustained. As stressed by one think-tank director, Richard Portes of CEPR, policy research is not bureaucracy-led but originates in the 'drives and priorities of fundamental research' (1988: 151).

Third, independent policy research institutes are dependent organisations. The interests of funders places limits on the autonomy of institutes and constrains research agendas. Most of the American institutes are sustained in large proportion by foundations as are some British institutes. In some degree, institutes are beholden to the funding priorities of foundations. Foundation executives and other sponsors have the ability to define what are emerging policy agendas (such as development studies in the 1960s, with the creation of bodies like the ODC with Rockefeller Foundation funding) and to legitimate particular kinds of professional expertise (Berman, 1983). In the interests of continued existence and financial viability, institutes need to accommodate some of the expectations of funders. Institutes are also reliant on the academic world for theoretical advances, for scholars to undertake policy analysis with these new theoretical insights, and for scholarly regeneration. Furthermore, it is the formally defined power holders – legislators, bureaucrats, party officials and the judiciary – who are responsible for the selection and the persistence of ideas in policy and indeed, their incorporation into policy networks. In the last instance, think-tanks are dependent on them for recognition and to see their policy recommendations implemented.

Fourth, the proliferation of think-tanks over the last two decades has diluted the impact of these organisations. It is not as feasible in contemporary circumstances for a new institute to have the same kind of impact that was once wielded by the older and wealthier policy institutes. With specialisation and intensified think-tank competition, the influence of any one organisation is not only likely to be more diffuse but also limited to a narrower policy domain. Many institutes remain small and unnoticed, such as the Institute of Muslim Minority Affairs in London or the Institute for Educational

Leadership in Washington DC, because they are engaged in localised or specific professional struggles. Furthermore, rather than a single policy institute acting as the prime site for intellectual innovation, in contemporary times it is more likely to be a number of institutes which act in conjunction with individuals spread throughout other different organisations.

Finally, it must be remembered that many think-tanks do not limit or concentrate their interests on policy analysis or see the state as the principal sphere within which to secure influence or direct their activities. The mission or goals of think-tanks are frequently more complex. Their relevance extends beyond policy-making. Some think-tanks regard effectiveness as the ability to bring alternative perspectives to light, that is, broadening debate or by articulating a counter-hegemonic discourse. Similarly, many think-tanks are also devoted to raising public awareness of new issues, for example, the educational campaigns of environmental think-tanks. Other institutes are more concerned to provide their membership with appropriate services. Additionally, as indicated in the previous chapter, a number of institutes seek to contribute to disciplinary developments in academe. The motivations of institute staff and the internally generated criteria of relevance and effectiveness within an institute broaden the way in which influence can be conceived.

Charitable Thought?

There is a good deal of scepticism about the value of think-tanks. Sometimes this attitude is justified. In particular, it is necessary to resist the temptation to exaggerate think-tank importance and utility. But the criticisms that have been levelled at think-tanks do not necessarily apply to all of them. The radical urge of some think-tanks, for instance the ASI, has ruffled some observers (Wheen, 1994). Yet most think-tanks are more mainstream in their approach. Extremism has given a minority of think-tanks some novelty value in the media. Their recommendations sacrifice political feasibility in an effort to shock civil servants and politicians out of their complacency and conservatism. Although think-tanks may well perform a valid role by being speculative and flying policy kites, sometimes the ideas emerging from such think-tanks are impractical. And there are many more criticisms that can be made of think-tanks, disputing their policy influence, highlighting their inefficiency or discrediting their charitable endeavours.

A number of think-tanks put too much emphasis on activities

extraneous to their goals and mission. Publicity seeking becomes an end in itself. Promotional hype and efforts to secure maximum exposure to the media and political world detracts time and resources from research and analysis although it may well assist in promoting the institute. It can cultivate in some think-tank activists an unwarranted image of self-importance that results from an exaggeration of the achievements and successes of the think-tank. A related issue is that think-tanks can too easily become a vehicle for the careers of directors and senior staff. In other words, the think-tank is used as an organisational launch pad for a more desirable and usually better paid career elsewhere.

Putting time and resources into activities promoting the public standing of an institute – whether it be for media contacts or recognition from Congressional staff – detracts from one of the key objectives of think-tanks, that is, to promote public understanding. This task appears to have been forgotten by some think-tanks in their quest for attention from political and opinion leaders. Some institutes are not even interested in informing the public. Rather, the focus of think-tanks like the Arms Control Association is the 'interested public', while the Atlantic Council is clearly élitist in its desire to incorporate professional, corporate and political leaders into its activities. The promotion of public understanding and education tends to be limited to a very narrow section of the community.

A frequent criticism is that the professional and scholarly standards of some think-tanks are quite poor. Instances of sloppy work are readily found. The Hudson Institute developed a reputation in the 1970s for not always finishing contracted work or delivering reports that were 'frivolous' (Smith, 1991: 156). Heritage Foundation issue briefs are thin in more than one sense of the word. Many of the smaller and poorer institutes do not have the resources to put together glossy, well-produced reports. Additionally, the work of an institute can become unbalanced with too much advocacy and insufficient research. A frequently heard complaint, usually from academics, is that reports and analyses are based on assertion rather than solid evidence or theory. However, the environment in which think-tanks operate often establishes a dynamic for polemic rather than of thoughtful debate and argument. The ideological task of providing intellectual legitimation to substantiate preferred policy positions does not require thoughtful research and analysis. Instead, it involves condensing serious academic arguments into a palatable format for research brokerage. In general, most think-tanks do not sponsor original research, especially if they are of the 'think-and-do' variety. Most are engaged in rehashing work. Waste – through the duplication of existing work – may well be the outcome. In other words, a substantial number of think-tanks belie their name. Not much thinking occurs in them.

From time to time think-tanks lose their critical edge. They become boring and predictable. Maintaining the impetus for creative research and innovative new ideas is rare. Organisational effectiveness is more likely to be met when scholars are bound together by a common world view and the consensual knowledge they create. The CFR, IPS, IEA, IFS, RIIA and Heritage Foundation were entrepreneurial and innovative when they were established. Their inception was a creative act in response to policy orthodoxies that were deemed unacceptable and which they wished to change. But the capacity for innovation is difficult to sustain in the long run. The ability to inform policy appears to be greatest in the first two or three decades of an institute's existence, before it grows large, staff become sedentary and bureaucratic inertia sets in. There is a reluctance to experiment. As a consequence, consumers of think-tank products are likely to gain the impression that they have seen it all before. That is, that the same analytical or ideological formula is being applied to qualitatively different policy questions. Nevertheless, it is quite feasible for an institute to experience growth and stability without doing anything new or interesting.

Another valid criticism is that the sheer number of think-tanks represents not merely an unnecessary luxury but a burden on society. In short, they are engaged in a diversion of resources that could be put towards more productive uses. As the majority of think-tanks are either charities in Britain or non-profit organisations with 501(c)(3) status in the USA, they benefit from certain tax exemptions. In other words, think-tanks can be construed as yet another indirect drain on the taxpayer. The general public are subsidising organisations and individuals who do not necessarily act in the public interest but serve the ends of governmental élites or vested interest. Similarly, a number of think-tanks are not truly engaged in charitable activity. Some are too closely affiliated with a political party or a sectional interest to warrant tax exempt status.

A frequently stated objective in the mission statements of think-tanks is the desire to improve public debate through reasoned analysis. There is little evidence to suggest that these organisations have improved the policy process, enriching the amount and quality of information available and thereby ensuring greater rationality. Instead, it can be argued that they detract from reasoned public debate. In Washington DC, in particular, decision-making would grind to a halt were those in power inclined to take on board all the unsolicited advice and analysis that originates from think-tanks let alone that which comes from interest groups, the political parties, media and within government as well. The plethora of independent analysis is cacophonic. Think-tanks supplement the din that surrounds government. Furthermore, the difficulties of waging policy discussions on serious substantive grounds become clear when investigating the activities of think-tanks. It is inadvisable to assume the importance of information in the decision-making process when there are other compelling factors influencing policy such as the ideological preferences and prejudices of decision-makers, the inertia of habit and the insularity of government processes.

Perhaps the most damning indictment of contemporary think-tanks is that they are becoming more like interest groups or are being drawn into interest group circles. This is particularly the case with the 'think and do' tanks. The majority of new institutes do not make a pretence of scientific, dispassionate and objective research and are open about their ideological disposition. But they draw a line at declaring an alliance with sectional interests in society. Yet, as think-tanks become more specialised in conjunction with the requirement to be adversarial in advocating policy advice and analysis, they appear to be in cahoots with clearly identifiable groups. The Washington Institute for Near East Policy has a good reputation for solid analysis on Middle East issues. It also has a clear affinity with the Jewish lobby in Washington DC and substantial financial support from the Jewish community. The Foundation for Manufacturing and Industry, a specialised institute in London, would also appear to serve the information and analysis requirements of that sector of capital in Britain. Advocacy blurs the distinctions in the motivations and activities of think-tanks and interest groups. Furthermore, with the increasing complexity of public policy-making, its segmentation into policy communities and the increased incorporation of scientific and social scientific advice in dealing with technical issues or developing reform agendas, interest groups activists are well aware that expertise is a new coin of currency in policy. 'Without access to expertise (or counter expertise), an interest group today cannot effectively participate in the policy process' (Fischer, 1993: 36). By necessity, interest groups will align themselves with certain think-tanks or support the establishment of new think-tanks, thereby accelerating the process of politicisation. The differences between a significant but small proportion of think-tanks and interest groups are blurring. At this point in time, it can still be said that think-tanks with features traditionally associated with independent policy research are in the majority. Over time, as the character of the advocacy think-tank evolves further, the boundaries may become even more fuzzy. As such, governments in Britain and the USA may feel compelled to introduce more stringent qualifications for the non-profit or charitable status that most institutes enjoy, which will undermine further their legitimacy as authoritative intellectual centres of research and analysis.

Appendix
Independent Policy Institutes in Britain and the USA

This Appendix provides a representative picture of the kinds of independent policy research institutes in Great Britain and the USA. It is preceded by a short discussion of the legal status of most think-tanks. The section concerning American institutes is divided into two parts: the first listing those organisations based in the Washington DC area, and the second listing institutes spread throughout the rest of the country. The information, and sometimes the wording, in the entries has been compiled from a number of sources, primarily annual reports but also pamphlets, brochures and other information material provided by institutes as well as other directories (Gale, 1991; Huberty and Hohbach, 1991; and Van Der Woerd, 1992).

A Note on Tax Regimes

Britain
Policy research institutes are usually considered as education charities, that is, organisations which embrace: i) any type of research useful to others; ii) the arts and museums; and iii) public schools (True, 1990). Charities are registered under a system operated by the Charity Commission. Charities are exempt from tax on the following kinds of receipts, if the funds involved are used only for charitable purposes: rents from land and property; interest and dividends; covenanted donations; single gifts by companies paid after tax has been deducted; grants from other charities; and chargeable gains (Inland Revenue, 1987: 4). Organisations which exist in order to influence government policy on particular issues cannot normally be regarded as charitable in law as political objects are not charitable. In relation to 'political' activity, 'politics' does not simply mean 'party politics'. According to the Charity Commissioners, it also includes seeking to influence government policy (local, central, at home or abroad), as well as advocating changes in the law or retention of the existing law. A non-charitable organisation such as, for example, the Fabian Society or the Centre for Policy Studies, has complete freedom to support any cause it wishes. A charity, by contrast, is confined to the objects of its trust.

Nevertheless, charities are permitted 'to influence opinion on particular public issues which are directly relevant to their objects and to their experience of the difficulties met in their field'. However, this activity must be conducted in a 'reasoned and relevant way, and not gratuitously seek to influence attitudes on fields beyond the direct objects of their charity' (Charity Commissioners, 1991: 2). Political activity must be entirely ancillary to the achievement of those objects. As a consequence, it is permitted for a charity concerned with particular issues, such as the environment, to present the government and others with reasoned arguments about the defects or virtues of environmental policy. This is because policy affects the environment, the condition and problems of which the charity exists to improve or remedy. However, it would not be proper for a charity concerned with the environment to campaign on some completely different cause such as apartheid or defence policy. It is also permissible for a charity to inform public thinking and debate by 'publishing material based on reasoned research and direct experience' (Charity Commissioners, 1991: 4). Yet it would not be proper for it to support a particular line of policy or legislative change, except in circumstances where the charity was helping to achieve its charitable purposes.

USA

All the American organisations listed in the appendix have, or have had, legal status as a 501(c)(3) non-profit organisation under the Internal Revenue Service (IRS) code. Within this category there are several quite diverse organisations. The Russell Sage Foundation, the Carnegie Endowment and the Twentieth Century Fund, for example, are general purpose operating foundations. The Progressive Policy Institute was a 501(c)(3) but since merging with the Democratic Leadership Council it has become the research arm of a larger 501(c)(4) organisation. Organisations that are involved in substantial political advocacy and lobbying are generally categorised under Section 501(c)(4) of the Code. They are prohibited for private foundations and are non-deductible for individuals.

US law regarding 501(c)(3) organisations is complex and has been subject to numerous interpretations. Tax deductibility is limited to 'religious, educational, charitable, scientific and literary' 501(c)(3) organisations. These organisations are barred from 'substantial political activity'. The meaning of 'substantial political activity' is somewhat ambiguous but has been clarified by IRS rulings and legislation. In 1966, the IRS ruled that non-profit organisations which convened public forums and debates on social, political and international matters qualified as exempt bodies regardless of whether or not they sparked controversy, provided that the primary purpose is to promote a fair and open-minded consideration of such questions. The charter of such organisations must specifically state that, firstly, it has no institutional point of view and is not responsible for the views expressed by its scholars, speakers or visitors, and secondly, its responsibility is to bring views expressed to the attention of the community (Hopkins and Summer, 1991: 8).

The major clarification of 'political' came in the Tax Reform Act of 1969. Congress defined 'politics' narrowly as direct involvement in campaign activity or attempts directly to influence Congress and the executive branch. Organisations may still legally appear and give testimony before Congress or administrative bodies provided such activities are 'educational', that is, factual and solicited by the governmental body in question, or if the activities represent an insubstantial portion of the organisation's endeavours. Charitable organisations are permitted to influence public policy through activities that are 'political' provided that the activities are not 'political campaign' activities. Charitable organisations are precluded from attempting to influence legislation. Such attempts include: i) contacting or urging the public to contact members of a legislative body for the purpose of proposing, supporting or opposing legislation; or ii) advocating the adoption or rejection of legislation. If a substantial portion of an organisation's activities are devoted to influencing legislation, the organisation is denominated an 'action' organisation which cannot qualify as an exempt entity. An organisation may analyse a subject of proposed or forthcoming legislation and prepare for the public an objective study of it, so long as it does not participate in the presentation of suggested bills to the legislature and does not engage in any campaign to secure enactment of the legislation.

United Kingdom

THE ADAM SMITH INSTITUTE – ASI
23 Great Smith Street
London SW1P 3BL

Established in 1977, the ASI is a market economics think-tank engaged in the analysis and development of public policy. The ASI recognises the wealth creating benefits of enterprise and searches for new ways of unleashing personal initiative with proposals that are both imaginative and practicable. The staff of the ASI fluctuates between four-and-a-half and seven. The two most important staff members are the President, Madsen Pirie, and the Director, Eamonn Butler. ASI contracts out most of its research and writing. The Institute's work is aided by a panel of approximately 200 leading academics and scholars. As a consquence, the organisation is run on a low budget (approximately £360,800 in 1991). Compared with the other policy institutes in the UK, the ASI is one of the newest and smallest. The Director and President have also decided to keep it small in order to remain flexible. It is the most advocacy- and media-oriented of the free market think-tanks and focuses on the practical applications of theory.

ARAB RESEARCH CENTRE
76/78 Notting Hill Gate
London W11 3HS

In view of the ever-increasing importance and influence of the Arab world, not only on the European stage but in the world as a whole as a result of the economic, social, commercial and cultural developments that have been taking place in recent years, it has been realised that there is an urgent need to study and analyse such developments and their future expansion. The Arab Research Centre has been established for the purpose of carrying out such research and objective studies in the various fields of knowledge with the help of scholars, thinkers and scientists not only from the Arab world but also from all over the world. The ARC was established in 1979 and has remained a small organisation with a staff of five.

BOW GROUP
92 Bishop's Bridge Road
London W2 5AB

Established in 1951, the Bow Group was formed to provide a Conservative counterweight to the intellectual socialism of the Fabian Society. The aim of the Group's founders was to create a policy research organisation of intellectual independence and authority that captured and nurtured the bright minds of young people who otherwise might not have had the opportunity to contribute so directly to the formulation of Conservative Party policies. Many of its members are Conservative Party politicians. The Bow Group is a small organisation in budgetary terms but is in the process of trying to expand into a much larger organisation by purchasing permanent accommodation to house full-time administrative and research staff. Currently it is producing a quarterly journal, Crossbow, in addition to research papers and reports.

CATHOLIC INSTITUTE FOR INTERNATIONAL RELATIONS
Unit 3, Canonbury Yard
190a New North Road
London N1 7BJ

Founded in 1940, the Catholic Institute works with people of any religious belief or none to overcome poverty and injustice in the Third World. CIIR believes that Third World poverty is caused by unjust political, social and economic structures and that development must involve a fair distribution of wealth and power. Through education and information work in Britain and Europe, CIIR seeks to increase understanding of struggles in the Third World for social justice and development. Staff are based in London and around the Third World and operated on a budget of over £3 million in 1994. CIIR is more of a 'think and do' tank. Only 20 per cent of its expenditure is devoted to education and research on international economic justice, human rights and democracy. The majority of funds are expended on local initiative schemes in conjunction with workers, communities and NGOs in Third World countries.

CENTRE FOR ECONOMIC POLICY RESEARCH – CEPR
25–28 Old Burlington Street
London W1X 1LB

The Centre is an economics networking organisation operating throughout Europe. Its purpose is to 'promote independent, objective analysis and discussion of open economies and the relations among them'. CEPR activities extend from the initiation to the funding, execution, administration and dissemination of research. The Centre emphasises theory and empirical work relevant to medium- and long-run policy formation for a wide range of macro-economic and micro-economic issues. Although with a budget of over £1 million and of moderate size (approx. 15 full-time staff), the Centre does not have an in-house research staff. Instead, it has 180 Research Fellows throughout Europe and the US who form a 'broad church' with no institutional line or policy positions. Founded in 1983, the Centre is modelled after NBER in the USA.

CENTRE FOR GLOBAL ENERGY STUDIES
17 Knightsbridge
London SW1X 7LY

Founded in 1990, the Centre carries out research into global energy issues and provides an active forum to encourage a greater degree of international energy co-operation in the interests of achieving a better world energy order. It represents neither energy producers, customers, governments nor energy organisations. The CGES brings together policy-makers and senior executives from all sides of the debate aiming to narrow the intellectual gap that exists among the various players on the world energy scene. The Centre's activities stem from the fundamental belief that energy-related issues should be viewed globally in the context of the international energy debate. On staff there are five researchers. The Centre also provides research fellowships. Publications include a bi-monthly *Global Oil Report* as well as the *Monthly Oil Report* and books.

CENTRE FOR POLICY ON AGEING
25–31 Ironmonger Road
London EC1V 3QP

The Centre was established in 1947 and was originally known as the National Corporation for the Care of Old People. In 1980 it changed its name and took on a new role as an independent unit aiming to formulate and promote social policies which will enable everyone to live the last third of life as fully as possible. It promotes informed debate about issues affecting older age groups, stimulates awareness of the needs of older people and encourages the spread of good practice among service providers. The Centre has co-published reports in conjunction with the voluntary organisation Help the Aged, and with another think-tank, the Family Policy Studies Centre.

CENTRE FOR POLICY STUDIES – CPS
52 Rochester Row
London SW1P 1JU

The CPS seeks to translate the belief in individual freedom, economic enterprise and social responsibility into the recommendation of policies which governments can carry out. Studies are despatched to Cabinet Ministers and Departments of State, to the media and to a wide circle of those engaged in the political life of Britain. Although the CPS enjoys links with Conservatives of most shades it is neither financed nor directed by the Party. The Centre sees itself as radical in the true sense: that is, as an organisation which seeks to change the way in which people have come to think. It places itself in the forefront of the battle of ideas, determined that intellect must be harnessed to the service of the politics of the day, and bear witness to a new age of both economic and social realism.

Established in 1974 as a limited company (the CPS is not a charity) by Margaret Thatcher and Sir Keith Joseph, the CPS is one the best known think-tanks in Britain. It is of modest size with a staff of seven and budget of approximately £300,000. Study groups or working parties are set up composed of men and women eminent in education, law, commerce, local government, nationalised industries, defence and other areas. Although the CPS adopts libertarian and free market approaches to economic policy, it is consevative on social and defence issues. It is more political than other free market and conservative institutes in Britain, having close but informal ties to the Conservative Party (see Burgess and Alderman, 1990; or Todd, 1993).

CENTRE FOR THE STUDY OF REGULATED INDUSTRIES
3 Robert Street
London WC2N 6BH

The Centre is an independent research centre of the Chartered Institute of Public Finance and Accountancy. CRI is politically neutral and aims to promote the objective investigation of the regulation of the privatised water, energy, transport and communications industries and the development of competitive markets in these industries, both in the UK and abroad. With a staff of five and supported by corporate sponsorship or income from conferences and consultancy, the Centre is administered alongside the Public Finance Foundation.

CITIZENS INCOME
St Phillips Building, Sheffield Street
London WC2A 2EX

Previously established in 1984 as the Basic Income Research Group, Citizens Income addresses all aspects of basic income and employment issues. It has a very small staff of two and survives on subscriptions, donations, and foundation support. It is an affiliate of the Basic Income European Network (BIEN).

CONSERVATIVE 2000 FOUNDATION
2 Wilfred Street
London SW1E 6PH

This organisation was established by John Redwood after unsuccessfully contesting John Major for leadership of the Conservative Party in mid 1995. Similar to the Bow Group it is a forum for debate and discussion for members of the Conservative Party. In particular, the Foundation adopts a sceptical position towards deepening European integration drawing attention to the dangers of over-regulation and over-government.

COUNCIL FOR ARMS CONTROL
Kings College
University of London
London WC2R 2LS

Founded in 1981, the Council initiates and conducts research into the arms control and disarmament fields and produces reports which are published and distributed to members and other interested individuals and organisations. The Council addresses issues which endanger peace and stability, especially the spread of weapons of mass destruction (nuclear, chemical and biological) and the trade in conventional arms. The Council works within, and in association with, the Centre for Defence Studies at King's College, University of London. It is composed of one self-employed director and survives on a very small budget. The *Bulletin of Arms Control* is issued quarterly.

DAVID HUME INSTITUTE
21 George Square
Edinburgh EH8 9LD

The aims and objectives of the Institute are to promote discourse and research on economic and legal aspects of public policy questions by a programme of publications, conferences and similar events. Created in

1985, the Hume Institute is another market liberal body. It has a very small staff of two and is reliant on adjunct writers for its monograph series and occasional papers.

DEMOS
9 Bridewell Place
London EC4V 6AP

Demos is not linked to any party or faction and not limited to the traditional concerns of politics and public policy. Demos includes radicals and innovators from across the political and occupational spectrums but is not focused narrowly on Parliament and Whitehall. Demos intends to 'to transform and revitalise the culture of political debate which has become too narrow, too enclosed and too self-referential; to develop strategic long-term solutions to the problems faced both by the UK and other advanced societies; and to provide a new energy and focus for the democratic ideal of a more open and mobile and participative society without privileges and vested interests'. Established in 1993, Demos has a small staff of around four and a budget of approximately £200,000 but has been relatively successful in attracting media attention for its reports.

EARTH RESOURCES RESEARCH – ERR
258 Pentonville Road
London N1 9JY

Since 1973, the ERR has been dedicated to both research and educational activities on topical environmental matters, and aims to provide technical and policy-oriented skills to statutory bodies, campaigning groups and the broader public. ERR's research focuses on environmental issues such as transport and environment; environmental pollution; forests and timber trade; agriculture, trade and resource use. Books and reports are its main products in addition to briefings for the media and other parties. ERR has a sizeable staff of 24 researchers and outside consultants, on only a small budget of £200,000 p.a.

ECONOMIC RESEARCH COUNCIL
239 Shaftesbury Avenue
London WC2H 8PJ

The Council was established in 1943 as the Joint Council for Economic and Monetary Research to promote education in the science of economics with particular reference to monetary practice. The Council's origins go back at least a decade earlier when a number of prominent persons, concerned with the poverty they witnessed around them, started questioning the use of the monetary system through the Economic Reform Club that was established in 1932. During the 1940s and 1950s the ERC promoted the ideas of J. M. Keynes. Today the Council has no paid staff – all are voluntary. Annual expenditure does not amount to more than £10,000 p.a. Earlier in its existence, the Council was a larger organisation. Today, the Council operates primarily for the dinner meetings and the production of its quarterly journal *Britain and Overseas*.

EMPLOYMENT POLICY INSTITUTE
Southbank House, Black Prince Road
London SE1 7SJ

Created in 1992, the Institute is an amalgamation of two older organisations, the Employment Institute (established 1984) and the Campaign for Work, an action trust, but remains a small body of approximately five people. According to its 1994 Development Plan, the Institute believes that a civilised society should not tolerate unemployment as a means of managing the economy and that the move from the social divisiveness of heavy unemployment to the social cohesion of full employment is the most pressing task on the national and international agenda. Its research field is all matters related to employment in Britain and Europe which it investigates through working groups and an annual conference.

EUROPEAN POLICY FORUM
20 Queen Anne's Gate
London SW1H 9AA

The EPF was established in 1992 to tackle the agenda for Britain and Europe. The Forum claims to have been assured of the active engagement of Whitehall and Community officials and key players from Westminster, the European Parliament, business organisations, permanent representations and embassies. It also draws upon the resources of the academic community. The EPF has four research programmes: Britain and Europe; constitutional and institutional issues; regulation, law and economics; policy innovation. It organises meetings, seminars and one-day conferences. The founding President and Director, Graham Mather (a Member of the European Parliament) and Frank Vibert, were both previously employed as the two senior executives of the IEA (see below).

FABIAN SOCIETY
11 Dartmouth Street
London SW1H 9BN

The Fabian Society consists of socialists. It therefore aims at the establishment of a society in which equality of opportunity will be assured and the economic powers and privileges of individuals and classes abolished through the collective ownership and democratic control of the economic resources of the community. It seeks to secure these ends by the methods of political democracy. Created in 1884, the Society is not a charity because of its affiliation to the Labour Party. Staff fluctuates between six and eight and expenditure amounted to £200,000 in 1994. During 1990, the Society ceased publishing *New Socialist* owing to readership decline and financial losses, and handed it to the Labour Party, which has since ceased its publication. The Society continues to publish pamphlets, discussion papers and has launched the new *Fabian Review*. Of all the British think-tanks, the Fabian Society is the oldest. Only since the 1980s, however, has its publicity material portrayed the Society as a think-tank. Its formal links with the Labour Party make it atypical of other organisations listed in this appendix. Its 'Golden Age' was during the 1930s and 1940s, particularly when the Labour Party was in office 1945–51 (see MacKenzie and MacKenzie, 1979). Since then, its influence in the party, and the political domain generally, has waned.

FAMILY POLICY STUDIES CENTRE
231 Baker Street
London NW1 6XE

Established in 1983 as a successor to the Study Commission on the Family, the Centre was set up to analyse and disseminate information about the family. It is concerned with exploring the association between family trends and public policy. In particular, it aims to interpret demographic trends and contemporary family patterns and analyse the impact of public policy on different kinds of families. The Centre is moderately large by British standards with a staff of eight in total. Expenditure in 1992–93 was £351,110 which put the Centre in deficit. Core funding is provided by a Department of Health grant representing 41 per cent of funding in 1992–93.

FEDERAL TRUST
158 Buckingham Palace Road
London SW1W 9TR

The Federal Trust was created in 1945 by the Federal Union, an organisation set up in Britain in the late 1930s to promote unity among democratic nations under threat from dictatorships. The Trust is the successor organisation to Federal Union's Research Institute which drew together, in the early days of the Second World War, a group of experts to work on plans for a post-war federation of Europe. Today, the Trust is concerned with European and world integration. The aim of the Trust is to study ways in which federal principles can be applied to allow new ways of states working together while safeguarding their diversity and identity. The Trust has a staff of eight on a small budget of £141,357 (1994). It conducts its research mainly through study groups although conferences are often arranged. The Trust was a co-funder of the Trans-European Policy Studies Association (TEPSA), based in Brussels, which links it with other similar research institutes in the European Union.

FOUNDATION FOR MANUFACTURING AND INDUSTRY
134 Buckingham Palace Road
London SW1W 9SA

The FMI is devoted to broadening understanding about the development of the British industrial and manufacturing base. Since 1993 it has been researching factors affecting industrial and commercial success; cultural factors affecting attitudes of both the general public and especially government, the media, academia and financial institutions to industry; and the impact of public policy on industry and commerce. It has initiated a discussion paper series, 'UK in the Global Economy' and holds research seminars and open meetings.

INSTITUTE FOR EUROPEAN DEFENCE AND STRATEGIC STUDIES
13–14 Golden Square
London W1R 3AG

The IEDSS was set up in 1980 to study political change in Europe and to assess its impact on strategic and defence issues. It is, therefore, particularly concerned with those developments which affect the future of the Western Alliance. It aims to be of interest to academics, politicians and others who have an impact on the formulation of policy, and by contributing to the exchange of ideas and information the Institute aspires to increase understanding of the complex issues involved. The Institute is widely regarded as conservative in its approach to security issues. With a budget of £150,000, it has a small staff of three. It produces the bi-monthly *European Security Analyst*, books and two monograph series.

INSTITUTE FOR EUROPEAN ENVIRONMENTAL POLICY – IEEP
158 Buckingham Palace Road
London SW1W 9TR

The Institute is an independent body for the analysis and advancement of environmental policies in Europe. It undertakes research on the European dimension of environmental protection, with a major focus on the development, implementation and evaluation of the European Community's environmental policy. The Institute was established in 1976 by the European Cultural Foundation in Amsterdam, but IEEP became independent in 1990. It retains a number of partner institutes in Europe: Institut für Europäische Umweltpolitik, Germany; Institut pour une Politique Européenne de l'Environment, France; Instituut voor Europees Milieubelied, Netherlands; Foundation for European Environmental Policy, Brussels. The Institute has a staff of nine and in 1992 had a budget of 503,000 ECU. It provides advice to UK government departments and agencies, Parliamentary committees and non-governmental organisations.

IPSET – EDUCATION UNIT
Warlingham Park School
Chelsham Common, Warlingham
Surrey CR6 9PB

The Education Unit – a market liberal body – was established in 1986 to propose, research and develop policies aimed at improving the quality of education for children and young people in the United Kingdom. The Education Unit was established in the Institute of Economic Affairs but operated as a separate, autonomous branch of the IEA. After four years, the Unit became legally and financially independent of the IEA, in mutual agreement, in an attempt to get better funding. The Education Unit was brought in under IPSET (the Independent Primary and Secondary Education Trust) with the permission of the Charity Commissioners. The Unit has not, as yet, been able to attract corporate support. Funds are extremely short which has meant reduced activity and publication. The Unit's staff is composed of one Director and a part-time secretary and volunteers.

INSTITUTE FOR AFRICAN ALTERNATIVES
23 Bevenden Street
London N1 6BH

Established in 1986 as a response to the prevailing African crisis, the institute is a network institute for policy research on alternative development strategies for the continent. It has links to NGOs in the North and South and with grass-roots organisations in Africa. It carries out research in ecology, politics and conflict. In addition to its office in London, there are centres in five African countries – Nigeria, Senegal, South Africa, Tanzania and Zimbabwe. Aside from publishing books, reports and a newsletter, the Institute arranges workshops (often in conjuction with the University of London), conferences and seminars. It conducts residential training programmes and adult education courses. The Institute also runs courses for certification in Africa-related subjects in conjunction with various universities.

INSTITUTE FOR FISCAL STUDIES – IFS
7 Ridgmount Street
London WC1E 7AE

The IFS is an independent centre for the study and discussion of fiscal policy. Since 1969, it has provided a focus for informed discussion of government policies on taxation and public spending. The IFS aims to bring academic rigour to policy discussion. It has five programmes of research: personal taxation and social security; corporate taxes and company behaviour; indirect taxes and consumer behaviour; local public finance; environmental taxes. The IFS has maintained a research staff of between 22 and 25 people, plus support staff, for some years. Expenditure in 1993 was £1,176,535. Publications include reports and commentaries, working papers, the quarterly journal *Fiscal Studies* and a newsletter. The IFS is distinctive in carrying out large-scale analysis of survey data and its quantitative research style. As IFS product is often original research, the Institute has an academic style.

INSTITUTE OF MUSLIM MINORITY AFFAIRS
46 Goodge Street
London W1P 1FJ

Since 1976, the objectives of IMMA have been three-fold. First, to draw attention to the importance of systematically and accurately investigating the conditions of life for Muslim minority communities. Second, to bring together in a close relationship Muslim and non-Muslim scholars to share information and exchange ideas. Third, to disseminate the results of such efforts through academic seminars and conferences as well as

through publications. The Institute is small in budgetary terms and had
a staff of only three in 1994. It survives on donations. Its major activity
is to produce the bi-annual *Journal of the Institute of Muslim Minority
Affairs* and a monograph series, as well as to arrange seminars and
conferences.

INSTITUTE FOR PUBLIC POLICY RESEARCH – IPPR
30/32 Southampton Street
London WC2E 7RA

IPPR promotes research into, and the education of the public in the
economic, social and political sciences and in science and technology,
including: the effects of moral, social, political and scientific factors on
public policy; and the effect of economic, social, financial, political,
environmental and international factors on the living standards of all
sections of the community. Founded in 1988, the IPPR has grown
relatively large quickly. It has a staff of twelve with an income of nearly
£700,000. IPPR was established to provide an alternative to the free
market think-tanks. IPPR is not committed to particular forms of public
provision. Instead, it argues that there is an urgent need to translate the
concept of the 'enabling state' into new kinds of intervention and to find
new ways of asserting the importance of community and co-operation in
our national life. The IPPR has informal links with the Labour Party.

INSTITUTE OF BUSINESS ETHICS
12 Palace Street
London SW1E 5JA

Founded in 1986, the Institute seeks to clarify ethical issues in business,
to propose positive solutions to problems and to establish common
ground with people of goodwill of all faiths. The Institute's audience is
primarily the business sector where it hopes to emphasise the essentially
ethical nature of wealth creation and promote the highest standards of
behaviour. The Institute has produced a number of reports on subjects
such as the management and health of employees; business takeovers;
good environmental practice; and codes of business ethics. The Institute
has a small staff of three people.

INSTITUTE OF ECONOMIC AFFAIRS – IEA
2 Lord North Street
London SW1P 3LB

The Institute was created in 1955 to improve public understanding of
economic principles and how they may apply to industry and commerce,

the professions and trade unions, government and international affairs. The Institute's characteristic approach, which differentiates it from many educational and research institutions, is to analyse the working or non-working of markets. For much of the Institute's existence, micro-economics has been overshadowed by Keynesian macro-economics. IEA studies have demonstrated the limits of macro-economics and shown the scope for individuals to exercise choice in priced markets, co-operating voluntarily and spontaneously in production, distribution and trade through the powerful and ingenious adaption which the market process makes possible.

The IEA has a staff of approximately 15 but is a networking organisation that draws on outside researchers. With income just over £1 million, the Institute has a substantial publications profile of monographs, papers, books and a bi-monthly magazine, *Economic Affairs*. The chief market comprises teachers and students in universities, technical colleges, schools and libraries who also make use of the IEA's Conferences, the Teachers Resource Center and economic videos. The IEA is one of the oldest institutes established with classical liberal and free market ethos (see Seldon, 1989). It was used as a model by one its founders, Antony Fisher, for the creation of a number of institutes in North America, namely the Manhattan Institute and Fraser Institute. Over the past few years the IEA has experienced division and conflicting views over its future role. It culminated in the departure of the previous General Director, Graham Mather and Deputy Director, Frank Vibert, who had wished to direct the IEA more in the style of the new partisan institutes. They have since established the European Policy Forum. The new General Director, John Blundell, was formerly President of the Atlas Foundation in the USA.

INSTITUTE OF EMPLOYMENT RIGHTS
112 Greyhound Lane
Streatham London SW16 5RN

Established in 1989, the Institute acts as a focal point for the spread of new ideas in the field of labour law. Think-tanks such as the Centre for Policy Studies, the Institute of Economic Affairs and the Adam Smith Institute have been waging ideological war against the trade unions for many years. The labour movement, on the other hand, had no equivalent think-tank to question this ideology and to develop and alternative approach around the specific area of labour law and industrial relations. The Institute of Employment Rights hopes to fill this perceived gap by making a constructive contribution to the debate on labour law and to expose attacks on trade unions. The Institute is small, with a staff of two people. Research work on labour law and industrial relations is commissioned and usually conducted on a voluntary basis. The IER is reliant on financial and other support from its membership which includes British trade union officials, labour law academics and practitioners, and other experts. Currently, the IER publishes annually the *Labour Law Review*, as well as other reports.

INSTITUTE OF RACE RELATIONS
2–6 Leeke Street
London WC1X 9HS

The Institute was founded as an independent body in 1958. It had its origin in the knowledge that race relations had become a fundamental factor throughout much of human society and that these relations deserved separate study. The main aims of the Institute are to promote the study of relations between groups racially defined, and the circumstances and conditions in which they live and work, to make available information on race to different groups, and to give advice on proposals for improving relations. IRR had a staff of five people in 1993 and maintained a small library on an income of only £86,645. It publishes a journal, *Race and Class*, books and pamphlets.

INTERNATIONAL INSTITUTE FOR ENVIRONMENT AND DEVELOPMENT
3 Endsleigh Street
London WC1H ODD

IIED seeks to promote sustainable patterns of world development through research, policy studies, consensus-building and public information. Focusing on the connections between economic development, the environment and human needs, the Institute's principal aim is to improve the management of natural resources so that countries of the South can improve living standards without jeopardising their resource base. Its work is undertaken with, or on behalf of, governments and international agencies, the academic community, foundations and non-governmental organisations, community groups and the people they represent. Research areas include sustainable development issues such as agriculture; tropical forestry; human settlements; drylands management; tropical forestry; environmental economics; climate change and institutional co-operation.

IIED was established in 1971 as the International Institute for Environmental Affairs. Since 1990 the Institute has grown rapidly and now has a staff of approximately forty people. Its income is close to £3 million p.a. Primary sources of support are governments and government agencies, foundations, international agencies and multilateral aid agencies and corporations. It collaborates with partner organisations in other continents such as the World Resources Institute in the USA. IIED also maintains a Register of Environmental and Sustainable Development Expertise, provides technical assistance, engages in project identification design and evaluation, and undertakes training of development workers.

INTERNATIONAL INSTITUTE FOR STRATEGIC STUDIES – IISS
23 Tavistock Street
London WC2E 7NQ

The aims of the Institute are:
– To provide a firm foundation of accurate information on and rigorous analysis of current and future problems, to assist the public comprehension of key international security and strategic issues.
– To promote professional debate and scholarship in international security matters by providing a forum for the exchange of views and facilities for members (for example, meetings, conferences, library and publications), by co-operating with other relevant institutes and individuals, and by actively encouraging younger contributions to the field.

Established in 1958, the IISS has become a large institute with a staff of twenty-five and expenditures of nearly £2 million. It publishes two annual reports, *The Military Balance* and *Strategic Survey*; the *Adelphi Papers*; a quarterly journal *Survival;* as well as books in areas such as regional security and conflict, European security after the Cold War, arms control and peace keeping, and non-military aspects of security. IISS was one of the first organisations to develop extensive links with other security and defence studies institutes and university centres, particularly through its surveys (see, for example, Van Der Woerd, 1992). Accordingly, it is an international organisation rather than domestically focused.

LOW PAY UNIT
29 Amwell Street
London EC1R 1UN

The Low Pay Unit was established in 1974 as a response to growing concern about the problems of the working poor. Its campaigns fuel the debate about low pay, poverty and inequality, both in the UK and in Europe. The Unit is working to make employees and employers aware of legal employment rights and ensure such rights are implemented; to challenge unfair discrimination at work against women, ethnic minorities and those with disabilities; and to influence the policy-making process in favour of greater social and economic justice. With nine full-time staff and expenditures of £143,004 (1992), the Unit publishes the *New Review of the Low Pay Unit* and booklets, as well as providing an

Employment Rights Advisory Service on pay and employment related issues.

NATIONAL INSTITUTE OF ECONOMIC AND SOCIAL RESEARCH
2 Dean Trench Street
Smith Square
London SW1P 3HE

The Institute's objective is to increase knowledge of the social and economic conditions of contemporary society. Created in 1938, the NIESR has grown to a staff complement of roughly fifty, of which three-fifths are research related. In 1993, expenditure was £1,738963. Books are usually published in association with Cambridge University Press and Gower Publishing Co. Ltd. The *National Institute Economic Review* is a quarterly journal which complements other occasional papers and reports. Its research activities include macro-economic analysis; studies of comparative industrial structure and efficiency; Britain in Europe; innovation and technology in eastern Europe; industrial productivity in the 1980s; skills shortage and mismatch in Germany and the UK; UK growth experience since 1920; economic aspects of demographic change; competitiveness of British financial services; economic effects of trade unions.

NEW ECONOMICS FOUNDATION
112–116 Whitechapel Road
London E1 1JE

Since 1986 the Foundation has been working to explore and promote an alternative vision – of ideas and practical schemes based on the needs of people and of the environment. The Foundation conducts research into, and the promotion of, innovative and effective approaches to economics that are socially just and environmentally sane.

OVERSEAS DEVELOPMENT INSTITUTE – ODI
Regents College, Inner Circle
Regents Park, London NW1 4NS

Since 1960 the ODI has been engaged in policy-related research on a wide range of issues which affect economic relations between North and South, and influence social and economic policies within developing countries. In particular, the ODI works closely with the All Parliamentary Group of Overseas Development and provides research and advice to both Houses of Parliament. It has a large staff of thirty people or more, and a budget of over £2.5 million. Financial support comes from commercial, voluntary and international organisations and the British Government. The ODI also runs a fellowship scheme, provides organisational and research support for the All Party Parliamentary Group on Overseas Development; maintains a library of 20,000 volumes, and organises the Agricultural Administration Unit which runs four formal networks linking 5,000 policy-makers, practitioners and researchers world wide.

PANOS INSTITUTE
9 White Lion Street
London N1 9PD

Established in 1986, Panos is an alliance of three institutes in London, Paris and Washington DC. Each institute works in partnership with non-governmental organisations, citizens groups and the media in the South. Research is conducted on global issues: i) health and social justice – AIDs, access to health care; racism, third world migration; ii) energy and environment – rural electrification, agroforestry, global warming, coral reefs, and forestry aid; iii) environment and security – narcotics, the 'green war' in the Sahel, and apartheid and environment; and iv) resettlement, biotechnology and biodiversity. There are no in-house research staff but there are approximately forty people employed in the three institutes with a budget of £2 million p.a. Support comes from Swedish, Dutch and Norwegian aid agencies; US foundations; government ministeries and agencies; non-governmental organisations; and individuals. Panos publications are various and include books, Panos Technical Reports, *Panos Features* – an English language publication co-syndicated in approximately 15 African/Asian languages, a bi-monthly magazine *Panoscope: PS* and a bi-monthly newsletter *WorldAids*, briefing documents for journalists, and a radio programme *Down to Earth*.

POLICY STUDIES INSTITUTE – PSI
100 Park Village East
London NW1

The PSI undertakes studies of economic, industrial and social policy, and the working of political institutions. PSI takes a politically neutral stance on issues of public policy, whatever political party forms the government. Its aim is to inform public policy by establishing facts through research, discussion and policy analysis. Originally established as Political and Economic Planning – PEP – in 1931, the Policy Studies Institute came into being as the result of a merger in 1978 between PEP and the Centre for the Study of Social Policy which was established in 1972. In 1994, PSI had approximately 80 staff of whom 60 were researchers. It had a budget in excess of £2 million p.a. in 1992. It produces reports, occasional papers and books as well as two quarterlies – *Policy Studies* and *Cultural Trends*. Its research field is broad and tackles issues in industrial development; employment and labour markets; industrial relations; social justice; social order; social security and family benefits; social care and community; health; transport, environment and conservation; local government; the arts.

POLITEIA
28 Charing Cross Road
London WC2H 0DB

Politeia is an independent foundation, established late 1995, dedicated to promoting informed public discussion about the relationship between the individual and the state.The founding Director, Dr Sheila Lawlor, was formerly a Deputy Director of the CPS.

PUBLIC FINANCE FOUNDATION
3 Robert Street
London WC2N 6BH

Established in 1984, the Foundation is the independent research arm of the Chartered Institute of Public Finance and Accountancy. The Foundation has a staff of six and a budget of half a million pounds. It provides an impartial forum for debate and the exchange of ideas on public expenditure and related aspects of public finance, and on the managment and administration of public services. The Foundation aims to promote objective and authoritative analysis and comment on these issues, drawing both on the work of the academic research community and on the practical knowledge and experience of senior financial and general managers from across the public sector. Publications include research reports, a quarterly journal, *Public Money and Management,* and a monthly review, *The Pay Forecasting Service.*

RESEARCH INSTITUTE FOR THE STUDY OF CONFLICT AND
TERRORISM
136 Baker Street
London W1M 1FH

The main aims of RISCT are: to research into the causes, manifestations and trends of political instability and conflict throughout the world; to study the activities of extremist organisations and their international links and support; and to publish balanced assessments of issues vital to international security. In 1989 RISCT was reconstituted from the Institute for the Study of Conflict which was founded in 1970. It has a staff of four but the majority of research and analysis is conducted by an international network of specialists. It produces a quarterly journal, *Terrorism and Political Violence*, a quarterly newsletter, *Conflict Bulletin*, books and a monograph series on matters such as global drug trafficking; prospects for regional security and co-operation in Southern Africa; regional security in the Middle East; and the impact of the AIDS epidemic.

ROYAL INSTITUTE FOR INTERNATIONAL AFFAIRS – RIIA
Chatham House
10 St James Square
London SW1Y 4LE

The aim of the Institute is to promote the study and understanding of all aspects of international relations. According to its Royal Charter, the Institute was established:

> To advance the sciences of international politics, economics, and jurisprudence, and the study, classification, and development of the literature of these subjects. To provide and maintain means of information upon international questions and promote the study and investigation of international questions by means of lectures and discussions and by the preparation and publication of books, records, reports or other works, or otherwise as may seem desirable. Generally to encourage and facilitate the study of international questions and to promote the exchange of information, knowledge and thought on international affairs and the understanding of the circumstances, conditions, and views of nations and peoples, and to do all things necessary or expedient for the proper and effective carrying out of the objectives aforesaid. To encourage and facilitate the formation of branches and committees throughout the Commonwealth.

Created in 1920 following the discussions among some members of the delegation to the Versailles Peace Conference, the RIIA today has an in-house staff of 84 people and a budget of nearly £3.5 million. Primary sources of support are foundations and corporations while government support is barely five per cent of income. The RIIA maintains links with other institutes of international relations throughout the Commonwealth and has engaged in collaborative research ventures with numerous institutes in Europe and Asia. Main publications include the monthly magazine, *The World Today,* and the quarterly journal, *International Affairs,* in addition to books and discussion papers. The meetings programme is a central activity which is complemented by ten to fifteen conferences each year.

SAFERWORLD
82 Colston Street
Bristol BS1 5BB

Although a small and relatively unknown institute, Saferworld claims to work behind the scenes advising and servicing governments, the press, academics and interested parties with timely and high quality public policy. Unlike most think-tanks, Saferworld wants to maintain a low profile as inappropriate or excessive publicity can close important doors. Since its inception in 1989, Saferworld has investigated ways in which human and financial resources can be diverted away from military confrontation. Research and policy work has focused on matters such as the arms trade, military aid, peace agreements, the defence industry and nuclear proliferation.

THE SOCIAL AFFAIRS UNIT
75 Davies Street
London W1Y 1FE

The Unit is a research and educational trust committed to the promotion of a lively and wide-ranging debate on social affairs. Its authors analyse the factors which make for a free and orderly society in which enterprise can flourish. Founded in 1980, the Unit maintains a staff of four and contracts people to do research and writing for its books and reports. It has a small annual income of around £120,000. Studies have included the reform of social security, the relation of education to business and enterprise, school standards, police accountability, criminal deterrence, housing, the media, the environment, regulation, family matters and the churches and social issues. The niche it has developed in Britain, distinct from the free market institutes which have tended to concentrate on economic affairs, has been to address the ethical, cultural and moral aspects of public issues. As a consequence, SAU authors are educationalists, philosophers, moralists, ethicists, sociologists, anthropologists and so forth.

SOCIAL MARKET FOUNDATION
20 Queen Anne's Gate
London SW1H 9AA

The central research task of the Social Market Foundation is to develop an orderly method of exploiting the key shifts in economic and political thinking which took place in the 1970s and 1980s. Of these, three stand out: a rebirth of faith in the market system; the realisation that market mechanisms can be applied to the public services as part of the attempt to make them accountable to their users; and the realisation that market economics is not enough. SMF's task is to develop the social market idea to the point where it can become an organising principle for social and economic policy. Created in 1989, the Foundation quickly generated publicity for itself and has attracted a stable of well reputed authors for its papers and reports.

TRADE POLICY RESEARCH CENTRE
University of Reading
Whiteknights Park, Reading RG6 2AA

The Trade Policy Research Centre was established in 1968 to promote independent analysis and public discussion of international economic policy issues. In general, the Centre provided a focal point for those in business, the universities and public affairs interested in the problems of international economic relations. During 1989, the Trade Policy Research Centre went into voluntary liquidation. From the mid-1980s, the Centre's deficit grew to unhealthy proportions. Although the Centre was increasingly successful in acquiring foundation grants, this was not accompanied with a commensurate rise in corporate support. Except for its journal which was acquired by Basil Blackwell Publishers, the Centre is now based at the University of Reading and receiving support from it, but remains independent of the University. The publications programme has been revived but it is no longer a membership organisation. The TPRC will have a broader focus than in the past but, as before, its principal objective is to promote work which is accessible to a wide readership.

United States of America

Policy Research Institutes within Washington DC

ACCF CENTER FOR POLICY RESEARCH
1750 K. Street, NW
Washington DC 20036

The Center for Policy Research is the education and research arm of the American Council for Capital Formation which created it in 1977. Through its economic analyses, publications and conference and seminar programme, the Center claims to provide the public, policy-makers and opinion shapers with timely, dependable and well-documented information on the importance of capital formation to the economy. The Center has a staff of four and a budget of over half a million dollars to initiate research or organise conferences on US economic growth; tax and environmental policies; waste management; corporate tax policies.

AMERICAN ENTERPRISE INSTITUTE FOR PUBLIC POLICY
RESEARCH – AEI
1150 17th Street, NW
Washington DC 20036

Originally known as the American Enterprise Association when established in 1943, the AEI sponsors original research on government policy, the American economy and American politics. AEI research aims to preserve and to strengthen the foundations of a free society – limited government, competitive private enterprise, vital cultural and political institutions and vigilant defence – through rigorous inquiry, debate and writing. The AEI is a large research institute with over one hundred people on staff and expenditures of nearly $12 million in 1993. Aside from a busy schedule of research conferences, lectures and seminars, the AEI has an extensive range of publications ranging from books and monographs to a bi-monthly magazine, *The American Enterprise*. There are three fields of research: domestic and international economic policy; foreign and defence policy; and social and political studies. The AEI is a neo-conservative organisation with a free market ethos, that is, 'the maintenance of a free and prosperous economic order, a resolute national defence, and tradition-proven cultural and political values'. Although its continued existence is not in doubt, the AEI has experienced financial difficulties since the mid-1980s. Nevertheless, it remains a leading American policy research institute.

ARMS CONTROL ASSOCIATION
1726 M. Street, NW
Washington DC 20036

Created in 1971, the ACA is dedicated to promoting public understanding and support for effective arms control policies. The ACA provides Congress, the media and the interested public with authoritative information and analyses on arms control proposals, negotiations and agreements, and a broad range of related national security issues. The ACA had a staff of eleven and a budget of $770,000 in 1994. Apart from reports and background papers, the ACA is best known for *Arms Control Today,* its monthly journal.

ATLANTIC COUNCIL OF THE US
1616 H. Street, NW
Washington DC 20006

A centre for the formulation of policy recommendations on the challenges and opportunities shared by the developed democracies of the Atlantic and Pacific communities, its purpose is to foster informed public debate about United States foreign, security and international economic policies. The Council engages the American Government, corporate, professional, and educational communities in an integrated programme of policy studies and round table discussions, dialogues and conferences designed to encourage its selected membership and other constituencies to reflect and plan for the future. Established in 1961, the Council has a staff of over thirty people and a budget in excess of $2 million. Its International Education programme aims to strengthen teaching of post-Second World War international relations in colleges and secondary schools in the USA and Europe. The Council has built a number of formal networks to facilitate liaison between the academic community, emerging leaders in government, business, law and the media as well as with business leaders. The Council describes itself as national in scope, rigorously bipartisan in orientation, and actively centrist and consensus-building in nature.

BROOKINGS INSTITUTION
1775 Massachusetts Ave, NW
Washington DC 20036

Brookings is devoted to research, education and publication in economics, government, foreign policy and the social sciences generally. Its principal purposes are to aid in the development of sound public policies and to promote public understanding of issues of national importance. The by-laws of the Institution state: 'It is the function of the Trustees to make possible the conduct of scientific research, and publication, under the most favorable conditions, and to safeguard the independence of the research staff in the pursuit of their studies and in the publication of the results of such studies. It is not a part of their function to determine, control, or influence the conduct of a particular investigations or the conclusions reached.' Brookings was established in 1927. It is an amalgamation of the Institute for Government Research (estab. 1916), the Institute of Economics (estab. 1922) and the Robert Brookings Graduate School of Economics and Government (estab. 1924). Today it is one of the largest independent research institutes in the USA with staff numbers bordering on 250 and expenses in excess of $20 million. Books and monographs are the main publications alongside the quarterly *The Brookings Review*. Brookings also sponsors conferences, seminars and other educational programmes for leaders in government, business and the professions.

CAPITAL RESEARCH CENTER – CRC
727 15th Street, NW
Washington DC 20006

The Capital Research Center was formed in 1984 to provide new perspectives on philanthropy in America. By challenging the progressive ideology of the public interest culture, the Center is helping the philanthropic community rediscover the bedrock principles of individual initiative and responsibility in a free society. The Center monitors and analyses the programmes, personnel, finances, goals and effects of key non-profit grant makers and recipients. With a staff of eight to ten people and a budget of approximately $700,000, the Center produces a number of reports, monographs and newsletters. Other activities include matching corporate givers with appropriate advocacy groups and think-tanks on its hotline. The CRC is a neo-conservative organisation with links to the Heritage Foundation. It maintains a considerable amount of information concerning other policy research institutes in the United States and acts as a reference centre.

CARNEGIE ENDOWMENT FOR INTERNATIONAL PEACE
2400 N. Street, NW
Washington DC 20037

Established in 1910 with a $10 million gift from Andrew Carnegie, the Carnegie Endowment conducts its own programmes of research, discussion, publication and education in international relations and US foreign policy. In 1993, the Endowment established a replica body, the Moscow Centre in Russia. Endowed with over $92 milion, it is one of the larger think-tanks in the USA and has sixty people on staff and expenses of $8,545,990 in 1993. It produces a well-regarded quarterly journal, *Foreign Policy*, as well as books and monographs covering issues such as American foreign policy and international security issues; nuclear non-proliferation; international migration; trade and national security; militancy in the developing regions of the world. The Endowment arranges occasional conferences; 'Face-to-Face' (invitation only, off the record) dinner discussions; breakfast meetings; luncheon seminars; as well as study groups and round tables to draw in and facilitate dialogue among a cross-section of key senior and working-level officials, former officials, media, business and industry, academics and others involved in the foreign policy processes.

CATO INSTITUTE
1000 Massachusetts Ave, NW
Washington DC 20001

Cato is dedicated to broadening the parameters of policy debate to allow consideration of more options that are consistent with the traditional American principles of limited government, individual liberty and peace. Toward that goal, the Institute strives to achieve a greater involvement of the intelligent, concerned lay public in questions of policy and the proper role of government in order to counter government's arbitrary intrusions into private economic transactions and its disregard for civil liberties. Originally located in San Francisco, California, the Cato Institute was established in 1977. The Cato Institute was informally linked with the Libertarian Party through the current Director and President, David Boaz and Ed Crane, who were both associated with the party until the 1980s. There is no longer any political connection. Once on the fringes, the Institute is now part of the intellectual mainstream in Washington DC, as its liberal position on homosexuality, pornography and drug legalisation combined with anti-communism and free market economics has become increasingly popular. Cato was staunchly against US involvement in the Gulf – a position which apparently lost it one of its major funders during 1991. Notwithstanding a few difficulties with some corporate funders, Cato is a steadily growing organisation with expenses in 1993 of an estimated $4,900,000. Cato has a staff of forty people and draws upon the intellectual support of 56 adjunct scholars. In order to maintain an independent posture the Institute accepts no government funding.

CENTER FOR DEFENSE INFORMATION – CDI
1500 Massachusetts Ave, NW
Washington DC 20005

CDI serves as an independent monitor of the military, analysing military spending, policies and weapons systems. The Center makes its reports available to journalists and the public and, on request, to government officials. The CDI opposes excessive expenditures for weapons and policies that increase the danger of nuclear war. CDI is committed to end the nuclear weapons build up, re-establish civilian control of the military and take the profit motive out of preparing for war. Founded in 1972, the 25 staff members of CDI are composed of retired military personnel and other researchers. The Center does not accept government funding or remuneration from military industries. It produces a periodical, *The Defense Monitor*, videos and a weekly television series 'America's Defense Monitor'.

CENTER FOR DEMOCRACY
1101 15th Street, NW
Washington DC 20005

The Center for Democracy seeks to promote and strengthen the democratic process in the United States and abroad. The Center claims to serve as a bridge linking the leadership of the two major American political parties. Created in 1984 by its current Director, Alan Weinstein, the Center has a staff of fifteen. It is affiliated with the International Center for Democracy in Strasbourg. The Center also maintains an office in Moscow. It produces a quarterly newsletter, *Democracy*, books and monographs on subjects such as democracy and the transition of societies to democracy. Its main activities, which make it more of a 'think-and-do' tank are conferences, election monitoring programmes, democratic legislative development, a Library of Democracy project for central and eastern European communities, the Young Leaders Programme and the provision of Freedom Scholarships.

CENTER FOR INTERNATIONAL POLICY
1755 Massachusetts Ave, NW
Washington DC 20036

The Center was founded during 1975 in the wake of the Vietnam War to define a more sympathetic US approach to the Third World. CIP seeks to convince US policy-makers that it is not in the long-term interests of the United States to embrace dictatorial rulers. CIP is a small institute of four salaried research staff and fluctuating income of approximately $300,000 p.a. The Center works within a web of organisations – church groups, labour groups, students and community goups with a common interest in Central America. The Center's role is to provide information which it does through public briefings, its *International Policy Report* and handbooks on US human rights law.

CENTER FOR NATIONAL POLICY – CNP
317 Massachusetts Ave, NE
Washington DC 20002

In the relationship between individual and government, the CNP believes the government has a positive role to play. Characterised as a 'liberal' think-tank, CNP describes itself as 'progressive-pragmatist'. It also sees itself as a forerunner to bodies such as PPI and EPI. The immediate past president of the CNP, Madelaine Albright, was appointed as Ambassador to the UN by President Bill Clinton. Formerly known as the Center for Democratic Policy, the CNP was created in 1981 by a group of people associated with the Democratic Party representing government, industry, labour and education. The Center is without resident research staff but draws on a roster of outside intellectual resources. With a budget of around $1 million, the CNP publishes occasional papers and books through CNP Press. It also runs a Campus Journal programme to assist students to start alternative opinion journals in addition to policy seminars, public symposium and invite-only Newsmaker Luncheons.

CENTER FOR POLICY ALTERNATIVES
2000 Florida Ave, NW
Washington DC 20009

The CPA is a policy centre for progressive policies and ideas in 50 states. The CPA chooses to work in the states since they are the place for action in a time of 'progressive federalism'. States incubate and test pragmatic solutions; together they create a horizontal wave of change from state to state which builds momentum for national action on shared problems. Established in 1975, the CPA has a staff of over 20 people and a budget of $1.5 million. It produces the quarterly *Ways and Means*, books, model legislation for state governments, a directory of progressive policy leaders, and policy papers. The Center undertakes research work on a diverse range of topics such as economic development, taxation, environmental security, barriers to voter registration, housing policy, sustainable agriculture, family and work, women's rights.

CENTER FOR POLICY ANALYSIS ON PALESTINE
2435 Virginia Avenue, NW
Washington DC 20037

The Center undertakes the study and analysis of the relationship between the United States and the Middle East, with particular emphasis on the Palestinian question and the Arab–Israeli conflict. The Center seeks to bring into focus the implications of US policies with regard to the Palestinian question ana the Arab–Israeli conflict and to provide a much needed Palestinian/Arab perspective that will address the political, media and academic establishments in Washington DC. The Center, established in 1990, is the educational arm of the Jerusalem Fund, a Washington DC based non-profit organisation. It is a small body with only two staff members.

CENTER FOR SECURITY POLICY
1250 24th Street, NW
Washington DC 20037

The Center emerged in 1988 as an uncompromising advocate of a strong national defence and a prudent foreign policy. The Center functions not as a traditional, research oriented think-tank but as a responsive policy information network in the Washington community focused exclusively on current foreign policy and defence issues. It seeks to disseminate its material through the most expeditious means available – primarily via fax but also by providing expert testimony to Congress. CSP is a conservative think-tank which exhibited a strong anti-Soviet orthodoxy. It is one of the most specialised think-tanks in Washington DC in terms of research focus, ideological stance and advocacy role. It operates with a small staff of four and a budget of $600,000.

CENTER FOR STRATEGIC AND INTERNATIONAL STUDIES – CSIS
1800 K. Street, NW
Washington DC 20006

The mission of the Center is to advance the understanding of emerging world issues in the areas of international security, politics, economics and business. The Center's commitment is to serve the common interests and values of the United States, its allies and other friends. From its inception in 1962, the CSIS was loosely affiliated with Georgetown University until 1987. Start-up was also assisted by the AEI. It did not accept federal funds in the past but now does so. The Center has a small endowment but is funded primarily from more than 300 US and foreign private sector corporations, individuals and foundations. Today, it has a staff of over 140 people and had operating costs of $13,776,026 in 1993.

Publications include, reports, monographs and papers, a newsletter, *The Washington Quarterly, Africa Notes* and *Soviet Prospect*. A crisis gaming centre has operated since 1981. Outreach involves Congressional study groups, briefings and testimonies, as well as seminars for senior corporate executives. In 1989, CSIS merged with Pacific Forum based in Hawaii, which is the hub of a network of 20 research institutes around the Pacific Rim.

CENTER FOR THE STUDY OF SOCIAL POLICY
1250 Eye Street, NW
Washington DC 20005

The Center is a research and policy analysis organisation established in 1979. It was conceived of as a place where contemporary social policies could be vigorously examined and where alternative strategies could be developed. Its mission is not to conduct pure research, but rather to work toward effecting change through thoughtful analysis of existing policies and the development of new ones. Much of the Center's work concentrates on financing and delivering human services in ways that cut across traditional programme boundaries and which use resources more effectively. In addition, the work focuses on inter-governmental aspects of social policy.

CENTER FOR WOMEN POLICY STUDIES
2000 P. Street, N
Washington DC 20036

Created in 1972, the Center is an independent policy research and advocacy organisation. The Center's central premises are that: all issues affecting women are interrelated; sex and race bias throughout society must be addressed simultaneously; and analyses of the status and needs of women must recognise their diversity – by race and ethnicity, by economic status, by disability, by sexual identity and by age. The Center's programmes combine advocacy, research, policy development and public education to advance the agenda for women's equality and empowerment. With a staff of seven and a budget of $500,000, the Center produces monographs and policy papers, a newsletter, videos, educational kits, and handbooks.

CENTER ON BUDGET AND POLICY PRIORITIES
777 N. Capitol Street, NE
Washington DC 20007

The Center is a leader in analysing public policies that affect low and moderate income Americans. Using data from the most reliable government sources, the Center analyses poverty trends and public policies. The primary concerns of the Center are income disparities, poverty, income and employment trends among minorities, low income housing, health care and food assistance issues, federal and state policies affecting low income households, options for reducing the federal deficit without increasing poverty, and strategies for lowering the poverty rate. A medium sized think-tank that was founded in 1981, the Center has a staff of over 20 on a budget of approximately $2 million. Publications include book chapters, reports and monographs, papers in professional journals and legal memoranda. Often described as an interest group, the Center is not a traditional scholarly think-tank but more advocacy driven.

COMPETITIVE ENTERPRISE INSTITUTE – CEI
1001 Connecticut Ave, NW
Washington DC 20036

The CEI is committed to advancing the principles of free enterprise and limited government. It was founded on the belief that free markets and competition best serve the public interest. CEI's programmes embrace a three-fold approach to implementing pro-market ideas: policy analysis; advocacy; litigation. With this 'triple threat' capability, CEI is able to advance the free market agenda and individual freedom wherever necessary. Established in 1984, the CEI has a fluctuating staff of between eight to twelve people on a budget of $500,000 or more. Aside from newsletters, reports, journal articles and book chapters, the CEI compiles the Competitive Enterprise Index – a record of how Congress members vote according to increased government intervention or spending. It is staffed by relatively young people and operates on a small budget. It maintains informal links with people at Heritage and Cato as well as other like-minded organisations, and is a member of StateNet.

COUNCIL ON HEMISPHERIC AFFAIRS
724 9th Street, NW
Washington DC 20001

The Council was founded in 1975 to promote the common interests of the hemisphere; raise the visibility and increase the importance of the inter-American relationship; and encourage the formulation of rational and constructive US policies towards Latin America. COHA supports open and democratic political processes, just as it condemns authoritarian regimes that fail to provide their populations with even minimal standards of political freedoms, social justice, personal security and civic guarantees. COHA publishes an Annual Survey of Press Freedom in Latin America in conjunction with the Newspaper Guild, and an Annual Human Rights Report. COHA is heavily reliant on volunteers and interns, and operated on a tiny budget of $75,000 in 1994.

DRUG POLICY FOUNDATION
4455 Connecticut Ave, NW
Washington DC 20008

The Foundation opposes the excesses of the world-wide war on drugs but supports the efforts to control drug related crime and corruption, to combat predatory criminal syndicates, to ameliorate the tragedies of drug abuse and to improve public health. Through research, education, legal action and public information programmes, the Drug Policy Foundation hopes to delineate rational modes of effective drug policy reform. The Foundation is not 'pro-drug' or a legalisation organisation. It sees itself as a resource centre and a leader in a growing reform movement. It seeks to counteract drug misinformation, such as through a weekly, half-hour television series on drug policy debate, *America's Drug Forum* and other television productions, and responds to numerous inquiries for information from the interested public, the media, state, federal and foreign legislators. The Legal Action Programme provides legal support for individuals and organisations. Civil libertarian in ethos, the Foundation was established in 1986 and by 1991 had 14 people on staff and a budget of $1 million. The Foundation neither seeks nor accepts government funding.

EAST–WEST FORUM
1455 Pennsylvania Ave, NW
Washington DC 20004

The East–West Forum aims to build a bridge between scholarship and policy making. It hopes to generate reliable information and high quality analyses that will prove useful to those engaged in the debates that shape US policy during a period of dramatic changes in East–West relations. Created in 1986, the Forum did not grow beyond a staff of two as a think-tank. By the 1990s, the Forum was phasing out traditional think-tank activities such as book publication, seminars and meetings in favour of educational activities, particularly for Eastern European individuals in the areas of business and management training, free market economic concepts and models and North American business practices and cultures, through intensive one year academic and practical training in US and Canadian universities and companies.

ECONOMIC POLICY INSTITUTE – EPI
1730 Rhode Island Ave, NW
Washington DC 20036

The EPI was conceived in 1984 by a group of people dissatisfied with the narrowness of the national dialogue on economics. Its founders felt that in an era of global competitiveness, new thinking was required for improving the opportunities and quality of life available to the people of America and the world. Accordingly, the EPI's programme of research and public education was established to broaden the public debate and to re-anchor that debate around the concerns of working Americans. In 1991, the EPI had a full-time staff of 30 – with additional research papers commissioned from a network of several hundred adjunct scholars – and expenses of $1,689,205. Start up funds came from eight unions. The EPI is a liberal alternative to the conservative and free market think-tanks in Washington DC.

ECONOMIC STRATEGY INSTITUTE – ESI
1100 Connecticut Ave, NW
Washington DC 20036

By challenging outmoded doctrines and examining the links between domestic and international economic policies, technological prowess, and global security issues, ESI aims to develop an integrated strategy that will halt erosion of the US economic base and assure the future of America's unique promise. Created in 1990, the ESI is a medium sized US think-tank with a staff of twelve and income of up to $3 million. Areas of research include: macro- and micro-economic policy; government–industry interaction; international trade policy; and the philosophy and structure of American business. Institute publications often advocate protectionist solutions to stem American economic decline. Accordingly, much of its financing comes from 'import sensitive US businesses'.

EMPLOYEE BENEFIT RESEARCH INSTITUTE – EBRI
2121 K. Street, NW
Washington DC 20037

Established in 1978, EBRI is a specialised think-tank that gathers, documents, analyses and communicates the facts that will shape the employee benefit programmes of the future. Its research programme strives to anticipate emerging benefit issues and to develop objective data relating to those issues before policy decisions are made. Thus, EBRI helps employers and employees, public officials and union leaders, scholars and the news media, as well as the general public, to intelligently assess health, welfare and retirement concerns. EBRI has a staff of 25 people or more, a budget of $2.75 million and approximately 300 member organisations. As a consequence, its publications are geared to the needs of this constituency and its interests in matters such as financing health care for the elderly; health care in the private sector; financial aspects of pension plans; tax policy and employee benefits; and retirement income security.

ENVIRONMENTAL AND ENERGY STUDY INSTITUTE
122 C. Street, NW
Washington DC 20001

The EESI was established in 1985 in co-operation with the leaders of the Congressional Environmental and Energy Study Conference (EESC), Congress's largest legislative service organisation with more than 90 Senators and 290 Representatives as members. Since 1991 EESI and EESC have operated as distinct and separate bodies. The EESI has a staff of 16 to 20 and a budget of $1 million. EESI is a member of Earth Share – a national federation of 27 non-governmental organisations with the joint commitment to safeguard environmental health, reduce pollution, save energy, preserve wilderness and protect wild life. The EESI is located close to the Capitol reflecting both its close contact with Congressional staff and its origins. It is rigorously bipartisan but its staff are generally characterised by a common commitment to ecologically sustainable modes of development.

ENVIRONMENTAL LAW INSTITUTE
1616 P. Street, NW
Washington DC 20036

Since 1969, the ELI has played a pivotal role in shaping the field of environmental law, management and policy, both domestically and abroad. Through its information services, training courses and seminars, research programmes and policy recommendations, the Institute reaches a broad constituency of environmental professionals in government, industry, the private bar, public interest groups and academia. With a staff of 60 and a budget of $5 million, the ESI is a large think-tank. It publishes the *Environmental Law Reporter* (monthly); the *National Wetlands Newsletter* (bimonthly); *The Environmental Forum* (bimonthly); monographs and occasional books. Like many other institutes, the ELI claims to be non-partisan and neither litigates nor lobbies.

ETHICS AND PUBLIC POLICY CENTER
1015 15th Street, NW
Washington DC 20005

The Center seeks to clarify and reinforce the bond between Judeo-Christian moral tradition and the public debate over domestic and foreign policy issues. Certain aspects of the Center's approach set it apart from other public policy organisations. First, it deals openly and explicitly with moral values in addressing contemporary issues. Second, the Center analyses the moral reasoning and public policy positions of organised religion. Third, the Center strives to deepen and broaden public debate on the ordering of our society and its relationship to the rest of the world, especially in areas where the positions of strident single-issue groups have received inordinate attention in the media and in the academy. Founded in 1976, the Ethics and Public Policy Center was originally located at Georgetown University but once it could survive independently, it was moved to a central Washington DC location. Unlike many of the new policy research institutes, the Center is relatively academic in style, mostly producing books. In 1993 it had a budget of just over $1 million and a staff of 13.

FAMILY RESEARCH COUNCIL
700 13th Street, NW
Washington DC 20005

The goal of the Council is not to find substitutes for the family but to restore to public esteem the private virtues of the family. Reminding legislators, judges and administrators of these traditional ideas – and buttressing them with fresh research and legislative initiatives – is a critical task. The family is also imperilled from without – by burgeoning bureaucracies that fail to recognise its worth, by radical forces that seek to redefine it and by commercial forces that profit from family break-up and sexual exploitation. The Council was created in 1983 and in 1988 it merged with Focus on the Family, another non-profit organisation committed to the preservation and strengthening of the family. The Council had a staff of 55 and income of $7 million in 1994.

FREE CONGRESS RESEARCH AND EDUCATION FOUNDATION
717 2nd Street, NE
Washington DC 20002

The Free Congress Foundation is dedicated to conservative governance, traditional values and institutional reform. The Foundation analyses issues of judicial reform, the electoral process, social welfare, foreign policy and education, particularly as they affect the family. Created in

1977, the Foundation evolved from the Committee for the Survival of a Free Congress, a political action committee established in 1974 by Paul Weyrich that provided conservative candidates with technical, informational and financial assistance in campaigns. Weyrich was one of the two founders of the Heritage Foundation. The Foundation maintains links with Heritage but is distinct in focusing more on social and cultural issues rather than economic affairs. With income in excess of $8 million the Foundation has grown into a large 'think-and-do' tank. In addition to the printed word (mostly newsletters), the Foundation brings together activists and leaders for training in the art of effective conservative governance and for periodic policy briefings on critical issues. In 1993, the Foundation launched NET – National Empowerment Television – its own full-time TV network.

GEORGE C. MARSHALL INSTITUTE
1730 M. Street, NW
Washington DC 20036

Since 1984, the George C. Marshall Institute has conducted technical assessments of scientific issues with an impact on public policy. Decisions are shaped by developments in and arguments about science and technology. However, even purely scientific appraisals are often politicised and misused by interest groups. The Marshall Institute seeks to counter this trend by providing policy-makers with rigorous, clearly written and unbiased technical analyses on a range of public policy issues.

GROUP RESEARCH INC.
2000 M. Street, NW
Washington DC 20005

Established in 1962, Group Research is similar in its research field and activities to the Capital Research Center but is liberal and almost exclusively devoted to monitoring the activities of right-wing organisations. The organisation has never expanded beyond two people and has been operating on a tiny budget by Washington DC standards.

THE HENRY L. STIMSON CENTER
21 Dupont Circle, NW
Washington DC 20036

Founded in 1989, the Center pursues research and public education on vital issues of arms control and international security, particularly difficult issues where policy, technology and politics intersect. The

Center involves executive branch officials, legislators and Capitol Hill
staff, non-governmental organisations in the US and abroad, diplomats
and the media in its programmes. The research interests of the Center
include multilateral verification of arms control agreements; politics of
treaty ratification; naval arms control; impact of declining defence
expeditures; new tools for peacekeeping; arms control in the Middle
East; confidence building measures.

HERITAGE FOUNDATION
214 Massachusetts Ave, NE
Washington DC 20002

The Heritage Foundation is dedicated to the principles of free
competitive enterprise, limited government, individual liberty and a
strong national defence. The Foundation's research and studies
programme are designed to make the voices of responsible conservatism
heard in Washington DC, throughout the US and in the capitals of the
world. Heritage publishes research in a variety of formats from books,
directories and journals (*Policy Review* – quarterly), to one-to-three page
issue briefs for the benefit of policy-makers, the media, the academic,
business and financial communities, and the public at large. Heritage was
set up in 1973 by Edwin Feulner and Paul Weyrich (now of the Free
Congress Foundation) in response to the perceived influence of liberal
organisations such as IPS and the Brookings Institution. Heritage has
become one of the largest conservative policy research institutes in
Washington DC. It has income of approximately $20 million and over
150 staff members. Its style of operation has also been emulated by
institutes such as the EPI and PPI as well as many of the state-based
conservative institutes, although none have been able to match it in size
or range of activity. Heritage has built up an International Resource Bank
of conservative scholars (and their areas of expertise), whom Heritage
attempts to promote in policy circles. In 1992, a branch office was
opened in Moscow to provide free market advice and assistance on
economic transition.

INSTITUTE FOR EDUCATIONAL LEADERSHIP
1001 Connecticut Ave, NW
Washington DC 20036

The IEL's purpose is to improve the quality of educational policy making
by linking people and ideas to address difficult issues. IEL serves state,
local and national educational leadership and others who have an impact
on education policy making. IEL has several objectives: improving
communications among policy-makers, educators and consumers of
educational services; offering mid-career training opportunities to

educational leaders; and providing educators, and the public-at-large a better understanding of key educational and social issues. The IEl was established in 1971 as an Institute of the George Washington University. In 1981, the Institute became a separate and autonomous non-profit organisation. Today it has a staff of 30.

INSTITUTE FOR INTERNATIONAL ECONOMICS – IIE
11 Dupont Circle, NW
Washington DC 20036

Since 1981, the IIE has been engaged in the study and discussion of international economic policy. The Institute is the only major research centre in the US devoted solely to international economic concerns such as the problems of world trade, money and finance, and debt and development. The IIE generally offers free trade prescriptions in its policy recommendations and is committed to multilateralism. IIE has been able to expand very quickly (by 1991, the IIE had a staff of 31, including visiting scholars, and a budget of $3.5 million) and has a high public profile in Washington DC. Fred Bergsten, founder of IIE, a former Treasury official in the Carter Administration and a scholar at Brookings, is an effective fund-raiser and promoter of the Institute and has been able to attract other officials and scholars. The Institute has also established links with other institutes throughout the world and sponsors a biennial conference for directors of international economic research institutes.

INSTITUTE FOR POLICY STUDIES – IPS
1601 Connecticut Ave, NW
Washington DC 20009

Created in 1963, the Institute serves as an independent centre of thought, action and social intervention in the nation's capital. Scholars and activists challenge the political pieties of the day and explore alternative directions to achieve real security, economic justice, environmental protection and grass-roots political participation. Independent of government, party, or political fashion, the Institute has put forward proposals for rethinking US–Soviet relations, for ending reliance on nuclear weapons, for achieving affordable health and housing for all Americans and for tackling other major public policy programmes. IPS was one of the first politically activist organisations, a style subsequently adopted to greater effect but different ideological purpose by the Heritage Foundation. It is a liberal progressive organisation, often portrayed as one of the most radical. In some accounts it is depicted as a communist front organisation (see Powell, 1987; Isaac and Isaac, 1983). The IPS experienced considerable organisational difficulties in the early 1980s from which it never fully recovered. Although it is a medium sized think-tank of 25 to 30 staff, income for the IPS in the 1990s has dropped from 1980s levels.

INSTITUTE FOR RESEARCH ON THE ECONOMICS OF TAXATION – IRET
1300 19th Street, NW
Washington DC 20004

IRET analyses the effects of government tax, spending and regulatory policies on the performance of the economy. Since its inception in 1985, IRET has promoted the free market system and opportunities for economic growth. It is a small classical liberal institute of less than ten staff members but with a budget of approximately $1 million.

INSTITUTE ON RELIGION AND DEMOCRACY
1313 H Street, NW
Washington DC 20005

Founded by Protestants and Catholics in 1981, the IRD promotes the spiritual renewal of the Church by insisting on the centrality of the proclamation of the gospel in the churches' ministry, and working for a more constructive Christian involvement in social and political issues. The IRD understands that faith must inform political judgements but the IRD cautions against the Church promoting extremist political positions which have not contributed to freedom or justice. The IRD is conservative and yet another institute with informal links to the Heritage Foundation as well as to the Ethics and Public Policy Center. It has staff of around eleven people and a budget below $1 million.

THE INTERNATIONAL CENTER
731 Eighth Street, SE
Washington DC 20003

Established in 1977, the International Center is a foreign policy organisation focused on relations with Asia, the former Soviet Union and promoting reforestation in developing countries around the world. It has a staff of twelve and a budget of $1,500,000. It produces books and directories as well as hosting foreign visitors or organising delegations of prominent Americans to other countries.

INTERNATIONAL FOOD POLICY RESEARCH INSTITUTE
1200 17th Street, NW
Washington DC 20036

IFPRI was established in 1975 to identify and analyse national and international strategies and policies for meeting food needs of the developing world on a sustainable basis, with particular emphasis on low income countries and on the poorer groups in those countries. The Institute's research programme reflects world-wide collaboration with governments and private and public intstitutions interested in increasing food production and improving the equity of its distribution. It is a large organisation with a staff of over 100 people plus visiting researchers. Its expenses in 1993 were $12,497,000. IFPRI operates as part of the Consultative Group on International Agricultural Research, a world-wide network of institutions that seeks to improve the productivity of agriculture, forestry and fisheries.

JOINT CENTER FOR POLITICAL AND ECONOMIC STUDIES
1090 Vermont Ave, NW
Washington DC 20005

The Center contributes to the national interest by helping black Americans participate fully and effectively in the political and economic life of our society. The Joint Center uses research and information dissemination to accomplish three objectives: to improve the socio-economic status of black Americans; to increase their influence in the political and public policy arenas; and to facilitate the building of coalitions across racial lines. The Center was created in 1970 as part of Howard University but is now completely autonomous. It has a staff of over 50 people and expenses nearing $4.5 million p.a. The Center maintains an on-line roster of black elected officials as well as on-line census and survey data. It produces radio and television programmes, works with minority elected officials and pinpoints resources that can be used to solve problems besetting socially and economically disadvantaged communities.

LINCOLN INSTITUTE FOR RESEARCH AND EDUCATION
1001 Connecticut Ave, NW
Washington DC 20036

The Lincoln Institute studies public policy issues that affect the lives of black middle America. The Institute aims to re-evaluate those theories and programmes of the past decades which were highly touted when introduced, but have failed to fulfil the claims represented by their sponsors – and in many cases, have been harmful to the long-range interest of blacks. The Institute demonstrates the futility of dwelling only on the differences instead of the many similarities that bind America's black minority to its white majority. The Institute prefers programmes like tuition tax credits, education vouchers, deregulation and strict law enforcement to affirmative action alternatives like quotas, busing and set-asides. Created in 1978, the Lincoln Institute is an average sized conservative think-tank of around ten to twelve people who produce books, monographs and the quarterly journal, *Lincoln Review*. While it is similar to the Joint Center in focusing on black American concerns, it does not have the same stature or public recognition as the Joint Center.

THE MEDIA INSTITUTE
1000 Potomac Street, NW
Washington DC 20007

The Media Institute is dedicated to the development of diverse news and information programming. The Institute conducts research studies and sponsors various seminars and programmes related to the First Amendment, business/media relations, Hispanic news media, commercial speech, environmental reporting and other communications policy issues. Created in 1976, the Media Institute pursues an active programme agenda that involves all sectors of the media, ranging from traditional print and broadcast outlets to the newer entrants such as cable, satellites and electronic databases. The Center seeks to promote a robust press and a dynamic communications industry and is ever mindful of the principles of free speech and free markets that animate its activities. In 1991, it had a staff of seven and a budget of $750,000.

NATHAN HALE INSTITUTE
422 First Street, SE
Washington DC 20003

The Institute was established in 1983 as the information and research arm of a now defunct advocacy organisation, the Hale Foundation. It provided support and encouragement for the US intelligence services at a time when they were under attack from hostile elements in Congress and the news media. Due to the end of the Cold War, the Institute's activities have been run down as funding has dried up. Although only ever a small think-tank, the Institute is no longer able to publish pamphlets, run a speakers bureau or hold conferences on intelligence and security issues.

NATIONAL ACADEMY OF PUBLIC ADMINISTRATION – NAPA
1120 G. Street, NW
Washington DC 20005

The Academy's mission is to improve the effectiveness of government at all levels chiefly by drawing upon the individual and collective experience of its own Fellows, as practitioners and students of government, to provide expert advice and counsel to government leaders. NAPA was founded in 1967. In 1984, NAPA acquired a Congressional Charter which requires it 'whenever called upon, to investigate, examine, experiment and report upon any subject of government', and to '... foresee and examine critical and emerging issues in governance and formulate practical approaches to their resolution'. NAPA has a budget of roughly $2 million and a staff of ten. Membership is made up of more than 400 current and former Cabinet officers, members of Congress, governors, mayors, legislators, jurists, business executives, public managers and scholars who have been elected as Fellows because of their distinguished practical or scholarly contribution to the nation's public life.

NATIONAL CENTER FOR PUBLIC POLICY RESEARCH
300 Eye Street, NE
Washington DC 20002

The National Center is a conservative 'think and do' tank with close links to Heritage, complementing its activities by undertaking grass-roots functions of mobilisation in addition to policy research on issues of immediate international and domestic interest. National Center materials (such as 'talking points cards', bumper stickers and 'how-to' manuals for activists) are designed for the use of conservative campus and community activists; for speakers, debaters and candidates; and for writers of op-ed pieces, research papers and policy statements. It was established in 1982. In 1991, the Center had a staff of four on an income that fluctuated around $300,000.

NATIONAL COMMITTEE FOR RESPONSIVE PHILANTHROPY
2001 S. Street, NW
Washington DC 20009

NCRP's purposes are to increase the accountability, accessibility and responsiveness of foundations, corporate giving programmes, United Ways and payroll education charity drives to social justice and progressive public interests. The NCRP is a watchdog on institutional philanthropy and advocate for social justice needs and progressive public interests. The Committee's field of interest is similar to that of the CRC (see above) albeit from a progressive ideological position. It was established in 1976. In 1993, it had a budget of $73, 836 and twelve full and part-time staff.

NATIONAL LEGAL CENTER FOR THE PUBLIC INTEREST
1000 16th Street, NW
Washington DC 20036

Since 1975, the National Legal Center has fostered knowledge about law and the administration of justice in a society committed to the rights of individuals, free enterprise, private ownership of property, balanced use of private and public resources, limited government and a fair and efficient judiciary. The Center does not accept state or federal funding.

NATIONAL PLANNING ASSOCIATION
1424 16th Street, NW
Washington DC 20036

The NPA is a forum where senior business, labour, agricultural and academic leaders come together on an on-going basis to focus on economic and social issues of mutual concern and national importance. NPA comprises a wide range of international and domestic policy committees that wrestle with the critical issues facing America and the world. Established in 1934, the NPA has a staff of around 25 and, in 1994, expenses of $1,817,257.

NATIONAL TAXPAYERS UNION FOUNDATION
713 Maryland Avenue, NE
Washington DC 20002

The Foundation was established in 1977 to fund and publish research, conduct symposia and undertake communication initiatives relating to fiscal and economic policy. The NTUF is the research affiliate of the National Taxpayers Union, a public interest advocacy organisation with 501(c)(4) status. The NTUF does not accept government funds.

NORTHEAST–MIDWEST INSTITUTE
218 D. Street, SE
Washington DC 20003

The Institute is a regional policy centre that works to ensure the future economic vitality of those states that historically have formed the nation's industrial heartland. The Institute is currently active in 19 states. In 1976, several members of Congress from the states within the region met to discuss items of common interest, from urban financial crises to rising energy costs. Their belief that the Northeastern and Midwestern states had much to gain from acting co-operatively on issues of regional concern led to the formation of the Northeast–Midwest Congressional and Senate Coalitions. Coalition members soon realised the need for information and public policy analysis as essential tools in identifying and furthering their mutual interests. The Institute was created in 1977 to provide the region's Senators and Representatives with up-to-date research in order to propose legislative solutions to regional problems. Today it has a staff of over ten people and a budget exceeding $1 million.

OVERSEAS DEVELOPMENT COUNCIL – ODC
1875 Connecticut Ave, NW
Washington DC 20036

Since 1969, the ODC's programmes have focused on US relations with developing countries. The ODC seeks to increase American understanding of the economic and social problems confronting the developing countries in an increasingly interdependent international system. ODC functions as:

- A centre for policy analysis. Bridging the worlds of ideas and action ODC translates the best academic research and analysis on selected issues of policy importance into information and recommendations for policy-makers in the public and private sectors.
- A forum for the exchange of ideas. ODC's programme of discussions of development issues at its conferences, seminars, workshops and briefings bring together legislators, business executives, scholars, and representatives of international financial institutions and non-governmental groups.
- A resource for public education. Through its publications, meetings, testimony, lectures and formal and informal networking, ODC makes timely, objective, non-partisan information available to an audience that includes but reaches far beyond the Washington policy-making community.

ODC has a permanent staff of 25 and expenditures over $2 million. A large organisation in its first decade, since the 1980s the ODC has become a smaller operation relying on scholars commissioned outside the organisation. A non-partisan and centrist body, it is often associated with advocating progressive views for US foreign policy towards developing nations.

POPULATION REFERENCE BUREAU
1875 Connecticut Ave, NW
Washington DC 20009

The PRB gathers, interprets and disseminates information about population trends and their public policy implications. PRB's programmes and publications reach a global audience with a special focus on those who can amplify the impact of its information – policy-makers in the United States and in the developing world, teachers and teacher trainers, an expanding network of journalists at home and abroad, as well as the concerned public. Technical support is also provided to organisations in developing countries. The PRB was created in 1929. In 1993 it had a staff of 50 and expenditures of over $3 million.

POTOMAC INSTITUTE
4323 Hawthorne Street, NW
Washington DC

The Potomac Institute promotes the development of policies and programmes designed to eliminate discrimination and realise the goal of equal opportunity for all Americans. It has sought to identify and help translate into action innovative approaches to the problems of racial and economic disadvantage. In 1991, the Potomac Institute was in the final phases of disbanding. Over its 30-year existence, when fully operational, the Institute fluctuated between 10 and 20 core staff.

PROGRESSIVE POLICY INSTITUTE – PPI
518 C. Street, NE
Washington DC 20002

Set up in 1989 the Institute seeks to adapt America's progressive tradition of individual liberty, equal opportunity and civic enterprise to the challenges of the post-industrial era. The PPI is the research arm of the Democrat Leadership Council and, as such, does not have 501(c)(3) status. PPI advocates growth-oriented economic policies designed to reverse America's competitive slide and foster a more inclusive, democratic capitalism; social policies that move beyond maintaining the poor to developing their personal capacities and independence; and a foreign policy based on protecting and spreading free institutions. The PPI has risen to greater significance since the presidential campaign of Bill Clinton. The PPI's *Mandate to Change* was considered to be one of the more influential transition documents.

RESOURCES FOR THE FUTURE – RFF
1616 P. Street, NW
Washington DC 20036

Established in 1952, RFF advances research and public education in the development, conservation and use of natural resources and in the quality of the environment. RFF research is concerned with the relationship of people to the natural environmental resources of land, water and air; with the products and services derived from these basic resources; and with the effects of production and consumption on environmental quality and on human health and well being. RFF is one of the first environmental think-tanks to emerge. It is also one of the largest think-tanks in Washington DC with expenditure of over $7 million in 1993. In addition to public advocacy and a diverse publishing programme, RFF is engaged in other activities. It distributes small grants to other organisations and individuals, offers research fellowships and four-week fellowships for professional development programmes, and awards a dissertation prize.

ROOSEVELT CENTER FOR AMERICAN POLICY STUDIES
316 Pennsylvania Ave, SE
Washington DC 20003

Established in 1982 and closed 1989, at its height the Center had a staff of 25. It researched the gamut of public policy. In addition it provided citizens guides on policy issues written for a general audience, conducted policy learning games and role playing exercises for secondary and college students and civic organisations, produced video presentations on policy issues for commercial and non-commercial distribution, and published curriculum guides and support materials for schools, colleges and community organisations.

TAX FOUNDATION
1250 H. Street, NW
Washington DC 20005

The Tax Foundation monitors tax and fiscal activities at all levels of government. In 1937, farsighted citizens envisioned an independent group of researchers who, by gathering data and publishing information on the public sector in an objective, unbiased fashion, could counsel government, industry and the citizenry on public finance. Through newspapers, radio, television and mass distribution of its own publications, the Foundation supplies objective fiscal information and analysis to policy-makers, business leaders and the general public. A medium sized think-tank of 12 to 15 people, the Foundation operated on a budget of $730,000 in 1990. The Tax Foundation describes itself as neither the voice of left or right, nor a voice of an industry or even of business in general, but as an advocate of a principled approach to tax policy. Nevertheless, it is of a broadly conservative ethos.

URBAN INSTITUTE
2100 M. Street, NW
Washington DC 20037

Created in 1968, the Institute's staff investigate the social and economic problems confronting the nation and develops public and private programmes designed to alleviate them. The Urban Institute was conceived as a domestic version of RAND at the instigation of Lyndon B. Johnson and his policy advisers. The Institute's objectives are to sharpen thinking about society's problems and efforts to solve them, improve government decisions and their implementation, and increase citizens' awareness about important public choices. Institute researchers evaluate existing policy options on a wide range of issues and offer conceptual clarification and technical assistance in the development of new strategies. The Urban Institute is large with a multi-disciplinary staff of about 200 and expenditure of over $17 million. It is academic in style, producing numerous books and reports of high scholarly standard. While it styles itself as a non-partisan and ideologically neutral organisation, it is generally perceived as liberal to centrist.

WASHINGTON INSTITUTE FOR NEAR EAST POLICY
1828 L. Street, NW
Washington DC 20001

Dedicated to providing research on the Middle East that is timely, of high quality and policy-relevant, the Washington Institute provides information and analysis on US interests in the Middle East. Established in 1985, the Institute grew quickly to a staff of 12 to 15 in-house research fellows, supplemented by visiting researchers and support staff in 1992. Of the organisations that are concerned exclusively with Middle Eastern affairs, the Washington Institute is the best financed and with the greatest public recognition. As a source of commentary and analysis, it became well known during the Gulf War. Its founding Director Martin Indyk went on to become Special Assistant to President Clinton on the Middle East and more recently US Ambassador to Israel.

THE WOMEN'S RESEARCH AND EDUCATION INSTITUTE
1700 18th Street, NW
Washington DC 20009

WREI's mission is to identify issues affecting women and their roles in the family, workplace and public arena, and to inform and help shape the public policy debate on these issues. WREI does not aim to be expert on all the important information about women being collected and analysed by researchers across this country. Rather, WREI seeks to strengthen the links between researchers, policy-makers, and opinion leaders so that research will be translated into action. WREI urges researchers to consider the public policy implications of their work, fosters the exchange of ideas and expertise between researchers and policy-makers, and promotes the informed scrutiny of policies regarding their effect on women, and encourages the development of policy options that recognise the circumstances of today's women and their families. Established in 1977 as the Congresswomen's Caucus Corporation, the Institute adopted its new name in 1979. It had a permanent staff of five and a budget of $700,000 in 1991–92.

WORLD RESOURCES INSTITUTE – WRI
1709 New York Ave, NW
Washington DC 20006

Through policy research and technical assistance, the World Resources Institute (established 1982) helps governments, the private sector, environmental and development organisations and others address how societies can meet human needs and nurture economic growth without destroying the natural resources and environmental integrity that make prosperity possible. In all its programmes, WRI strives to build bridges between scholarship and action, bridging the insights of scientific research, economic analysis and practical experience to political, business and other leaders around the world. In 1989 WRI merged with the Institute for International Environment and Development-North America. The amalgamation with IIED-North America strengthened the ability of both organisations to work at the country level in the developing world. With a 100-member interdisciplinary staff and a budget of approximately $11,500,000 budget in 1991, the WRI is a large scholarly think-tank. It collaborates with research institutions in 50 other nations.

WORLDWATCH
1776 Massachusetts Ave, NW
Washington DC 20036

From 1974, the Worldwatch Institute has sought to inform policy-makers and the general public about the interdependence of the world economy and its environmental support systems. Issues are analysed from a global perspective and within an integrated, interdisciplinary fashion. Research interests include environment; energy; food policy; population; development; technology; human resources; economics. WorldWatch publishes papers, the annual *State of the World Report* (sales approaching 300,000 p.a. and appearing in 27 languages), a bi-monthly magazine *Worldwatch* and books. It has a staff of over 30 and a budget of approximately $3.5 million. Worldwatch does not accept funding from any government.

Policy Research Institutes outside the Washington DC Area

ACTON INSTITUTE FOR THE STUDY OF RELIGION AND LIBERTY
161 Ottawa Street, NE
Grand Rapids, Michigan 49503

The mission of the Acton Institute is to identify and promote the ethical underpinnings of liberty by educating religious leaders about the ethical foundations of political liberty and free market economics. The goal is to foster a culture of active religious communities, strong families and wide ownership of property with constant reference to transcendent concerns. Established in 1990, it has a staff of nine and a budget in 1994 approaching $1,000,000. Generally regarded as a conservative body, it has links to the IEA in Britain through its Director, the Revd. Sirico.

ALAN GUTTMACHER INSTITUTE
111 Fifth Avenue
New York, NY 10003

Established in 1968, the AGI continues, through its research, policy analysis and public education activities, to build a firm base of substantive information to guide and shape the public debate about reproductive health and rights. The AGI is a specialised research institute addressing issues related to human reproduction especially regarding the socially and economically disadvantaged, that is, family planning, sex education, abortion, teenage pregnancy, maternal and prenatal care, contraceptive development and use, and reproductive health services. A division of Planned Parenthood Federation of America until 1977, the Institute is now a 'special affiliate' employing approximately 50 people.

AMERICAN INSTITUTE OF PACIFIC RELATIONS – AIPR

The Institute for Pacific Relations was an international organisation established in 1925 for the study of the conditions of the Pacific peoples with a view to the improvement of their mutual relations. It consisted of independent national councils in Australia, Canada, China, Great Britain, Japan, the Netherlands, New Zealand, the Philippines and the Soviet Union in addition to the USA. The international secretariat was established in New York and housed with the American Council of the IPR. The Institute was initially a leader in the field of Asian studies and particularly well known through its two journals *Pacific Affairs* and the *Far Eastern Survey*. However, the organisation ran into considerable difficulty after the Second World War with McCarthyite accusations of communist infiltration. National councils gradually disbanded when the American branch and international secretariat encountered funding difficulties as these bodies were the prime funding source for other Councils. The Institute was disbanded in 1961 (see Thomas, 1974).

ASPEN INSTITUTE
Box 222, Carmichael Road
Queenstown, Maryland 21658

The Aspen Institute is an international organisation founded in 1950. Its programmes are designed to enhance the ability of leaders in business, government, the non-profit sector, academia and the media to understand and act upon the issues that challenge the national and international community. The Institute helps leaders deepen their thinking and broaden their perspectives for decision making by convening them in seminars and conferences that address topics of current interest, but place the debate and discussion of such issues within the context of the universal and enduring values and ideas that traditionally define civilisation. Income of the Aspen Institute exceeds its expenditures of roughly $2.2 million p.a. substantially. It maintains additional offices in Washington DC; Aspen, Colorado; Germany; France; Italy; Britain; Japan. It produces *The Aspen Institute Quarterly* and reports.

ATLAS FOUNDATION
4210 Roberts Road
Fairfax, Virginia 22032

Atlas was established in 1981 for the purpose of creating, advising, supporting and developing independent public policy research institutes throughout the world. It helped establish and advises over 60 institutes in more than 30 countries. Atlas seeks to combat and challenge the conventional belief that government can best solve the economic and social problems of mankind. Each institute in the Atlas world-wide network shares the belief that the world's social, economic and political problems can be ameliorated by relying on some fundamental concepts of the free society: the rule of law, the institution of private property, contracts, the advocacy of the ideal of voluntarism in all human relations, and support of the unhampered market mechanism in economic affairs. Atlas operates with a small staff of five. Government support is not accepted. The Foundation conducts a yearly international workshop for research institutes and provides advisory services for free enterprise public policy units worldwide.

BARRY GOLDWATER INSTITUTE FOR PUBLIC POLICY RESEARCH
1109 South Plaza Way
Flagstaff, Arizona 86001

The Institute's mission is to marshal the best research and analysis on governmental, economic and educational issues which face Arizona now and into the twenty-first century. The Goldwater Institute concentrates on providing Arizona legislators and opinion leaders with the important and timely information that will help them implement public policies based on free market and limited government principles in Arizona.

CARNEGIE COUNCIL ON ETHICS AND INTERNATIONAL AFFAIRS
Merrill House, 170 East 64th Street
New York, NY 10021

Since its beginnings in 1914, the Council has asserted a strong belief that ethics, as informed by the world's principal moral and religious traditions, are an inevitable and integral component of any policy decisions, whether in the realm of economics, politics, or national security. The interrelationship of ethics and foreign policy is thus a unifying theme of all Carnegie Council programmes. The Council had a staff of 16 and a budget of $1,506947 in 1993. In addition to the publication of books, papers and an annual journal, *Ethics and International Affairs,* the Council is also engaged in college level curriculum development and runs case-study projects on classic problems in international affairs. The Carnegie Leadership Programme involves drawing together corporate executives, government officials, lawyers and consultants in luncheon and dinner seminars so as to contribute to informed policy and management decision-making.

CATALYST INSTITUTE
33 North LaSalle Street
Chicago, IL 60602

Created in 1984 as the Mid America Institute, the Catalyst Institute now claims to be the world's leading think-tank dedicated to improving public policy and business decisions affecting financial markets and institutions, and to raising the efficiency and effectiveness not only of these markets and institutions but also of governments and related agencies.

CENTER FOR THE STUDY OF DEMOCRATIC INSTITUTIONS
10951 Pico Boulevarde
Los Angeles, CA 90064

The Center was a progressive body and this ethos continues to be reflected through *New Perspectives Quarterly (NPQ)*. Originally established in Santa Barabara, in 1959 the Center brought together authoritative figures from the arts, academia, government, media and busines for open forums and discussion. Over time and after the death of its founder, Robert Hutchins, the Center lost funding and faced closure. In the 1980s it merged with a journal *(NPQ)*. Since the merger with *NPQ*, the Center exists only as a publisher.

CLAREMONT INSTITUTE FOR THE STUDY OF STATESMANSHIP AND POLITICAL PHILOSOPHY
4650 Arrow Highway D6
Montclair, CA 91763

Fellows at the Institute see an essential connection between free government and free enterprise, between good character among the people and the prevalence of strong families. 'We believe it essential to defend the nation against tyranny. We believe it necessary to prepare an overpowering defence in this time of unsettled and dangerous "peace", that no temptations be offered to potential aggressors. The Claremont Institute would recover the original principles of America and restore them to their preeminent place in the common mind of the nation'. A conservative body, the Institute was established in 1979. It has a staff of approximately 20 people and a budget of over $1 million.

COMMITTEE FOR ECONOMIC DEVELOPMENT – CED
477 Madison Avenue
New York, New York 10022

Since 1942, the CED has been devoted to policy research and the implementation of its recommendations by the public and private sectors. Its mission is to identify the most important and persistent economic problems confronting business and the nation, to develop constructive and realistic solutions to these problems, and to build a national consensus to convert its ideas into action. CED is unique among business-oriented organisations. Its 250 trustees – mostly heads of major corporations and university presidents – personally formulate and vote on policy recommendations and speak out forcefully for the adoption of these recommendations by government and business. CED has a staff of approximately 45 research and support personnel and, in 1993, expenses of $4,389,800.

COMMONWEALTH FOUNDATION FOR PUBLIC POLICY
ALTERNATIVES
600 North Second Street
Harrisburg, Pennsylvania 17101

From its inception in 1988, the Foundation has been committed to furthering the goals of economic growth and individual opportunity in Pennsylvania. Affirming the belief that market competition enhances the public interest by creating growth and prosperity for all, the Foundation's programmes attempt to foster an economic climate where entrepreneurship and private initiative can flourish. The Foundation is a small institute of about four people. It does not accept state or federal government grants. In addition to policy research, the Foundation has conducted statewide polls, built an academic resource bank and speakers bureau, and established the Pennsylvania Privatisation Council. The Commonwealth Foundation is a member of the StateNet network of institutes.

CONFERENCE BOARD
845 Third Avenue
New York, NY 10022

The Conference Board's two-fold purpose is to improve the business enterprise system and to enhance the contribution of business to society. To accomplish this, the Conference Board strives to be the leading global business membership organisation that enables senior executives from all industries to explore and exchange ideas of impact on business policy, and practices. With a staff of 250 and expenditures of over $24 million in 1993, the Board is a very large think-tank. It is also affiliated with the Conference Board of Canada and maintains a European office in Brussels.

COUNCIL ON FOREIGN RELATIONS – CFR
Harold Pratt House, 58 East 68th Street
New York, NY 10021

The CFR is a non-partisan membership organisation dedicated to improving understanding of American foreign policy and international affairs through the free exchange of ideas. The Council's membership is composed of men and women with experience in American foreign policy who are leaders in education, public service, business and the media. As a leader in the expanding community of institutions concerned with American foreign policy, the Council recognises its responsibility to contribute to the public dialogue on significant international issues. Established in 1921, the Council has over 40 researchers on staff plus support. In 1993, its expenditure was $13 million. The CFR has no affiliation with, receives no funding from and does no contract research for the US Government or any other government. The Council benefits from a sizeable endowment of over $55 million.

EMPIRE FOUNDATION FOR POLICY RESEARCH
130 Washington Avenue
Albany, NY 12210

The Foundation was created in 1991 and is a member of StateNet, the conservative network of state based think-tanks. Its research interests are tax issues, welfare reform and New York state issues. The Foundation does not accept government support.

FLAGSTAFF INSTITUTE
PO Box 986
Flagstaff, Arizona 86002

Founded in 1976, the objectives of the Institute are to research, discuss, publish and present information to support and improve world trade; to encourage, foster and stimulate commerce, world trade and business; and to obtain and distribute reliable information and promote co-operation and exchange between countries and businessmen; to acquaint and inform the public and various governmental agencies of the benefits of improved world trade. It is a small think-tank of only five people.

FOREIGN POLICY RESEARCH INSTITUTE
3615 Chestnut Street
Philadelphia, PA 19104

The FPRI is devoted to advanced research and public education on international affairs. FPRI seeks to shape the intellectual climate in which US foreign policy is made and thereby contribute to the spread of representative governments and the rule of law. FPRI was established at the University of Pennsylvannia in 1955 but has been independent since 1970. It has 20 in-house employees. It produces two quarterly journals, *ORBIS* and *AGORA*, papers and books.

FOUNDATION FOR RESEARCH ON ECONOMICS AND THE ENVIRONMENT
4900 25th Avenue
Seattle, WA 98105

Since 1986 FREE has developed innovative solutions to environmental problems based on the classical liberal principles of private property and the market process. With a staff of seven it publishes a newsletter, project reports and books on topics such as endangered species, Federal natural resource management, global warming, waste management, and scientific developments in environmental issues.

THE HEARTLAND INSTITUTE
800 East Northwest Highway
Palatine, IL 60067-6516

Heartland develops and promotes free-market solutions to state and local public policy problems. Heartland solicits research from academics and professional policy analysts, edits and packages the results for popular audiences and aggressively promotes its findings to legislators and (through the news media) the public. Heartland is another think-tank that does not accept government funding. Established in 1984, the Institute has a staff of twelve and had a budget of $1.2 million in 1993.

THE HOOVER INSTITUTION ON WAR, REVOLUTION AND PEACE
Stanford University
CA 94305

Established in 1919, the Hoover Institution is a centre for advanced study in domestic and international affairs. It contains one of the largest private archives and most complete libraries in the world on economic, political and social change in the twentieth century, as well as a major scholarly press. Affiliated with the Institution are five Nobel laureates and a host of distinguished statesmen. More than 100 resident scholars examine major issues in economic, political science, sociology, education and history. It had a budget of approximately $20 million in 1992 and an endowment of $120 million. It is based at, but is independent of, Stanford University.

THE HUDSON INSTITUTE
PO Box 26-919
Indianapolis, Indiana 46226

Hudson specialises in the study of policy problems and options for the public and private sectors. Hudson analysts take an approach to research which embodies scepticism about conventional wisdom, optimism about solving problems, a steadfast commitment to free institutions and individual responsiblity, and a 'realistic' view of threats to national security. Hudson was established in 1961. Today it has a budget of approximately $5 million. Originally, the Hudson Institute was located in New York State. It relocated to Indianapolis as a means to overcome funding and administration problems.

THE INDEPENDENCE INSTITUTE
14142 Denver West Parkway
Golden, Colorado 80401

The Institute offers state and local government a forward-looking, non-partisan agenda that builds on the principles established by the Founding Fathers to create the nation – limited government, economic freedom and individual responsibility. It has served Colorado and the nation since 1985 by seeking to build consensus on strategies for resolving today's governmental, economic and educational issues consistent with the truths of the Declaration of Independence. The Independence Institute was one of the first state-based libertarian policy organisations and, accordingly, a prototype and mentor for nascent free market think-tanks in other states. It is a member of StateNet.

INDIANA POLICY REVIEW FOUNDATION
320 North Meridian Street
Indianapolis, Indiana 46204-1719

'Our mission is to marshal the best research on governmental, economic and educational issues at the state and municipal level. We seek to accomplish this in ways that: exalt the truths implied in the Declaration of Independence, especially those concerning the interrelated freedoms of religion, enterprise and speech; emphasize the primacy of the individual in solving public concerns; and recognize that equality of opportunity is sacrificed in the pursuit of equality of results.' Established in 1989, the Foundation has a staff of five and had a budget of half a million dollars in 1993.

INSTITUTE FOR AMERICAN VALUES
1841 Broadway
New York, NY 10023

The Institute is devoted to research, publication and public education on major issues of family well being, family policy and civic values. The Institute's primary mission is to examine the status and future of the family as a social institution. Through its publications and other educational activities, the Institute bridges the gap between scholarship and policy making, bringing new analyses to the attention of policy-makers in government, decision-makers in the private sector, and opinion-makers in the media. Founded in 1987, the Institute is small with a staff of four and budget of $400,000.

INSTITUTE FOR CONTEMPORARY STUDIES
243 Kearny Street
San Francisco, CA 94108

Since 1974, the ICS has specialised in anticipating policy issues, mobilising the best academic talent, publishing for policy-makers in language they can understand. The ICS was set up to aid Ronald Reagan in his run for the Presidency by providing fresh ideas. The links were to cost ICS later, for many of its staff went to Washington DC when Reagan was elected, decimating the analytic base of the organisation. During this period it did little other than publish books and monographs. The Institute has regained much ground since the early 1990s and has a staff of approximately 25 and a budget of approximately $3 million. It has, however, become less academic in style and more populist and engaged in adocacacy oriented activities. ICS is a conservative organisation of the market liberal variety.

INSTITUTE FOR DEFENSE AND DISARMAMENT STUDIES
675 Massachusetts Avenue
Cambridge, Massachusetts 02139

Established in 1979, the IDSS addresses the need and opportunity, in the wake of the cold war, for nations to adopt common security policies that would demilitarise international relations, reduce the risk of war, and strengthen democratic institutions. With a budget of around $1 million and a staff of ten people in 1991, the Institute produces papers, edits books, provides a monthly reference service, *Arms Control Reporter*, a monthly bulletin, *Defense and Disarmanent Alternatives*, and *WeaponWatch Data on Disk*. Other activities include engaging in dialogue with diplomats, civilian officials, military officers and analysts, media liaison, and support for professional and public interest groups.

INSTITUTE FOR ENERGY RESEARCH
6219 Olympia
Houston, Texas 77057

The IER was founded in 1989 to offer a free market voice in the energy debate. Policy issues concerning oil, gas, and electricity have been dominated by industry firms and trade groups, the environmental lobbies and self-styled consumer groups – all supporting government intervention to address energy problems. IER has sought to add a consistent private property rights/voluntary exchange perspective as well. The IER is a tiny organisation with only two staff members and had a budget of $35,000 in 1994. It has links with the Cato Institute and Competitive Enterprise Institute.

INSTITUTE FOR FOOD AND DEVELOPMENT POLICY
145 9th Street
San Francisco, CA 94103

The Institute conducts policy research on issues such as aid, poverty, food insecurity, Third World development and environment. Created in 1975, it is a small organisation of seven people and had a budget of $575,000 in 1993.

INSTITUTE FOR GLOBAL SECURITY STUDIES
225 North 70th Street
Seattle, WA 98103

The Institute was founded with the belief that, in the past, 'security' has signified only military strength. The Institute believes that 'genuine security' can only exist by defending human rights, encouraging sustainable development and reversing militarisation. Created in 1986, the Institute is a very small body of three people and had a budget of approximately $86,000 in 1992. It produces a quarterly *Pacific Security Report* which addresses issues such as arms control, human rights and sustainable development.

INSTITUTE FOR FOREIGN POLICY ANALYSIS
675 Massachusetts Avenue
Cambridge, Massachusetts 02139

Since 1976, the Institute has provided a forum for the examination of political-economic, national security and defence-industrial issues confronting the US and its allies in a rapidly changing world. IFPA's programmes are based on the realisation that decision-makers, whether in government or industry, cannot make adequate choices without the benefit of a strategic perspective. Indispensable to such an approach is the integration of defence issues, economic factors, technological trends and political dimensions. IFPA is conservative in ethos and seeks to preserve and strengthen a national consensus in support of American foreign policy. With a staff of 20, it had a budget of $2.1 million in 1991.

INSTITUTE OF THE AMERICAS
10111 North Torrey Pines Road
La Jolla, CA 92037

The Institute is dedicated to promoting co-operation and information exchange among the countries of the Americas and to finding effective responses to some of the major challenges facing the Western hemisphere: consolidating democracy and market-oriented economic reform; extending free trade; finding alternative sources of energy and halting environmental deterioration. The Institute was established in 1983. It had a budget of $1 million in 1993. It conducts private sector oriented conferences and is the official secretariat of the US–Mexico Environmental Business Committee.

INSTITUTE ON RELIGION AND PUBLIC LIFE
156 Fifth Avenue
New York, NY 10010

'America desperately needs a public philosophy and practical guidelines for sustaining this Republic's experiment in a free and virtuous public order. The three component parts of such an order are politics, economics and culture. Of the three, culture is the most important and is today the most embattled. By culture we mean the available ideas by which a society understands itself, its problems and its possible futures. At the heart of culture is religion. By religion we mean the morally binding ideas in a society – whether or not they are identified as "religious".' The goal of RPL is to make persuasive and effective connections between public policy, culture and religion. The predecessor organisation of the Institute was the Center on Religion and Society – established in 1984. The new Institute was operational from 1990. In

1993, it had revenue of $1,400,000 and a staff of five under the President, Father Richard Neuhas.

INTERNATIONAL PEACE ACADEMY
777 United Nations Plaza
New York, NY 10017

The IPA is devoted to peaceful and multilateral approaches to the resolution of international and internal conflicts. In fulfilling its mission, the IPA works closely with the UN, regional and other international organisations, government and parties to conflicts. With a staff of 16, its output of policy oriented research is focused on the evolving peace and security role of the UN. The Academy also provides training seminars on peacemaking and UN collective security.

JAMES MADISON INSTITUTE FOR PUBLIC POLICY STUDIES
Post Office Box 13894
Tallahassee, Florida 32317

'The mission of the Madison Institute is to cause those who influence and make public policy in the Southeastern states to give greater consideration to the timeless principles of the United States Constitution. Those principles have been expressed clearly and forcefully by Jefferson, Madison, Monroe and others.' The Institute is committed to free enterprise and a market economy, limited government, federalism, strengthening the family and traditional values. Founded in 1987, the Institute is another think-tank that does not accept government funding and is a member of the StateNet organisation.

JOHN LOCKE FOUNDATION
PO Box 17822
Raleigh, North Carolina 27619

The Foundation seeks to advance understanding of society based on principles of individual liberty, the voluntary exchanges of a free market economy and limited government. Founded in 1990, the John Locke Foundation is one of the smallest state-based policy institutes. Accordingly, it is reliant on a network of scholars based outside the institute in universities or other think-tanks as contributors to its newsletter and reports. It is also a member of StateNet.

KEYSTONE CENTER
PO Box 606
Keystone, CO 80435

Founded in 1975, the Center focuses on science and public policy. As a conflict resolution organisation, it provides facilitation and mediation services on controversial environmental, health, natural resource, scientific and technological issues and offers educational and professional programmes to encourage and enhance scientific enquiry. The Center seeks to bring people together to solve problems, to enhance understanding and appreciation of the natural world, to encourage scientific inquiry, and to develop consensus on important, complex and controversial public policy issues. In 1993, it had expenses of nearly $7.5 million.

LEHRMAN INSTITUTE INC.
42 East 71st Street
New York, NY 10021

The Institute is now defunct. It was created in 1972 as an operating foundation. Books addressed contemporary economic, social and foreign policy issues, for example, the international monetary system, US foreign economic policy since 1945, economic and trade relations with Japan, politics of international debt, and New York City/state financial problems.

LOCKE INSTITUTE
5188 Dungannon Road
Fairfax, Virginia 22030

The Institute is named after John Locke, philosopher and political theorist, who based his theory of society on natural law which required that the ultimate source of political sovereignty was with the individual. Founded in 1990, the Locke Institute seeks to engender a greater understanding of the concept of natural rights, its implications for constitutional democracy and for economic organisation in modern society. The Institute encourages high quality research utilising modern theories of property rights, public choice, law and economics, and institutional economics as a basis for a more profound understanding of important and controversial issues in political economy.

MACKINAC CENTER FOR PUBLIC POLICY
119 Ashman
PO Box 568
Midland, Michigan 48640

The Center seeks to challenge the prevailing consensus with alternatives to more government spending and regulation. Formerly known as the Michigan Research Institute, the Center was created in 1987. The Center is a state based, conservative and market liberal think-tank with links to the Heritage Foundation. It is also a member of StateNet.

MANHATTAN INSTITUTE FOR POLICY RESEARCH
52 Vanderbilt Avenue
New York, NY 10017

The Manhattan Institute was established in 1978. It made headlines early in its existence through its promotion of George Gilder's *Wealth and Poverty* and *Losing Ground* by Charles Murray. During the 1980s, Gilder became the Institute's programme director and a key promoter of the supply-side economic philosophy. The Institute's broad field of research interest is national and international policy such as civil justice reform and housing. While maintaining research interest in national issues, the Institute has developed greater policy strength in issues relating to New York City. The usual approach of the Institute, which has only a small staff of ten, is to commission books written by academics.

NATIONAL BUREAU OF ECONOMIC RESEARCH
1050 Massachusetts Avenue
Cambridge, MA 02138

Founded in 1920, the NBER is dedicated to promoting greater understanding of how the economy works. The NBER is committed to promoting and disseminating unbiased economic research among public policy-makers, business professionals and the academic community. Much of its research is of a technical and statistical nature. For example, studies of productivity, capital formation, taxation, pensions and social insurance, business cycles, financial institutions and processes, international economic relations, the economics of health and of aging, and quantitative analyses of the US economy. Its staff is composed of 280 research associates and 100 Faculty Research Fellows spread through US universities. Since 1992 it has enjoyed a budget in excess of $10 million.

NATIONAL CENTER FOR POLICY ANALYSIS
12655 N. Central Expy
Dallas, Texas 75243

The NCPA supports free enterprise, low taxes, limited government and a strong national defence. Its primary goal is to uncover and promote alternatives to government regulation and control, solving problems by relying on the strengths of the competitive, entrepreneurial private sector. The motto of the NCPA, 'Making Ideas Change the World', reflects the belief that ideas have the power to change the course of human events. Established in 1983, the NCPA has a national focus but has ties with the state based conservative, free market institutes through StateNet. Its revenue in 1993 exceeded $2 million. It has a small staff of eleven but an extensive list of over 60 adjunct scholars.

NATIONAL INSTITUTE FOR PUBLIC POLICY
3031 Javier Road
Fairfax, VA 22031

Founded in 1981, the Institute provides a wide-ranging strategic perspective – integrating political, military, historical, social and economic analysis – for both public and private clients. As part of its role in informing public policy, staff of the National Institute regularly engage in interacting with the US Governmental community. Research topics include arms control and disarmament, nuclear decision making, uses of space, naval strategy, peace and security education. Other activities include in-service training seminars for high school teachers and production of school textbooks on international relations and global education.

PACIFIC FORUM
1001 Bishop Street
Honolulu, Hawaii 96813

Pacific Forum conducts policy-focused discussions and studies on issues of national and international importance in the Pacific Basin. It promotes mutual understanding of such vital international issues as economic development, investment, trade, resources and technology, and threats to security proposed by political, economic and military tensions. In 1989, Pacific Forum merged with the CSIS in Washington DC. It remains an autonomous organisation with a staff of 14. Aside from books and policy papers, the Forum has become the international secretariat for the Pacific Basin Economic Council (PBEC) which serves as the private sector's voice in the region. In 1991, a new division of Pacific Forum was established – the Ocean Policy Institute. It will address environmental and ocean issues in the Asia-Pacific.

PACIFIC INSTITUTE
1204 Preservation Parkway
Oakland, CA 94612

Underlying all of the Pacific Institute's work is the recognition that the pressing problems of environmental degradation, regional and global poverty, and political tension and conflict are fundamentally interrelated, and hence long-term solutions must consider all of these issues in an interdisciplinary manner. Established in 1987, the Pacific Institute strives to conduct, to encourage and to disseminate research that acknowledges the breadth and the long-term nature of both the problems and the necessary solutions.

PACIFIC RESEARCH INSTITUTE FOR PUBLIC POLICY
177 Post Street
San Francisco, CA 94108

Founded in 1979, the Pacific Research Institute investigates critical policy issues and provides solutions which apply the fundamental principles of market process, property rights, and public choice theory. The Institute's Center for Applied Jurisprudence charts the course to a principled rule of law based on individual natural rights and the Constitution. The Institute's environmental programme explores the potential for enhanced environmental quality and economic efficiency through free market incentives, accountable institutions, and enforceable property rights. The Institute does not conduct in-house research. By 1991 the Institute had published 31 books which have been adopted for over 460 courses at more than 220 colleges, universities, and graduate schools nationwide.

PIONEER INSTITUTE FOR PUBLIC POLICY RESEARCH
21 Custom House Street
Boston, MA 02215

Government funded academic research has dominated political and intellectual discourse in Massachusetts. The Pioneer Institute seeks to change this by inspiring the academic community, the media and state and local officials to reconsider the strongly held notions about education, automobile insurance, health care and welfare reform to move the intellectual debate toward market-based policy reforms and cost-conscious government.

POLITICAL ECONOMY RESEARCH CENTER
502 South 19th Street
Bozeman, Montana, MT 59715

Established in 1980, PERC employs public choice perspectives and other free market approaches to assess environmental issues and is libertarian in ethos. PERC seeks to inform policy in the areas of energy, minerals, taxation, productivity, water; forestry and wildlife. Its publications frequently argue that government 'protection' of natural resources and the environment is a myth and that private protection is often more effective. Many of its books are distributed by the Pacific Research Institute.

RAND
1700 Main Street
Santa Monica, CA 90407

RAND has its origins in the Second World War when it was established, and then contracted, by the Air Force division of the Army as a research unit. In 1948, it sought and acquired independent status from the Air Forces by successfully attracting Ford Foundation funding. RAND is an acronym for Research and Development (see Smith, 1966 for an early history). It is engaged in research and analysis of matters affecting national security and the public welfare. Work involves most of the major disciplines in the physical, social and biological sciences with an emphasis on their application to problems of policy and planning in domestic and foreign affairs. RAND's objectives are to further and promote scientific, educational and charitable purposes, for the public welfare and security of the United States of America.

RAND is a very large organisation. It has over 1000 employees while funding, which mostly comes from government, was in excess of $110 million in 1993. Research projects are managed within four research divisions: Project AIR FORCE, Army Research, National Security Research and Domestic Research. RAND does not conduct commercial research. RAND Graduate School, founded in 1970, is an accredited doctoral institution.

THE REASON FOUNDATION
3415 S. Sepulveda Blvd.
Los Angeles, CA 90034

The United States was founded on principles of private property, a market economy, civil liberties, and democracy, yet maintaining the institutions that uphold those principles is an ongoing process. The Reason Foundation plays a unique and important role in that process with its concern about impacts of current policies on basic political and economic institutions. The Reason Foundation was established in 1978. It has a staff of approximately 20 and a budget over $2 million, but does not accept nor seek government grants or contracts. Its research covers government and the private sector, and privatisation and deregulation in the areas of tollways, airports, solid waste management, and air quality. Reason also produces Midnight Economist – a syndicated radio programme.

ROCKFORD INSTITUTE
934 North Main Street
Rockford, IL 61103

The purpose of the Rockford Institute is to rebuild an American ethical consensus rooted in the fundamental ideas and traditions of Western civilisation. Through research, conferences and publications, the Institute seeks to influence the moral and intellectual forces that shape social and cultural trends and public issues. The Institute has programmes in the general areas of religion and society, the family and literature. Created in 1976, the Institute has a staff of 17 and expenses in 1993 of $1.3 million. The Institute does not accept government funds. The Institute has expanded in scope from an initial focus on educational curricula to broader policy issues.

THE RUSSELL SAGE FOUNDATION
112 East Sixty-fourth Street
New York, NY 10021

The Russell Sage Foundation was established in 1907 for the improvement of social and living conditions in the United States. Since the Second World War the Foundation has devoted its efforts to strengthening the social sciences as a means of achieving more informed and rational social policy. To that end, Russell Sage has established a research center at its headquarters in New York where visiting social scientists can pursue their writing and research. The Foundation also supports external research projects. The Foundation's agenda includes research on the causes and consequences of various social problems as well as basic research aimed at improving the methods, data and theoretical foundation of social science. In 1991, the Foundation expended $5.6 million.

SOUTH CAROLINA POLICY COUNCIL
1419 Pendleton Street
Columbia, South Carolina 29201

The Council is a centre for research on issues of importance to the peoples of South Carolina. Founded in 1986, its goal is to generate new ideas and prompt policy change that will, spur economic growth, enhance individual opportunity, empower citizens with greater control over their government, and defend traditional South Carolina values.

STATENET
PO Box 25010
Fort Wayne, Indiana 46825

StateNet grew out of the Madison Group – an informal network of state-based conservative and market liberal policy institutes. StateNet came into being in 1992 and has a membership of approximately 40 institutes. Membership in StateNet is open to any 501(c)(3) policy organisation devoted exclusively or primarily to research on state policy issues. Other criteria include support for:

- economic freedom, citizen empowerment, and traditional American values,
- research on a broad range of public policy subjects of relevance to the state in which it is located,
- an established place of business,
- high quality programmes such as publications, seminars and other educational activities,
- developing and maintaining a sufficiently broad base of members and supporters and to prevent undue influence on the objectivity of research and maintain financial stability.

StateNet is primarily responsible for fund-raising for market liberal institutes and for mounting national public relations programmes to raise awareness of the state policy movement. It aims to provide pension and health insurance plans for staff of policy institutes, printing services and access to electronic data services as well as volume purchasing agreements for equipment. StateNet will also provide matching grants to assist in the start-up of new state policy research organisations along with technical support and management development services such as manuals on how to start a policy organisation. To facilitate communication, StateNet provides an on-line repository of state policy research and an on-line state policy 'bulletin board'.

TEXAS PUBLIC POLICY FOUNDATION
8626 Tesoro Drive, Suite 203
San Antonio, Texas 78217

Established in 1989, the Foundation seeks to generate new ideas, gather
accurate facts, analyse these thoroughly and set down their findings and
recommendations in the clear light of truth, integrity and fairness.

TWENTIETH CENTURY FUND
41 East Seventieth Street
New York, NY 10021

The Twentieth Century Fund was conceived during 1911 in an effort to
help bridge the gap between the world of ideas and the world of affairs.
Its roots were in the progressive movement that dominated much of
American public policy thinking during the early decades of this century.
It is concerned with issues such as the role of government in an
overwhelmingly private-sector economy, the international mission of the
United States, and the management of many of significant economic and
social institutions. The Fund is an operating foundation. It had an
endowment of approximately $50 million in 1991 and an annual budget
of around $3 million. It has a staff of 20 people plus adjunct scholars
under contract to the Fund to conduct research and write books.

WASHINGTON INSTITUTE FOR POLICY STUDIES
999 Third Avenue
Seattle, WA 98104

The Institute supports national, state and local policies based on limited
government, individual freedom, free enterprise and more accountability
for how tax dollars are spent. It is committed to streamlining
government bureaucracy, cutting red tape, holding down taxes and
getting taxpayers more value for their money. A major responsibility of
the Washington Institute is to bring new ideas to the political arena that
will strengthen the state economy and improve the efficiency of
government. The Washington Institute was set up in 1985 and is one of
the new breed of conservative, state based think-tanks involved in
StateNet.

WISCONSIN PUBLIC POLICY RESEARCH INSTITUTE INC.
3107 North Shepard Ave
Milwaukee, WI 53211

Founded in 1987, the goal of the Institute is to provide non-partisan
research on key issues affecting citizens living in Wisconsin so that their

elected representatives are able to make informed decisions to improve the quality of life and future of the state. The major priority of WPRI is to improve the accountability of Wisconsin's government.

WORLD POLICY INSTITUTE
777 United Nations Plaza
New York, NY 10017

The Institute focuses on international economic and security issues, challenging Cold War assumptions and advancing a concept of international security grounded not in military might but in policies that foster world economic growth. Although focused on the US political debate, the Institute emphasises the development of 'world policies' – initiatives that reflect America's common security and development with other nations. The Institute was established in 1948, but in 1990 WPI became an affiliate of the New School for Social Research in New York thereby revoking its independent status. During the 1980s, the WPI was experiencing financial difficulties, especially maintaining a cash flow over the summer months. The merger provides financial stability, although the WPI still needs to raise its own budget of about $1 million. Its major publication is the *World Policy Journal*.

YANKEE INSTITUTE FOR PUBLIC POLICY STUDIES
117 New London Turnpike
Glastonbury, Connecticut 06033

The Yankee Institute works to mobilise the power of ideas to discipline the power of government and thus enhance the freedom and quality of life for all citizens of Connecticut. The Yankee Institute is a tiny think-tank with a staff of one to two and a budget under $100,000. The Institute is a member of StateNet.

Interviews

Digby Anderson, Director, Social Affairs Unit, 20 January 1992.

Peter Andreas, Research Scholar, and John Cavanagh, Fellow, Institute for Policy Studies, 31 October 1991.

Tom Atwood, Director of Resource Bank, Heritage Foundation, 8 September 1994.

Thomas Bayard, Research Fellow and Deputy Director, Institute for International Economics, 22 October 1991.

Rinelda Bliss-Walters, Special Assistant, Center for Security Policy, 18 September 1991.

David Boaz, Executive Vice-President, Cato Institute, 10 October 1991.

Brock Bower, Director of Public Affairs, Center for Stratagic and International Studies, 8 September 1994.

Susan Brown, Special Assistant to the President, Sarah Ingram, Director of Public Affairs and Laura Wilcox, Public Affairs, Urban Institute, 17 October 1991.

Eammon Butler, Director, Adam Smith Institute, 17 January 1992.

Richard Caplan, Acting Director, World Policy Institute, 13 November 1991.

John Chipman, Director of Studies and Gerard Segal, Senior Fellow, International Institute for Strategic Studies, 20 January 1992.

Betsy Cole and Charlie Gershenson, Center for the Study of Social Policy, 15 October 1991.

Christine Contee, Director of Public Affairs and Fellow, Overseas Development Council, 1 November 1991.

John Cooper, President, James Madison Institute for Public Policy Studies, 3 December 1991.

James Cornford, Director, Institute for Public Policy Research, 16 January 1992.

Simon Crine, General Secretary, Fabian Society, 17 January 1992.

Nancy Cuniff, Program Officer, Russell Sage Foundation, 12 November 1991.

Bill Daniel, Director, Policy Studies Institute, 16 January 1992.

Elizabeth Ellis, Director of Media Relations, Free Congress Foundation, 29 October 1991.

Eleanor Farrar, Executive Vice-President, Joint Center for Political and Economic Studies, 2 October 1991.

Jeff Faux, President, Economic Policy Institute, 10 October 1991.

Chris Files, Assistant to the President, Institute for Policy Studies, 5 December 1991.

Harold Fleming, President, Potomac Institute, 5 December 1991.

Robert Fri, President, Resources for the Future, 20 September 1991.

Gerald Frost, Director, Centre for Policy Studies, 9 November 1994.

Jeffrey Gayner, Counsellor for International Relations, Heritage Foundation, 7 October 1991.

Gloria Gilbert-Stoga, Director – Privatization Project, Carnegie Council, 6 September 1994.

Sam Harper, Chief Operating Officer, Institute for Contemporary Studies, 26 August 1991.

Owen Harries, Editor, *The National Interest*, 19 November 1991.

Linda Harsh, Assistant Director – Washington, Council on Foreign Relations, 5 October 1991.

Carl Helstrom, Director of Program Development, and Jo Ann Kwong, Director of Public Affairs, Atlas Foundation, 18 October 1991.

John Hyde, Executive Director, Institute for Public Affairs, Australia, 1 May 1992.

Martin Indyk, Executive Director, Washington Institute for Near East Policy, 8 November 1991.

Kent Jeffreys, Director of Environmental Studies, Competitive Enterprise Institute, 25 September 1991.

Carolyn Jones, Director, Institute of Employment Rights, 9 November 1994.

Stanley Kiaer, Director, Institute of Business Ethics, 10 November 1994.

John Kirkland, National Institute of Social and Economic Research, 9 November 1994.

Michael Krepon, President, Henry L. Stimson Center, 27 September 1991.

Bruce MacLaury, President, Brookings Institution, 16 October 1991.

Will Marshall, President, Progressive Policy Institute, 20 September 1991.

Francis McGlone, Senior Researcher, Family Policy Studies Centre, 10 November 1994.

Lawrence Mone, Director of Research, Manhattan Institute, 15 November 1991.

James Montgomery, Director, International Affairs, East–West Forum, Joseph E. Seagram and Sons, 20 September 1991.

Amy Moritz, President, National Center for Public Policy Research, 9 December 1991.

James Morrell, Director of Research, Center for International Policy, 27 November 1991.

Roderick Nye, Deputy Director, Social Market Foundation, London, 11 November 1994.

Michael O'Hare, Director of Finance and Administration, Carnegie Endowment for International Peace, 16 September 1991 and 7 September 1994.

Van Dorn Ooms, Senior Vice-President and Director of Research, Committee for Economic Development, 27 November 1991.

Deidre F. Parker, Director: Research and Membership, American Enterprise Institute, 24 September 1991.
Elissa Parker, Director – Research and Training, Environmental Law Institute, 23 October 1991.
Madsen Pirie, President, Adam Smith Institute, 9 November 1994.
Richard Portes, Director, Centre for Economic Policy Research, 22 January 1992.
Bob Roll, Director – Washington Operations, RAND Corporation, 9 October 1991.
James Rollo, Royal Institute for International Affairs, 22 January 1992.
Robert Royal, Vice-President for Research, Ethics and Public Policy Center, 4 November 1991.
Harry Rudday, Director of Communications, Center for Strategic and International Studies, 20 November 1991.
John Samples, Assistant Director for Programs, Twentieth Century Fund, 12 November 1991.
Chris Sigur, Vice President – Asian Programs, Carnegie Council on Ethics and International Affairs, 13 November 1991.
Thomas Skladony, Director of Communications, American Enterprise Institute, 9 September 1994.
Jack Spence, Director of Studies, Royal Institute for International Affairs, 15 January 1992.
Debra Springley, Research Assistant, Pacific Research Institute, 26 August 1991.
Maureen Steinbrunner, Executive Vice-President, Center for National Policy, 25 September 1991.
Robert Stumberg, Associate Director – Policy, Center for Policy Alternatives, 28 October 1991.
Jan Erik Surotchak, Coordinator of Washington Programs, Institute for Foreign Policy Analysis, 20 November 1991.
Greg Taylor, Director of Information, Cato Institute, 8 September 1994.
Arnold Trebach, Director, and Pam Griffin, Drug Policy Foundation, 27 September 1991.
Norman Ture, President, Institute for Research on the Economics of Taxation, 2 October 1991.
Frank Vibert, Deputy Director, Institute of Economic Affairs, 23 January 1992.
Steven Webb, Programme Coordinator, Institute for Fiscal Studies, 14 January 1992.
David Willetts, Director of Studies, Centre for Policy Studies, 21 January 1992.
Donna Wise, Director of Policy Affairs, World Resources Institute, 8 October 1991.
Michael Witt, Project Coordinator, Environmental and Energy Study Institute, 9 October 1991.
Laurianne Zwart, Executive Secretary, TransNational Institute, Amsterdam, 7 January 1992.

Bibliography

Abelson, Donald E. (1992) 'A New Channel of Influence: American Think Tanks and the News Media', *Queens Quarterly*, 99 (4): 849–72.

Abshire, David. (1993) 'Thirty Years After Our Founding: Reflections on CSIS, the New World Disorder, and Two Burkes – Arleigh and Edmund', Washington DC, Center for Strategic and International Studies.

— (1987) 'CSIS Conceptual and Operational Framework: The Way Ahead As An Independent Institution', Report submitted to the Board of Trustees, Center for Strategic and International Studies, 24 September, Washington DC, Center for Strategic and International Studies.

— (1982) 'Twenty Years in the Strategic Labryinth', *Washington Quarterly*, 5 (1): 83–105.

Adam Smith Institute – ASI (1990) *The First Hundred: 'Ideas Have Consequences'*, London, Adam Smith Institute.

— (1988) *ASI Bulletin*, newsletter, Adam Smith Institute.

— (1985) *The Omega File*, London, Adam Smith Institute.

Adler, Emanuel (1992) 'The Emergence of Cooperation: National Epistemic Communities and the International Evolution of the Idea of Arms Control', *International Organization,* 46 (1): 101–45.

Adler, Emanuel, and Haas, Peter (1992) 'Conclusion: Epistemic Communities, World Order, and the Creation of a Reflective Research Program', *International Organization*, 46 (1): 367–90.

Allen, Gary (1972) *None Dare Call It Conspiracy*, California, Concord Press.

Alpert, I. and Markusen, A. (1979) 'The professional production of policy, ideology and plans: Brookings and Resources for the Future', *The Insurgent Sociologist*, 9 (2–3): 94–106.

Anderson, Terry L. (1991) *The Market Process and Environmental Amenities*, CIS Occasional Papers 34, Sydney, Centre for Independent Studies.

Andrews, John K. (1989) 'So You Want to Start A Think Tank', *Policy Review*, 49: 62–65.

Ascher, Kate. (1987) *The Politics of Privatisation: Contracting Out Public*

Services, London, Macmillan.

Atlas Economic Research Foundation (1991) *16th International Workshop and 10th Anniversary Celebration*, conference brochure.

— (1988) *Highlights*, newsletter, summer.

Bachrach, P. and Baratz, S. M. (1962) 'Two Faces of Power', *American Political Science Review*, 56: 947–52.

Bailey, Stephen (1993) 'Public Choice Theory and the Reform of Local Government in Britain', *Public Policy and Administration*, 8(2): 7–4.

Barry, N. B. (1987) *The New Right*, London, Croom Helm.

Beer, Samuel H. (1980) 'In Search of a New Public Philosophy', in A. King, *The New American Political System*, Washington DC, American Enterprise Institute.

Bell, Daniel (1992) 'The Cultural Wars: American Intellectual Life, 1965–1990', *Quadrant*, 36 (7–8): 8–27.

Bell, Geoffrey (1991) 'Privatization in a Capital-Short World', Carnegie Council/DRT International Privatization Project, No. 3, New York, Carnegie Council on Ethics and International Affairs.

Bennett, Colin J. (1992) 'The International Regulation of Personal Data: From Epistemic Community to Policy Sector', Paper Presented at the 1992 Annual Meeting of the Canadian Political Science Association, Prince Edward Island.

— (1991) 'Review Article: What is Policy Convergence and What Causes It?' *British Journal of Political Science*, 21: 215–33.

Berle, Adolf A. (1986) *Leaning Against the Dawn: 1919–69*, New York, Twentieth Century Fund.

Berman, Edward H. (1983) *The Ideology of Philanthropy: The Influence of the Carnegie, Ford and Rockefeller Foundations on American Foreign Policy*, Albany, State University of New York Press.

Bernstein, Peter W. (1984) 'Brookings Tilts Right', *Fortune*, 23 July: 96.

Berry, Jeffrey M. and Hula, Kevin W. (1991) 'Interest Groups and Systematic Bias'. Paper presented to the 1991 Annual Meeting of the American Political Science Association, 29 August–1 September, Washington DC.

Bierstaker, Thomas J. (1992) 'The "Triumph" of Neoclassical Economics in the Developing World: Policy Convergence and Bases of Governance in the International Economic Order', in J. N. Rosenau and E-O. Czempiel (eds.) *Governance Without Government: Order and Change in World Politics*, Great Britain, Cambridge University Press.

Bethall, T. (1984) 'Liberalism, Stanford Style', *Commentary*, 77 (1): 42–47.

Blackstone, T. and Plowden, W. (1988) *Inside the Think Tank: Advising the Cabinet 1971–1983*, London, Heinemann.

Blumenthal, Sidney (1986) 'The Left Stuff: IPS and the Lonely? Left Wing Thinkers', *Washington Post*, 30 July.

Blundell, John (1990) 'Waging the War of Ideas: Why There Are No

Shortcuts', *The Heritage Lectures*, 245: 1–9.

Boal, J. (1985) 'Great Thinkers Get the Word Out', *American Way*, 5 March.

Bonafede, Dom (1982) 'Issue Oriented Heritage Foundation Hitches Its Wagon to Reagan's Star', *National Journal*, 20 March: 502–7.

Borins, Sanford (1988) 'Public Choice: "Yes Minister" Made it Popular, But Does Winning the Nobel Prize Make It True?' *Canadian Public Administration*, 3 (1): 12–26.

Bremner, Robert H. (1988) *American Philanthropy*, Chicago, University of Chicago Press.

Brookings Institution (1991) *Annual Report*, Washington DC, Brookings Institution.

Brooks, Stephen (1990) 'The Market for Social Scientific Knowledge: The Case of Free Trade in Canada' in S. Brooks and A-G. Gagnon (eds.), *Social Scientists, Policy and the State*, New York, Praeger.

Brooks, Stephen and Alain-G. Gagnon (eds.) (1990) *Social Scientists, Policy and the State*, New York, Praeger.

Bruce-Briggs, B. (ed.) (1981) *The New Class?* New York, McGraw Hill Books.

Buchanan, James (1990) *Socialism is Dead but Leviathan Lives On*, CIS Occasional Paper No. 30, Sydney, Center for Independent Studies.

Bulmer, Martin (1987a) 'The governmental context: interaction between structure and influence', in M. Bulmer (ed.), *Social Science Research and Government: Comparative Essays on Britain and the United States*, Cambridge, Cambridge University Press.

— (1987b) 'The social sciences in an age of uncertainty', in M. Bulmer (ed.), *Social Science Research and Government: Comparative Essays on Britain and the United States*, Cambridge, Cambridge University Press.

Burgess, Simon and Alderman, Geoffrey (1990) 'The Centre for Policy Studies: The Influence of Alfred Sherman', *Contemporary Record*, 4 (2): 14–15.

Butler, Eamonn (ed.) (1992) *Privatization East and West*, Conference proceedings, London, Adam Smith Institute.

Butler, Eamonn and Pirie, Madsen (1989) *The Manual On Privatisation*, London, Adam Smith Institute.

Butler, Stuart M. (1989) 'Privatization and the Management of Public Policy', *National Civic Review*, March/April: 114–26.

Capital Research Center – CRC (1990) *Annual Report 1990*, Washington DC, Capital Research Center.

Carnegie Council on Ethics and International Affairs (1989) *Annual Report 1988–89*, New York, Carnegie Council in Ethics and International Affairs.

Caporaso, James A. and Levine, David P. (1992) *Theories of Political Economy*, Cambridge, Cambridge University Press.

Carnoy, Martin (1984) *The State and Political Theory*, Princeton, New

Jersey, Princeton University Press.
Center for Policy Alternatives – CPA (1991) *Mission Statement* (draft), Washington DC, Center for Policy Alternatives, 20 September.
Centre for Policy Studies – CPS (1988) *The Power of Ideas*, Annual Review, London, Centre for Policy Studies.
Center for Security Policy – CSP (1990) *1990 Annual Report*, Washington DC, Center for Security Policy.
Center for Strategic and International Studies – CSIS (1989) *CSIS and the Issues 1990*, Washington DC, Center for Strategic and International Studies.
Chabal, Pierre (1992) 'Advice giving, time constraints and ministerial efficiency', in B. Guy Peters and Anthony Barker (eds.), *Advising West European Governments: Inquiries, Expertise and Public Policy*, Edinburgh, Edinburgh University Press.
Charity Commissioners (1991) 'Political Activities by Charities', Explanatory Leaflet CC9, London, Charity Commissioners.
Chernogorodsky, Valeri. (1991) 'Privatization in the Republic of Russia', Carnegie Council/DRT International Privatization Project, No. 5, New York, Carnegie Council on Ethics and International Affairs.
Chote, Robert (1991) 'Thatcher fallout buffets IEA', *The Independent*, 16 September.
Clinton, John (1987) 'Trends in Foundation Giving', *The Foundation Directory*, 11th edition, New York, The Foundation Center.
Cobb, Roger *et al.*, (1976) 'Agenda Building as a Comparative Political Process', *American Political Science Review*, 70 (1): 126–38.
Cockett, Richard (1994) *Thinking the Unthinkable: Think Tanks and the Economic Counter-Revolution, 1931–1983*, London, Harper Collins.
Cohen, Michael D., March, James G. and Olsen, Johan P. (1972) 'A Garbage Can Model of Organizational Choice', *Administrative Science Quarterly*, 17 (1): 1–25.
Cohn, Carol (1987) 'Sex and Death in the Rational World of Defense Intellectuals', *Signs*, 12 (4): 687–718.
Coleman, David A. (1991) 'Policy Research – Who Needs It?' *Governance: An International Journal of Policy and Administration*, 4 (4): 420–55.
Coleman, Peter (1989) *The Liberal Conspiracy: The Congress for Cultural Freedom and the Struggle for the Mind of Post-War Europe*, New York, Free Press.
Commonwealth Foundation for Public Policy Alternatives (n.d.) *Supplying the Ideas for Change*, Harrisburg, PA, Commonwealth Foundation.
Conference Board (1993) *Annual Report*, New York, Conference Board.
Conway, Thomas (1990) 'Background Reading: The Crisis of the Policy Sciences', in S. Brooks and A-G. Gagnon (eds), *Social Scientists, Policy and the State*, New York, Praeger.
Cornford, James (1990) 'Performing Fleas: Reflections from a Think

Tank', *Policy Studies*, 11 (4): 22–30.

Crane, Edward H. (1988) 'America's Counter-revolution', *Cato's Letters* No. 5: 1–18.

Critchlow, D. T. (1985) *The Brookings Institution, 1916–52: Expertise and the Public Interest in A Democratic Society*, Dekalb, Northern Illinois Press.

Culleton Colwell, M. A. (1980) 'The Foundation Connection: Links Among Foundations and Recipient Organizations', in R. F. Arnove (ed.), *Philanthropy and Cultural Imperialism: The Foundations At Home and Abroad*, Boston, MA, G.K. Hall and Co.

Cyert, Richard M. and March, James G. (1963) *A Behavioural Theory of the Firm*, New Jersey, Prentice-Hall, Inc.

Dalby, Simon (1990) *Creating the Second Cold War: The Discourse of Politics*, London, Pinter Publishers.

Daniel, W. W. (1989) 'PSI: A Centre for Strategic Research', *Policy Studies*, 9 (4): 24–33.

Davis, Howard R. and Salasin, Susan E. (1978) 'Strengthening the Contribution of Social R&D to Policy Making', in L. E. Lynn (ed.), *Knowledge and Policy: The Uncertain Connection*, Washington, National Academy of Sciences.

Davis Smith, Justin (1989) 'Commentary', in Judith McQuillan (ed.), *Charity Trends*, Tonbridge, Charities Aid Foundation.

Desai, Rhadika (1994) 'Second-hand Dealers in Ideas: Think Tanks and Thatcherite Hegemony', *New Left Review*, No. 203: 27–64.

Diamond, Sara (1990) 'Rumble on the Right', *Z Magazine*, December.

Dickie, John (1992) *Inside the Foreign Office*, London, Chapman Publishers.

Dickson, Paul (1971) *Think Tanks*, New York, Atheneum.

Dionne, E. J. jnr. (1991) *Why Americans Hate Politics*, New York, Simon and Schuster.

Doherty, William H. (1991) 'Labor's View of Privatization', Carnegie Council/DRT International Privatization Project, No. 1, New York, Carnegie Council on Ethics and International Affairs.

Domhoff, William G. (1978) *The Powers That Be: Processes of Ruling Class Domination*, New York, Vintage Books.

— (1980) 'Introduction', *The Insurgent Sociologist*, 9(2–3): 3–7.

— (1983) *Who Rules America Now? A View for the 1980s*, New Jersey, Prentice Hall.

Drake, William and Nicolaidis, Kalypso (1992) 'Ideas, Interests and Institutionalization: "trade in services" and the Uruguay Round', *International Organization*, 46 (1): 37–100.

Dreier, Peter (1982) 'Capitalists *vs* the media: an analysis of an ideological mobilization among business leaders', *Media, Culture and Society*, 4: 111–32.

Dror, Y. (1984) 'Required breakthroughs in think tanks', *Policy Sciences*, 16: 199–225.

— (1980) 'Think tanks: A new invention in government', in C. H. Weiss and A. H. Barton (eds), *Making Bureaucracies Work*, Beverley Hills, Sage.
Dryzek, John S. (1992) 'How Far Is It From Virginia and Rochester to Frankfurt? Public Choice as Critical Theory', *British Journal of Political Science*, 22: 397–417.
Dunleavy, P. (1991) *Democracy, Bureaucracy and Public Choice: Economic Explanations in Political Science*, London, Harvester.
Dunleavy, P. and O'Leary, B. (1987) *Theories of the State: The Politics of Liberal Democracy*, London, Macmillan.
Durst, Samantha L. and Thurber, James A. (1989) 'Studying Washington Think Tanks: In Search of Definitions and Data'. Paper presented to the American Political Science Association Annual Meeting, Atlanta, 31 August–3 September.
Dye, Thomas R. (1987a) 'Organizing Power for Policy Planning: The View From the Brookings Institution', in G. William Domhoff and Thomas. R. Dye (eds.), *Power Elites and Organizations*, Beverly Hills, Sage.
— (1987b) *Understanding Public Policy*, New Jersey, Prentice Hall.
— (1978) 'Oligarchic tendencies in national policy making: The role of private planning organisations', *Journal of Politics*, 40 (May): 309–31.
Dyer, Hugh C. and Mangasarian, Leon (eds) (1989) *The Study of International Relations: The State of the Art*, London, Macmillan in association with *Millennium: Journal of International Studies*.
Eakins, D. (1972) 'Policy planning for the establishment', in R. Radosh and M. Rothbard (eds), *A New History of Leviathan*, New York, E. P. Dutton.
Earth Resources Research – ERR (1992) *Report of Activities 1990–92*, London, Earth Resources Research.
Easterbrook, Greg (1986) 'Ideas Move Nations', *The Atlantic Monthly*, January: 60–80, mimeo: 1–12.
The Economist (1992) 'The Good Think-Tank Guide: The Joys of Detached Involvement', 21 December 1991–3 January 1992: 79–85.
— (1991) 'Think-Tanks: The Carousels of Power', 25 May: 23–26.
Edelman, Murray (1985) 'Political Language and Political Reality', *PS: Political Science and Politics*, 18 (1): 10–19.
— (1977) *Political Language: Words That Succeed and Policies That Fail*, New York, Academic Press.
— (1973) 'Mass Responses to Political Symbols' in Philip. H. Melanson (ed.), *Knowledge, Politics and Public Policy: Introductory Readings in American Politics*, Cambridge MA, Winthrop Publishers Inc.
Evans, Medford (1975) 'The CFR Elite: Making A Deal on the Mountain Top', *American Opinion*, April: 39–48.
Fabian Society (1985) *Annual Report 1984–85*, London, Fabian Society.
Fabian, Larry L. (1985) *Beginnings*, Washington DC, Carnegie

Endowment for International Peace.

Fabricant, Solomon (n.d.) *Toward a Firmer Basis of Economic Policy: The Founding of the National Bureau of Economic Research*, Cambridge, MA, National Bureau of Economic Research.

Fauriol, George A. (1984) 'Think Tanks and U.S. Foreign Policy', in T. B. Lee (ed.), *Ideology and Practice: The Evolution of US Foreign Policy*, Taipei, Tamkang University.

Feulner, Edwin (1985) 'Ideas, Think-Tanks and Government', *Quadrant*, November: 22–26.

— (1991) 'Building the New Establishment', an interview with Adam Meyerson, *Policy Review*, 58: 6–17.

Fischer, Frank (1993) 'Policy Discourse and the Politics of Washington Think Tanks', in F. Fischer and J. Forester (eds), *The Argumentative Turn in Policy Analysis and Planning*, London, UCL Press.

Fischer, Frank and Forester, John (1993) 'Editors' Introduction', in F. Fischer and J. Forester (eds), *The Argumentative Turn in Policy Analysis and Planning*, London, UCL Press.

Fisher, Dorian D. (1983) *Atlas Economic Research Foundation Manual: Some Do's and Dont's for Public Policy Institutes*, Notes from the Atlas Foundation Seminar, 2–3 September 1983, San Francisco, California, Atlas Foundation.

Fly, R. (1986) 'What's In For Presidential Hopeful: Think Tanks', *Business Week*, 12 May: 61–62.

Ford, Patrick (1992) 'American Enterprise Institute for Public Policy Research' in C. Weiss (ed.), *Organizations for Policy Advice: Helping Government Think*, California, Sage.

Foreman, Carol Tucker and Steinbruner, Maureen (1991) 'Righting the Record on Regulation: An Introduction', in Carol Tucker Foreman (ed.), *Regulating for the Future: The Creative Balance*, Washington DC, Center for National Policy Press.

Forsyth, Michael (1982) *Reserving Health*, London, Adam Smith Institute.

— (1980) *Reservicing Britain*, London, Adam Smith Institute.

Foster, Leonie (1986) *High Hopes: The Men and Motives of the Australian Round Table*, Victoria, Melbourne University Press in association with the Australian Institute of International Affairs.

Friedman, John. S. (ed.) (1983) *First Harvest: The Institute for Policy Studies*, 1963–1983, New York, Grove Press.

Furhman, Susan H. (1992) 'The Center for Policy Research in Education: An Overview', in C. Weiss (ed.), *Organizations for Policy Advice: Helping Government Think*, California, Sage.

Gaffney, John. (1991) 'Political Think Tanks in the UK and Ministerial "Cabinets" in France', *West European Politics*, 14 (1): 1–17.

Gagnon, Alain-G. (1990) 'The Influence of Social Scientists on Public Policy', in S. Brooks and A-G. Gagnon (eds), *Social Scientists, Policy and the State*, New York, Praeger.

Gale Research Inc. (1991) *Research Centers Directory*, 15th edition, Detroit, Gale Research International Limited.

Galston, William A. (1990) 'Knowledge and Power', *PS: Political Science and Politics*, 23 (3): 431.

Gamble, Andrew (1989a) 'Ideas and Interests in British Economic Policy', in A. Gamble, *et al.*, *Ideas, Interest and Consequences*, London, Institute of Economic Affairs.

— (1989b) *The Free Economy and the Strong State: The Politics of Thatcherism*, London, Macmillan.

Gellner, Winand (1990) 'Political Think Tanks: Functions and Perspectives of a Strategic Elite', Paper delivered to the 1990 Annual Meeting of the American Political Science Association, 30 August –2 September.

Gill, Stephen (1990) *American Hegemony and the Trilateral Commission*, Cambridge, Cambridge University Press.

Goodman, John C. (1985) 'Introduction', in John C. Goodman (ed.), *Privatization*, Dallas, Texas, National Center for Policy Analysis.

Goodman, John C. and Nicholas, Alistair J. (1990) *Voluntary Welfare: A Greater Role for Private Charities*, Sydney, Centre for Independent Studies.

Goodwin, Craufurd D. (1990) *Report on the US–European Economics Program*, German Marshall Fund Strategic Review Trustee Committee #1, Washington DC, July, mimeo.

Gray, Colin S. (1978) 'Think Tanks and Public Policy', *International Journal*, 33 (1): 177–194.

— (1971a) 'What RAND Hath Wrought', *Foreign Policy*, 7: 111–129.

— (1971b) 'The Rise and Fall of Academic Strategy', *RUSI Journal*, June (16): 54–57.

— (1970–71) 'Strategists: Some Views Critical of the Profession', *International Journal*, 26: 771–90.

Green, David (1987) *The New Right: The Counter Revolution in Political, Economic and Social Thought*, Great Britain, Wheatsheaf Books Ltd.

Griggs, Edwin (1991) 'The Politics of Health Care Reform in Britain', *Political Quarterly*, 62 (4): 419–27.

Groom, John (1974) *British Thinking About Nuclear Weapons*, London, Frances Pinter.

Gunn, Simon (1989) *The Revolution of the Right: Europe's New Conservatives*, London, Pluto Press in association with the TransNational Institute.

Guttman, D. and Willner, B. (1976) *The Shadow Government*, New York, Pantheon Books.

Gwartney, James D. and Wagner, Richard E. (eds) (1988) *Public Choice and Constitutional Economics*, Greenwich, Connecticut, JAI Press.

Haakonssen, Knud (1985) 'Foreword' in *Hayek's Serfdom Revisited*, CIS Readings No. 7, Sydney, Centre for Independent Studies.

Haas, Ernst B. (1990a) *When Knowledge is Power: Three Models of Change In International Organizations*, Berkeley and Los Angeles, University of California Press.

Haas, Peter (1992a) 'Introduction: Epistemic Communities and International Policy Coordination', *International Organization*, 46 (1):1–35.

— (1992b) 'Banning Chlorofluorocarbons: Epistemic Community Efforts to Protect Stratospheric Ozone', *International Organization*, 46 (1): 187–224.

— (1990b) 'Obtaining International Environmental Protection Through Epistemic Consensus', *Millennium*, 19(3): 347–63.

— (1989) 'Do Regimes Matter? Epistemic Communities and Evolving Policies to Control Mediterranean Pollution', *International Organization*, 43 (3): 377–403.

Hajer, Maarten (1993) 'Discourse Coalitions and Institutionalization of Practice: The Case of Acid Rain in Great Britain', in F. Fischer and J. Forester (eds), *The Argumentative Turn in Policy Analysis and Planning*, London, UCL Press.

Hall, Peter A. (1990) 'Policy Paradigms, Experts, and the State: The Case of Macroeconomic Policy-Making in Britain', in S. Brooks and A-G. Gagnon (eds), *Social Scientists, Policy and The State*, New York, Praeger.

— (1989) *The Political Power of Economic Ideas: Keynesianism Across Nations*, Princeton, NJ, Princeton University Press.

Hallow, Ralph Z. (1985) 'Donations fuel think-tank battle to control field of policy ideas', *The Washington Times*, 26 November.

Ham, Christopher and Hill, Michael (1993) *The Policy Process in the Modern Capitalist State*, London, Harvester Wheatsheaf.

Hames, T. and Feasey, R. (1994) 'Anglo-American think tanks under Reagan and Thatcher', in A. Adonis and T. Hames (eds), *A Conservative Revolution? The Thatcher–Reagan Decade In Perspective*, Manchester, Manchester University Press.

Hanke, Steve H. (ed.) (1987) *Privatization and Development*, San Francisco, ICS Press.

Harley, Kevin F. (1991) 'The State Budget Crisis: An Opportunity for Leadership', *Issue Brief* (June), Harrisburg PA, Commonwealth Foundation.

— (1989) 'The Local Privatization Movement in America', Harrisburg, PA., The Commonwealth Foundation for Public Policy Alternatives.

Hart, Benjamin (ed.) (1987) *The Third Generation: Young Conservative Leaders Look to the Future*, Washington DC, The Heritage Foundation.

Hayek, F. A. (1990) *The Intellectuals and Socialism*, Fairfax, Virginia, The Institute for Humane Studies, George Mason University.

— (1967) *Studies in Philosophy, Politics and Economics*, London, Routledge & Kegan Paul.

Heald, David (1983) *Public Expenditure: Its Defence and Its Reform*, Oxford, Martin Robertson.

Heclo, H. (1989) Book review of J. Peshek, *Policy Planning Organizations: Elite Agendas and America's Rightward Turn*, in *The American Journal of Sociology*, 94 (5): 1222–24.

— (1980) 'Issue Networks and the Executive Establishment', in A. King (ed.), *The New American Political System*, Washington DC, American Enterprise Institute.

Henig, J. H., Hamnett, C. and Feigenbaum, H. B. (1988) 'The Politics of Privatization: A Comparative Perspective', *Governance*, 1 (4): 442–68.

Higgott, Richard. (1992) 'Susan Strange and the Development of International Political Economy' . Paper for ISA Senior Scholars Panel honouring Susan Strange, Vancouver, Mimeo.

— (1993) 'Economic Cooperation: Theoretical Opportunities and Practical Constraints', *Pacific Review*, 6 (2): 103–17.

Higgott, Richard. and Stone, Diane. (1994) 'The Limits of Influence: Foreign Policy Think Tanks in Great Britain and the USA', *Review of International Studies*, 20 (1) 1994: 15–34.

Hill, Christopher. (1994) 'Academic International Relations: The Siren Song of Policy Relevance', in C. Hill and P. Beshoff (eds.), *Two Worlds of International Relations: Academics, Practitioners and the Trade in Ideas*, London, Routledge and London School of Economics.

— (1989) 'The Study of International Relations in the United Kingdom' in Hugh Dyer and Leon Mangasarian (eds), *The Study of International Relations: The State of the Art*, London, Macmillan in association with *Millennium: Journal of International Studies*.

Himmelstein, Jerome L. (1990) *To The Right: The Transformation of American Conservatism*, Berkeley, University of California Press.

Hodgkinson, Virginia Ann and Weitzman, Murray S. (1989) *Dimensions of the Independent Sector: A Statistical Profile*, Washington DC, Independent Sector.

Hollis, Martin and Smith, Steve (1990) *Explaining and Understanding International Relations*, Oxford, Clarendon Press.

Holmes, A. (1986) 'Think tanks: Hit or myth?' unpublished M. Public Administration thesis, Department of Government, University of Queensland.

Holmes, Martin (1990) 'The Thatcher Government and Privatisation', Seminar Series Paper No. 1, Melbourne, Tasman Institute.

Hoogerwerf, Andries (1992) 'The market as a metaphor of politics: a critique of the foundations of economic choice theory', *International Review of Administrative Sciences*, 58: 23–42.

Hoover, K. and Plant, R. (1987) *Conservative Capitalism in Britain and the United States*, United Kingdom, Routledge.

Hopkins, Bruce R. and Summers, Elyse I. (1991) 'Using Charitable Dollars To Affect Public Policy', Working Paper Series No. 44,

Washington DC, Washington Legal Foundation.

Howard, Michael (1989) 'IISS – The First Thirty Years: A General Overview', *Adelphi Papers*, 235 (1): 10–19.

Huberty, Robert and Hohbach, Barbara D. (1991) *The Annual Guide to Public Policy Experts*, Washington DC, The Heritage Foundation.

Hyland, William G. (1992) 'Foreign Affairs at 70', *Foreign Affairs*, 71 (4): 171–93.

Ikenberry, John G. (1992) 'A world economy restored: expert consensus and the Anglo-American post war settlement', *International Organization*, 46 (1): 289–321.

— (1990) 'The International Spread of Privatization Policies: Inducements, Learning and "Policy Bandwagoning"', in E. Suleiman and J. Waterbury (eds), *The Political Economy of Public Sector Reform and Privatization*, Boulder, Westview Press.

Inland Revenue (1987) 'Tax Reliefs for Charities', leaflet IR 75, Bootle, Inland Revenue.

Institute for Defense and Disarmament Studies – IDDS (1990) *Celebrating a Decade of Work for Peace and Democracy*, 1990 Annual Report, Cambridge, MA, Institute for Defense and Department Studies.

Institute for International Economics – IIE (1991) *Publications 1991*, Washington DC, Institute for International Economics.

Institute for Public Policy Research – IPPR (1991) *Annual Report 1990–1991*, London, Institute for Public Policy Research.

Institute for Research on the Economics of Taxation – IRET (1991) *1991 Program*, Washington DC, Institute for Research on the Economics of Taxation.

Institute of Economic Affairs – IEA (1989) *The IEA's Distinctive Approach: The Institute for Economic Affairs Progress Report 1988–1989*, London, Institute of Economic Affairs.

Irvine, Kenneth (1987) *The Right Lines*, London, Adam Smith Institute.

Isaac, Rael Jean and Isaac, Erich (1983) *The Coercive Utopians: Social Deception By America's Power Players*, Chicago, Regnery Press.

Isserlis, A. R. (1981) 'Plus Ça Change ...' in J. Pinder (ed.), *Fifty Years of Political and Economic Planning: Looking Forward 1931–1981*, London, Heinemann.

James, Estelle (1987) 'The Nonprofit Sector in Comparative Perspective', in W. Powell (ed.), *The NonProfit Sector: A Research Handbook*, New Haven, Yale University Press.

James, Michael (1991) 'New ideas for old', *Policy*, 7 (4): 47–8.

— (1985) *Parliament and the Public Interest*, Critical Issues No. 1., Perth, Australian Institute for Public Policy.

James, Simon (1993) 'The Idea Brokers: The Impact of Think Tanks on British Government', *Public Administration*, 71(Winter): 491–506.

Jenkins, J. Craig (1987) 'Nonprofit Organizations and Policy Advocacy', in W. Powell (ed.), *The NonProfit Sector: A Research Handbook*, New

Haven, Yale University Press.

Jenkins, J. Craig and Eckert, Craig M. (1989) 'The Corporate Elite, the New Conservative Policy Network and Reagonomics', *Critical Sociology*, 16 (2-3): 121–44.

Jordan, Grant and Ashford, Nigel (eds) (1993) *Public Policy and the Impact of the New Right*, London, Pinter Publishers.

Jordan, Grant and Schubert, Klaus (1992) 'A Preliminary Ordering of Policy Network Labels', *European Journal of Political Research*, 12: 7–27.

Judis, John B. (1990a) 'Tokyo spending big bucks to swing US policies to its favour', *The Straits Times*, 24 April: 28.

— (1990b) 'The Conservative Crackup', *The American Prospect*, Fall: 30–42.

Kaldor, N. (1982) 'The Economic Consequences of Mrs Thatcher', Fabian Tract No. 486, London, Fabian Society.

Kasper, W. (1987) 'Comments', in M. James (ed.), *Restraining Leviathan*, Sydney, Centre for Independent Studies.

Kay, J. A. (1989) 'Research and Policy: The IFS Experience', *Policy Studies*, 9 (3): 20–26.

Kedourie, Elie. (1984) *The Chatham House Version and Other Middle Eastern Studies*, Hanover, University Press of New England.

Kendle, John E. (1975) *The Roundtable Movement and Imperial Union*, Toronto, University of Toronto.

King-Hall, Stephen (1937) *Chatham House: A Brief Account of the Origins, Purposes, and Methods of the Royal Institute for International Affairs*, London, Oxford University Press.

Kingdon, J. (1984) *Agendas, Alternatives and Public Policies*, Boston, Little Brown and Co.

Kissinger, Henry A. (1957) *Nuclear Weapons and Foreign Policy*, New York, Council on Foreign Relations.

Knoke, David (1990) *Political Networks: The Structural Perspective*, Cambridge, Cambridge University Press.

Knutsen, Torbjorn L. (1992) *A History of International Relations Theory*, Manchester, Manchester University Press.

Kondracke, Morton (1978) 'Home for Hardliners', *The New Republic*, 4 February: 21–25.

Kornhauser, Anne (1988) 'Diverse Groups Hoping for a Piece of the Action', *Legal Times*, 29 August: 4–5.

Kraft, Joseph (1958) 'School for Statesmen', *Harper's*, July, mimeo.

Krippendorff, Ekkehart. (1989) 'The Dominance of American Approaches in International Relations', in Hugh Dyer and Leon Mangasarian (eds), *The Study of International Relations: The State of the Art*, London, Macmillan in association with *Millennium: Journal of International Studies*.

Kriz, M. E. (1988) 'Providing A New Forum For Liberal Economists', *National Journal*, 17 September.

Kuttner, Robert (1989) 'The Perils of Privatization: False Profit', *New Republic*, 6 February: 21–23.

Kwong, JoAnn (1991) Personal correspondence from the Director of Public Affairs, Atlas Foundation, 18 June.

Lagemann, Ellen Condliffe (1989) *The Politics of Knowledge: The Carnegie Corporation, Philanthropy and Public Policy*, Middletown, CT, Wesleyan University Press.

Landers, Robert K. (1986) 'Think Tanks: The New Partisans', *Editorial Research Reports*, 1 (23): 455–72.

Langford, John W. and Brownsey, K. Lorne. (1991) 'Think Tanks and Modern Governance' in John W. Langford and K. Lorne Brownsey (eds.), *Think Tanks and Governance in the Asia-Pacific Region*, Canada, Institute for Research on Public Policy.

Lawrence, Philip (1992) 'US Nuclear Policy: The Dialectic of Myth and Reality', *Paradigms*, 6 (2): 106–22.

Lefever, Ernest W., English, Raymond. and Schuettinger, Robert L. (1982) *Scholars, Dollars and Public Policy: New Frontiers in Corporate Giving*, Washington DC, Ethics and Public Policy Center.

Levine, Charles H. (1985) 'Where Policy Comes From: Ideas, Innovations, and Agenda Choices', *Public Administration Review*, January/February: 255–58.

Levitan, Sar A. and Cooper, Martha (1984) *Business Lobbies: The Public Good and the Bottom Line*, Baltimore, Johns Hopkins University Press.

Levitas, Ruth (1986) 'Ideology and the new right', in R. Levitas (ed.), *The Ideology of the New Right*, Oxford, Polity Press.

Light, Paul C. (1983) *The President's Agenda: Domestic Policy Choice from Kennedy to Carter (With Notes on Ronald Reagan)*, Baltimore, Johns Hopkins University Press.

Lindblom, Charles (1990) *Inquiry and Change: The Troubled Attempt to Understand and Shape Society*, New Haven, Yale University Press.

Linden, P. (1987) 'Powerhouse of Policy', *Town and Country*, January.

Lindquist, Evert A. (1993) 'Think Tanks or Clubs? Assessing the Influence and Roles of Canadian Policy Institutes', *Canadian Public Administration*, 36 (4): 547–79.

— (1990) 'The Third Community, Policy Inquiry and Social Scientists', in S. Brooks and A-G. Gagnon (eds.), *Social Scientists, Policy and the State*, New York, Praeger.

— (1989) *Behind the Myth of Think Tanks: The Organization and Relevance of Canadian Policy Institutes*, unpublished doctoral thesis, Berkeley, University of California.

Lindsay, Kenneth (1981) 'PEP through the 1930s: Organisation, Structure, People', in J. Pinder (ed.), *Fifty Years of Political and Economic Planning: Looking Forward 1931–1981*, London, Heinemann.

Lowi, Theodore J. (1992) 'The State in Political Science: How We

Become What We Study', *American Political Science Review*, 86 (1): 1–7.

Machin, Howard (1987) 'Advice on Economic and Foreign Policy', in W. Plowden (ed.), *Advising the Rulers*, Oxford, Basil Blackwell.

MacKenzie, Norman and MacKenzie, Jeanne (1979) *The First Fabians*, London, Quartet Books.

MacLennan, Carol (1988) 'The Democratic Administration of Government', in Levine, Marc V. *et al., The State and Democracy: Revitalizing America's Government*, New York, Routledge, Chapman and Hall Inc.

Maddox, G. and Hagan, S. (1987) 'A new sophistry: The rhetoric of the New Right', *Politics*, 22 (2): 29–35.

Mandelstam, E. F. (1989) 'Shrinking Spheres of Influence', *The New York Observer*, 11 December.

Manhattan Institute (1989) *Ten Year Review 1980–1989*, New York, Manhattan Institute.

Marsh, Ian (1991) *Globalisation and Australian Think Tanks: An Evaluation of their Role and Contribution to Governance*, CEDA Information Paper No. 34, February, Melbourne and Sydney, CEDA.

— (1980) *An Australian Think Tank?* NSW, New South Wales University Press Ltd.

Martino, Antonio (1990) 'Are We Winning?', *CIS Occasional Paper* No. 29, Sydney, Centre for Independent Studies.

Matlack, Carol (1991) 'Marketing Ideas', *National Journal*, 22 June: 1552–1555.

McCloskey, Donald N. (1985) *The Rhetoric of Economics*, Madison, Wisconsin, University of Wisconsin Press.

McDowell, Stephen D. (1994) 'Policy Research Institute and Liberalized International Services Exchange', in S. Brooks and A-G. Gagnon (eds.), *Social Scientists, Policy Communities and the State*, Westport, CT, Praeger Publishers.

McGann, James G. (1992) 'Academics to Ideologues: A Brief History of the Public Policy Research Industry', *PS: Political Science and Politics*, 25 (4): 733–40.

Melnyk, Andrew (1989) 'On Ideas and Interests', in A. Gamble *et al., Ideas, Interests and Consequences*, London, Institute of Economic Affairs.

Meyerson, Adam (1991) 'Building the New Establishment – An Interview with Edwin Feulner', *Policy Review*, No 58: 6–16.

Middleton, Melissa (1987) 'Nonprofit Boards of Directors: Beyond the Governance Function', in W. Powell (ed.), *The NonProfit Sector: A Research Handbook*, New Haven, Yale University Press.

Mills, C. W. (1959) *The Power Elite*, Oxford, Oxford University Press.

Moe, Ronald C. (1987) 'Exploring the Limits of Privatization', *Public Administration Review*, 47 (6): 453–60.

Moore, B. and Carpenter, G. (1987) 'Main players' in K. Coghill (ed.),

The New Right's Australian Fantasy, Melbourne, McPhee Gribble/ Penguin Books.

Moore, John (1992) *Privatisation Everywhere: The World's Adoption of the British Experience*, Winter Address, London, Centre for Policy Studies.

— (1988) 'Local Right Thinkers', *National Journal*, 1 October: 2455–2459.

Moore, Stephen and Butler, Stuart. (1988) *Privatization: A Strategy for Taming the Federal Budget, Fiscal Year 1988*, Washington DC, The Heritage Foundation.

Morgan, Roger (1979) 'To Advance the Sciences of International Politics ... Chatham House's Early Research', *International Affairs*, 55 (2): 240–51.

Moritz, Amy (1991) *List of Conservative Groups*, Memorandum, August, Washington DC, National Center for Public Policy Research.

Murray, Charles (1984) *Losing Ground: American Social Policy, 1950–1980*, New York, Basic Books.

Muscatine, A. (1986) 'Georgetown's Media Profs', *Washington Post*, 11 May.

Nagorski, Zygmunt (1977) 'A Member of the CFR Talks Back', *National Review*, 12 September: 1416–1418.

National Bureau of Economic Research – NBER (n.d.) *National Bureau of Economic Research*, Cambridge MA, National Bureau of Economic Research.

The National Center for Policy Analysis – NCPA (1990) *NCPA Case Statement and Five Year Plan*, Dallas, Texas, National Center for Policy Analysis.

National Committee for Responsive Philanthropy – NCRP (1994) *Responsive Philanthropy*, winter, Washington DC, National Committee for Responsive Philanthropy.

— (1991) 'Burgeoning Conservative Think Tanks', *Responsive Philanthropy*, Special Report, Spring: 1–20.

Nurick, John (1990) 'The Adam Smith Bicentennary', *Policy*, 6 (4): 46–47.

— (1987) 'Editorial: The future of the think tanks', *Clear Thinking*, 24 (November).

O'Connell, Brian (ed.) (1983) *America's Voluntary Spirit*, New York, The Foundation Center.

Olsen, Mancur (1989) 'How Ideas Affect Societies: Is Britain the Wave of the Future', in A. Gamble *et al.*, *Ideas, Interests and Consequences*, London, Institute of Economic Affairs.

— (1982) *The Rise and Decline of Nations*, New Haven, CT, Yale University Press.

Olson, William C. and Groom, A. J. R. (1991) *International Relations Then And Now: Origins and Trends in Interpretation*, London, HarperCollins Academic.

Orlans, Harold (1972) *The Non-Profit Research Institute: Its Origins, Operation, Problems and Prospects*, New York, Carnegie Commission on Higher Education, McGraw Hill.

Overseas Development Institute – ODI (1985) *Twenty Five Years in Development*, London, Overseas Development Institute.

Pacific Research Institute (1992) *Pacific Research Institute for Public Policy*, San Francisco, Pacific Research Institute, fact sheet.

Pal, Leslie A. (1990) 'Knowledge, Power, and Policy: Reflections on Foucault', in S. Brooks and A-G. Gagnon (eds), *Social Scientists, Policy and the State*, New York, Praeger.

Palmer, Tom G. (1991) *Philanthropy in Central and Eastern Europe: A Resource Book for Foundations, Corporations and Individuals*, Fairfax, Virginia, The Institute for Humane Studies, George Mason University.

Panos Institute (1991) *Annual Report 1991*, London, Panos Institute.

Parmar, Inderjeet (1995) 'The Issue of State Power: The Council on Foreign Relations as a Case Study', *Journal of American Studies*, 29 (1); 73–95.

Pearce, Edward (1993) 'The Prophet of Private Profit', *Guardian*, 19 April: 8–9.

Pemberton, Jo-Anne (1988) '"The end" of economic rationalism', *Australian Quarterly*, 60 (2): 188–199.

Peschek, J. S. (1987) *Policy Planning Organizations: Elite Agendas and America's Rightward Turn*, Philadelphia, Temple University Press.

Peterson, M. J. (1992) 'Whalers, Cetologists, Environmentalists, and the International Management of Whaling', *International Organization*, 46 (1): 147–86.

Pinder, J. (1981) '1964–1980: From PEP to PSI', in J. Pinder (ed.), *Fifty Years of Political and Economic Planning: Looking Forward 1931–1981*, London, Heinemann.

Pines, Burton Yale (1982) *Back to Basics: The Traditionalist Movement That is Sweeping Grass-Roots America*, New York, William Morrow and Co.

Pirie, Madsen (1988) *Micropolitics*, Hants, England, Wildwood House Ltd.

— (1985) *Privatization: The facts and the fallacies*, Sydney, Centre 2000.

Plowden, W. (ed.) (1987) *Advising the Rulers*, Oxford, Basil Blackwell.

Polsby, Nelson (1993) 'Foreign Policy Establishment Moves to Middle', *Public Affairs Report*, 34 (1): 1, 12–13.

— (1984) *Political Innovation in America: The Politics of Policy Initiation*, New Haven: Yale University Press.

— (1983) 'Tanks but no Tanks', *Public Opinion*, April/May: 14–16, 58–59.

Pomeroy, Brian W. (1991) 'An Assessment of Privatization in the UK: Mistakes, Successes and Future Prospects', Carnegie Council/DRT International Privatization Project, No. 4, New York, Carnegie

Council on Ethics and International Affairs.

Poole, Robert (1990) 'The Local Privatization Revolution', *The Heritage Lectures*, No. 258: 1–6.

— (1985) 'Privatization from the Bottom Up', in John C. Goodman (ed.), *Privatization*, Dallas, Texas, National Center for Policy Analysis.

Portes, Richard (1988) 'Priorities for Economic Policy Research', in P. Deane (ed.), *Frontiers of Economic Research*, Proceedings of Section F (Economics) of the British Association for the Advancement of Science, Oxford, Macmillan.

Powell, Steven S. (1987) *Covert Cadre: Inside the Institute for Policy Studies*, Illinois, Green Hill Publishers Inc.

Prestowitz, C., Morse, R. A. and Tonelson, A. (eds) (1991) *Powernomics: Economics and Strategy After the Cold War*, Lanham, Maryland, Madison Books.

Quiggin, John (1991a) 'The Private Interest Theory of Politics: Liberal or Authoritarian?', *Policy*, 7 (1): 51–54.

— (1991b) 'Rejoinder', *Policy*, 7 (2): 50–51.

Rauch, Jonathon (1988) 'Giving Wings to Ideas', *National Journal*, 22 October: 2655–2659.

— (1989) 'The Counterrevolution', *National Journal*, 2 October: 2142–2145.

Reason Foundation (1991) *Annual Report*, Los Angeles, Reason Foundation.

Redwood, John (1988) *Signals from a Railway Conference*, London, Centre for Policy Studies.

Reilly, A. M. (1981) 'Reagan's Think Tank', *Dun's Review*, 117 (4): 110–14.

Reimnitz, C. (1992) 'Privatizing Eastern Germany: A Report from the Treuhand', Carnegie Council/Deloitte Touch Tomatsu Privatization Project, No. 11, New York, Carnegie Council on Ethics and International Affairs.

Resources for the Future – RFF (1991) 'Since 1952, independent research and policy analysis about natural resources and the environment ...', Washington DC, Resources for the Future, promotional pamphlet: 1–13.

Restivo, Sal and Loughlin, Julia (1987) 'Critical Sociology of Science and Scientific Validity', *Knowledge: Creation, Diffusion, Utilization*, 8 (3): 486–508.

Rhodes, R. A. W. and Marsh, David (1992) 'New Directions in the Study of Policy Networks', *European Journal of Political Research*, 21: 181–205.

Ricci, David (1993) *The Transformation of American Politics: The New Washington and the Rise of American Politics*, New Haven, Yale University Press.

Rich, S. (1988) 'Think Tank Survives Lean Times', *Washington Post*, 15 May: H13.

Richards, Huw (1993) 'Dry as wind-blown dust', *Times Higher Education Supplement*, 19 February: 6.

Richardson, J. J. (1994) *Doing Less By Doing More: British Government 1979–93*, European Public Policy Institute occasional papers, University of Warwick, No: 93/2.

Richardson, J. J. and Jordan, A. G. (1979) *Governing Under Pressure: The Policy Process in a Post Parliamentary Democracy*, Oxford, Martin Robertson.

Riddell, Peter (1994) 'Ideology in Practice', in A. Adonis and T. Hames (eds), *A Conservative Revolution? The Thatcher–Reagan Decade In Perspective*, Manchester, Manchester University Press.

Rivlin, Alice M. (1992) 'Policy Analysis at the Brookings Institution' in C. Weiss (ed.), *Organizations for Policy Advice: Helping Government Think*, California, Sage.

Robinson, William H. (1992) 'The Congressional Research Service: Policy Consultant, Think Tank and Information Factory', in C. Weiss (ed.), *Organizations for Policy Advice: Helping Government Think*, California, Sage.

Robinson, Bill (1990) 'The Early Days of IFS', *Fiscal Studies*, 11 (3): 1–11.

The Roe Foundation (1990) *The 1989 Roe Foundation Report on Twelve State Public Policy Institutes*, South Carolina, The Roe Foundation.

Rose, Richard (1993) *Lesson-Drawing in Public Policy: A Guide to Learning Across Time and Space*, Chatham, NJ, Chatham House Publishers.

— (1991) 'What is Lesson-Drawing?' *Journal of Public Policy*, 11 (1): 3–30.

Rosenau, James N. (1990) *Turbulence in World Politics: A Theory of Change and Continuity*, Princeton, NJ, Princeton University Press.

Rosenau, Pauline (1992) *Post-Modernism and the Social Sciences: Insights, Inroads, and Intrusions*, Princeton NJ, Princeton University Press.

Roth, Gabriel (1989) 'Bringing Efficiency to the Third World Through Private Provision of Public Services', Backgrounder No. 739, Washington DC, Heritage Foundation.

Sabatier, Paul (1991) 'Political Science and Public Policy', *PS: Political Science and Politics*, 24 (2): 144–56.

— (1987) 'Knowledge, Policy Oriented Learning, and Policy Change: An Advocacy Coalition Framework', *Knowledge: Creation, Diffusion, Utilization*, 8 (4): 649–92.

Salamon, Lester E. (1989) 'Introduction' in Lester E. Salamon (ed.), *Beyond Privatization: The Tools of Government Action*, Washington DC, Urban Institute Press.

Salinas, Roberto (1990) 'Privatization in Mexico: Good, But Not Enough', Backgrounder No. 797, Washington DC, Heritage Foundation.

Salisbury, Robert (1990) 'The Paradox of Interest Groups in Washington: More Groups, Less Clout', in A. King (ed.), *The New American Political System*, London, Macmillan.

Saloma, J. S. (1984) *Ominous Politics: The New Conservative Labryinth*, New York, Hill and Wang.

Sarup, Madan (1993) *Post-Structuralism and Post-Modernism*, Herts, Hemel Hempstead, Harvester Wheatsheaf.

Saunders, C. B. (1966) *The Brookings Institution: A Fifty Year History*, Washington DC, Brookings Institution.

Sawer, Marian (1990) *Public Perceptions of Multiculturalism*, Centre for Immigration and Multicultural Studies, Research School of Social Sciences, Australian National University.

Sawicky, Max (1991) *The Poverty of the New Paradigm*, EPI Briefing Paper, Washington DC, Economic Policy Institute.

Schneider, Anne and Ingram, Helen (1988) 'Systematically Pinching Ideas: A Comparative Approach to Policy Design', *Journal of Public Policy*, 8 (1): 61–80.

Schulzinger, Robert D. (1984) *The Wise Men of Foreign Affairs: The History of the Council on Foreign Relations*, New York, Columbia University Press.

Sclar, Elliott D., Schaeffer, K. H. and Brandwein, Robert (1989) *The Emperor's New Clothes: Transit Privatization and Public Policy*, Washington DC, Economic Policy Institute.

Scruton, R. (1983) *A Dictionary of Political Thought*, London, Pan Books in association with Macmillan.

Seldon, A. (1989) 'Economic Scholarship and Political Interest: IEA Thinking and Government Policies', in A. Gamble *et al.*, *Ideas, Interests and Consequences*, London, Institute of Economic Affairs.

Self, Peter (1993) *Government By the Market? The Politics of Public Choice*, London Macmillan.

Seymour-Ure, Colin (1987) 'Institutionalization and Informality in Advisory Systems', in W. Plowden (ed.), *Advising the Rulers*, Oxford, Basil Blackwell.

Shapiro, Isaac, Porter, Kathryn, and Greenstein, Robert (1992) 'The Center on Budget and Policy Priorities', in C. Weiss (ed.), *Organizations for Policy Advice: Helping Government Think*, California, Sage.

Sharkansky, Ira (1989) 'Policy making and service delivery on the margins of government: The case of contractors', in Harold W. Demone and Margaret Gibelman (eds.), *Services for Sale: Purchasing Health and Human Services*, New Jersey, Rutgers University Press.

Shaw, Jane (1987) 'James Buchanan and Public-Choice Economics', *Dialogue*, No. 77: 22–25.

Shenoy, S. (1987) 'The urgency of profitable losses', *Economic Affairs*, February/March: 22–24.

Shoup, L. (1977) 'The Council on Foreign Relations and America's

Policy in Southeast Asia', *The Insurgent Sociologist*: 19–30.
Shoup, L. and Minter, W. (1977) *Imperial Brain Trust: The Council on Foreign Relations and United States Foreign Policy*, New York, Monthly Review Press.
Silk, L. and Silk, M. (1980) *The American Establishment*, New York, Basic Books.
Singer, Otto (1990) 'Policy Communities and Discourse Coalitions', *Knowledge: Creation, Diffusion, Utilization*, 11 (4): 428–58.
Smith, Bruce (1977) 'The Non Governmental Policy Analysis Organization', *Public Administration Review*, 3 (May/June): 253–58.
Smith, Bruce (1966) *The RAND Corporation: Case Study of a Non Profit Advisory Corporation*, Cambridge, MA, Harvard University Press.
Smith, C. S. (1987a) 'Networks of influence: the social sciences in Britain since the war', in M. Bulmer (ed.), *Social Science Research and Government: Comparative Essays on Britain and the United States*, Cambridge, Cambridge University Press.
Smith, Fred (1987b) 'Privatization at the federal level' in S. H. Hanke (ed.), *The Prospects for Privatization*, Proceedings of the Academy of Political Science, 36 (3): 190–206.
Smith, Fred L. Jnr. (1986-87) 'The Public Choice Approach to Dismantling Big Government', *Economic Affairs*, December–January: 29–30.
Smith, James A. (1993a) *Strategic Calling: The Center for Strategic and International Studies 1962-1992*, Washington DC, Center for Strategic and International Studies.
— (1991a) *The Idea Brokers: Think Tanks and the Rise of the New Policy Elite*, New York, The Free Press.
— (1991b) *Brookings at Seventy Five*, Washington DC, Brookings Institution.
— (1989) 'Think tanks and the politics of ideas', in David Colander (ed.), *The Spread of Economic Ideas*, Canada, Cambridge University Press.
Smith, Martin (1993b) *Pressure, Power and Policy: State Autonomy and Policy Networks in Britain and the United States*, Hemel Hempstead, Harvester Wheatsheaf.
Smoot, D. (1963) *The Invisible Government*, Belmont, MA, Western Islands/The Americanist Library.
Solomon, Burt (1986) 'Ivory Tower Input', *National Journal*, 2 November: 2837–2841.
Spence, Jack (1992) ' The House that Research Built', *RTZ Review*, 22 June.
Stanfield, Rochelle L. (1990) 'The Golden Rolodex', *National Journal*, 10 March: 552–57.
Stang, Alan (1975) 'The CFR: House Organ of the New World Order', *American Opinion*, March: 25–94.
Starr, P. (1990) 'The New Life of the Liberal State: Privatization and the

Restructuring of State-Society Relations', in E. N. Suleiman and J. Waterbury (eds), *The Political Economy of Public Sector Reform and Privatization*, Boulder, Westview Press.

— (n.d.) *The Limits of Privatization*, Washington DC, Economic Policy Institute.

Steinfels, P. (1979) *The Neo-Conservatives: The Men Who Are Changing America's Politics*, New York, Simon and Schuster.

Stone, Diane (1991) 'Old Guard versus New Partisans: Think Tanks in Transition', *Australian Journal of Political Science*, 26 (2) 1991: 197–215.

Suggs, Robert E. (1989) *Minorities and Privatization: Economic Mobility at Risk*, Washington DC, Joint Center for Political Studies Press.

Sundquist, James L. (1978) 'Research Brokerage: The Weak Link', in L. E. Lynn (ed.), *Knowledge and Policy: The Uncertain Connection*, Washington DC, National Academy of Sciences.

Thomas, David (1984) 'An alternative think tank', *New Society*, 8 March.

Thomas, John N. (1974) *The Institute of Pacific Relations: Asian Scholars and American Politics*, Seattle, University of Washington Press.

Thomas, P. (1988) 'In Washington's Marketplace of Ideas, Think Tanks Are The Strongest Sellers', *Los Angeles Times*, 6 November: V.

Thompson, G. (1993) 'Network Coordination', in R. Maidment and G. Thompson (eds), *Managing the United Kingdom: An Introduction to Its Political Economy and Public Policy*, London, Sage.

Thorne, Christopher (1978) 'Chatham House, Whitehall and Far Eastern Issues: 1941–45', *International Affairs*, 54(1): 1–29.

Throgmorton, J.A. (1993) 'Survey Research As Rhetorical Trope: Electrical Power Planning Arguments in Chicago', in F. Fischer and J. Forester (eds), *The Argumentative Turn in Policy Analysis and Planning*, London, UCL Press.

Timmins, Nicholas (1990a) 'Right's think-tanks see rosy future in post-Thatcher era', *The Independent*, 12 December: 5.

— (1990b) 'Think-tank guides Labour towards "market mechanism"', *The Independent*, 9 July: 7.

Todd, Michael J. (1991) 'The Centre for Policy Studies: Its Birth and Early Days', *Essex Papers in Politics and Government*, No. 81, Department of Government, University of Essex.

Tomkin, R. (1990) 'Japanese "think tanks": An imperfect hybrid', *The Japan Economic Journal*, 24 February: 26.

Toner, Robin (1985) 'New Day Dawns for Think Tanks', *The New York Times*, 27 December.

Towle, Nick (1994) 'Exporting the Law to Emerging Markets'. Paper presented to the *Privatisation – Maintaining the Momentum Conference*, London, Centre for Policy Studies, July.

Trade Policy Research Centre (1988) *Twenty Years in the Theatre of Economic Diplomacy*, London, Trade Policy Research Centre.

TransNational Institute – TNI (1991) *Programme Report*, Amsterdam, Trans National Institute.

True, Nicholas (1990) 'Giving: how to encourage charities more', *CPS Policy Study No. 113*, London, Centre for Policy Studies.

Tullock, Gordon *et al.* (1983) *The Economics of Bureaucracy and Statutory Authorities*, Policy monograph No. 1, Sydney, Centre for Independent Studies.

Urban Institute (1991) 'Privatizing State Rental Housing in Hungary', *The Urban Institute Policy and Research Report*, 21 (2): 24.

Useem, M. (1984) *The Inner Circle: Large Corporations and the Rise of Business Political Activity in the US and UK*, Oxford, Oxford University Press.

Van Der Woerd, Nicoline (1992) *World Survey of Strategic Studies Centres*, London, International Institute for Strategic Studies.

Van Dyne, Larry (1985) 'Idea Power', *The Washingtonian*, 20 (April): 102–09; 151–65.

Van Waarden, Frans (1992) 'Dimensions and Types of Policy Networks', *European Journal of Political Research*, 21: 29–52.

Veljanovski, Cento (ed.) (1989) *Privatisation and Competition: A Market Perspective*, London, Institute of Economic Affairs.

— (1987) *Selling the State: Privatisation in Britain*, Great Britain, Weidenfeld & Nicolson.

Vibert, Frank (1992) 'Notes for Breakfast Club meeting in Paris', Institute of Economic Affairs, 21 January.

Victor, Kirk (1988) 'After the Victory', *National Journal*, 24 September: 2389–2394.

Waldman, Steven (1986) 'The King of Quotes', *The Washington Monthly*, 18 (11): 33–40.

Wallace, William (1994) 'Between Two Worlds: Think Tanks and Foreign Policy', in C. Hill and P. Beshoff (eds.), *Two Worlds of International Relations: Academics, Practitioners and the Trade in Ideas*, London, Routledge and London School of Economics.

— (1990) 'Chatham House at 70: to the 1990s and beyond', *The World Today*, 46 (5): 75–77.

Ware, Alan (1990) *Between Profit and the State: Intermediate Organisations in Britain and the United States*, Princeton University Press.

Weaver, R. K. (1989) 'The Changing World of Think Tanks', *PS: Political Science and Politics*, September: 563–78.

Weaver, R. K. and Rockman, B. A. (1993) 'Assessing the Effects of Institutions', in R. K. Weaver and B. A. Rockman (eds), *Do Institutions Matter? Government Capabilities in the United States and Abroad*, Washington DC, Brookings Institution.

Webb, Keith (1994a) 'Academics and Practitioners: Power, Knowledge and Role', in M Girard, W-D. Eberwein and K. Webb (eds), *Theory and Practice in Foreign Policy-Making: National Perspectives on*

Academics and Professionals in International Relations, London, Pinter Publishers.

— (1994b) 'Academics and Professionals in International Relations: A British Perception', in M. Girard, W-D. Eberwein and K. Webb (eds), *Theory and Practice in Foreign Policy-Making: National Perspectives on Academics and Professionals in International Relations*, London, Pinter Publishers.

Weiss, Carol (1992a) 'Preface' in C. Weiss (ed.), *Organizations for Policy Advice: Helping Government Think*, California, Sage.

— (1992b) 'Introduction: Helping Government Think: Functions and Consequences of Policy Analysis Organizations' in C. Weiss (ed.), *Organizations for Policy Advice: Helping Government Think*, California, Sage.

— (ed.) (1992c) *Organizations for Policy Advice: Helping Government*, California, Sage.

Weller, Pat (1987) 'Types of Advice', in W. Plowden (ed.), *Advising the Rulers*, Oxford, Basil Blackwell.

Wheen, F. (1994) '... goes to war against policy units and think tank battalions', *Life*, 9 October: 86.

Wheeler, Charles (1986) 'Think Tanks Following the Issues Home', *Insight*, 22 December: 50–51.

Whittle, Richard (1985) 'Journalists fill up at think tanks', *Morning News Dallas*, 10 November.

Wickham-Jones, Mark (1992) 'Monetarism and its Critics: The University Economists' Protest of 1981', *The Political Quarterly*, 63 (2): 171–85.

Wilentz, Amy (1986) 'On the Intellectual Ramparts', *Time*, 1 September: 22–23.

Willetts, David (1987) 'The role of the (UK) Prime Minister's policy unit', *Public Administration*, 65 (4): 443–54.

Williams, Barbara R. and Palmatier, Malcolm. A. (1992) 'The RAND Corporation', in C. Weiss (ed.), *Organizations for Policy Advice: Helping Government Think*, California, Sage.

Williams, Roger M. (1989) 'Capital Clout: The White House–Heritage Foundation Connection', *Foundation News*, 30 (4): 15–19.

Wilson, J. Q. (1981) '"Policy Intellectuals" and Public Policy', *The Public Interest*, Summer, 64: 31–46.

Wolman, Harold (1992) 'Understanding Cross National Policy Transfers: The Case of Britain and the US', *Governance*, 5 (1): 27–45.

Wood, John B. (1987) 'Unintended Outcomes', *Economic Affairs*, April/May.

World Resources Institute – WRI (1991) *At A Glance*, Washington DC, World Resources Institute.

World Watch Institute (n.d.) *Fact sheet*, Washington DC, World Watch.

Wright, John (1994) 'UK Export Opportunities'. Paper presented to the *Privatisation – Maintaining the Momentum Conference*, London,

Centre for Policy Studies, July.

Wright, T., Rodriguez, F. and Waitzkin, Howard (1985) 'Corporate Interests, Philanthropies and the Peace Movement', *Monthly Review*, 36: 19–34.

Wyszomirski, Margaret J. (1989) 'Administrative Agents, Policy Partners, and Political Catalysts: A Structural Perspective on the Interactions of Governmental and Nonprofit Organizations', *Teaching Political Science*, 16 (3): 122–30.

Yoffe, E. (1980) 'The domains of eminence: Great minds do not always think alike', *Washington Journalism Review*, Reproduced by Washington Communications Corp.

Young, Hugo (1989) *One of Us*, London, Macmillan.

Zacher, Mark W. (1992) 'The Decaying Pillars of the Westphalian Temple: Implications for International Order and Governance', in James N. Rosenau and Ernst-Otto Czempiel (eds), *Governance Without Government: Order and Change in World Politics*, Cambridge, Cambridge University Press.

Index

A

ACCF Center: 135, 161
Acton Institute: 54
Adam Smith Institute (ASI): 44, 68,
108, 109, 123, 125, 127, 142; and
conservatives, 45, 47–48; ideological
stance, 14, 21, 22, 148, 222; and
privatisation, 171–72, 175, 177, 179,
181–83
advocacy: 13–14, 23, 96, 113, 121, 122,
146, 162, 225
advocacy coalitions: 90–92, 103
agenda setting: 1, 3, 30, 33, 89–91,
92–94, 96, 110, 111, 113, 122, 136,
145, 163, 180, 218–20
alternative policy advice: 2, 3, 45, 105,
112, 119, 222
American Enterprise Institute (AEI): 39,
71, 101, 124, 125, 141, 143, 158,
207–08; and conservatives, 24, 149;
and epistemic communities, 95, 97;
ideological stance, 20, 32;
management of, 65, 66, 80, 81, 118
Arab Research Centre: 121
Arms Control Association: 129, 209,
223
Aspen Institute: 9
Atlantic Council: 16, 18, 200, 206, 210,
223
Atlas Foundation: 51, 54, 128, 130–31,
134, 138, 216

B

Barry Goldwater Institute for Public
Policy Research: 142
Bow Group: 48
Brookings Institution: 5, 29, 32, 51,
71–72, 103, 121, 134, 143; academic
style, 18, 19, 67, 109; ideological
stance, 79, 101, 117, 125; financing,
39, 60, 80, 116

C

Capital Research Center (CRC): 132,
149
Carnegie Council on Ethics and
International Affairs: 19, 176, 179,
185, 200, 204, 205
Carnegie Endowment for International
Peace: 13, 19, 39, 52, 55, 66, 80, 129,
134, 185, 208–09, 211
Cato Institute: 48, 63, 68, 102, 114, 134,
154, 157; market liberal ethos, 21, 55,
100, 129, 148; and privatisation, 174,
175, 179
Center for Defense Information (CDI):
119, 195
Center For Democracy: 22, 109, 121
Center for International Policy: 23, 196
Center for National Policy (CNP): 49,
67, 116, 117, 159, 174
Center for Policy Alternatives: 131
Center for Security Policy: 62, 72, 124,
195, 201
Center for Strategic and International
Studies (CSIS): 19, 51, 55, 69, 71,
121, 123, 191, 193, 206, 207–08; and
strategic thinking, 191, 194, 211; and
universities, 60, 204, 214
Center for the Study of Democratic
Institutions: 20, 124
Center for the Study of Social Policy: 63
Center for Women Policy Studies: 115
Center on Budget and Policy Priorities:
22
Central Policy Review Staff (CPRS): 26,
43
Centre for Economic Policy Research
(CEPR): 22, 39, 51, 62, 67, 112, 123,
211
Centre for Global Energy Studies
(CGES): 22, 161
Centre for Policy Studies (CPS): 44,
65–66, 67, 111, 125, 126, 134, 140,
141, 142, 159, 160; and Conservative

government, 23, 27, 45, 47, 102, 117;
ideological stance, 21–22, 33, 114,
148; and privatisation, 170–71, 177,
181
charitable activity and institutions: 14,
46, 115, 118, 120, 222–25
civil service (UK): 28, 42–45, 47, 105,
122, 126, 186, 200
classical liberalism: 25, 99, 136–39,
145–46
Committee for Economic Development
(CED): 18, 34, 39, 71, 72, 80, 103,
161
Commonwealth Foundation: 176, 180
Competitive Enterprise Institute (CEI):
66, 67, 121, 129, 134, 157, 174, 176
Conference Board: 19, 34, 72, 97, 101,
103, 161
consensual knowledge: 74, 85, 88, 94,
96, 99, 122, 198, 220; and policy
innovation, 95, 98, 224; about
privatisation, 167, 168–69, 171, 177
Conservative Party: 22, 23, 47–48, 65,
102, 126, 169–70, 177, 182
conservative think-tanks: 14, 20, 21, 23,
29, 47, 84, 115, 118, 127, 139, 148,
150, 158, 167, 176, 191, 195, 204
consultancy companies: 13, 14, 27, 71,
102, 180
corporate relations with think-tanks:
29–30, 34, 53, 117, 149–50, 160
Council on Foreign Relations (CFR): 4,
5, 18, 31, 50, 70, 83, 95, 185, 188–89,
195, 198, 199, 200, 208, 224; as
exclusive Establishment body, 16, 29,
32, 39, 72; and study of IR, 205,
208–09, 210
Council on Hemispheric Affairs: 196

D
David Hume Institute: 22, 140, 142
Democratic Party: 9, 49, 117, 125
Demos: 38, 67
Dickson, Paul: 10, 11, 14, 124
diplomacy: 185, 197, 199, 200–01, 214
discourse: 36, 90, 100, 110, 115, 118,
122, 136, 140–41, 145, 147–48, 152,
163–6, 218, 222; coalition, 3, 90, 94,
121, 159, 220; institutionalisation, 94,
165; structuration, 94, 162, 180
Dror, Yehezkel: 11–12, 20, 41, 50, 105
Drug Policy Foundation: 102–103, 110,
115, 116

E
Earth Resources Research (ERR): 19,
21, 44, 204
East–West Forum: 23, 121
Economic Policy Institute (EPI): 21, 49,
60, 67, 68, 117, 159, 176, 197
Economic Strategy Institute (ESI): 62,
196
élite theorists: 5, 26, 29–31, 35, 36,
63–64
Employee Benefit Research Institute
(EBRI): 34
Employment Policy Institute: 110
Environmental and Energy Study
Institute (EESI): 21, 50, 54, 112, 116,
124–25, 129, 131
Environmental Law Institute: 129
epistemic communities: 6, 85, 88, 117,
122, 125, 127, 132, 137, 162–63, 218;
definition and theory of, 3, 36–37,
86–91, 94–104; in foreign and
defence policy, 95, 184, 189, 191–93,
197–98; and privatisation, 167,
180–81, 183
Ethics and Public Policy Center (EPPC):
21, 60, 125, 149
European Policy Forum (EPF): 60, 62,
65, 125, 126, 195, 200
exceptionalism, US: 38, 40–42, 50–51, 217
experts: 3, 103, 113–14, 120, 121,
131–32, 137, 150, 213 (see also
epistemic communities)

F
Fabian Society: 18, 20, 48, 55, 60, 68,
117, 133, 138–39, 173, 217
Feulner, Edwin: 41, 61, 69, 108, 129,
140, 141

financial autonomy/dependence of think-tanks: 11, 12, 14, 16, 53–61, 116, 220, 221
Fisher, Antony: 51, 128, 138
Foreign Policy Research Institute (FPRI): 18, 95, 191, 200, 210
Foundation for Manufacturing and Industry (FMI): 225
foundations: 13, 45–47, 52, 54–55, 65, 125, 130, 131, 133, 138–39, 144, 149, 161, 221; withdrawal of funding, 61, 64, 65, 130; Rockefeller, 54, 188, 221
Free Congress Foundation: 21, 23, 55, 127, 129
free market think-tanks: 6, 23, 28, 33, 51, 118, 159, 165, 169, 170, 172, 177, 180

G

Gamble, Andrew: 2, 27, 33–34, 125, 145, 164
government contract research: 19, 42, 53, 55, 62, 71, 116, 144, 215
Gray, Colin: 13, 14, 42, 191, 195

H

Haas, Ernst: 73, 79, 80, 83, 84
Haas, Peter: 6, 86–90, 95, 96, 183, 197
Hayek, F. A: 128, 136–40, 141, 146, 170
Heartland Institute: 22, 130, 176, 180
hegemony: 32, 33, 114, 141, 165, 222
Henry L. Stimson Center: 195, 206
Heritage Foundation: 32, 39, 48, 55, 72, 84, 108, 114, 125, 133–34, 141, 143, 155, 156–58, 224; and Congress, 23, 68, 71, 132; and conservatives, 65, 101, 118, 126–27, 132, 148, 150–51; ideological stance, 14, 21, 24, 25; networks, 129, 133–34, 216; and privatisation, 171–72, 174–75, 177, 179; publications, 68, 69, 131, 209, 223
Hoover Institution: 20, 39, 48, 60, 84, 101, 191, 194, 208
Hudson Institute: 19, 39, 55, 62, 81, 204, 223

I

idealism: 19, 184, 185, 190–91, 213
ideas: 1; battle of, 138, 139, 152, 158; diffusion of, 2, 37, 120, 139, 167–69, 177, 180, 183, 217, 220; marketing of, 23, 123, 136, 140, 218; market place of; 33, 53, 102, 110, 143–45, 149, 155
independence: organisational, 10, 14–16, 33, 43, 111, 117; academic, research and scholarly: 11, 13, 15, 16, 55, 69, 116–17; political and bureaucratic: 12, 14, 16, 34, 119, 120, 216
Independence Institute: 119, 121, 156
influence: methodological question of proof, 4–5, 29, 105, 107–08, 111, 113, 219; limits of, 183, 184, 199–200, 218–22; on policy, 6, 16, 30, 55, 68–69, 86, 89, 94, 106–111, 134, 137, 215, 219
Institute for American Values (IAV): 54, 121
Institute for Contemporary Studies (ICS): 32, 48, 67, 68, 116, 175
Institute for Defense and Disarmament Studies: 195, 211
Institute for Educational Leadership: 221
Institute for Energy Research: 54
Institute for European Defence and Strategic Studies (IEDSS): 195
Institute for European Environmental Policy (IEEP): 39, 196
Institute for International Economics (IIE): 22, 61–62, 95, 96, 97, 107, 123, 196, 197, 200–01, 204, 211
Institute for Fiscal Studies (IFS): 22, 43, 83, 173, 224
Institute for Foreign Policy Analysis (IFPA): 39, 200
Institute for Policy Studies (IPS): 18, 20, 81–82, 84, 85, 103, 115, 129, 150–51, 194, 207, 224
Institute for Public Policy Research (IPPR): 24, 28, 48, 67, 76, 103, 117, 133, 139, 173
Institute for Research on the Economics

of Taxation (IRET): 63, 71, 101, 107, 129, 157, 174
Institute of Economic Affairs (IEA): 18, 60, 65–66, 67, 100, 116, 126, 128, 130, 140, 141, 157, 158–59, 198, 224; and Conservative governments, 27, 33, 45, 47–48, 102, 111, 114, 117; and market ethos, 20, 21, 22, 51, 138–39, 143; and privatisation, 169–70, 172, 176, 181, 182
Institute of Employment Rights: 21, 103, 115
Institute of Muslim Minority Affairs: 221
Institute of Pacific Relations (IPR): 20, 70, 77–78, 186, 203, 205, 214
Institute of Race Relations: 103
Institute on Religion and Public Life: 65
IPSET – Education Unit: 130
interest groups: 13, 27, 37, 41, 87, 91, 94, 103, 133, 150, 153–54, 211; and think-tank politicisation, 71, 117, 121, 216, 225–26
International Center: 201
International Institute for Environment and Development (IIED): 39, 55, 60, 129, 196, 200
International Institute for Strategic Studies (IISS) 18, 39, 51, 63, 96, 146, 190–91, 208, 213, 216
International Peace Academy: 200
issue networks: 90, 98, 102

J
James Madison Institute: 22, 121, 128
John Locke Foundation: 142, 176
Joint Center for Political and Economic Studies: 19, 21, 61, 63, 119, 176

K
Keynesianism: 20, 33, 42, 83, 87, 99–102, 136, 145, 159, 182
Keystone Center: 129
Kingdon, John: 1, 93, 100, 103, 122, 169, 183, 218,
knowledge/politics dynamic: 29, 36–37, 93, 113–15, 120, 122–23, 136, 212–14, 218

L
Labour Party: 24, 48, 117, 133, 173
learning: 50, organisational, 73–74, 82–85, 95, 189–190, 224; policy learning, 6, 91, 190; social learning, 96, 168, 178, 181, 216, 220 (*see* consensual knowledge)
Lehrman Institute: 77,
libertarian think-tanks: 14, 47, 127, 137, 139–40, 146, 164 (*see* free market and market liberal think–tanks)
Lincoln Institute: 21
Lindquist, Evert: 10, 15, 50, 103, 108, 161
Locke Institute: 155

M
Mackinac Center: 176
Major, John: 47, 48, 114, 171, 174, 187
Manhattan Institute 51, 124, 128, 155, 157
market liberal think-tanks: 6, 20, 21, 22, 25, 55, 110, 115, 148, 152, 160, 169
media: 23, 33, 44, 55, 71–72, 96, 102, 103, 107, 118–19, 120, 124, 133, 150, 222–23,
The Media Institute: 150
metaphors: 113, 120, 136, 139–46, 152, 155, 163, 165, 218
monetarism: 102, 152, 180
Monterey Institute: 196

N
Nathan Hale Institute: 81
National Bureau of Economic Research (NBER): 18, 19, 51, 54, 55, 96, 103, 117
National Center for Policy Analysis (NCPA): 107, 134, 177
National Center for Public Policy Research (NCPPR): 129, 132, 141
National Committee for Responsive Philanthropy: 127
National Institute of Economic and Social Research (NIESR): 18, 44, 55, 103, 123, 125, 159

National Institute for Public Policy: 42, 195
National Planning Association: 101, 121
neo–marxist theories: 5, 31–34, 35, 36, 114
networking: 16, 63, 67, 88, 96, 103, 122, 127–34, 160
New Class: 29, 33, 142, 148–51, 158
'new partisan' institutes: 18, 21–24, 38, 49, 72, 79, 109, 21
New Right: 2, 21, 22, 24, 27, 33, 148, 180
non–profit organisations (NPOs): 2, 5, 11, 15, 45, 53, 63, 70, 93, 105, 115, 119, 215, 224
Northeast–Midwest Institute: 50

O

'old guard' institutes: 18–21, 24, 54, 55, 60, 66, 68, 71, 79–80, 159, 176, 196, 205, 217
opinion formation: 3, 29, 32, 61, 68, 96, 110, 126, 220
organisational adaption: 73–74, 79–82, 85, 189, 224
organisational decline: 74–78, 85
Outer Circle Policy Unit (OCPU): 76–77
Overseas Development Council (ODC): 20, 54, 66, 68, 121, 195
Overseas Development Institute (ODI): 111–12, 129, 210, 221

P

Pacific Forum: 199
Pacific Institute: 198
Pacific Research Institute: 51, 128, 157, 175
Panos Institute: 39, 198
parliamentary systems: 29, 38, 42–45, 47, 126, 217
permeability: 4, 41, 44, 45, 51, 125, 217
philanthropy: 38, 45–47, 53, 217
pluralist perspectives: 5, 26, 27–29, 36, 119
policy communities: 2, 3, 23, 44, 90–91, 93, 98, 100, 102, 121, 153, 168, 217, 220, 225

policy entrepreneurs: 6, 61–62, 93, 108, 121, 122, 124, 137, 141, 145–46, 215
policy networks: 3, 36, 90, 92, 93, 215, 220, 221
policy paradigm: 101–02, 103, 112, 137, 141, 145, 147, 148, 162, 182
policy process: 4, 7, 30, 34–36, 39, 43, 87, 168, 215, 224
policy relevance: 13, 15, 64, 86, 105, 109, 199, 216
Policy Studies Institute (PSI): 13, 18–19, 20, 81, 103, 111, 121, 169
Political and Economic Planning (PEP): 18–19, 81
Political Economy Research Center (PERC): 156–57, 164, 175, 177, 179, 198
political parties: 11, 17, 27, 37, 38, 40–41, 47–50, 71, 112, 117, 153, 216
politicisation: 28, 50, 69, 71, 102, 121, 152, 216, 221, 225
Polsby, Nelson: 9, 13, 27, 41, 108
Potomac Institute: 76, 78, 84
privatisation: 6, 100, 155, 157, 166, 167–83
progressive liberalism: 25, 29, 49, 71, 82, 131, 148–50
progressive liberal think-tanks: 20, 49, 81, 131, 150, 167, 194–95
Progressive Policy Institute (PPI): 9, 49, 117, 121
public choice theory: 6, 139, 151, 152, 152–66, 172–73, 176–7, 218
public service motivation: 15, 16, 34–35, 105, 115–16, 119, 160, 162, 210, 222–23, 224–25

R

RAND: 5, 9, 18–19, 39, 72, 95, 194, 203, 208; and US Government connection, 70, 83–84, 116, 191, 193, 201; and strategic theory, 147, 190, 191–93, 203, 213; funding of, 19, 24, 144
rationality: 11, 20, 101, 117–18, 146–47, 153, 162, 217, 224

Reagan administration: 48, 52, 55, 77, 79, 108, 114, 115, 173–74, 178

Reason Foundation, The: 121, 175, 178–79, 180

Republican Party: 48–49, 81, 125, 133

research brokerage: 6, 97, 122–27, 151, 155, 162, 165, 179–80, 197, 220, 223

Research Institute for the Study of Conflict and Terrorism (RISCT): 195, 200, 204, 208

Resources For the Future (RFF): 19, 63–64, 66, 81, 116, 123, 129

Ricci, David: 12, 13, 14, 41

Rockford Institute: 64–65

Roosevelt Center: 77

Round Table: 18, 74–76, 185

Royal Institute for International Affairs (RIIA, also Chatham House): 4, 18, 50–51, 66–67, 70, 75, 80, 83, 95, 97, 121, 125, 130, 134, 185, 200, 204, 224; and government relations, 186–87, 189, 207; and the study of international relations, 96, 205–06, 208, 209–11

Russell Sage Foundation (RSF): 13, 18, 52, 55, 80, 159

S

Saferworld: 72, 195

Smith, James: 12, 19, 21, 27, 28, 38, 41, 42, 62, 124, 204, 223

Social Affairs Unit (SAU): 22, 60, 67, 130

Social Market Foundation (SMF): 111, 125, 160

socialism or socialists: 25, 136–39, 142, 146, 149

socialist think-tanks: 20, 24, 167

state-based think-tanks: 22, 84, 127–28, 176

Stone, Diane: 9, 24, 39, 83

T

Tax Foundation: 19

tax status: 38, 45–47, 105, 118, 161, 217, 220, 224

Texas Public Policy Foundation: 128

Thatcher government: 27, 47, 111, 114, 117, 172, 187

Thatcher, Margaret: 27,33, 43, 45, 47, 106, 115, 117, 126, 170, 178, 182

'think and do' tanks, 22–23, 223, 225

think-tanks: competition among, 22, 33, 39, 50, 74, 79, 143, 161, 200, 221; definition and key features, 5, 9–12, 17, leadership of, 61–62, 63, 74, 80, 82–83, 123; membership of, 55, 116, 189, 205, 222; neutrality, 29, 49–50, 115, 117–18, 120, 126, 187, 217, 225; proliferation of: 110, 112, 115, 134, 150, 221; publications of, 68–71, 124, 131–32, 204, 205–206, 208–10; research standards, 11–12, 15–16, 115–16, 123, 221; scholarly and scientific reputation of, 12, 20, 115–17, 123, 165, 209, 213–14, 217, 220; specialisation, 19, 21–22, 54, 99, 130, 195, 199, 200, 216, 221, 225; staff, 66–68, 82, 99, 117, 124–25, 129, 160, 215, 223; vanity tanks, 61–62, 77, 216

Trade Policy Research Centre (TPRC): 95, 97–98, 103–04, 172, 197

trade unions: 24, 32, 60, 71, 103, 115, 164, 182

Trilateral Commission: 31, 32

Twentieth Century Fund: 19, 121, 185

U

universities: 11, 13, 14, 15, 27, 33, 42, 54, 95, 122, 138, 149, 156, 203–14; academic think-tank exchange, 38, 60, 64, 66–67, 207, 208, 214, 221, 222; Asian studies, 78, 203, 214; environmental studies; 66, 81, 204, 211; international relations and strategic studies, 190, 203–205, 209, 210–12

Urban Institute: 18, 20, 42, 52, 55, 123, 144, 169, 178

V

Versailles peace conference: 4, 50, 185, 202

W

'war of ideas': 6, 140–48, 150–51, 152, 156, 218
Washington Institute for Near East Policy: 21, 196, 225
Washington Institute for Policy Studies: 176

Weaver, Kent: 4, 13, 18, 27, 39, 50, 121
Weiss, Carol. 2, 13–14, 15, 24, 39–41
Women's Research and Education Institute: 21, 115
World Policy Institute (WPI): 68, 81, 84
World Resources Institute (WRI): 21, 39, 63, 96, 111, 129, 132, 196
Worldwatch: 62, 196, 204

Y

Yankee Institute: 128

9 780714 642635